Mastering AI System Design

Architect, Build and Deploy AI Systems Using 10 Domain Driven Blueprints and Interview Strategies

Soudamini Sreepada

www.orangeava.com

First Published: December 2025

Published By: Orange Education Pvt Ltd, AVA®

Address: 9, Daryaganj, Delhi, 110002, India

275 New North Road Islington Suite 1314 London,
N1 7AA, United Kingdom

ISBN (PBK): 978-93-49888-74-6
ISBN (E-BOOK): 978-93-49887-22-0

Scan the QR code to explore our entire catalogue

www.orangeava.com

Dedicated To

My Beloved Parents,

Sripada Peri Sastry

And

Sripada Syamala.

About the Author

Soudamini Sreepada is a distinguished leader in Artificial Intelligence, education, and research, with over 18 years of experience in the technology industry. She teaches AI system design through DesignYourAI - https://www.designyourai.in. Her projects and resources are available on GitHub at https://github.com/soudaminigit/

After earning her M.Tech. in Computer Science from IIT Bombay in 2003, she built a remarkable career at Microsoft India Pvt. Ltd., where she held roles such as Software Engineer, Manager, and Principal Data Scientist. At Microsoft, she contributed to flagship products including Windows and Bing, spearheading initiatives that combined large-scale engineering with applied AI to create intelligent systems used by millions, worldwide. She received national innovation awards and was recognized as a Best Manager during her tenure.

Soudamini holds multiple U.S. patents and has published research in Natural Language Processing, Computer Vision, and Generative AI. Renowned for her innovation and real-world problem-solving, she is a sought-after speaker on topics such as Machine Learning, Deep Learning, presenting at events like the Codess, GraceHopper Conference and Microsoft Research Conferences.

She is passionate about bridging the gap between academia and industry. Soudamini teaches and mentors at Cognida.ai and Jain University, and also guides aspiring AI professionals globally through platforms such as Topmate. Her teaching philosophy centers on hands-on learning and system-level thinking, empowering learners to design, build, and deploy production-ready AI systems.

Beyond her professional achievements, Soudamini is a published Telugu short story writer, a trained Carnatic vocalist, and a tarot reader, reflecting her diverse interests and creative pursuits.

About the Technical Reviewer

Amanpreet Singh Bhogal is an AI Engineer specializing in Machine Learning (ML), Deep Learning (DL), and Model Context Protocol (MCP). His work focuses on designing and deploying scalable AI systems that bridge the gap between research and real-world applications. With expertise in building ML pipelines, fine-tuning models, and orchestrating AI workloads on modern infrastructure, Amanpreet ensures that all his solutions are both technically robust and business-driven.

He has collaborated with cross-functional teams to deliver AI-enabled automation, decision-making, and digital transformation initiatives. By leveraging MCP, Amanpreet emphasizes structured and contextualized AI workflows that enhance adaptability, precision, and efficiency. His strong background in cloud-native development and orchestration further strengthens his ability to deliver end-to-end AI solutions at scale.

Passionate about innovation and continuous learning, Amanpreet is dedicated to advancing AI adoption, and contributing to intelligent system design that creates meaningful and measurable impact on real-world scenarios.

Acknowledgments

Firstly, I would like to express my deepest gratitude to my parents, Sripada Peri Sastry and Sripada Syamala, whose unwavering encouragement and passion for learning instilled in me a lifelong curiosity and drive to think beyond boundaries. I am equally thankful to my brother, Sripada Balamukund, for his constant support and guidance throughout my professional journey.

I owe immense gratitude to my husband, Venkata Ramgopal Sahasranamamula, for his steadfast encouragement and patience during the writing of this book. His belief in my vision and his constant support made this endeavor possible. My heartfelt thanks goes to my daughter, Pravallika Sahasranamamula, for her valuable insights and feedback from a college student's perspective that helped enhance the content and relevance of several sections. I am deeply appreciative of my son, Venkata Sai Prateek Sahasranamamula, whose curiosity, inquisitive nature, and probing questions have been a continual source of inspiration.

I would also like to extend my appreciation to Microsoft India (R&D) Pvt. Ltd. for providing me the opportunity to work on scalable products such as *Windows* and *Bing* - experiences that greatly deepened my understanding of real-world engineering and product design. I am grateful to Cognida.ai for their partnership, and for keeping me connected with the latest advancements in the AI industry.

My sincere thanks goes to Dr. Mangathayaru Nimmala, Head of the IT Department at VNR *Vignana Jyothi Institute of Engineering & Technology, Hyderabad*, and Dr. G.N.V.G. Sirisha, Associate Professor, Dept CSE at S.R.K.R. *Engineering College*, for involving me in the academic journey of the engineering students.

My special thanks goes to Amanpreet Singh Bhogal for dedicating his valuable time to provide a detailed technical review and feedback that greatly enhanced the quality of this book. I am also grateful to all my mentees at Preplaced and Topmate, whose questions and concerns helped me recognize the gaps in how ML system design interviews are understood and prepared for. I would also extend my heartfelt gratitude to Chetna Shahi for creating the beautiful illustrations featured in Chapter 7 of this book.

Finally, I am thankful to everyone who contributed directly or indirectly to the successful completion of this work. Their inspiration, collaboration, and faith in my vision made this journey truly meaningful!

Preface

Artificial Intelligence (AI) has evolved from a purely academic discipline into a cornerstone of modern industry, where success relies not only on theoretical understanding but also on the ability to design practical and scalable systems. However, many students and aspiring AI professionals continue to face challenges in bridging the gap between conceptual knowledge and real-world implementation. This book is designed to address that gap, equipping readers with the skills needed to design, build, and deploy AI systems that meet industry standards.

Designed for both students and industry professionals, this book guides readers through the entire AI lifecycle–from data design and preparation to model selection, deployment, and monitoring. Through ten comprehensive case studies, it brings to life a diverse spectrum of AI applications, ranging from supervised learning systems and recommendation engines to multimodal transformers and large language models. Each case study highlights architectural design, trade-offs, evaluation metrics, and emerging trends, offering readers a rare glimpse into how theoretical principles are transformed into production-grade systems.

Hence, whether you are preparing for AI system design interviews, transitioning into the AI domain, or seeking to deepen your understanding of modern machine learning infrastructure, this book serves as your roadmap. It seamlessly blends academic rigor with industry relevance, empowering readers to think like system architects, reason like data scientists, and build like engineers!

Overview of the Book's Structure

This book offers a comprehensive guide to designing, building, and deploying advanced AI systems for real-world applications. It bridges foundational AI concepts with practical industry implementation, covering everything from system design principles and prompt engineering for generative AI to specialized architectures such as Retrieval-Augmented Generation (RAG) and multi-modal transformers. Readers gain hands-on guidance in fine-tuning Large Language Models (LLMs), building domain-specific models, and implementing both supervised and unsupervised learning systems across diverse applications such as finance, e-commerce, healthcare, and edge computing.

Through a combination of theoretical insights, practical workflows, and case studies, the book equips readers to handle challenges in data processing, model evaluation, explainability, ethical AI, and deployment strategies. From recommendation engines and sequence-to-sequence systems to custom LLMs and multi-modal AI, it provides a holistic blueprint for creating scalable, efficient, and impactful AI solutions across industries.

Chapter 1: Introduction to AI System Design

This chapter establishes the essential principles, and addresses the key challenges of AI system design, serving as a bridge between academic learning and real-world industry expectations. It introduces a structured framework to help readers effectively approach and solve AI system design problems.

Chapter 2: Crafting Intelligent Systems Using Prompt Engineering

This chapter focuses on the transformative potential of Generative AI, guiding readers through prompting techniques and frameworks such as Hugging Face and OpenAI APIs. Through real-world case studies, it demonstrates how to design intelligent systems using large language models, and equipping readers with practical skills for building advanced AI solutions.

Chapter 3: Developing Retrieval-Augmented Generation Systems

This chapter demystifies RAG architectures that integrate information retrieval with generative models. It provides detailed guidance on database selection, explores toolkits such as LangChain and Llama Index, and discusses deployment trade-offs. The concepts are reinforced through case studies and interview scenarios, offering readers practical insights into real-world applications.

Chapter 4: Enhancing Systems Through LLM Finetuning

This chapter provides readers with hands-on experience in advanced fine-tuning methods such as PEFT, LoRA, and instruction tuning. It bridges these fine-tuning strategies to real-world business applications, demonstrating how to adapt large models for specialized tasks and practical deployment scenarios.

Chapter 5: Designing Financial Risk Prediction Systems Using Supervised Learning

This chapter presents a comprehensive, end-to-end journey in designing supervised machine learning systems for financial risk analysis. It guides readers through vital stages such as data processing, model evaluation, explainability, and privacy considerations. The chapter concludes with practical deployment strategies and domain-specific case studies, offering actionable insights for real-world applications.

Chapter 6: Implementing Unsupervised Learning Systems

In this chapter, readers explore unsupervised learning methods, including clustering and topic modeling. The discussion emphasizes embedding strategies, evaluation techniques, and practical CRM applications for customer segmentation and actionable insights.

Chapter 7: Building Recommendation Systems for E-Commerce

This chapter traces the evolution of recommendation systems, guiding readers from collaborative filtering approaches to advanced graph-based models. It places special emphasis on ethical AI, explainability, experimentation, and effective deployment strategies, providing a comprehensive perspective on building modern recommendation engines.

Chapter 8: Building Image Classification Models for Edge Devices

This chapter teaches readers how to design optimized computer vision systems specifically for resource-constrained environments. It covers essential topics such as data annotation, model architecture, optimization techniques, and deployment strategies for mobile and edge devices, all illustrated with real-life case examples.

Chapter 9: Designing Sequence-to-Sequence Systems

This chapter examines sequence-to-sequence models that drive applications such as translation, summarization, and speech recognition. It guides readers through key topics including data challenges, LSTMs, transformer-based design, and performance evaluation, all illustrated with a practical summarization case study.

Chapter 10: Building Domain-Specific LLMs from Scratch

This chapter offers an in-depth exploration of building customized LLMs, guiding readers through data curation, transformer architecture, distributed training, and evaluation. It presents a comprehensive blueprint for developing specialized LLMs, exclusively tailored to meet the industry requirements.

Chapter 11: Building Multimodal Applications for Healthcare

The final chapter delves into multi-modal AI architecture, guiding readers through dataset preparation, architectural alignment, and deployment trade-offs. It culminates with a comprehensive healthcare case study and an interview guide.

Get a Free eBook

We hope you are enjoying your recently purchased book! Your feedback is incredibly valuable to us, and to all other readers looking for great books.

If you found this book helpful or enjoyable, we would truly appreciate it, if you could take a moment to leave a short review with a 5 star rating on Amazon. It helps us grow, and lets other readers discover our books.

As a thank you, we would love to send you a free digital copy of this book, and a **30%** discount code on your next cart value on our official websites:

www.orangeava.com

www.orangeava.in (For Indian Subcontinent)

☑ **Here's how:**

Leave a review for the book on Amazon.

Take a screenshot of your review, and send an email to **info@orangeava.com** (it can be just the confirmation screen).

Once, we receive your screenshot, we will send you the digital file, within 24 hours.

Thank you so much for your support – it means a lot to us!

Downloading the code bundles and colored images

Please follow the links or scan the QR codes to download the ***Code Bundles and Images*** of the book:

https://github.com/ava-orange-education/Mastering-AI-System-Design

The code bundles and images of the book are also hosted on ***https://rebrand.ly/552c8b***

In case there's an update to the code, it will be updated on the existing GitHub repository.

Errata

We take immense pride in our work at **Orange Education Pvt Ltd,** and follow best practices to ensure the accuracy of our content to provide an indulging reading experience to our subscribers. Our readers are our mirrors, and we use their inputs to reflect and improve upon human errors, if any, that may have occurred during the publishing processes involved. To let us maintain the quality and help us reach out to any readers who might be having difficulties due to any unforeseen errors, please write to us at :

errata@orangeava.com

Your support, suggestions, and feedback are highly appreciated.

DID YOU KNOW

Did you know that Orange Education Pvt Ltd offers eBook versions of every book published, with PDF and ePub files available? You can upgrade to the eBook version at **www.orangeava.com** and as a print book customer, you are entitled to a discount on the eBook copy. Get in touch with us at: **info@orangeava.com** for more details.

At **www.orangeava.com**, you can also read a collection of free technical articles, sign up for a range of free newsletters, and receive exclusive discounts and offers on Print Books and eBooks.

PIRACY

If you come across any illegal copies of our works in any form on the internet, we would be grateful if you would provide us with the location address or website name. Please contact us at **info@orangeava.com** with a link to the material.

ARE YOU INTERESTED IN AUTHORING WITH US?

If there is a topic that you have expertise in, and you are interested in either writing or contributing to a book, please write to us at **business@orangeava.com**. We are on a journey to help developers and tech professionals to gain insights on the present technological advancements and innovations happening across the globe and build a community that believes Knowledge is best acquired by sharing and learning with others. Please reach out to us to learn what our audience demands and how you can be part of this educational reform. We also welcome ideas from tech experts and help them build learning and development content for their domains.

REVIEWS

Please leave a review. Once you have read and used this book, why not leave a review on the site that you purchased it from? Potential readers can then see and use your unbiased opinion to make purchase decisions. We at Orange Education would love to know what you think about our products, and our authors can learn from your feedback. Thank you!

For more information about Orange Education, please visit **www.orangeava.com**.

Table of Contents

1. Introduction to AI System Design **1**
Introduction 1
Structure 1
System Design for AI 2
Challenges in AI System Design 3
Evolution of System Design 5
Rule-Based Versus Machine Learning 5
Scenario: Email Spam Filtering 5
Machine Learning Versus Deep Learning 7
Trade-offs between ML and DL System Design 8
Traditional Machine Learning System Design 9
Using Large Language Models 10
Stage 1. Pre-trained Models 10
Stage 2. Generative Models 10
Stage 3. Multi-modal LLMs 10
Stage 4. Small Language Models (SLMs) 11
Steps in Designing AI Systems with LLMs 11
AI System Design Interviews 14
Preparing for the Interview 14
Research the Organization 14
Stay Updated on AI Trends 15
The Interview Format 15
Template for AI System Design Questions 16
Conclusion 18
Points to Remember 18
Multiple Choice Questions 19
Answers 19

2. Crafting Intelligent Systems Using Prompt Engineering 20

Introduction 20

The Prompt Engineering Edge 20

The Power of Hugging Face and Open-Source Tools 21

Structure 21

Introduction to LLMs and Hugging Face 21

LLM Ecosystem and Access Options 23

Hugging Face Hub and Transformers 23

Offline and Local Workflows 24

Command-Line Engines and Quantization 24

Hosted APIs and Hardware Backends 24

Ecosystem Integrators 24

Prompt Engineering Techniques 24

Zero-shot Prompting 25

Lazy Prompting 25

Few-Shot Prompting 26

Chain-of-Thought (CoT) 26

Self-Consistency 27

Least-to-Most (LtM) 27

Multi-Task Prompting 28

Role Prompting 28

Meta-Prompting 29

Tree-of-Thought (ToT) 29

Graph-of-Thought (GoT) 29

Advanced Prompting Techniques 31

Prompt Templates and Parameters 31

Prompt Template 31

Prompt Parameters 32

Prompt Optimization 32

Guardrails 33

Input Guardrails 33

In-Process (Prompt-Level) Guardrails 34

Output Guardrails........ 34

Setting up private/public LLMs........ 35

Private LLM Deployment (On-Prem or Private Cloud)........ 35

Public LLM Deployment (Cloud APIs)........ 36

Hybrid Deployment........ 36

Best Practices and Principles........ 37

Case Studies........ 37

Case Study 1: Finance – Automated EarningsCall Summarizer with CoT Prompting........ 38

Case Study 2: Medical – Triage Support Assistant Using Meta and Role Prompting........ 38

Case Study 3: CRM – Personalized Customer Reply Generator Using Few-shot Prompting........ 39

Case Study 4: Agriculture – Pest Diagnosis Assistant Using LoM Prompting........ 40

Case Study 5: Law – Legal Clause Risk Assessment Using ToT Prompting........ 40

Conclusion........ 41

Further Reading and References........ 42

3. Developing Retrieval-Augmented Generation Systems........ 43

Introduction........ 43

Structure........ 44

Introduction to Different Databases........ 44

Relational Databases........ 45

Document Databases (NoSQL)........ 46

Vector Databases........ 47

Graph Databases........ 48

Redis as a Fast Knowledge Store........ 50

RAG Architecture........ 51

Advanced RAG Architectures........ 53

Techniques to Improve Semantic Matching in RAG........ 55

Handling Big Data in RAG Systems........ 56

Chunking Strategy........ 56

Distributed Embedding Generation 56

Scalable Storage 56

Index Maintenance 57

Hybrid Retrieval Architecture 57

Caching and Routing 57

Evaluation and Monitoring 57

Libraries for RAG Support 57

llamaIndex 58

LangChain 58

LangGraph 61

Deploying RAG Systems 62

Modular and Microservices-Based Architecture 62

Containerization with Docker 63

Kubernetes Orchestration 63

Case Studies 64

Legal Domain – Automating Legal Document Search and Summarization 64

Healthcare – Clinical Decision Support System 65

Customer Support – AI Knowledge Assistant for Telecom Company 65

Mock Interview 66

Conclusion 68

References 69

4. Enhancing Systems Through LLM Finetuning **70**

Introduction 70

Structure 71

Using LLMs for Different Business Applications 72

The Power of Specialization 72

E-Commerce: Personalization at Scale 72

Education and EdTech: Adaptive Learning Assistants 72

LLM Fine-tuning Techniques 73

*Instruction Fine-Tuning: Teaching the Model to "**Follow Orders**"* 76

Parameter-Efficient Fine-Tuning: More with Less 76

Adapter Layers: Plug-and-Play Intelligence 77

Low-Rank Adaptation: Elegant Efficiency 77

Quantized LoRA (QLoRA) 78

Prompt-Tuning and Prefix-Tuning (Lightweight but Limited) 79

Full Fine-Tuning - The Heavyweight Approach 79

Evaluation Strategies 80

Text Quality Metrics (Language Modelling and Generation) 82

Task-Specific Metrics 82

LLM-Specific Metrics 83

Example Business Case-Studies 83

Healthcare: Med42 – Parameter-Efficient Fine-Tuning for Medical Q&A 83

Finance: Prefix-Tuned Summarization of Financial News 84

Legal: LegiLM – Domain-Specific Instruction Tuning for GDPR Compliance 85

Customer Support: ChatGPT for Telecom Helpdesks 85

Libraries and Implementation Strategies 85

LLM Fine-Tuning and Deployment: Best-of-Breed Stack 87

Fine-Tuning (Hugging Face Transformers + PEFT) 87

Scaling Training (Deep Speed) 88

Inference and Deployment - Text Generation Interface 88

API Layer (Fast API) 89

Monitoring (Weights and Biases - W and B) 89

Conclusion 90

References 91

Fun Riddles to Test Your Understanding 92

Answers 93

5. Designing Financial Risk Prediction Systems Using Supervised Learning **94**

Introduction 94

The Risks We Are Trying to Solve 94

Structure 95

Business Case Studies 96

Exploratory Data Analysis 97

Collecting Finance Data 97

Storing Finance Data 97

Cleaning the Data 98

Handle Missing Values 98

Normalization or Scaling 98

Labeling the Data 99

Ethical Considerations (Explainability and Privacy) 100

Compliance with GDPR and CCPA 100

Explainability 101

Introduction to Supervised Machine Learning and Algorithms 103

Regression Versus Classification 103

Key Supervised Machine Learning Algorithms 104

Linear Regression 104

Logistic Regression 105

Decision Trees 105

Gradient Boosting 106

Random Forest 107

Support Vector Machines (SVMs) 109

Neural Networks 111

Comparison of ML Algorithms 112

Explanation of the Table 112

Evaluation Criteria 113

Offline Metrics 114

Classification Metrics 114

Regression Metrics 115

Online Metrics 115

Efficiency Metrics 116

Mock Interview: Building a Loan Prediction Classification System 117

Conclusion 129

Key Points 130

References 130

6. Implementing Unsupervised Learning Systems 132

Introduction 132

Structure 132

Overview and Examples 133

Real-Life Examples of Unsupervised Learning 133

Embedding and Distance Algorithms 134

Distance Algorithms 136

Hamming Distance 136

Euclidean Distance 137

Manhattan Distance 137

Cosine Similarity 138

Mahalanobis Distance 138

Real-World Explanation 140

Embeddings for string Data 141

Embeddings for Image data 142

Using HOG Features as Image Embeddings 142

Clustering Algorithms 142

K-Means Algorithm (Partition Algorithm) 143

Hierarchical Clustering (Agglomerative and Divisive Methods) 144

Density-based Clustering: DBSCAN, OPTICS 145

Gaussian Mixture Model (GMM) 146

Latent Dirichlet Allocation (LDA) 148

Evaluation Criteria 150

Silhouette Coefficient 150

Coherence......151

Purity......152

Business Case Studies......152

Topic Modeling......153

Applications in CRM......153

Customer Segmentation......154

Applications in CRM......154

Anomaly Detection......154

Case Study: Topic Modeling for CRM......155

Business Requirement......155

Data Curation......155

Feature Engineering......156

Algorithm Selection......157

Model Evaluation......160

Deployment......160

Evaluation and Iteration......160

Conclusion......161

Multiple Choice Questions......161

Answers......163

References......163

7. Building Recommendation Systems for E-Commerce......164

Introduction......164

Structure......165

Recommendation Systems and Real-Life Use Cases......165

How Recommendation Systems Became a Game-Changer......165

Netflix: A $1 Billion Algorithm......165

Amazon: The Master of Cross-Selling......166

Spotify: Understanding Musical Tastes......167

Why Recommendation Systems Matter......167

The Challenge: Making Recommendations Smarter and Fairer......167

Evolution of Recommendation Algorithms 168

Rule-Based Systems (Early Days) 169

Content-Based Filtering 169

Collaborative Filtering (User Based and Item Based) 170

User-based Collaboration 170

Item-based Collaboration 171

Matrix Factorization 172

Original User-Item Matrix 173

Popular Matrix Factorization Techniques 173

User Matrix (U) 173

Item Matrix (V) 174

Predicted User-Item Ratings Matrix 174

Two-Tower Network 175

Architecture Overview 175

Workflow 176

Deep Learning-Based Approaches 177

Neural Collaborative Filtering 177

Autoencoders for Latent Representation Learning 177

Use in Recommendation Systems 178

Transformer-Based Models (BERT4Rec) 178

Graph Neural Networks for Recommendations 179

Architecture 179

Measuring the Success of a Recommendation System 183

Accuracy-Based Metrics 183

Recall 183

F1-Score: Finding the Right Balance 184

Precision@K 184

Normalized Discounted Cumulative Gain (NDCG): Prioritizing Highly Relevant Items 184

Engagement Metrics 185

Business KPIs 185

Cold Start Problem Handling 185

New Users: Personalization without History......185
New Items: No Interaction Data Available......186
Cross-Domain Knowledge Transfer......186
Promotions: Leveraging Engagement Data......186
Diversity, Ethical AI, and Explainability......187
Diversity and Serendipity: Avoiding Filter Bubbles......187
Fairness and Bias Mitigation: Addressing Algorithmic Bias......189
Explainability: Making Recommendation Logic Transparent......190
Privacy and Security Considerations: Handling User Data Responsibly......191
Experimentation, User Feedback, and Data Drifts......192
Mock Interview Example......193
Business Requirements......193
Data Collection and Labelling......194
Knowledge Graph Construction......195
Algorithm......195
Ranking......196
Offline Processing (Precomputed Features and Matching)......197
Online Processing (Real-Time Inference and Ranking)......198
Hybrid Approach (Balanced Trade-Off)......199
Evaluation Metrics......200
Conclusion......200
Multiple Choice Questions......201
Answers......202
References......202
8. Building Image Classification Models for Edge Devices......203
Introduction......203
Structure......204
Introduction to Image Classification......204
Types of Image Classification......206

Designing an Image Classification Model 206
Image Annotation Techniques 207
Challenges in Image Annotation 208
Annotation Tools for Image Classification 208
Techniques to Reduce Annotation Time 209
Architecture Evolution 209
Classical Machine Learning for Image Classification 210
Feature Extraction Techniques 210
Traditional Machine Learning Models 210
Convolutional Neural Networks (CNNs) 211
CNNs Overview 211
Key CNN Architectures 212
Lightweight CNN Variants for Edge Deployment 212
Vision Transformers (ViTs) and Modern Approaches 213
Introduction to Vision Transformers 213
Efficient Vision Transformers for Edge Deployment 214
Tradeoffs between Latency and Performance 214
Data Processing Architectures: Edge versus Cloud versus Hybrid 215
Architectural Components: End-to-End Flow 216
Model Optimization and Deployment Strategies 218
Data Optimization Techniques 218
Quantization 219
Functionality 219
Mixed Precision 220
Functionality 220
Pruning 221
Functionality 221
Knowledge Distillation 222
Lightweight Model Design 225
Hardware Aware Training 226
Sparsity and Low-Rank Approximations 227

Real-Life Case Studies 228

Agriculture: Pest Classification on Edge Devices 228

Agriculture: Precision Farming 229

Remote Medical Diagnosis: Detecting Diabetic Retinopathy 229

Industrial Defect Detection and Predictive Maintenance 230

Wildlife Conservation: Species Identification in Remote Forests 230

Mock Interview 231

Requirements Gathering 231

Data Collection 232

Model Selection 233

Evaluation Metrics 234

Deployment Considerations 234

Conclusion 236

References 237

9. Designing Sequence-to-Sequence Systems 238

Introduction 238

Structure 239

Applications of Sequence-to-Sequence Models 239

Machine Translation 239

Speech Transcription 240

Summarization in Media and Research 240

From Questions to Insight 240

Machines That Talk Back 240

The Pattern behind the Magic 241

Data Creation and Annotation Challenges 242

Solutions to Annotation Challenges 243

Doccano 245

Label Studio 246

Prodigy (Commercial) 246

LightTag (Commercial) 247

ELAN 247
Architecture Evolution 247
The Recurrent Neural Networks Era (2014) 248
Long Short Term Memory Networks 249
LSTMs are Better for Long Sequences 251
Learning to Focus: The Rise of Attention (2015) 252
The Transformer Revolution: Attention is All You Need (2017) 254
Pretraining and the Modern Seq2Seq Renaissance 255
Bidirectional Encoder Representations from Transformers 256
Bidirectional and Auto-Regressive Transformers 256
Designing Encoders and Decoders for Transformers 257
Common Encoder Architectures 258
Choosing the Right Decoder 259
Choosing the Right Tokenizer 259
Choosing the Right Positional Encoding 260
Choosing the Correct Attention Mechanism 261
Evaluation Strategies 264
Automatic Metrics 264
Bilingual Evaluation Understudy (BLEU) 264
Recall-Oriented Understudy for Gisting Evaluation (ROUGE) 264
Embedding-Based and Learned Metrics 265
Human Evaluation 266
Case Study of Building a Summarization Engine 266
Dataset and Setup 267
Data Preprocessing 267
Fine-Tuning the Model 269
Testing the Summarization Model 270
Serving and Deployment 271
Model Serving with FastAPI 271
Scaling and Optimization for Serving 273

Monitoring the Summarization Service ... 273
Example in Our Context ... 274
Real-World Effectiveness ... 275
Tips for Further Improvement ... 275
Wrapping Up the Case Study ... 276
Trivia ... 276
Answers ... 277
Conclusion ... 277
References ... 278

10. Building Domain-Specific LLMs from Scratch ... 280
Introduction ... 280
Structure ... 281
Data Creation ... 281
Sourcing Domain-Specific Data ... 282
Preprocessing and Normalization ... 284
Format Normalization ... 284
Noise Removal and Filtering ... 284
Deduplication ... 284
Preserving Structural Markers ... 285
Best Practices in Tokenization ... 285
Supervised Learning ... 288
Privacy, Licensing, and Ethical Considerations ... 288
Privacy and PII Removal ... 289
Licensing and Copyright ... 289
Ethical Use and Bias ... 289
Compliance and Legal Constraints ... 290
Open Source vs Proprietary Considerations ... 290
Transformer Architecture in Depth ... 291
Encoder and Decoder: Decoded ... 292
Multi-Head Self-Attention (Shared by Encoder and Decoder) ... 294
Encoder and Decoder Layers ... 296

Full Transformer (encoder-decoder) 297

Model Size: Layers, Heads, and Hidden Dimensions 299

Design Recommendations for Domain-Specific LLMs 301

Distributed Training 302

Data Parallelism 302

Model Parallelism 304

Pipeline Parallelism 305

Tensor Parallelism 306

ZeRO and Sharded Optimizers 306

Strategic Considerations and Trade-offs 307

Frameworks 307

Evaluation and Deployment 308

General Metrics 308

LLM Evaluation Frameworks 309

Deployment Strategies 309

Case Study: Building a Legal LLM from Scratch 310

Data Collection and Preparation 310

Model Design 311

Training Process 311

Evaluation 311

Deployment and Usage 312

Conclusion 312

References 313

11. Building Multimodal Applications for Healthcare 315

Introduction 315

Structure 316

Multimodal Dataset Preparation 316

Data Preprocessing 318

Audio Processing 318

Video Data and Multimodal Representations 319

Decomposing Video into Modalities 319

Multimodal Embeddings and Alignment 319

Early Fusion 320
Late Fusion 321
Contrastive Learning 322
Projection Networks 324
Cross-Modal Attention 325
Multimodal Architectures 327
Contrastive Language–Image Pre-training (CLIP) 327
Weekly Supervised Speech Recognition (Whisper) 328
A Large-Scale ImaGe and Noisy-Text Embedding (ALIGN) 330
Bootstrapping Language-Image Pre-training (BLIP) 331
Facebook AI (FLAVA) 331
VideoBERT 332
Evaluation Strategies 332
Image–Text Retrieval 333
Image Captioning 333
Visual Question Answering (VQA) 334
Visual Grounding (Referring Expression Comprehension) 334
Speech Recognition (ASR) 334
Speech Translation (ST) 334
Video Captioning 334
Video Retrieval (Video–Text Retrieval) 335
Video Question Answering 335
Text-to-Image Generation 335
Audio-to-Text Generation (Audio Captioning) 336
Best Practices and Pitfalls 336
Business Case Studies in the Healthcare Segment 337
Radiology + EHR Fusion 337
Neurodegenerative Disease Diagnosis 338
Video + Sensor Input in Vestibular Diagnosis 338
Cardiology: ECG + Echocardiography Fusion 338
Oncology: Prostate Cancer Treatment Planning 338
Clinical Workflows + Admin Support 338

Key Takeaways 338
Deployment Trade-Offs 339
Decoupled Model Splitting (Image versus Text Nodes) 340
Co-locating Stages 340
Latency versus Throughput 340
Edge versus Cloud Deployment 340
Cost and Scalability 341
Best Practices 341
Mock Interview 341
Interview Question 341
Conclusion 345
References 346
Index 347

CHAPTER 1
Introduction to AI System Design

Introduction

AI system design lies at the intersection of technology, innovation, and problem-solving. This chapter sets the stage for understanding the foundational principles and complexities involved in building AI systems. We begin by exploring the core aspects of system design for AI, shedding light on the unique challenges that arise when transitioning from traditional software systems to intelligent, learning-driven architectures.

The journey of AI system evolution is examined, from rule-based systems to machine learning models, and further to the transformative power of deep learning and large language models (LLMs). Through this, we aim to highlight the paradigm shifts in capabilities and applications that have redefined how AI systems are designed.

For aspiring professionals preparing for AI system design interviews, this chapter provides actionable insights into the interview process, including typical formats, key preparation strategies, and a structured template to approach design questions effectively. By merging technical depth with practical guidance, this chapter equips readers to tackle the complexities and leverage the opportunities presented by modern AI system design.

Structure

In this chapter, we will cover the following topics:

- System Design for AI
    - Challenges in System Design
- Evolution of System Design
    - Rule-Based Versus Machine Learning
    - Machine Learning Versus Deep Learning

    - Using Large Language Models
- AI System Design Interviews
    - Preparing for the Interview
    - Interview Format
    - Template for AI System Design Questions

System Design for AI

System design often feels like a daunting, mythical challenge—but the reality is far simpler. Designing AI systems is not just about training models but extends beyond the process of model training—it encompasses the integration of those models into real-world environments, where data is imperfect, user expectations are high, and computational resources are both finite and costly.

While AI system design shares the foundational principles of traditional software engineering—such as defining requirements, architecting components, and ensuring scalability—the key distinction lies in its dynamic, data-driven nature. Unlike conventional systems, which operate on fixed logic and produce consistent outputs, AI systems are probabilistic and evolve through feedback loops. Their performance depends not only on code but also on the quality, quantity, and timeliness of data, requiring mechanisms for continuous learning, monitoring, and adaptation. This also extends to deployment, where trade-offs must be carefully evaluated: cloud-based deployments may offer scalability and ease of integration but can raise latency, privacy, and cost concerns, while on-premise or edge deployments enhance control and responsiveness at the expense of hardware investment and maintenance overhead. Effective AI system design, therefore, must balance adaptability, reliability, and deployment strategy to ensure long-term performance and value.

Imagine designing a robot that brews the perfect coffee for everyone in your college/ office. It is not just about programming the robot to pour coffee; it is about:

- **Understanding preferences**: Gathering and analyzing data about individual tastes.
- **Training the robot's "*taste buds*"**: Using machine learning to teach it what "*perfect coffee*" means. The training data could include measurable attributes such as the coffee-to-water ratio, brewing temperature, grind size, milk type, sugar level, and brewing time, combined with user feedback on each cup's taste.
- **Making the perfect brew**: Ensuring precision and consistency in every cup and offering the best taste.
- **Improving over time**: Optimizing based on user feedback.

- **Avoiding costly mistakes**: Implementing safeguards, such as preventing spills on the supervisor's laptop.

Building AI products means designing systems that do not just function but adapt, improve, and deliver value under real-world constraints.

This mix of creativity, logic, and engineering is what makes system design for AI both exciting and challenging.

Figure 1.1: *Imaginative picture of a personalized AI coffee maker*

Challenges in AI System Design

Designing AI products presents a set of challenges that go far beyond those encountered in traditional software development. One of the most pressing challenges is the rapid evolution of the field. New research breakthroughs, architectures, and terminologies emerge at a dizzying pace, making it difficult for teams to stay current and evaluate which innovations are truly impactful versus those that are transient trends. This constant change means that design decisions made today may be outdated in a matter of months, demanding agility in both technology choices and product strategy.

- Another complexity stems from the **numerous alternatives** available when building AI solutions. Practitioners can choose from cutting-edge large language models (LLMs), specialized deep learning architectures, or more classical machine learning algorithms–each with different strengths, limitations, and operational costs. Navigating these options is not trivial; even experienced AI engineers can find themselves weighing trade-offs between model complexity, interpretability, scalability, and domain fit.

- The **quality of data** poses yet another challenge. Unlike academic environments, where datasets are often curated, balanced, and well-documented, real-world data is imperfect or incomplete, and at times biased. In many cases, the data is also scarce or difficult to collect, forcing engineers to devise strategies for augmentation, cleaning, and validation to ensure the model can perform reliably in production.
- **Resource constraints** further complicate the process. While state-of-the-art AI models can demand vast computational power and specialized hardware, most industry applications must be optimized for cost-effectiveness and energy efficiency. This creates a tension between adopting the most accurate, complex models and deploying solutions that can run within practical infrastructure and budgetary limits.
- Finally, successful AI system development requires looking **beyond the model** itself. A high-performing algorithm is only one piece of the puzzle. Teams must manage the entire lifecycle–data collection, preprocessing, training, deployment, monitoring, and iteration–while also addressing trade-offs between accuracy, latency, scalability, and cost. Building an AI product is thus an exercise in systems thinking; where engineering, design, and business considerations must all align to deliver a solution that is both technically sound and operationally viable.

Figure 1.2: *Depicting the complexity of AI system design*

Evolution of System Design

The past decade has witnessed a remarkable transformation in AI system design. Initially, the transition from logic-driven algorithms to data-driven methodologies marked a paradigm shift, laying the foundation for modern AI. This shift introduced both opportunities and challenges, as academic research and industry adoption drove the evolution of system architectures.

The advent of deep learning was a pivotal moment, enabling breakthroughs in tasks such as complex image recognition and natural language understanding. This era marked the first significant transition toward more powerful AI capabilities. The emergence of pre-trained models and large language models (LLMs) further accelerated the pace of innovation, redefining the landscape of AI system design. These models, with their ability to generalize across tasks, have rapidly become the cornerstone of modern AI solutions.

Organizations now face the challenge of balancing cost-efficiency, performance, and suitability for specific system requirements. The evolution of system design reflects the dynamic interplay between technological advancements and practical constraints.

Rule-Based Versus Machine Learning

In the early days of machine learning evolution around 2015, engineering managers were concerned about using machine learning models. They were used to the engineering systems that operate on '*logic*' or code that they write. Using systems that operate on '*data*' was difficult to digest for them. Also, they felt that machine learning-based systems were difficult to explain. Developers will not have control over what happens inside the ML systems. Also, rule-based systems will be 100% accurate. ML-based systems may work or may not work. It is difficult to explain "*when do they work?*"

Developers/Managers used to resort to a '**`rule`**' based system as much as possible. Let us consider the following example.

Scenario: Email Spam Filtering

Initially, an organization builds a spam filter using a rule-based system. Rules are hardcoded based on patterns observed in spam emails, such as:

- Emails containing specific keywords (for example, "**`win`**", "**`lottery`**", "**`free money`**").
- Emails from suspicious domains (for example, *@spamdomain.com).
- Emails with excessive punctuation or uppercase letters (for example, "**`!!!WIN NOW!!!`**").

The rule-based system is simple to implement and effective for clearly identifiable spam patterns.

However, there are certain challenges with scaling the Rule-Based System.

- **Evolving Patterns**: Spammers continually adapt, using synonyms ("`prize`" instead of "`win`") or obfuscating keywords ("`w!n`").
- High False Positives/Negatives:
  - Legitimate emails flagged as spam due to overly broad rules.
  - Sophisticated spam bypasses rules by mimicking legitimate content.
- **Complexity Management**: As spam patterns evolve, maintaining and updating thousands of rules becomes unmanageable.
- **Personalization**: Rules do not account for user-specific preferences (for example, what one user considers spam may be valuable to another).

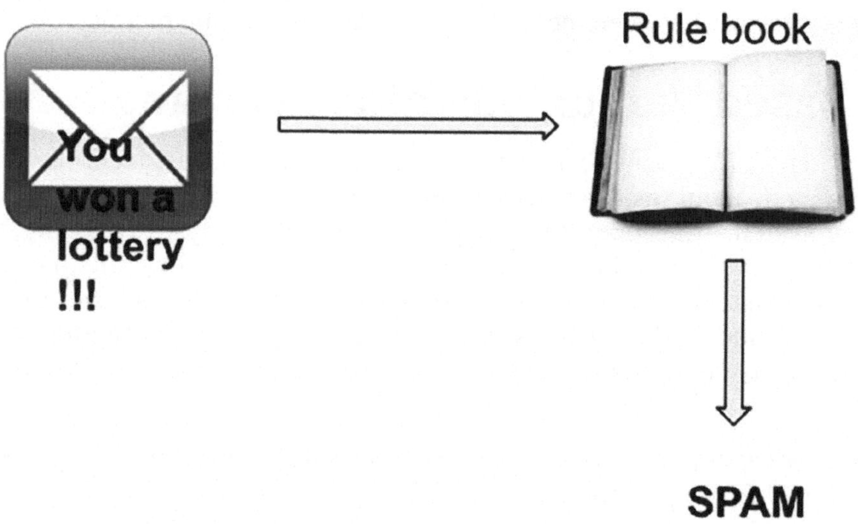

Figure 1.3: *Depicting rule-based SPAM filtering*

To address these challenges, the organization transitions to an ML-based spam filtering system.

How ML Solves the Problem

- **Data-Driven Learning:**
  - ML models (for example, Naive Bayes, Support Vector Machines, or deep learning) are trained on a labeled dataset of spam and non-spam emails.

- Models learn nuanced patterns beyond simple keywords, considering context and combinations of features.

- **Continuous Adaptation**: ML systems can be retrained periodically to adapt to evolving spam techniques.
- **Scalability**: Unlike rules, ML models handle complexity and scale well without manual intervention for every new spam type.
- **Personalization**: User-specific filters are enabled by training models on individual users' email preferences.

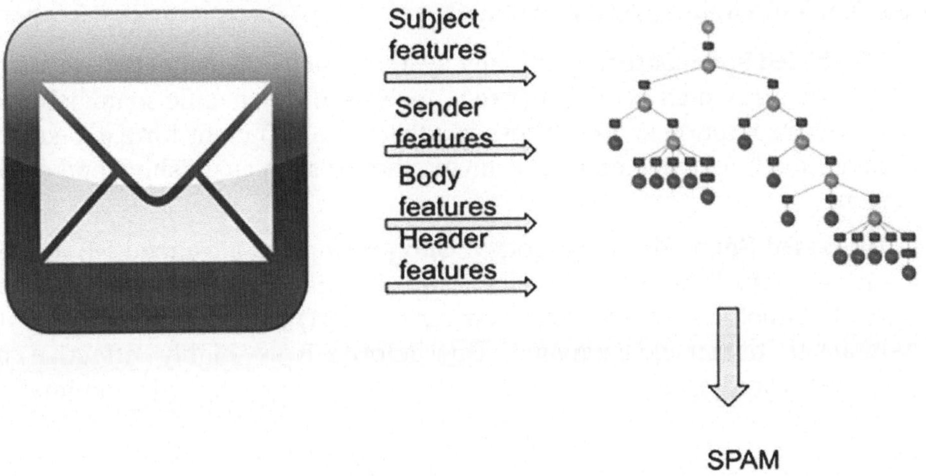

Figure 1.4: *Spam filtering using machine learning*

Machine Learning Versus Deep Learning

Deep learning introduced a new paradigm for solving NLP and computer vision problems. Instead of relying heavily on hand-crafted features, the focus shifted to building rich, multi-layered neural networks that could automatically learn features from data. Tasks such as translation, speech recognition, and image understanding became not only feasible but also significantly more precise with deep learning frameworks. However, this shift brought its own set of challenges for developers:

- **Data Requirements**: Deep learning models require vast amounts of labeled data for training. Developers needed to ensure the data was a realistic representation of the real world.

  Example: Training a sentiment analysis model on product reviews requires diverse and balanced datasets to avoid bias.

- **Computational Demands**: Deep learning models demand significant computing resources for training, introducing challenges around cost and latency.

Example: Training a complex model such as GPT-3 involves thousands of GPUs running for weeks, which is prohibitively expensive for most organizations.

- **Deployment Challenges**: Deploying large deep learning models remains a critical challenge, particularly for real-time applications. The size and complexity of these models introduce latency and cost concerns during inference.

  Example: Serving a real-time chatbot powered by a large model requires low-latency responses, which can be difficult with traditional deep learning setups.

Example: Real-World Integration in Gmail

- **ML-Based Spam Filtering:** Initially, systems such as Gmail relied on ML models with features such as email content analysis, user-specific spam behavior, and sender reputation scores. These models were sufficient for early-stage spam detection but struggled with evolving tactics such as phishing and contextual spam.
- **DL-Based Spam Filtering:** Today, Google employs advanced DL models that analyze email content, metadata, and user interaction patterns, leveraging models such as Transformers (similar to BERT) to understand the contextual nuances of email language. This approach is highly effective against sophisticated spam tactics and can adapt dynamically with minimal manual intervention.

Trade-offs between ML and DL System Design

Let us take a look at the comparison between ML and DL System design approaches.

Aspect	ML-Based Approach	DL-Based Approach
Model Type	Traditional ML models such as Naive Bayes, SVM, or Random Forest.	Deep learning models such as RNNs, CNNs, or Transformers.
Feature Engineering	Requires significant manual effort to extract features such as keywords, sender reputation, or email metadata.	Learn features automatically from raw data such as email text or metadata.
Data Dependency	Performs well with smaller datasets when features are carefully designed.	Requires large-scale labeled data to train effectively.
Contextual Understanding	Limited contextual understanding, relying on predefined features and simple patterns.	Captures complex relationships and semantics, such as nuanced language usage or context.

Processing Speed	Faster to train and deploy due to lower complexity.	Training and inference can be computationally expensive and slower.
Adaptability	Needs regular manual updates to feature sets as spam tactics evolve.	Automatically adapts to new patterns with retraining, leveraging its ability to learn representations.
Scalability	Easier to scale with moderate computational requirements.	Requires significant computational resources and optimized infrastructure for scalability.
Explainability	Easier to interpret predictions based on known features.	Harder to explain due to the "*black box*" nature of deep learning models.
Performance on Complex Spam	Struggles with sophisticated or evolving spam strategies.	Excels in detecting complex and context-sensitive spam messages.

Table 1.1: *Comparison between ML and DL system design approaches*

While ML-based approaches are simpler and resource-efficient, DL-based approaches dominate in accuracy and robustness, especially in large-scale systems such as Google's spam filtering, where adaptability and contextual understanding are paramount.

Traditional Machine Learning System Design

Designing a traditional machine learning (ML) or deep learning (DL) system is not just about training a model–it is a structured process that moves from understanding raw data to delivering a production-ready solution. Building traditional machine learning/deep learning systems involved the following stages:

1. **Data Collection, Analysis, and Pre-processing:** Fetching the data, analyzing the data, and labeling the training data are done during this phase.
2. **Model building:** In this phase, we will train and build the model from scratch.
3. **Model Evaluation:** The models are evaluated using the right evaluation metrics.
4. **Experimentation and selecting the right model:** The model behavior is monitored during the experimentation phase, and the right model is designed using latency/cost tradeoff considerations, feedback, and business results.
5. **Deployment:** The model is deployed into production and monitored.

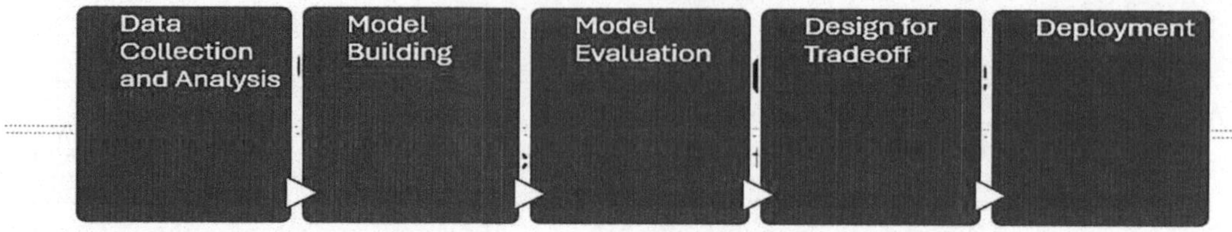

Figure 1.5: *Bottom-up design using machine learning/deep learning*

Using Large Language Models

Large Language Models (LLMs) have dramatically transformed the way we work, starting with ChatGPT and followed by an ever-growing lineup of generative models. These include LLaMA from Meta, Gemini from Google, Phi from Microsoft, Claude from Anthropic, and many others. The landscape of LLMs expands almost weekly, with each iteration bringing enhanced capabilities and broader applicability.

The journey of LLMs can be traced back to the introduction of BERT, which set the stage for modern AI's evolution. Let us look at this evolution stage-by-stage:

Stage 1. Pre-trained Models

These models were trained on vast amounts of text data to solve tasks such as Masked Language Modeling (MLM). For example, BERT is pre-trained to predict masked words in a sentence, such as:

- **Input**: "*The [MASK] is blue.*"
- **Prediction**: "*The sky is blue.*"

Stage 2. Generative Models

Models such as GPT-2 and beyond introduced generative capabilities. Pre-trained on vast datasets, they can perform multiple tasks such as translation, summarization, and creative text generation without additional task-specific training. For instance, ChatGPT can generate a poem, summarize a legal document, or write a software snippet.

Stage 3. Multi-modal LLMs

Models extend beyond text to include image understanding, speech recognition, and even video generation. For example, OpenAI's DALL-E generates images based on textual prompts, while models such as Gemini from Google process text, images, and speech simultaneously.

Stage 4. Small Language Models (SLMs)

Designed to run efficiently on CPU environments, these models, such as Microsoft Phi-mini, sacrifice some accuracy for lower latency and cost, making them suitable for resource-constrained settings.

In this book, for simplicity, we collectively refer to these diverse models as Large Language Models (LLMs).

While LLMs have revolutionized how we approach problems, organizations face a critical challenge: integrating these models into practical, scalable systems.

The process typically starts with evaluating existing models and fine-tuning them if necessary. Only when trade-offs such as accuracy, latency, or cost are not met do companies consider building custom models from scratch. Many common problems, such as text classification or image classification, can now be solved with popular LLMs.

Here is a breakdown of how different models are utilized:

- Open-source models such as LLaMA, GPT-OSS enable customization through fine-tuning with specific datasets.
- Small models such as Phi-mini offer low-latency and cost-efficient solutions, often at the expense of some accuracy.
- Commercial models such as those from OpenAI deliver high precision but come with higher operational costs.

Steps in Designing AI Systems with LLMs

Unlike traditional ML pipelines that begin with raw data and build upward, the top-down approach with LLMs starts from the end goal (the application) and works backward to design the system. The design of AI systems using LLMs typically follows these stages:

1. **Data Collection:** Collecting relevant, clean, and diverse data tailored to the task at hand. For spam detection, this could include labeled datasets of emails marked as "*spam*" or "*not spam*," ensuring diversity in languages, topics, and spam strategies.
2. **Model Evaluation:** Assessing available models for trade-offs in cost, accuracy, and latency. For instance, a small model such as Phi-mini might suffice for a lightweight email app, while OpenAI models may be better for enterprise-level spam detection.

3. **Fine-tuning:** Enhancing a pre-trained model's performance by fine-tuning it with domain-specific data. For example, using email datasets that include regional spam patterns or phishing scams to improve spam filtering accuracy.
4. **Optimization:** Reducing model size or computation requirements through techniques such as quantization or distillation, ensuring the model meets real-world latency or cost constraints.
5. **Deployment:** Rolling out the model to production, integrating it into pipelines such as Gmail spam filtering, and monitoring for feedback.

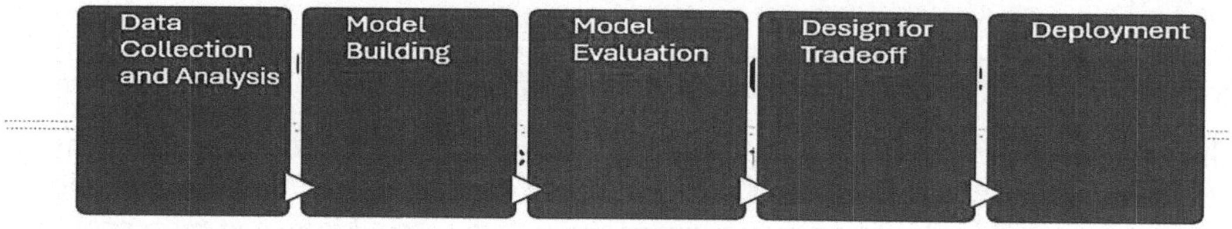

Figure 1.6: *AI System design using LLMs*

Example: Spam Detection with LLMs

Spam detection can leverage the power of LLMs, specifically generative and fine-tuned models:

- **Using Generative Models:** A model such as ChatGPT or Claude can be trained to classify an email as spam or not by examining its tone, structure, and keywords. For example, it can detect phishing emails by understanding context, such as financial urgency or suspicious links.
- **Enhancing Contextual Understanding:** Unlike traditional ML models that rely on static features (for example, the presence of specific keywords), LLMs understand semantics. They can identify subtle patterns, such as formal language disguising spam content.
- **Real-time Adaptability:** LLMs can adapt to new spam trends by fine-tuning with updated datasets, reducing the risk of outdated rules or patterns.
- **Multi-modal Advantage:** Multi-modal LLMs could extend spam detection to analyze images or attachments embedded in emails, detecting hidden threats such as malicious links in images.

Now, we will learn how to apply these approaches for different applications. We will learn these applications in detail in the upcoming chapters.

Use Case	Rule-Based Approach	Machine Learning (ML)	Deep Learning (DL)	LLM-Based Approach
1. Customer Churn Prediction	Method: Rules on usage decrease or complaints.	Method: Logistic Regression, Decision Trees. Pros: Good for tabular KPIs & clear factors.	Method: Deep nets for sequential usage behavior.	Method: LLM summarizes customer feedback, sentiment & acts as reasoning engine.
2. Document Classification	Keyword-matching, regex logic.	Word Vectors + ML algorithms.	BERT/RoBERTa LLM fine-tuning.	Zero-shot classification using generative AI.
3. Sentiment Analysis	Lookup lists of positive/negative words.	Classical ML with word vectors.	Transformers (BERT/RoBERTa).	LLMs interpret sarcasm, nuanced sentiment without training.
4. Recommendation System	If user likes X → recommend Y (manual mapping).	Collaborative filtering, matrix factorization.	Deep recommender systems (Neural CF, Transformers).	LLM-based conversational recommendation powered by RAG.
5. Medical Diagnosis Support	If symptoms → possible disease mapping.	ML using diagnostic KPIs.	CNNs for X-ray, MRI, ECG.	LLM interprets reports, summarizes EHR, reasons clinically (with guardrails).
6. Image Classification (Defect detection)	Manual visual check rules.	ML algorithms with hand-crafted features.	CNN-based models (ResNet, EfficientNet).	LLM agents orchestrate vision models + interpret root causes.
7. OCR / Text Extraction	Rule-based template matching.	Classical ML (SVM on character images).	Deep CNN/RNN OCR engines (Tesseract 5 w/DL).	LLM corrects extracted text, interprets noisy OCR.
8. Text Summarization	Manually written summary templates.	Extractive ML methods.	Transformer-based abstractive models.	GPT-like large models with near-human summarization.

9. Product Categorization (E-commerce)	Regex rules.	ML with word vectors.	BERT fine-tuning.	LLM zero-shot classification.
10. Topic Modelling	Manual keyword grouping	Clustering algorithms	BERTopic (Transformer embeddings)	LLMs auto-label topics + cluster using embeddings.

***Table 1.2**: Comparison of different approaches for common use-cases*

AI System Design Interviews

The primary goal of a system design interview is to assess whether the candidate can practically apply theoretical concepts to real-world scenarios. Additionally, it evaluates the depth and breadth of the candidate's knowledge. These interviews typically involve **open-ended questions** with multiple possible solutions. By presenting these scenarios and challenging the candidate to think on their feet, the interviewer gains insight into their problem-solving approach, technical expertise, and creativity.

Understanding the interviewer's intent is key to succeeding in a system design interview. The interviewer might be tackling a specific ML problem in their organization and could have already considered basic solutions. In such cases, they are often looking for:

- **Foundational knowledge**: Does the candidate understand the standard approaches?
- **Innovative thinking**: Can the candidate suggest new, efficient, or innovative solutions beyond the basics?

Preparing for the Interview

Nailing the ML System Design interview is never a cakewalk. It's where algorithms meet real-world constraints, data pipelines meet scalability, and your thinking meets the company's expectations. Let's uncover the mindset, tools, and tactics you need to crack it.

Research the Organization

Before the interview, spend time learning about the company and its AI initiatives. Visit their website, LinkedIn page, and job postings to understand their projects and focus areas.

- **Example Insights by Industry:**
    - **Indeed**: Works on AI for job/resume matching, fraud detection in

resumes or job descriptions, and personalized job recommendations for applicants.

  - **Microsoft**: Focuses on building AI copilots for products such as Bing, Office, and Azure. Their NLP solutions include autosuggest, translation, and speech recognition for Bing, while Office teams work on security, compliance, and privacy AI solutions.
  - **Amazon**: Heavy on e-commerce, with AI initiatives in product catalog enrichment, recommendation systems, and supply chain optimizations.
  - **Finance Organizations (for example, CRED)**: Develop credit risk forecasting models, risk portfolio assessment tools, and explainable AI solutions for financial analysis.

By researching the company's past and present AI solutions, you can anticipate the kinds of problems they are tackling and align your preparation accordingly.

Stay Updated on AI Trends

The AI field evolves rapidly, and staying informed about the latest developments can give you an edge in interviews. However, the sheer volume of information can be overwhelming, so focus on reliable, concise resources:

- **Alphasignal/The rundown AI**: A daily newsletter covering the latest AI updates.
- **Paperswithcode(Huggingface)**: Tracks trending research papers and state-of-the-art benchmarks.
- **Daily Dose of Data Science**: Industry-oriented insights in a digestible format.

Whether you are preparing for a system design interview or aiming to build similar AI solutions, this book serves as a **comprehensive guide**. It bridges the gap between theoretical knowledge and practical implementation, helping you approach system design problems with confidence and clarity.

The Interview Format

Let us talk about what to expect in a typical AI system design interview:

- **The Problem Statement**: You will be given a real-world problem, such as designing a movie recommendation system or a fraud detection pipeline. Your job is to break it down into smaller, manageable chunks.
- **Discussion Phase**: This is where you shine. You will discuss trade-offs, brainstorm ideas, and impress the interviewer with your understanding of the problem.

- **Whiteboarding/Diagramming**: Here is your chance to show your visual flair. Sketch out the system architecture, data flow, and interactions.
- **Follow-Up Questions**: Be ready for curveballs! Interviewers love to ask about edge cases, scaling issues, and optimization opportunities.

Template for AI System Design Questions

Templates are like recipes for cooking–they help you organize your ingredients and steps so you do not accidentally serve a burnt *Biryani*. In system design, a good template ensures you do not miss any critical aspects of the system.

Here is a stage-wise collection of ML system design questions designed to reflect how interviews progress in real companies – from defining the problem to scaling and productionizing the solution.:

1. **Understand the Problem**
    a. Clarify requirements: Functional and non-functional.
    b. Ask questions: Is the system real-time? What is the scale?
    c. Define success metrics: Accuracy, latency, scalability, and so on.
2. **Data Pipeline**
    a. Where is the data coming from?
    b. How will you clean, preprocess, and store it?
    c. Which database to choose from and how to design it?
    d. How to ensure the privacy of the data?
    e. Any statistical techniques applied to the data?
3. **Data Labeling**
    a. Do we need labeled data? (Supervised versus unsupervised problem)
    b. How to increase the data points?
    c. How do we label the data?
    d. How to prepare training and testing data?
    e. Are we using online/offline features?
    f. How do we measure bias in the data?

4. **Model Selection and Training**
    a. What kind of model suits the problem (for example, deep learning, classical ML)?
    b. What are the different model design options?
    c. What are the compute and storage requirements?
    d. Do we need to build a model from scratch or use pre-trained models?
    e. How to tune the hyperparameters?
    f. How to versionize the models?
    g. What evaluation metrics are used? How to select the best model?
5. **Model Optimization**
    a. Where do we want the model to be deployed?
    b. What are some model optimization techniques?
6. **Model Serving**
    a. How will you deploy the model (batch, real-time, edge devices)?
    b. What is your latency and budget?
    c. How do we design the system to meet the latency/throughput/cost?
    d. Any caching strategies?
    e. What are the deployment strategies?
7. **Experimentation**
    a. How will we run the experiments?
    b. Which online metrics are used to measure the model's performance?
    c. How to measure the experimentation success?
8. **Monitoring and Feedback**
    a. How will you track model performance in production?
    b. How to detect data drifts?
    c. What is the plan for retraining and updates?
    d. How to integrate the model into CI/CD pipelines?

9. **Scaling and Optimization**
    a. How will you handle increasing user demands?
    b. What are your optimization strategies (cost versus performance)?
    c. How to deploy the model on a large scale using cloud/Kubernetes?
10. **Edge Cases and Failures**
    a. How will the system behave under extreme conditions?
    b. What is the fallback mechanism?
11. **Explainability and Responsibility**
    a. How do we make the model explainable?
    b. Are we using Responsible AI practices?

Conclusion

System design for AI is like putting together the ultimate puzzle—except the pieces keep changing. This chapter sets the stage for your journey into mastering the art of AI system design. You have seen why it matters, what the interview process looks like, and a handy template to guide you.

As you move forward, remember: this is not just about landing a dream job. It is about thinking like an architect, solving real-world challenges, and creating systems that make life better (or at least more interesting).

We will discuss diverse scenarios and the system design solutions to address various real-world problems in the coming chapters. Stay tuned!

Points to Remember

- **AI System Design involves a holistic approach**: It integrates data engineering, machine learning, software engineering, and system architecture.
- **Understand the trade-offs**: Accuracy versus interpretability, cost versus performance, latency versus accuracy.
- **Templates help structure responses**: Structure the response in a template for the data pipeline till deployment.

Multiple Choice Questions

1. What is the primary difference between rule-based systems and ML systems?
    a. Rule-based systems require training data; ML does not.
    b. ML systems rely on predefined rules.
    c. Rule-based systems rely on human-defined logic, and ML systems learn from data.
    d. Rule-based systems are scalable; ML systems are not.
2. Which of the following is a key challenge in AI system design?
    a. Data preprocessing
    b. Scalability
    c. Data privacy
    d. All of the above
3. Which is NOT a feature of deep learning models?
    a. Designed for unstructured data
    b. Low computational requirements
    c. Use of neural networks
    d. Complex architecture for feature extraction

Answers

1. c
2. d
3. b

CHAPTER 2
Crafting Intelligent Systems Using Prompt Engineering

Introduction

Imagine having an assistant that understands your industry, thinks critically, and communicates fluently—all at the speed of thought. Welcome to the revolution powered by Large Language Models (LLMs) and prompt engineering. Today, we stand at a tipping point: where language intelligence is not just a tool—it is a collaborator.

Why LLMs Matter Now

- **Unparalleled versatility**: From drafting emails and writing code to reasoning through complex problems and analyzing multimodal data, LLMs have become Swiss Army knives for modern workflows.
- **Accessible innovation**: Open-source ecosystems and powerful cloud APIs mean that organizations big and small can harness these capabilities in hours, not months.
- **Creative thinking at scale**: By crafting smart prompts, we can guide these models to not only follow instructions—but to think methodically, adaptively, and contextually.

The Prompt Engineering Edge

While LLMs bring raw intellect, prompt engineering gives them direction. It is the subtle art of shaping their output—crafting the right question, guiding the thinking process, constraining for consistency, or steering their "*persona*." From zero-shot prompts to advanced techniques such as Chain-of-Thought, Tree-of-Thought, Graph-of-Thought, meta-prompts, and beyond, the prompts we design define the quality of our interactions.

The Power of Hugging Face and Open-Source Tools

At the heart of this transformation is a rich ecosystem of open-source models and deployment tools:

- **Hugging Face Hub**: A vibrant marketplace of models–from quirky community creations to giants such as Llama, Gemma, DeepSeek, Qwen, and Mistral.
- **Local tooling**: Use llama.cpp, Ollama, vLLM, or quantized GGUF formats to run these models offline, privately, and efficiently.
- **Hardware and orchestration**: Whether we tap into Groq's lightning-fast LPU accelerators or build advanced pipelines using services and frameworks such as LangChain and Langroid, the paths are many.

Structure

In this chapter, we will cover the following topics:

- **Prompting Mastery:** All the latest techniques, explained with clarity and depth
- **Prompt Templates and API Tuning:** Harnessing structure, creativity, and control
- **LLM Deployment:** From cloud APIs to private servers, across formats, speeds, and cost points
- **Real-World Scenarios:** Embedded prompts show how these tools come alive in business

By the end of this chapter, we will not only understand the building blocks but also know exactly how to assemble them. You will be outfitted to craft systems that think critically, speak convincingly, and operate intelligently across any domain.

Introduction to LLMs and Hugging Face

As of mid-2025, the state-of-the-art in large language models spans proprietary powerhouses and open-source challengers, each with unique strengths:

- **GPT-4o (GPT-4 Omni):** OpenAI's flagship multimodal model offering human-like multimodal interaction with top-tier reasoning and sub-300 ms response time. Evolved from GPT-4 Turbo; introduced voice-to-voice and vision capabilities; added structured output and expanded token length by November 2024. Achieved 88.7 MMLU (Massive Multitask Language Understanding), outperforming GPT-4's 86.5, and introduced new state-of-the-art results in multilingual and audio/vision tasks.
- **o1 / o3-mini**: OpenAI's specialist reasoning models optimized for rigorous STEM and logical tasks; they trade low latency for deep analytical ability.

o3-mini is lightweight; o1/o3 models optimized for reasoning. Excel on hard reasoning tasks (Deep Research reveals deeper problem-solving), achieving ~87% accuracy on AIME (AI Model for Medical Information Extraction).

- **Llama 4 (Scout/Maverick):** Meta's massive MoE (mixture-of-experts) family, with Scout offering open-source 109B-model performance and Voyager contextual memory via 10M token windows. It is a state-of-the-art open-source performer on reasoning/cognition benchmarks, comparable to proprietary models.
- **Gemma 3 and 2:** Google's multimodal models available under open source licenses, balancing vision-language capabilities efficiently. It has strong performance in vision-language tasks.
- **Mistral Large 2/Pixtral:** Mistral AI's 123B parameter models with extensive context (128K tokens), especially strong in multilingual and multimodal tasks. It is among the top open-source models for general-purpose and multimodal tasks.
- **DeepSeek-R1/V3 and Qwen family:** Open-source models comparable to GPT-4o in performance, optimized for reasoning-heavy and multilingual workflows.
- **Claude 3.7 Sonnet**, **Gemini 2.5 Pro**, **GPT-4.5**, **Grok 3:** Proprietary models offering polished API ecosystems, high reliability, specialized domains (for example, developer support), and multimodal capabilities.

The performances of different large language models.

Model	**Params/Context**	**Source**	**Key Strengths**
GPT-4o	Unreleased/128 K	OpenAI	Multimodal, reasoning, multilingual
o1/o3-mini	Small/Unreleased	OpenAI	Deep mathematics and logical reasoning
Llama 4 (Scout/ Voyager)	109 B/10 M	Meta (open)	Expert-level memory, open-source reasoning
Gemma 3 and 2	~Unknown/ Medium	Google (open)	Vision-language, multimodal
Mistral Large 2 / Pixtral	123 B/128 K	Mistral AI-open	Multilingual, multimodal performance
DeepSeek-R1 / R1-distills	671 B >70 B	DeepSeek-open	Reasoning, efficient Mixture-of-Experts
Claude 3.7 Sonnet	Unknown	Anthropic	Scratchpad reasoning, safety

Gemini 2.5 Pro	Unknown	Google DeepMind	Multimodal proficiency, code, reasoning
GPT-4.5	Unreleased	OpenAI	Refined GPT-4 performance
Grok 3	Unknown	xAI	Developer support, code assistance

***Table 2.1**: Comparison of different LLMs*

Now, let us understand which models are appropriate for the given task.

Category	Key Models	Performance Highlights
Cognitive and General QA	GPT-4o, Llama 3/4, Gemma 3, Meta Llama 3.1	Meta Llama 3.1 leads open-source performance
Language Generation	Llama 3, Gemma 3, Mistral Large 2	Matches closed systems for fluency; proprietary models offer tighter control
Code Generation	GPT-4o, Claude, Gemini, CodeLlama	60–75% accuracy on HumanEval; Gemini 2 achieves 94% on design patterns
Long Context Handling	Llama 3.1 405B, Gemini 1.5 Pro	Supports 128K tokens; Gemini handles context length in millions
Hybrid/Reasoning Control	Claude 3.7 Sonnet, OpenAI o3-mini-high	Variable depth reasoning; 87% accuracy on AIME

***Table 2.2**: Suitability of LLMs for different tasks*

LLM Ecosystem and Access Options

Let us understand different ways to access the LLMs–through command line, APIs, UX, and workflows. Hugging Face provides a versatile environment to explore, deploy, and customize LLMs–with both cloud and local-first strategies:

Hugging Face Hub and Transformers

- Hugging Face is like an **app store for AI models**.
- It has thousands of models (from small ones such as GPT-2 to big ones such as LLaMA-4 and Gemma).
- We can load a model in just a few lines of Python:

```
from transformers import AutoModelForCausalLM, AutoTokenizer
model = AutoModelForCausalLM.from_pretrained
("meta-llama/Llama-4-scout-109B")
tokenizer = AutoTokenizer.from_pretrained(...)
```

Offline and Local Workflows

We can download a model once and then use it without the internet. This is useful for secure or private environments.

```
tokenizer.save_pretrained("./local-model")
model.save_pretrained("./local-model")
```

- Some models (such as LLaMA-4) need you to request access and use a special token to unlock them.

Command-Line Engines and Quantization

- Tools such as **`llama.cpp`** or **`Llamafile`** let you run compressed ("quantized") models that work on normal CPUs or GPUs.
- Ollama makes it very easy: you install once, then run models with a single command. It even provides an API similar to OpenAI's.
- Tools such as vLLM or **`text-generation-webui`** give you simple web interfaces or REST APIs to host models locally.

Hosted APIs and Hardware Backends

- **Hugging Face Inference API**: Lets you call any model on their hub through a simple web request.
- **GroqCloud**: Runs models on special super-fast chips (LPUs), supporting LLaMA-3, Mistral, Gemma, and so on.
- **OpenAI, Anthropic, Google Vertex AI**: Big companies offer ready-to-use, secure APIs at a global scale.

Ecosystem Integrators

- **LangChain**, **Langroid**, **Open WebUI**, **AnythingLLM**: Abstract access across all backends–enabling multi-model apps, agent pipelines, and memory tools.

Prompt Engineering Techniques

Imagine the Alladdin genie in the hand, which is the LLM. How do we command the LLM to get the complex tasks done? That is the beauty of prompt engineering. Let us understand different prompting techniques. It is very important to make sure that the LLM reasons well and also does not hallucinate.

Figure 2.1: *Fun interpretation of Prompt Engineering (Credits: supermeme.ai)*

Zero-shot Prompting

Provide a task instruction directly—no examples needed. The model leverages its general knowledge to respond.

Example:

```
Classify sentiment: "I loved the movie."
```

The model infers the task is sentiment classification and responds: **Positive**.

Lazy Prompting

Minimal context is provided—enough to let the model infer intent.

Andrew Ng describes it best:

> "when debugging code, many developers copy-paste error messages… Most LLMs are smart enough to figure out that you want them to help understand and propose fixes"
>
> **Example:** User pastes a compiler error without explanation, prompting the model to detect and fix the bug.

```
Uncaught TypeError: Cannot read properties of undefined
(reading 'map')
    at UserList (UserList.jsx:23)
```

Few-Shot Prompting

Sometimes, prompts cannot understand the task. Providing a few examples to define the task, then request inference: One-shot prompting means one example, and the few-shot technique involves giving a few examples.

```
Q: 'I feel cold' → Negative
Q: 'Best day ever' → Positive
Now classify: 'Could be better.'
```

Model continues the pattern: **Negative**.

Chain-of-Thought (CoT)

Chain-of-Thought prompting guides a model to "*think out loud*" by providing intermediate reasoning steps before giving the final answer. This technique, introduced by Google Brain (Wei et al., 2022), boosts performance on complex tasks such as math problems, logical puzzles, and common sense questions.

Why it works:

- Breaks down complex tasks into manageable steps.
- Encourages the model to build on each step, improving reasoning accuracy.
- Makes output more transparent and interpretable.

Example:

```
If you start with 23 apples, use 20, then buy 6 more, how many?
Think step by step.
```

Model outputs intermediate reasoning:

1. 23 - 20 = 3
2. 3 + 6 = 9

   Answer: 9

Usage Tips:

a. Include clear cues such as "*Let's think step-by-step*" or numbered steps.

b. For complex tasks, combine with a **few-shot examples** demonstrating the CoT style.

c. After CoT reasoning, enforce a concise final answer to avoid verbosity.

Self-Consistency

Self-Consistency builds on CoT by generating multiple reasoning chains for the same prompt and selecting the answer that appears most frequently (majority vote). It addresses the unreliability of single-path reasoning by aggregating multiple "*opinions*" to improve accuracy.

Example:

```
Q: When I was 6, my sister was half my age. Now I'm 70. How old
is my sister?
```

Why single CoT fails sometimes?

A greedy answer might wrongly compute "70 : 2 = 35," missing the consistent age gap logic.

Workflow

Prompt the model with CoT instructions (for example, "*Let's think step by step*") multiple times.

Collect N separate answers.

Apply a majority vote to choose the most frequent answer.

Hypothetical outputs:

```
Chain 1: "Age gap is 3, so sister is 67."
Chain 2: "Half-age method says 35."
Chain 3: "Age gap remains 3, answer: 67."
```

The answer 67 appears twice versus 35 once—so 67 is selected via majority vote

This significantly boosts accuracy on arithmetic and logic benchmarks (+11–18%).

Usage Tips:

- Use higher temperatures (0.5–0.7) or top-k (for example, k=40) to ensure chain diversity.
- 5–10 paths balance cost versus gains; accuracy plateaus around 40.
- Larger models (>100B parameters) benefit most from CoT and self-consistency.
- Consider Adaptive-Consistency to dynamically stop sampling once consensus emerges.

Least-to-Most (LtM)

Least-to-Most (LtM) prompting refines CoT by breaking a complex problem into smaller subproblems, and solving them sequentially, using previous answers to inform the next step.

- **Stage 1**: Decompose the problem (often via few-shot examples).
- **Stage 2**: Solve each subproblem in order, passing along context.

This approach excels at easy-to-hard generalization, outperforming CoT on tasks that require multiple reasoning steps.

Example:

```
Q: Elsa has 5 apples; Anna has 2 more. How many apples do they
have together?
```

Workflow:

- `How many apples does Anna have?`
- `What is the total of Elsa and Anna together?`

Solve Subproblem 1:

"Anna has 5 + 2 = 7 apples."

Solve Subproblem 2:

"Together they have 5 + 7 = 12 apples."

Final Answer: 12

Example (from research):

Solving "SCAN" tasks via sub-tasks boosts accuracy from 16% to ~99%. SCAN is a benchmark that tests whether models can systematically generalize by mapping simple language commands to action sequences.

Multi-Task Prompting

Combine several instructions in one prompt:

```
1) Translate this into French.
2) Provide estimated word count.
Text: "Welcome to Hyderabad."
```

The model returns both the translation and word count in a single response.

Role Prompting

Assign the model a persona to shape tone and style:

```
As a financial analyst, summarize the quarterly earnings below.
```

The output is structured with analyst-level insight.

Meta-Prompting

Meta Prompting is a structural, abstract approach to prompt engineering. Instead of specifying content, it defines the form, syntax, and flow of tasks. Think of it as teaching the LLM *how* to construct a prompt or organize reasoning, rather than what content to include. It is like prompting the model to *program itself* to solve problems.

Example:

```
Solve the problem as follows:
1. Restate the problem.
2. Identify knowns and unknowns.
3. Outline solution strategy.
4. Give step-by-step reasoning.
5. Present final answer.
```

If we feed any prompt to LLM, it responds in the same structure.

Tree-of-Thought (ToT)

ToT enhances CoT by enabling the model to explore multiple reasoning paths simultaneously, evaluate them, and backtrack if a branch is unpromising–much like a human solving a puzzle.

How It Works

- **Propose** multiple candidate steps at each decision point.
- **Evaluate** each possibility (for example, "sure", "maybe", "impossible").
- **Search strategy** (BFS/DFS/beam search) guides exploration and pruning

Example:

```
Imagine 3 different experts are answering this question. The first
one performs addition, the second one performs subtraction, and
the third one performs multiplication. We start with numbers
5,10,15. Will we receive any negative number after a certain
number of operations?
```

The LLM should perform all operations (+, - , *) across the three numbers 5,10,15, and should return the answer as YES.

Example (solving Game of 24):

ToT raises solving accuracy from 4% (CoT) to 74%.

Graph-of-Thought (GoT)

GoT generalizes reasoning beyond trees by forming a graph of thought nodes, capturing interdependent insights, feedback loops, merges, and revisions—closer to human-like reasoning.

- Nodes represent individual "**`thoughts`**" or sub-solutions.
- Edges represent dependencies, support, or evolution of ideas.
- Allows merging, refining, and revisiting nodes via feedback loops.
- Outperforms ToT on tasks such as sorting by +62% quality and lowers cost by 31%

Example:

```
A farmer has 3 types of animals: chickens, cows, and pigs. He has 30
animals in total. Chickens have 2 legs, cows and pigs have 4 legs each.
The total number of legs is 100. How many chickens, cows, and pigs are
there?
```

In sorting tasks, GoT constructs a dependency graph of comparisons, enabling the model to select consistent ordering by analyzing graph structure, outperforming ToT significantly. Let's revise the important prompting techniques - CoT, GoT, ToT and Self-consistency.

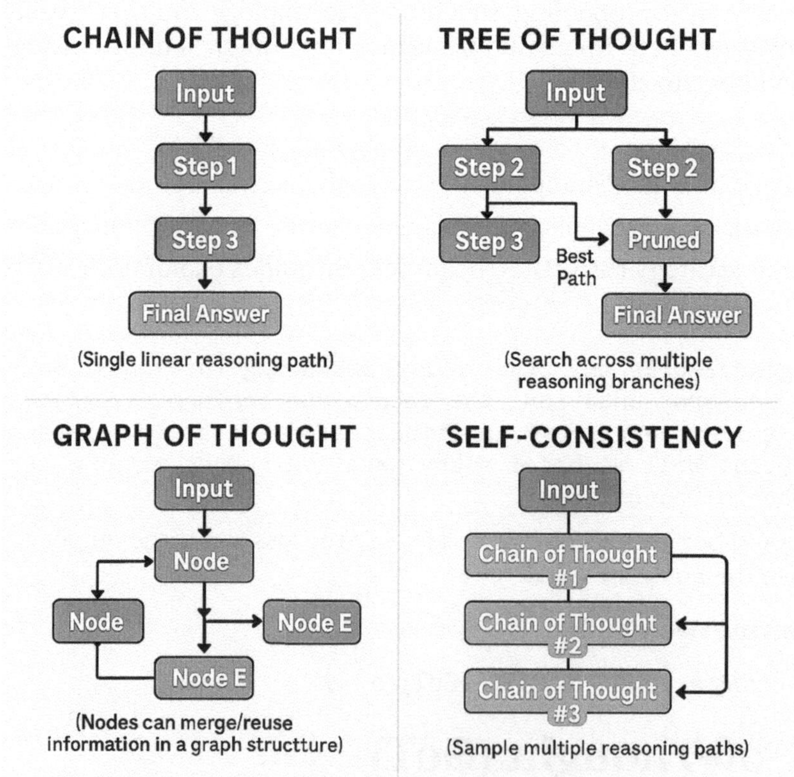

Figure 2.2: *Comparing different prompting techniques*

Advanced Prompting Techniques

- **Prompt Ensembling:** Use multiple prompt versions and combine their answers.
- **ReAct (Reason+Act):** Combining reasoning with API/tool
- **Auto Prompting:** Automatically learn prompting using gradient search
- **Active Prompting:** Dynamically generate better prompts using feedback.
- **Zero-shot CoT**: Add "*Let's think step-by-step*" to a zero-shot prompt
- **Auto-CoT**: LLM drafts its own CoT exemplars for future use
- **Multimodal CoT**: Applies CoT reasoning with images + text inputs

Prompt Templates and Parameters

We have seen how to frame the prompt to solve difficult tasks. Let us understand the prompt structure and what are the different parameters that can be tuned to get the desired response.

Prompt Template

- Role: Role of the Prompt
- Instruction: The Exact instruction to LLM
- Example: Input and Output
- Context: Provide the context of the task
- Question: Ask the final task

Example:

```
January 1, 2005: Fractured right arm playing basketball. Treated
with a cast.
February 14, 2010: Diagnosed with hypertension. Prescribed aten-25.
October 10, 2015: Developed pneumonia. Treated with antibiotics
and recovered fully.
March 1, 2020: Sustained a concussion in a car accident. Admitted
to the hospital and monitored for 48 hours.
You are a doctor. Read this medical history and predict risks for
the patient.
```

Prompt Parameters

Combine structured prompts with hyperparameters for reliability:

Parameter	**Purpose**
`temperature`	Controls output randomness
`top_p`	Sets nucleus sampling for diversity
`max_tokens`	Limits response length
`stop_sequences`	Prevents over-generation

Table 2.3: *LLM API parameters*

Tree of Thoughts (ToT) and Graph of Thoughts (GoT) often need a higher temperature for breadth, followed by self-consistency deduplication. Meta-prompts benefit from low temperature for a deterministic structure.

Best Practices:

- Include details in your query to get more relevant answers
- Ask the model to adopt a persona
- Use delimiters to clearly indicate distinct parts of the input
- Specify the steps required to complete a task
- Provide examples
- Specify the desired length/style of the output

Prompt Optimization

Since the context length for LLMs is limited, prompt optimization becomes important. Prompt optimization/prompt compression techniques help in reducing the prompt length.

Use Abbreviated Few-Shot Examples

Instead of long-winded few-shot examples, make them:

- Compact
- Task-specific
- Use bullet points or keywords

"English → French":

I am a student → Je suis étudiant

Truncate or Summarize Context

If we include user history or documents:

- Use extractive summarization (for example, sumy, spacy, nltk)
- Retain only the most relevant parts of the conversation/document
- Use tools such as LangChain, LlamaIndex, or Haystack to dynamically fetch/reduce content

Example:

```
# LangChain style
retriever = vectorstore.as_retriever(search_type="similarity", k=3)
context = retriever.get_relevant_documents(query)
```

Prompt Compression techniques:

- If we use repeated patterns, use prompt caching
- Tokenize the prompts
- Use summarization-based compression on the prompt
- Splits long documents into manageable chunks
- Keyword filtering based on heuristics or self-information (perplexity) scores.
- Compress the prompt using AutoEncoder
- Prompt compression using Reinforcement Learning.

Guardrails

Guardrails ensure your LLM operates within safe, ethical, and domain-appropriate boundaries by intercepting unwanted input/output at three levels:

- **Input guardrails** prevent malicious or off-topic input from reaching the model.
- **In-process (prompt-level) constraints** embed rules directly into system prompts.
- **Output guardrails** filter or modify the model's response before it reaches users.

Input Guardrails

Goal: Block or sanitize harmful or irrelevant queries before the LLM sees them. Use the guardrails before calling the LLM API.

Example – Regex Filtering:

```
import re
blocked = [r"ignore all previous instructions", r"bypass
security", r"generate fake id"]
```

```
def sanitize(user_input):
    for pat in blocked:
        if re.search(pat, user_input, re.IGNORECASE):
            return "Your request is blocked due to policy
violation."
    return user_input
```

This filters known prompt-injection phrases before forwarding the input.

In-Process (Prompt-Level) Guardrails

Goal: Embed constraints directly into the system prompt to guide the LLM's behavior.

Example – Role + Behavioral Guardrail:

```
You are a virtual travel agent.
- Only respond to questions about flights, hotels, or sightseeing.
- If the user asks about anything else, reply: "I'm sorry, I can
only help with travel-related questions."
```

This ensures the model stays on-topic and refuses unrelated requests.

Output Guardrails

Goal: Catch and clean any inappropriate or unwanted content produced by the LLM. Use the guardrails after calling the API.

Example – Keyword Filter:

```
def filter_output(text):
    disallowed = ["hate", "violence", "explicit"]
    for w in disallowed:
        if w in text.lower():
            return "Response removed due to content policy."
    return text
```

This post-processes the LLM's answer to ensure safe delivery.

Guardrail Best Practices

- **Multi-layer strategy**: Combine input, prompt, and output guardrails
- **Red-teaming**: Use adversarial testing to identify vulnerabilities before deployment
- **Human-in-the-loop:** Include oversight for sensitive content or borderline cases
- **Audit and Logs:** Maintain logs for all input/output to support compliance and review

- **Iterative tuning** – Guardrails should evolve with new threats and domain requirements

Setting up private/public LLMs

Large language models (LLMs) have become indispensable tools for businesses, powering everything from chatbots and customer support to document analysis and code generation. Choosing how to access and deploy an LLM is critical—not just for performance and scalability, but also for data security, compliance, and cost control. In this chapter, we will explore the two main deployment models—private (self-hosted or on-premise) and public (cloud APIs)—highlighting their advantages, limitations, technical setup, and hybrid architectures. Understanding these trade-offs is the first step toward building a robust, scalable AI system.

Private LLM Deployment (On-Prem or Private Cloud)

Deploying a LLM in a private or controlled environment, instead of relying on public cloud APIs. This is done for data privacy, security, regulatory compliance, or low-latency needs.

Benefits

- **Data Control and Compliance**: Ideal for regulated industries handling sensitive or personal data—everything stays in-house.
- **Low Latency and Customization**: Locally deployed models reduce network delays and support advanced fine-tuning, quantization, or model editing.

Setup Paths

- **CLI and Local Servers**: Tools such as Ollama, llama.cpp, vLLM, and text-generation-webui facilitate running open-source models (for example, Llama, Mistral) with OpenAI-compatible APIs.
- **Containers and Orchestration**: Dockerized deployments with Kubernetes/KServe allow scalable, production-grade serving.
- **Hardware Requirements**: A capable on-prem setup includes GPUs (for example, NVIDIA RTX series with ≥12GB VRAM), 16–32 GB of RAM, and 256–512 GB SSD storage.

Key Challenges

- **Upfront Infrastructure Costs**: Hardware setup and GPU provisioning can be expensive. Scaling requires thoughtful load forecasting.

- **Operational Management**: Ongoing responsibilities include deploying updates, patching, logging, monitoring, and debugging.
- **Security Risks**: Self-hosted endpoints can be vulnerable if not configured correctly–default configurations often expose open APIs. Studies show many public LLM endpoints lack TLS or authentication.
- **Governance Limitations**: Traditional row/column ACLs do not map to model inference–fine-grained data access control remains unsolved.

Public LLM Deployment (Cloud APIs)

Using LLMs through managed cloud services or public APIs instead of hosting them locally. This allows easy access to powerful models without managing infrastructure.

Benefits

- **Fast & Easy**: No server provisioning–just sign up and start using REST APIs (OpenAI, Anthropic, Hugging Face Inference, GroqCloud, Vertex AI).
- **Scalable on Demand**: Provides auto-scale to meet demand, supporting dynamic workloads seamlessly.
- **Access to Cutting-Edge Models**: Immediately available access to the latest, most capable models without local setup.

Core Limitations

- **Data Privacy Concerns**: Your inputs traverse third-party networks, raising compliance risks under GDPR, HIPAA, and similar regulations.
- **Unpredictable Costs and Lock-In**: Pay-as-you-go pricing can escalate unexpectedly. Switching providers often requires code rework and data migration.
- **Latency and Availability**: Network delays and regional outages can affect performance; some use cases require consistent low-latency that the cloud may not guarantee.
- **Bias and Accountability**: Embedded biases and a black-box ecosystem make responses inconsistent and auditing difficult.

Hybrid Deployment

Hybrid deployment combines private/local LLMs with public/cloud LLMs.

- Sensitive or proprietary data can stay on-premises.
- Less-sensitive or heavy workloads can use cloud services for scale.

Benefits

- **Balanced Architecture**: Hosting sensitive operations locally while offloading burst or non-sensitive workloads to the cloud reduces risk and cost.
- **Flexibility and Efficiency**: Elastically mix resources to accommodate peak demands, without over-provisioning hardware.

Practical Drawbacks

- **Complex Integration**: Requires secure data routing, encryption across environments, and orchestrating consistent model versions.
- **Governance Overhead**: Must monitor compliance, access controls, and policy enforcement on both sides of the firewall.

Best Practices and Principles

- **Resource Efficiency**: Quantize models (Q4/Q8, INT8) to reduce memory and inference cost; use batching and caching.
- **Secure-by-Default**: Always enable TLS and user authentication; regularly audit configurations for open access.
- **Robust LLMOps Process**: Implement version control, monitoring, drift detection, fallback routing, and rollbacks.
- **Adaptive Orchestration**: Use local private inference first, fall back to cloud during peaks or complex cognition tasks.
- **Governance Tools**: Apply access control, encryption, and audit logging across all stages. Public API keys should be secured; private data should never leave the trusted perimeter.

Deploying LLMs is not just a technical decision—it is strategic. Private deployments offer control and compliance at the cost of operational overhead. Public APIs provide speed and scalability, but compromise privacy and cost predictability. Hybrid models attempt to have the best of both worlds but demand complex orchestration and management. By understanding these trade-offs—and following best practices in security, optimization, and governance—you can architect LLM systems that are robust, performant, and aligned with your organizational goals.

Case Studies

Let us take a look at different case studies across multiple domains for understanding the power of prompt engineering.

Case Study 1: Finance – Automated Earnings Call Summarizer with CoT Prompting

Objective: Help investment analysts quickly summarize and interpret quarterly earnings reports and transcripts using an LLM.

Prompting Techniques Used:

- Chain-of-Thought (CoT)
- Role Prompting
- Meta Prompting

Prompt Example:

```
You are a senior equity analyst. Your task is to:
1. Summarize key financial metrics from the earnings call below.
2. Highlight any forward-looking statements by the company.
3. Identify risks and market sentiments.

Earnings Call Transcript:
<PASTE_TEXT_HERE>
Think step-by-step.
```

Example Output:

- `Revenue grew 12% YoY to $1.2B.`
- `CEO mentioned increased R&D in AI-based personalization.`
- `Risks include macroeconomic uncertainty and global supply chain costs.`

Business Outcome: This prompt structure helps LLMs provide multi-level, coherent breakdowns useful for both junior and senior analysts, saving hours of work.

Case Study 2: Medical – Triage Support Assistant Using Meta and Role Prompting

Objective: Aid nurses in identifying the urgency of incoming patient complaints via chat.

Prompting Techniques Used:

- Role Prompting

- Meta Prompting
- Guardrails (Embedded and post-filtering)

Prompt Example:

```
You are a triage nurse assistant. For each case:
1. Classify urgency (Emergency, Urgent, Routine)
2. Justify classification
3. Suggest next action
Symptoms: Patient reports shortness of breath, dizziness, and
chest pain.
Format:
Urgency: [Level]
Reason: [Justification]
Action: [Recommendation]
```

Example Output:

```
Urgency: Emergency
Reason: Classic indicators of myocardial infarction
Action: Advise immediate emergency room visit
```

Implementation Note: System prompt enforces strict format. Output guardrails ensure no medical diagnosis is given directly—only action-oriented suggestions.

Case Study 3: CRM – Personalized Customer Reply Generator Using Few-shot Prompting

Objective: Generate personalized responses to customer service emails.

Prompting Techniques Used:

- Few-shot Prompting
- Zero-shot with Temperature Control

Prompt Example:

```
Q: "My internet has been down for 2 days. I'm very upset."
A: "We're truly sorry for the inconvenience. Let us make this
right immediately."

Q: "I was double-billed for my last subscription."
A: "Thanks for alerting us. We've reversed the extra charge and
updated your account."

Now generate a response to:
"I ordered a phone case a week ago, but it still hasn't arrived."
```

Output: "We apologize for the delay. Your order is on its way and should arrive shortly. We've also issued a 10% discount on your next purchase."

Why It Works: Few-shot context sets tone, structure, and empathy. The prompt supports dynamic adaptation to sentiment and topic.

Case Study 4: Agriculture – Pest Diagnosis Assistant Using LoM Prompting

Objective: Help field officers diagnose crop disease based on image and symptom descriptions.

Prompting Techniques Used:

- Least-to-Most (LoM)
- Multimodal Inputs (Image + Text)

Prompt Example:

```
You are an agricultural scientist.
Step 1: Identify the crop
Step 2: Analyze visible symptoms
Step 3: Cross-reference with known diseases
Step 4: Suggest probable diagnosis and mitigation
Image: <CROP_IMAGE>
Description: "The cotton leaves have brown spots with yellow
halos, and plant growth is stunted."
```

Output:

```
1. Crop: Cotton
2. Symptoms: Brown circular spots with yellow halos
3. Match: Alternaria leaf spot (Alternaria macrospora)
4. Recommendation: Apply Mancozeb; remove infected leaves
```

Note: *Can be integrated with a mobile field app with offline LLM capabilities using quantized models via Ollama.*

Case Study 5: Law – Legal Clause Risk Assessment Using ToT Prompting

Objective: Assist contract reviewers in identifying high-risk clauses in legal documents.

Prompting Techniques Used:

- Tree-of-Thought (ToT)
- Meta Prompting

Prompt Example:

```
As a legal analyst, review the clause below for potential risk:
Clause:
"The vendor may terminate the agreement without penalty or notice
for any reason."
Break down your reasoning into alternatives. For each:
- Assess risk level
- Explain legal implications
- Suggest a revised version
Choose the most balanced path.
```

Example Output:

- **Path 1:** `Risk: High. Unilateral termination clause exposes the company to sudden service loss.`
- **Path 2:** `Risk: Medium. Could be negotiated with a 30-day notice clause.`
- **Best Revision:** `"Vendor may terminate with 30-day notice and mutual agreement."`

Impact: ToT prompting explores multiple risk paths and helps select a defensible, actionable outcome—useful for junior legal teams.

Conclusion

In a world increasingly driven by intelligent automation, prompt engineering has emerged as the essential interface between human intent and machine reasoning. Unlike traditional programming, where logic is hardcoded, prompt engineering allows us to communicate goals, constraints, and context through natural language—transforming static models into adaptive, interactive systems.

This chapter has journeyed through the entire lifecycle of crafting intelligent systems using prompts—starting with the foundational understanding of large language models (LLMs) and their access paradigms, progressing through state-of-the-art prompting techniques, and culminating in domain-specific case studies.

On the deployment front, we explored the landscape of public APIs (for example, OpenAI, Anthropic, Groq), open-source model hosting (for example, Hugging Face, Ollama, llama.cpp), and hybrid strategies—each with trade-offs in latency, privacy, cost, and control. We also outlined guardrails as a design imperative, ensuring safety and reliability through layered input, prompt, and output validation mechanisms.

Through our case studies across Finance, Healthcare, CRM, Agriculture, and Law, it became clear that prompt engineering is not only a technical tool, but also a medium for encoding business logic, ethics, and workflow intelligence—bridging LLMs with real-world requirements.

As generative AI continues to evolve, the prompt will remain central—not just as a request, but as a *contract* between the user and the model. Mastering prompt engineering is mastering the language of intelligent systems. In the next chapter, we will discuss grounding LLMs using RAG systems.

Further Reading and References

Foundational Papers and Techniques

- Wei, J. et al. (2022). *Chain-of-Thought Prompting Elicits Reasoning in Large Language Models.* arXiv:2201.11903
- Yao, S. et al. (2023). *Tree of Thoughts: Deliberate Problem Solving with Large Language Models.* arXiv:2305.10601
- Zhang, S. et al. (2023). *Graph of Thoughts: Solving Elaborate Problems with Large Language Models.* arXiv:2310.01835
- Kojima, T. et al. (2022). *Large Language Models Are Zero-Shot Reasoners.* arXiv:2205.11916

Prompting Guides and Tools

- Prompting Guide by OpenPrompt: https://promptingguide.ai
- OpenAI Cookbook: https://github.com/openai/openai-cookbook
- Awesome Prompt Engineering: https://github.com/dair-ai/Prompt-Engineering-Guide
- Guardrails.AI: https://www.guardrailsai.com
- NVIDIA NeMo-Guardrails: https://github.com/NVIDIA/NeMo-Guardrails

LLM Deployment Frameworks

- Hugging Face Transformers & Inference Endpoints: https://huggingface.co
- Ollama (Run models locally via Docker): https://ollama.com
- llama.cpp (Lightweight inference): https://github.com/ggerganov/llama.cpp
- vLLM (Fast Transformer Inference): https://github.com/vllm-project/vllm
- GroqCloud (High-speed inference APIs): https://groq.com

Benchmarks and Evaluation

- HELM (Holistic Evaluation of Language Models): https://crfm.stanford.edu/helm/latest/
- Open LLM Leaderboard (by Hugging Face): https://huggingface.co/spaces/HuggingFaceH4/open_llm_leaderboard
- MT-Bench (Multitask evaluation benchmark): https://huggingface.co/datasets/lmsys/mt_bench

Chapter 3
Developing Retrieval-Augmented Generation Systems

Introduction

Imagine asking a smart assistant about a specific policy update, a niche scientific concept, or an obscure line from a century-old legal document–and getting an accurate, detailed, and source-cited answer instantly. Traditional large language models (LLMs), no matter how advanced, often stumble in such situations. They are powerful, yes, but bound by their training data and the finite window of context they can hold. What if these models could access an external brain, real-time, structured knowledge that enhances their native capabilities?

This is the promise of Retrieval-Augmented Generation (RAG). Instead of relying solely on what a model "*remembers*," RAG lets it look things up, fetch information from external databases, and reason using that retrieved knowledge–all in real time. It is a bit like giving a world-class writer instant access to a personalized research assistant.

This chapter explores the world of RAG: what makes it powerful, how to build it, which tools to use, and the architectural decisions that underpin successful deployments. From understanding databases and retrieval mechanisms to evaluating trade-offs in deployment and learning from real-world case studies, this chapter is your guide to engineering intelligent, context-aware AI systems that stay current, grounded, and reliable.

Figure 3.1: *RAG for grounding. Credits: Generated by GPT-4*

Structure

In this chapter, we will cover the following topics:

- Introduction to Different Databases
- RAG Architecture
- Libraries for RAG Support
- Deploying RAG Architectures, Tradeoffs
- Case-studies and Real User Scenarios
- Mock Interview

Introduction to Different Databases

Modern RAG systems thrive on external knowledge, but the real question is: how do we actually feed that knowledge to an LLM? Think of RAG as an intelligent bridge that connects the model to vast, ever-changing sources of information. Instead of simply storing documents, these systems use external databases as powerful engines for semantic search, metadata-based filtering, relevance scoring, and session-aware retrieval. By pulling the right context at the right moment, RAG transforms scattered data into precise, actionable knowledge—ensuring that the LLM generates responses that are accurate, grounded, and deeply informed.

But the choice of database is not one-size-fits-all. Depending on the use case, we may need to store high-dimensional vectors, execute keyword searches, represent knowledge graphs, or manage session data. Moreover, as data volume grows, these systems must scale in performance and throughput. This section explores the database landscape for RAG, explaining how different types of databases store and retrieve knowledge, how to perform knowledge insertion, and how to architect solutions that scale to big data.

Relational Databases

An **RDBMS** stores data in structured tables (rows and columns) with predefined schemas, ensuring strong consistency and support for ACID (Atomicity, Consistency, Isolation, Durability) transactions. It uses SQL for queries and is highly reliable for applications requiring strict data integrity.

Examples: PostgreSQL, MySQL, and SQLite

RDBMSs are best suited for structured tabular data such as metadata, document attributes (for example, author, topic, date), and user interaction history. They play an important role in the filtering and enrichment phase of RAG.

This is a typical schema definition of a PostgreSQL query:

```
CREATE TABLE documents (
    id SERIAL PRIMARY KEY,
    title TEXT,
    category TEXT,
    chunk_id INT,
    embedding_id INT,
    created_at TIMESTAMP
);
```

RDBMS System Principles:

- Data is organized as tables, with the identifier as the primary key
- Relationships are maintained using foreign keys and joins
- Uses normalization rules
- Adheres to ACID properties

Knowledge Insertion:

- Use Object Relational Mapping (ORM) frameworks (FastAPI - SQLAlchemy, Django ORM) or raw SQL.
- Index frequently queried fields (for example, category, tags).

Document Databases (NoSQL)

Pre-2000s: Relational databases (RDBMS) dominated with rigid schemas and ACID properties.

Post-2000: Web-scale applications such as e-commerce, social media, and IoT required more flexible, horizontally scalable storage.

A **Document Database** stores data as JSON-like documents instead of rigid tables. Each document can have a flexible schema, making it well-suited for handling semi-structured or unstructured data such as articles, logs, or case files. Queries are typically based on key-value lookups, filters, and nested attributes.

Disadvantages of SQL Databases:

- **Rigid Schema Requirements**
    - RDBMS requires predefined table schemas.
    - Any structural change (such as adding a new field) requires altering the schema, which can be disruptive.
- **Poor Fit for Semi-Structured or Nested Data**
    - JSON-like hierarchical or flexible data is hard to represent using flat tables.
    - Storing embedded objects or arrays needs normalization (joins, multiple tables).
- **Scalability Challenges**
    - Horizontal scaling (adding more machines) is hard with RDBMS due to strong ACID constraints.
    - Difficult to distribute large-scale read/write workloads.
- **Complexity in Handling Evolving Applications**
    - Agile development environments need rapid schema changes.
    - Applications such as content management, user profiles, and IoT telemetry generate diverse, nested data, not ideal for SQL tables.
    - NoSQL: A family of non-relational databases, including:
        - Document (for example, MongoDB)
        - Key-Value (for example, Redis)
        - Columnar (for example, Cassandra)
        - Graph (for example, Neo4j)

Document databases became popular for their ability to store semi-structured data (such as JSON), aligning closely with how modern applications model data.

Key Principles of Document DB:

- **Schema-less**: Each document (usually in JSON/BSON format) can have a different structure.
- **Self-contained records**: Related data is stored together in one document.
- **Horizontal scalability**: Designed to scale out using sharding across multiple nodes. **Sharding** is a database scaling technique where a large dataset is split into smaller, more manageable pieces called shards, and each shard is stored on a separate server or database instance.
- **Eventual consistency**: Eventual consistency is a consistency model used in distributed systems where updates to data are not immediately visible across all nodes, but given enough time and no new updates, all replicas will converge to the same state. Most prioritize availability and partition tolerance over strict consistency.
- Adheres to **BASE** (Basically Available, Soft state and Eventual consistency) principles.

Vector Databases

A vector database is a specialized database designed to store, index, and search high-dimensional vector embeddings generated by AI models. Unlike traditional databases that handle structured or text data, vector databases enable similarity search–finding items that are most semantically similar to a given query. They are the backbone of modern AI applications such as Retrieval-Augmented Generation (RAG), recommendation systems, image search, and anomaly detection.

Pre-2010s: Early Nearest Neighbor Search (NNS):

- Concepts such as K-Nearest Neighbors (KNN) and vector similarity search were well known in classical machine learning and information retrieval.
- Libraries such as Fast Library for Approximate Nearest Neighbors (FLANN) were used in computer vision (for example, for image feature matching).
- 2017–2020 has given birth to Vector Databases.
- Researchers and engineers began building dedicated systems for large-scale embedding, storage, and similarity search.

Use Case: Semantic search on text/image embeddings.

Examples: FAISS (local), Pinecone, Weaviate, Qdrant, Milvus, and so on.

Guiding principle:

- Traditional databases store structured data (such as names, dates).
- A Vector DB stores numerical representations of text, also called embeddings.

- These embeddings are like a mathematical fingerprint of the meaning of a sentence.

Example:

- `"I like dogs" → [0.12, 0.98, -0.34, ...]`
- `"Dogs are great pets" → [0.13, 0.99, -0.32, ...]`

These two embeddings are close together in the vector database, meaning they are similar in meaning.

Cosine and Euclidean Distance

These are mathematical formulas to measure how close two vectors are:

- **Cosine similarity:** Measures the angle between two vectors (used for meaning-based comparison).
- **Euclidean distance:** Measures the straight-line distance (such as GPS distance between two points).

The smaller the distance or the larger the similarity, the more related the texts are.

Data Insertion Workflow:

1. Split documents into overlapping chunks.
2. Generate embeddings (for example, using OpenAI, Cohere, Sentence Transformers).
3. Store vectors with metadata (title, chunk ID, topic).

Hybrid Search: Some vector DBs (for example, Weaviate, Qdrant) support hybrid search–combining vector similarity with keyword filters.

Graph Databases

A **graph database** is a type of database designed to store and query data as nodes (entities) and edges (relationships) rather than rows and tables. Unlike relational databases that focus on tabular joins, graph databases emphasize the connections between data, making them powerful for use cases where relationships are as important as the data itself.

Examples: Neo4j, Amazon Neptune, TigerGraph

- With the internet, social media, and recommendation systems, data became more interconnected.
    - Social graphs
    - Knowledge graphs

    - Linked data (semantic web)
- These relationships were first-class citizens, but RDBMS could not efficiently represent or query them.

Data is Naturally a Graph

Real-world entities and their relationships often form a graph:

- People connected to people
- Webpages linked to webpages
- Devices interacting in networks

Relational Databases Struggle with Deep Relationships:

- Modeling multi-hop relationships (such as friends-of-friends) in SQL requires complex joins.
- Performance degrades exponentially with depth.

  Example: Finding the shortest path between two people in a social network is trivial in a graph DB, but inefficient in SQL.

Need for Flexibility:

- In graphs, schemas can be dynamic and flexible.
- New types of relationships or properties can be added without changing table structures.

High-Performance Traversal:

- Graph DBs optimize for depth-first or breadth-first traversals.
- Useful for:
    - Route optimization
    - Knowledge inference
    - Pattern detection (for example, fraud)

Graph databases excel at expressing entities and relationships, such as author-to-paper, drug-to-disease, or law-to-case. This is especially useful in domain-specific RAG systems, such as legal or scientific assistants.

Knowledge Insertion:

- Convert text to structured triples using NLP tools
- Ingest triples using batch Cypher or Gremlin scripts

```
CREATE (doc:Document {title:"AI and Law"})
CREATE (topic:Topic {name:"Legal Ethics"})
CREATE (doc)-[:RELATES_TO]->(topic)
```

Let us assume we have a simple customer, order, and product entity. Customers place orders for products. Let us understand the data schema in RDBMS, document database, and Graph databases using this example schema in the following diagram:

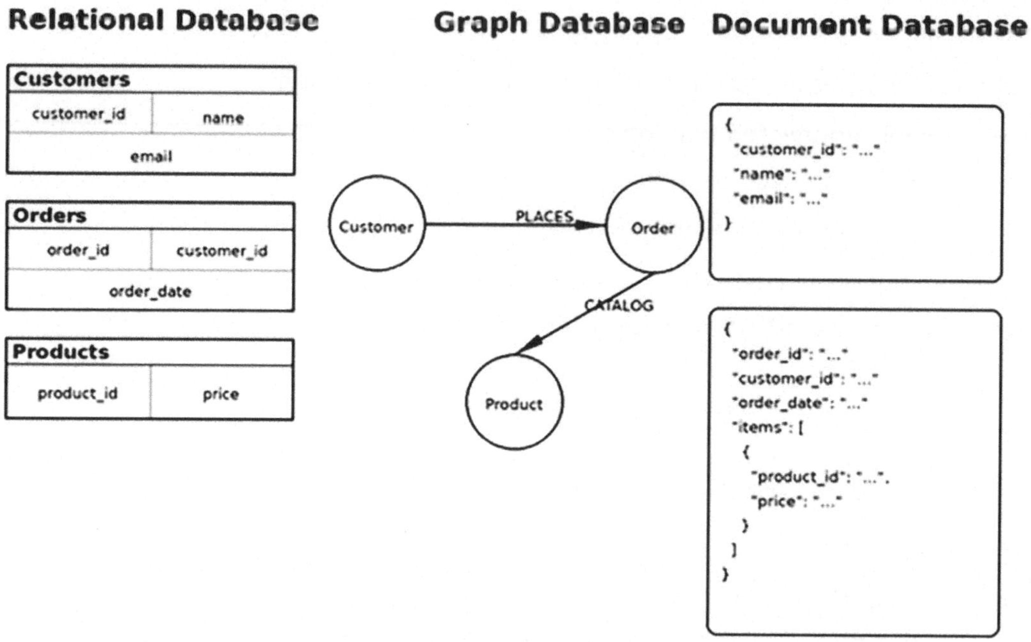

Figure 3.2: *Representation of RDBMS, Graph DB, and Document Databases*

Redis as a Fast Knowledge Store

Redis is an in-memory key-value database known for its speed, simplicity, and versatility. It stores data directly in memory rather than on disk, enabling sub-millisecond responses, which makes it ideal for real-time applications. Redis supports various data structures such as strings, hashes, lists, sets, and sorted sets, going beyond a simple key-value store.

Examples: Redis, KeyDB

- Web applications grew rapidly, demanding:
  - Faster session management
  - Low-latency data access
  - High availability
- Engineers began using lightweight key-value stores for these scenarios.
- Salvatore Sanfilippo created REmote DIctionary Server (Redis) as an in-memory key-value store with extra data structures (lists, sets, hashes).
- It was designed for performance, simplicity, and real-time data handling.

Redis is a key-value, in-memory store ideal for storing temporary knowledge: cached retrievals, user sessions, recent queries, or token usage logs.

Example Usage:

```
SET "query:latest ai news" "chunk_0234, chunk_0456"
```

Knowledge Insertion:

- Use Redis as a complement, not a primary store.
- Serialize documents as JSON or pickle serialization formats.
  - **JSON**: A lightweight, human-readable serialization format used for data interchange across systems and languages.
  - **Pickle**: A Python-specific serialization format that converts objects into byte streams, mainly for persistence and quick loading, but less portable.

RAG Architecture

Let us take a look at a simple RAG architecture.

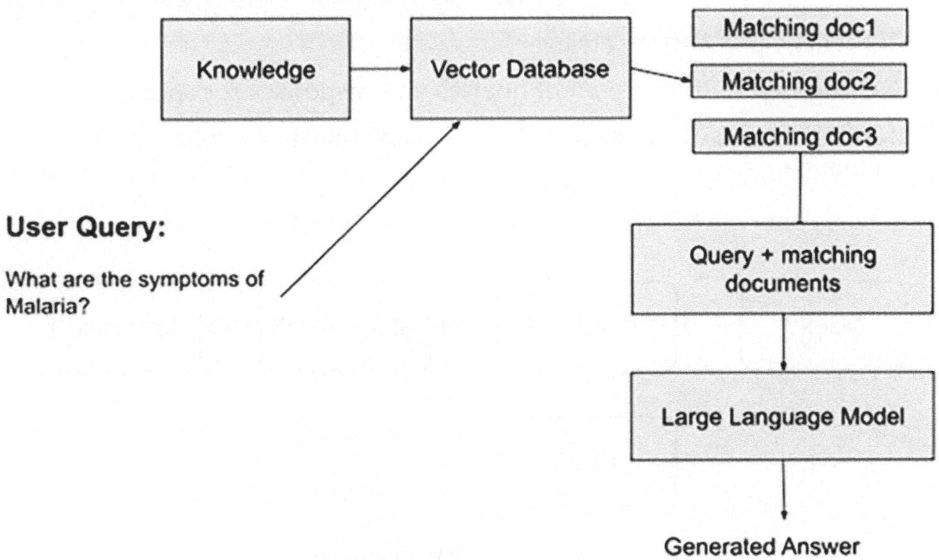

Figure 3.3: RAG *simple architecture*

Let us understand the flow of the RAG system illustrated in the preceding picture.

User submits a query ("*What are the symptoms of Malaria?*").

- The knowledge of the medical database is split into chunks. The embedding for the chunks is computed and stored in the vector database.

- The user query is embedded into a high-dimensional vector using an LLM or embedding model.
- The Vector Database performs a similarity search to find the top-k (the k most relevant) relevant document embeddings. In the diagram, we can see the matching documents as matching doc1, matching doc2, and matching doc3.
- These retrieved documents are then assembled into a prompt, often concatenated or structured with the query.
- The LLM generates a response based on the augmented prompt.
- The answer is returned to the user, grounded in the retrieved content.

Let us elaborate on each component, add the additional components, and generalize the architecture.

Additional components:

- **Indexing Pipeline**: Preprocess and embed documents in advance before storing them. Knowledge insertion happens in this module.
- **Filtering/Metadata**: Use vector DB filters to narrow down search (for example, by date, author).
- **Re-ranking**: Optionally re-rank retrieved documents using another model. This will help in better retrieval.
- **Caching Layer**: Store frequent queries and responses for speed.
- **Monitoring**: Track metrics such as latency, relevance, and correctness post-deployment.

We can draw a generic RAG architecture diagram as follows:

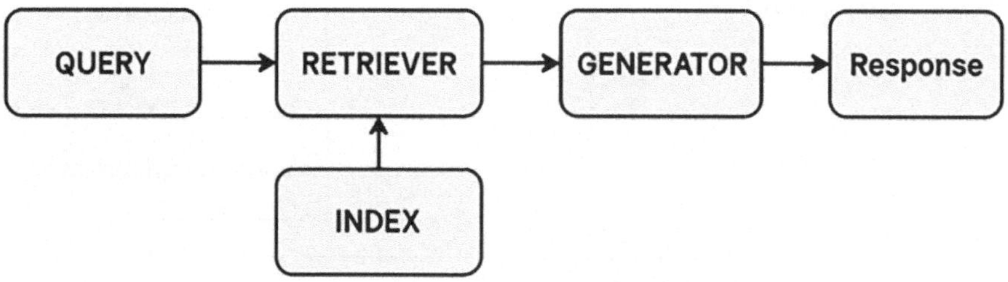

Figure 3.4: *Generic RAG architecture*

Let us understand each of the components in the diagram:

QUERY:

- This is the user input or question.
- It can be a natural language prompt, such as: "*What are the causes of climate change?*"

RETRIEVER:

- This module takes the query and searches a document index to find the most relevant pieces of information (contexts).
- It uses a similarity search technique, often based on dense vector embeddings (for example, FAISS, Elasticsearch, or vector DBs such as Pinecone).
- The retriever returns top-k relevant chunks/documents from the index.

INDEX:

- This is a pre-processed and vectorized representation of the knowledge base or document corpus.
- It supports fast lookup and retrieval by converting documents into embeddings (using a model such as Sentence-BERT or OpenAI embeddings).

GENERATOR:

- This is the LLM (such as GPT, T5) that takes both the original query and the retrieved documents as context.
- It generates a coherent and context-aware response.

RESPONSE:

- The final output from the generator.
- It answers the query using both its internal knowledge and the retrieved external context.

Advanced RAG Architectures

There has been a lot of research in the RAG space to make it more effective and relevant to the scale of applications. The following are some interesting architectural variations and advanced RAG architectures as proposed effectively by the research community.

- **Retrieve-and-Rank RAG:** In scenarios where the retrieval step produces a large set of potentially relevant documents, not all of them are equally useful for answering the query. Retrieve-and-Rank RAG addresses this by introducing an additional ranking step. First, a broad pool of documents is retrieved based on semantic similarity. Then, a second model – often a re-ranker trained with relevance judgments is applied to sort and prioritize the results. Finally, only the top-ranked documents are passed to the LLM for generation. This ensures that the context provided to the LLM is concise, highly relevant, and less noisy. The method improves both efficiency and the quality of the generated responses.

Benefits: By filtering out irrelevant or weakly related documents, Retrieve-and-Rank RAG reduces information overload and delivers sharper, contextually aligned answers.

- **Multi-Stage/Iterative RAG:** Some queries are complex and require step-by-step reasoning rather than a single retrieval. Multi-Stage or Iterative RAG tackles this by alternating between retrieval and generation in several rounds. In each cycle, the LLM refines or reformulates the query based on partial answers, which in turn drives a new round of retrieval. This feedback loop allows the system to progressively narrow in on the correct or most detailed response. For instance, answering a legal or scientific query might require multiple iterations to gather supporting evidence and synthesize it correctly.

  Benefits: This approach mimics human reasoning, enabling deeper comprehension and richer responses for multi-layered or ambiguous queries.

- **Agentic and Multi-Agent RAG:** Agentic RAG involves a single intelligent agent that dynamically routes queries, decides when retrieval is needed, and selects tools for reasoning. The agent acts as an orchestrator, ensuring that only relevant knowledge sources are consulted. In contrast, Multi-Agent RAG uses a team of specialized agents, each with a distinct role. For example, one agent may be a retrieval specialist, another a summarizer, and another an integrator, all coordinated by a master agent. This division of labor makes it possible to handle more complex tasks that require different skill sets.

  Benefits: Agentic setups provide flexibility and adaptiveness, while multi-agent setups introduce collaboration, making the system more robust and modular.

- **Speculative and Corrective RAG:** Speculative RAG emphasizes speed by generating a draft answer immediately, even before all retrieval operations are complete. Once retrieval finishes, the draft is refined with the final context, balancing speed with accuracy. Corrective RAG (CRAG), on the other hand, prioritizes reliability. After generating an answer, it validates the response against the retrieved context. If inconsistencies are detected, the system either corrects the answer or regenerates it entirely. This ensures factual accuracy and reduces hallucinations from the LLM.

  Benefits: Speculative RAG improves responsiveness in real-time systems, while Corrective RAG ensures higher trustworthiness and correctness of answers.

- **Multimodal RAG:** Traditional RAG pipelines rely solely on text-based embeddings and retrieval. Multimodal RAG extends this by incorporating embeddings from different modalities such as images, audio, video, or even sensor data. This makes the system capable of handling diverse inputs and generating richer responses. For example, a user might upload an image of a product along with a text query, and the system can jointly retrieve relevant documents across both modalities.

Benefits: By fusing multiple data types, Multimodal RAG delivers more contextually rich and comprehensive responses, opening possibilities for domains such as healthcare, e-commerce, and media.

Techniques to Improve Semantic Matching in RAG

One of the key challenges with the RAG architectures is the semantic similarity. Since we use the Vector Database to fetch the semantic similarity, sometimes the context/domain knowledge might be missing. The following are some architectural variations to provide high semantic similarity.

- **High-Quality Embeddings**

  Use state-of-the-art or domain-specific embedding models:

  - Use OpenAI embeddings or Sentence-BERT for a strong general-purpose.
  - Use fine-tuned embeddings for specialized domains (for example, legal, medical).

- **Semantic Chunking**

  Break documents into semantically coherent chunks rather than fixed sizes:

  - Use embeddings to find natural boundaries (for example, paragraphs, sentence clusters).
  - Use sliding windows with an overlap to maintain context.

  Benefits: clearer chunks, less noise, better retrieval relevance

- **Query Transformation and Expansion**

  Enhance user queries before retrieval:

  - Add synonyms to reformulate using LLMs.
  - Split complex queries into sub-queries for multi-hop retrieval.

- **Multi-Vector and Embedding Ensembles**

  Represent documents across multiple semantic dimensions:

  - Embed titles, summaries, and detailed text separately.
  - Combine multiple models into hybrid indexes for robust coverage.

- **Feedback and Active Learning**

  Incorporate user feedback to adjust retrieval:

  - Track relevance metrics and fine-tune the retriever based on corrections
  - Use active learning loops for domain-specific improvement

Handling Big Data in RAG Systems

When RAG systems are used in small projects, it is easy to manage a handful of documents and run quick searches. But in enterprise settings, the scale is completely different. Imagine a legal firm with millions of case files, or a healthcare provider with years of medical reports, or even a bank processing billions of financial records daily. In such cases, the challenge is not only to retrieve the right document but to do it quickly, accurately, and consistently—even as the data grows every day.

To make this possible, RAG systems need carefully designed strategies for storage, retrieval, and performance. This involves splitting documents into manageable chunks, using distributed systems for embedding, ensuring scalable storage, and combining different databases to cover all types of search needs. It also requires caching, routing, and continuous monitoring to keep the system efficient as the workload increases.

Chunking Strategy

Instead of feeding whole documents, break them into smaller overlapping parts (such as 1–2 paragraphs each). This makes searching and matching easier. For huge collections of files, use tools that can process many documents at the same time (such as Spark or Dask).

Why it matters: If you do not chunk properly, the system might miss important context or return irrelevant results.

Distributed Embedding Generation

To turn text into embeddings (vectors), process in batches and spread the work across multiple machines or GPUs. Save these embeddings in cloud storage (such as S3 or MinIO) and connect them to your vector database.

Why it matters: Without parallel processing, embedding millions of documents would take weeks. This makes it practical and faster.

Scalable Storage

Pick vector databases that are designed to handle billions of records (such as Milvus or Weaviate). Use metadata tags (for example, "`finance`", "`2024`", "`India`") so you can quickly narrow down which documents to search before doing the heavy vector lookup.

Why it matters: Saves time and money, because you do not need to search the *entire* database every time.

Index Maintenance

Update the database regularly so search results stay accurate. If a document changes, run background jobs to refresh its embedding and re-index it.

Why it matters: If indexes are outdated, your system will give wrong or stale answers.

Hybrid Retrieval Architecture

Do not rely on just one type of database. Use the right tool for the right job:

- `Vector DB → understands the meaning of text`
- `Elasticsearch → great for keyword-based filtering`
- `RDBMS → good for structured business rules`
- `Redis → quick caching for repeated questions`
- `Graph DB → maps relationships (for example, "Company → Subsidiary → CEO")`

Why it matters: Real-world queries often mix structured rules (dates, IDs) with semantic meaning. A hybrid approach balances speed and accuracy.

Caching and Routing

Store the most frequently asked queries in a cache (such as Redis) so they return instantly. Also, direct questions to specialized indexes (for example, legal queries to a "**`law`**" index, medical queries to a "**`health`**" index).

Why it matters: Makes the system both faster and cheaper to run.

Evaluation and Monitoring

Track how long retrieval takes and how relevant the answers are. Use dashboards to monitor query patterns, token usage, and whether the AI is grounding answers in the retrieved context.

Why it matters: Without monitoring, you will not know if your system is slowing down, wasting resources, or giving bad answers.

Libraries for RAG Support

Modern Retrieval-Augmented Generation (RAG) systems require multiple components working together: document loading, chunking, embedding, retrieval, generation, evaluation, and sometimes orchestration across tools or agents. Several libraries have emerged to simplify and structure this process.

This section compares LlamaIndex, LangChain, and LangGraph – the three most prominent and complementary libraries in the RAG ecosystem.

llamaIndex

LlamaIndex is purpose-built for RAG pipelines, providing modular tools to transform raw documents into queryable indexes. It is often used as the *retrieval engine* in LLM-based systems.

Key Features:

Capability	**Description**
Data Loaders	Prebuilt connectors for PDFs, Notion, websites, APIs, SQL, Google Docs, and so on.
Text Chunking	Advanced chunking strategies with metadata awareness.
Indexing	Supports vector indexes, keyword indexes, graph indexes, and composite indexes.
Retrievers	Pluggable retrievers with hybrid search (vector + keyword + metadata).
Query Engines	Support for querying via natural language, structured queries, or tools.
Callback System	Logging, tracing, and observability hooks (integrates with OpenTelemetry).
LLM-Agnostic	Works with OpenAI, Anthropic, Cohere, Ollama, HuggingFace, and so on.
Composable	Combine multiple retrieval strategies and indexes.

Table 3.1: *Features of the llama index*

LangChain

LangChain is a general-purpose framework for orchestrating LLM-based applications. It supports chaining prompts, integrating tools, managing memory, agents, and combining LLMs with retrieval and structured APIs.

Here is a small code snippet for RAG implementation using the langchain library.

Let's first install all the required libraries:

```
pip install langchain faiss-cpu openai
from langchain.embeddings import OpenAIEmbeddings
from langchain.vectorstores import FAISS
```

```
from langchain.chains import RetrievalQA
from langchain.llms import OpenAI
```

Now, let's create some sample documents as sentences.

```
documents = [
    "Paris is the capital of France.",
    "The Eiffel Tower is located in Paris.",
    "London is the capital of the UK.",
    "Big Ben is a famous landmark in London."
]
```

Step 1: Create OpenAI embeddings for the documents. We will use FAISS as the Vector Database.

```
embeddings = OpenAIEmbeddings()  # Make sure OPENAI_API_KEY is set
vector_store = FAISS.from_texts(documents, embeddings)
```

Step 2: Lets create a retriever block using similarity search.

```
retriever = vector_store.as_retriever(search_type="similarity",
search_kwargs={"k":2})
```

Step 3: Initialize the GPT 3.5 as LLM and Langchain RetrievalQA chain module

```
llm = OpenAI(temperature=0)  # GPT-3.5 by default
qa_chain = RetrievalQA.from_chain_type(
    llm=llm,
    retriever=retriever,
    chain_type="stuff"  # simple concatenation of retrieved docs
)
```

Step 4: Ask a query and get the response from LLM based on our knowledge.

```
query = "Where is the Eiffel Tower located?"
answer = qa_chain.run(query)
print("Query:", query)
print("Answer:", answer)
```

Summary of the code:

1. **Documents:** A small list of text documents serves as the knowledge base (for example, facts about cities and landmarks).
2. **Embeddings:**
    a. Each document is converted into a vector embedding using OpenAI embeddings.
    b. Embeddings capture the semantic meaning of the text.

3. **Vector Store (FAISS):**
    a. Embeddings are stored in **FAISS**, an efficient vector similarity search engine.
    b. Allows fast retrieval of documents most relevant to a query.
4. **Retriever:** A retriever object fetches the top k most similar documents for a user query.
5. **LLM and Chain:**
    a. OpenAI (GPT-3.5) acts as the generator.
    b. RetrievalQA combines retrieved documents with the LLM to produce a natural language answer.
6. **Query Execution:**
    a. User enters a query.
    b. Relevant documents are retrieved from FAISS.
    c. LLM generates the answer based on the retrieved context.
7. **Output:** The system outputs an accurate and human-readable answer to the user's query.

Let us understand the important features of the langchain library.

Capability	**Description**
Chains	Compose sequences of steps (for example, input → LLM → output parser).
Agents	Use LLMs to decide which tools or APIs to use next.
Memory	Buffers, summaries, or entity memories for chat context.
Tool Integration	Built-in support for APIs, SQL, vector DBs, code execution, and so on.
Output Parsers	Extract structured data from LLM outputs (JSON, Pydantic, and so on).
Vector Store Connectors	Integrates with Pinecone, Chroma, Qdrant, FAISS, and so on.
LangSmith Integration	Powerful for experiment tracking and prompt evaluation.
Model Flexibility	Supports OpenAI, Cohere, HuggingFace, Claude, and local LLMs.

Table 3.2: *Features of the langchain library*

LangGraph

LangGraph is a newer addition to the ecosystem, developed by the creators of LangChain, designed for stateful, multi-step, multi-agent workflows. It provides a graph-based execution model for building LLM workflows that are:

- Re-entrant (can resume)
- Reactive (respond to new data)
- Stateful (track context across steps)
- Deterministic (clear control flow)

Capability	**Description**
Graph-Based Execution	Define nodes and edges as steps in a workflow (such as DAGs).
Reactivity	Nodes can respond to new inputs at runtime.
Stateful Memory	Track workflow progress and conversation state in memory.
Multi-Agent Support	Define workflows involving multiple agents (for example, researcher + summarizer).
Integration with LangChain	Can use chains and agents inside nodes.
Ideal for	Multi-round planning, tool-chaining, RAG with decision logic.

Table 3.3: *Summary of langgraph features*

Now, let us take a comparison of different frameworks at the time of writing this book.

Feature Capability	**LlamaIndex**	**LangChain**	**LangGraph**
Primary Purpose	RAG document indexing and querying	LLM orchestration (tools, memory, chains)	Graph-based orchestration for LLM workflows
Data Loaders	Yes (many built-in)	Limited	Depends on LangChain integration
Vector Store Support	Full (pluggable)	Full	Via LangChain
Retrieval Logic	Native retrievers, hybrid search	Uses retrievers via a wrapper	Uses LangChain inside graph nodes
Index Types	Vector, keyword, list, tree, graph	Relies on external indexes	Delegates to LangChain or LlamaIndex

Prompt Chaining	Limited, experimental	Core Feature	Fully supported as graph edges
Agents	Not supported	Powerful agent support	Multi-agent support
Workflow Execution	Linear/callable functions	Sequential or conditional chains	Graph-based, stateful
Memory Support	Basic chat memory	Multiple memory types	Full state across nodes
Observability/ Tracing	Built-in callbacks	LangSmith	LangSmith-compatible
Ease of Use	Very high	Medium (more flexible but verbose)	Requires understanding of graph architecture
Best For	RAG pipelines with structured docs	Agents + APIs + LLM tools orchestration	Multi-step workflows, planning, and agents

Table 3.4: *Comparison of RAG frameworks*

Deploying RAG Systems

Deploying RAG systems means making the integrated retrieval and generation components of the AI model operational and accessible for real-world use, allowing it to answer queries by first searching a knowledge base and then generating responses based on the retrieved information. We have different paradigms for deploying the RAG systems:

- Deploy it as a standalone service with a combination of microservices.
- Deploy it as a container using a containerization platform such as Docker.
- Use Kubernetes for scaling it to large systems.
- Use CI/CD to integrate the systems into the build system for Agile system integration.

Modular and Microservices-Based Architecture

Instead of one giant application, microservices break systems into smaller, independent services that talk to each other. This makes applications easier to scale, update, and maintain without shutting everything down.

- Ingestion service handles document parsing, embedding, and storing vectors in a Vector DB.

- Inference service processes queries: embeds the question, retrieves top documents, constructs a prompt, and calls an LLM.
- Embedding service might be a separate service if embeddings are generated asynchronously or at scale.

Why microservices:

- Enables scalability per component (for example, inference needs more replicas under load)
- Follows the separation of concerns: each service is lightweight and independently deployable.

Containerization with Docker

If we create a service and deploy it in production, it may or may not work due to the dependencies on the deployment servers. How do we make sure that our service is consistent and portable across all servers? Containers are the answer for that. Docker packages applications and all their dependencies into lightweight containers. This ensures your app runs the same way everywhere—on the laptop, a server, or the cloud.

Each service is packaged as a Docker container.

- Dockerfiles define each microservice (ingestion, inference).
- Containers ensure consistent environments across **`dev`**, **`test`**, and **`prod`**.

Microservices are deployed via Docker Compose in early testing and pushed to Docker images for production.

Kubernetes Orchestration

Now, let's think about scale. If we are building a large-scale system, someone needs to manage the containers and ensure that service always runs. Kubernetes is like the traffic controller for containers. It manages, scales, and heals containerized applications automatically, so large systems stay reliable even under heavy loads.

On Kubernetes (for example, GKE, EKS, AKS):

- Deploy each microservice as a Deployment with multiple replicas
- Use Services for internal communication (for example, inference↔vector DB)

CI/CD Pipeline

CI/CD automates how code changes move from a developer's laptop to production. It continuously tests, integrates, and deploys updates so features reach users faster and with fewer errors.

Typical flow for microservices deployment:

1. Code pushed to GitHub/GitLab triggers CI build.
2. CI runs tests, builds a Docker image, and pushes to the registry.
3. CD pipeline applies updated manifests to Kubernetes.
4. Kubernetes rolls out updated Deployments.

Case Studies

Let us walk through real-world use cases and how RAG systems can be built to solve the problem. We will study three different real-life cases in legal, healthcare and customer support segments.

Legal Domain – Automating Legal Document Search and Summarization

Imagine, you have to fight a legal battle and you will consult the law firm. Law firms often deal with hundreds of contracts and legal documents when preparing for a case. Manually reviewing documents for relevant clauses, precedents, and compliance regulations is time-consuming and error-prone. How do we add legal knowledge to the chatbots?

Solution: We can implement a RAG-based legal assistant to answer legal queries using internal databases of contracts, case law, and statutes.

Implementation:

- **Document Corpus**: Internal legal contracts, court rulings, compliance guidelines.
- **Indexing**: Legal documents were chunked by clauses/sections and embedded using Sentence-BERT. Indexed using FAISS.
- **Retriever**: Uses dense vector similarity to fetch relevant clauses or legal precedents.
- **Generator**: A fine-tuned T5 model with legal vocabulary generates simplified answers.

  Example Use: A lawyer asks, "*Is there a clause about data protection in the client's contract?*"

```
 → The retriever fetches the correct clause; the generator
rewrites it in plain language.
```

Results:

- Document review time reduced by 70%
- Improved legal compliance checks
- Lawyers used the system interactively during client consultations

Healthcare – Clinical Decision Support System

Doctors and medical researchers struggle to keep up with constantly evolving medical literature, patient histories, and treatment protocols. Making evidence-based decisions quickly is difficult. How do we simplify the diagnosis procedure for the doctors?

Solution: Build a RAG-powered assistant that supports clinicians by retrieving relevant studies and patient records for diagnosis or treatment queries.

Implementation:

- **Document Corpus**: Clinical trial data, patient EHRs, research publications (PubMed).
- **Indexing**: Split into paragraphs, vectorized with BioBERT, stored in Pinecone.
- **Retriever**: Context-aware retriever prioritizes documents based on patient condition.
- **Generator**: Fine-tuned GPT-Neo model produces concise suggestions or summaries.

  Example Use: A doctor asks, "*What are treatment options for drug-resistant* TB *in diabetics?*"

  `→ Retrieves latest case studies + patient-specific data to produce tailored recommendations.`

Results:

- 30–40% faster treatment plan formulation
- Reduction in redundant tests and manual literature review
- System integrated into the hospital EMR interface

Customer Support – AI Knowledge Assistant for Telecom Company

Customer support agents at a large telecom company struggle with slow information retrieval from a vast, disorganized knowledge base (FAQs, technical docs, historical tickets). How do we make the customer support agent bots more knowledgeable?

Solution: Deploy a **RAG-based virtual assistant** to retrieve and generate precise support responses using internal knowledge documents.

Implementation:

- **Document Corpus**: Support tickets, internal KBs, training manuals, API documentation.
- **Indexing**: Used OpenAI embeddings, indexed in Weaviate with metadata tags.
- **Retriever**: Query-specific search across topics such as "*billing*", "*SIM activation*", "*5G issues*".
- **Generator**: GPT-OSS with prompt-tuning for tone and compliance.
- **Use Case**: An agent types, "*Customer cannot activate eSIM on iPhone 14 Pro*".

  ```
  → Retrieves matching resolutions from past tickets and generates a step-by-step reply.
  ```

Results:

- Average call handling time reduced by 35%
- Improved Customer Satisfaction (CSAT) by 18%
- System learned over time from ticket resolutions

Mock Interview

While facing the real deal, imagine yourself as the interviewer and unfold the drama in the interview room.

Interviewer: How would you design the document ingestion pipeline for Indian law texts such as Bharatiya Nyaya Samhita?

You:

I would break ingestion into stages:

1. **Parsing and Cleaning**: Extract text from PDF using OCR if scanned, clean headers/footers, and remove non-textual artifacts.
2. **Segmentation**: Split into semantically meaningful chunks (for example, by section, article, or clause).
3. **Embedding Generation**: Convert chunks into dense vector embeddings using a legal-domain embedding model.
4. **Storage**: Store in a vector database (for example, FAISS, Weaviate, Pinecone) along with metadata such as *Act Name*, *Section*, and *Chapter*.

   This ensures efficient retrieval at section-level granularity, while maintaining legal context.

Interviewer: How do you prevent hallucinations in RAG for legal documents?

You:

- Limit model output strictly to retrieved text.
- Inject system prompts such as: "*Answer* ONLY *using the retrieved* Acts. *If unsure, cite the section.*"
- Use fact-verification modules that cross-check generated answers against retrieved snippets.
- Provide citations by default so users can verify.

Interviewer: If the Acts are updated in the future, how would you update the RAG system without downtime?

You:

- Maintain a document update pipeline:
    - New PDFs → parse & embed → store in staging DB.
- Use versioned vector stores: old index (v1), new index (v2).
- During cutover, queries are routed to v2 while v1 stays as a backup.
- This enables zero-downtime updates.

Interviewer: What are the risks of using an open-source LLM such as LLaMA-2 in legal applications?

You:

- **Legal Liability**: If a model hallucinates, wrong legal advice may cause harm.
- **Bias:** Trained on generic data → may miss legal nuances.
- **Performance**: Larger LLaMA (13B+) requires high compute for inference.
- **Security**: If fine-tuned improperly, it may leak confidential queries.

  Mitigation:
- Always ground answers in retrieved text.
- Add legal disclaimers.

Interviewer: How would you log and monitor queries for improvement in a legal RAG system?

You:

- Log queries + retrieved sections + model responses.
- Capture feedback signals (thumbs up/down).
- Track metrics:

    - Retrieval precision/recall.
    - Answer groundedness.
    - Latency (retrieval + generation).
- Build a feedback loop to fine-tune retrievers and prompts.

Interviewer: If the system is queried in Hindi, how would you handle retrieval and generation?

You:

- Use multilingual embeddings (for example, LaBSE, mUSE).
- Store bilingual embeddings of Acts (Hindi + English).
- If Hindi query → embed in Hindi → retrieve → LLM generates in Hindi.
- Optionally, fallback: Hindi query → translate to English → retrieve → generate → translate back.

This ensures accessibility across languages.

Conclusion

Retrieval-Augmented Generation (RAG) is revolutionizing how large language models interact with dynamic, domain-specific, and frequently updated knowledge sources. By combining the semantic understanding of generative models with the precision of retrieval systems, RAG addresses key limitations such as hallucination, outdated knowledge, and lack of domain adaptation.

In this chapter, we explored the fundamental architecture of RAG—comprising the retriever, indexer, and generator—and how each component contributes to building a grounded and responsive AI system. We also examined various deployment strategies, from microservices to serverless environments, leveraging tools such as Docker, Kubernetes, and Helm for scalability and resilience.

The real-world case studies across legal, healthcare, and customer service domains demonstrate the versatility of RAG systems. These implementations not only improved accuracy and reduced operational overhead but also enhanced user trust and productivity. Whether it is assisting doctors with evidence-based decisions or helping customer service agents with fast, relevant answers, RAG has proved to be a robust solution across sectors.

The future of RAG systems will go beyond text, blending hybrid retrievers, adaptive learning, and multi-modal grounding that connects language with images, audio, and beyond. As AI continues to mature, the ability to design and deploy powerful RAG pipelines will not just be a technical skill—it will be a cornerstone of building AI systems that are scalable, explainable, and truly trustworthy. For today's practitioners, mastering RAG means stepping into the frontlines of shaping how the next generation of AI will think, reason, and serve society.

Fine-tuning large language models is about adapting powerful pre-trained models to specific tasks or domains, making them more accurate, efficient, and aligned with real-world needs. The next chapter explores the key techniques, strategies, and tools that transform general-purpose LLMs into domain experts.

References

1. **Lewis, P., et al. (2020).** *Retrieval-Augmented Generation for Knowledge-Intensive NLP Tasks*. NeurIPS. https://arxiv.org/abs/2005.11401
2. **OpenAI Documentation:** Using embeddings and retrieval in GPT-based applications. https://platform.openai.com/docs/guides/embeddings
3. **LangChain Documentation:** Framework for building RAG pipelines. https://docs.langchain.com
4. **LlamaIndex Documentation:** Indexing and querying LLM-ready data structures. https://www.llamaindex.ai
5. **Kubernetes Documentation:** Deploying applications in a scalable microservices environment. https://kubernetes.io/docs/home/
6. **Docker Documentation:** Containerizing AI and RAG workloads. https://docs.docker.com/

Chapter 4
Enhancing Systems through LLM Finetuning

Introduction

On launch day, a fintech startup celebrated the integration of a cutting-edge language model into its customer service platform. The excitement was short-lived—within days, tickets piled up again, not because the model was silent but because it was confidently wrong. It offered US tax advice to Indian users, confused PAN numbers with postal codes, and generally failed to grasp the context of the domain it was serving. This story highlights a fundamental limitation: while LLMs such as GPT-4, LLaMA, and Claude are powerful, they are trained on broad, internet-scale data. They know a little about many things, but without domain grounding, their responses risk being misleading or even harmful.

For businesses, this creates a paradox—LLMs are too powerful to ignore, yet too generic to rely on out of the box. Pre-trained models often hallucinate details, mismatch tone, misinterpret cultural nuances, or deliver inconsistent results despite prompt engineering or retrieval augmentation. The solution lies in fine-tuning: adapting a general-purpose model to a specific domain, dataset, or tone. Fine-tuning builds on the strong foundation of an existing model to improve accuracy, reliability, and domain fluency, while reducing hallucinations and latency. In the following sections, we explore how organizations are leveraging fine-tuning techniques, supported by real-world case studies, to transform general LLMs into specialized, trustworthy systems.

Structure

In this chapter, we will cover the following topics:

- Using LLMs for Different Business Applications
- LLM Fine-Tuning Techniques
- Evaluation Strategies
- Example Business Case-Studies
- Libraries and Implementation Strategies

Is building LLM fine-tuning a simple task? The picture below depicts the complexities of LLM fine-tuning. LoRA (Low Rank Adaptation)/Prefix Tuning are different fine-tuning techniques.

Figure 4.1: *Fun interpretation of challenges with respect to LLM fine-tuning. Credits: Meme concept and generation by ChatGPT AI*

Using LLMs for Different Business Applications

In a modest clinic in Bengaluru, a nurse speaks into a mobile app: "*Male, 62, diabetic, presenting with chest pain and shortness of breath.*" Within seconds, the app converts her spoken notes into a structured clinical summary using standard ICD-10 terms. The doctor is already reviewing treatment suggestions generated by the AI, cross-referenced with the patient's history. All of this is powered by a fine-tuned language model—not a generic one, but one trained on years of medical notes, local guidelines, and patient outcomes from that very clinic network.

The Power of Specialization

Fine-tuning enables a model to understand our world, not just the world in general. In practice, this means:

- Understanding the terminology that the business uses.
- Following the workflow and regulatory requirements.
- Adapting to your audience's expectations and domain complexity.

Let us walk through a few domains where fine-tuning can make a substantial impact.

E-Commerce: Personalization at Scale

An e-commerce platform fine-tunes an LLM to write product descriptions. A blue cotton kurti is not just "*a kurti*" but "*a breathable, summer-friendly ethnic wear piece tailored for urban Indian women.*" Conversion rates rise. Customer reviews improve.

Use Case: Product description generation, dynamic pricing summaries, personalized marketing copy.

Education and EdTech: Adaptive Learning Assistants

A competitive exam platform fine-tuned its LLM on UPSC previous papers. The assistant can now not only answer, but also ask questions in the same pattern as the exam. It even generates hints and step-by-step answers personalized to the learner's pace.

Use Case: Quiz generation, syllabus-aligned tutoring, multilingual question explanations. Let us visualize how an AI tutor would take the world.

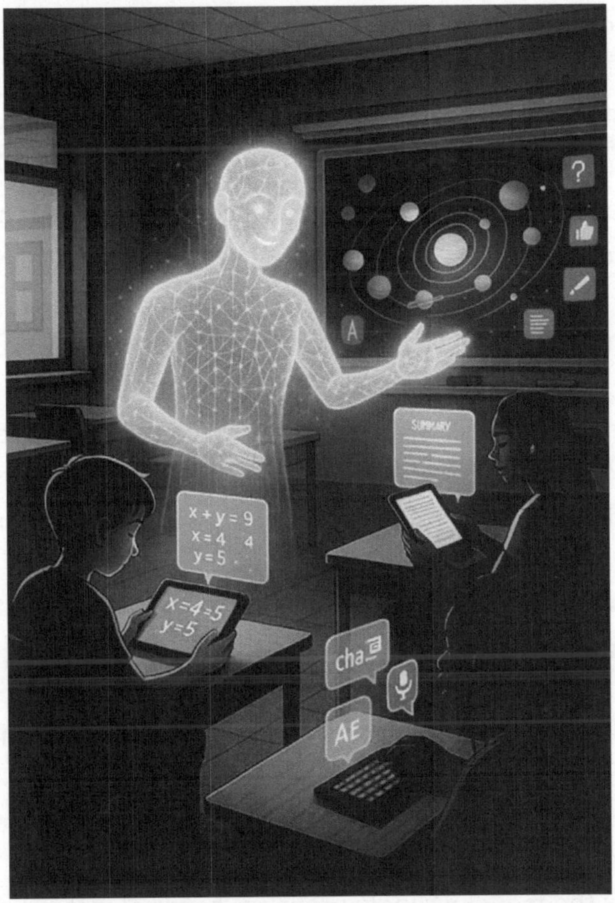

Figure 4.2: *An AI hologram teaching the students. Credits: Sora*

As part of my tutoring classes, I have to teach AI to different experience levels and different types of learners. Some like pictures, some would like in-depth mathematics, some would want practical exposure, and many like to learn with fun. AI helps me to bring all these aspects into content preparation, along with fun assessments such as Pictionary, trivia, riddles, and so on.

LLM Fine-tuning Techniques

Think of the LLM like a team of magical workers inside the library. Each worker has a role:

1. **The Tokenizer (the word cutter):** When you ask, "*What is AI?*", the tokenizer chops your sentence into smaller pieces called **tokens** (like LEGO blocks of words).

   Example: `"What is AI?" → ["What", "is", "AI", "?"]`

2. **The Embedding (the meaning finder):** Each token is then turned into a vector that captures its meaning.
3. **The Transformer (the thinking process):** This is the brain of the LLM.
   - Imagine a tall tower with many floors.
   - On each floor, there are workers called **Attention Mechanisms**.
   - Their job is to figure out: "*Which other words should I pay attention to when understanding this word?*"

   Example: In "*The cat sat on the mat*", when thinking about "*sat*," it pays attention to "*cat*."
4. This attention system allows the machine to connect ideas across the sentence, just like how we remember context in conversation.
5. **The Decoder (the storyteller):** After thinking deeply, the model predicts the next word step by step.
   - **Example**: If you say, "*Once upon a...*", the model predicts "*time*."
   - Then it predicts the next word, and the next, until you get a full answer.

Inside the LLM machine, there are millions (or even billions) of tiny workers. Each worker has a parameter (such as a dial or switch) that controls how strongly it connects words, ideas, and meanings.

- During training, the model trains the parameters to get better at predicting the right word.

  Example: If the model wrongly predicts "*banana*" instead of "*queen*," training nudges the parameters so next time it is closer to "*queen*."

When you hear about a **7B model** or **13B model**, it is talking about how many knobs (parameters) the model has:

- **7B (7 billion parameters):** The library has **7 billion** parameters to tune. It is powerful, but still compact enough to run on smaller machines.
- **13B (13 billion parameters):** Now the library has **13 billion** parameters.

  More parameters → more memory for patterns, relationships, and subtle details.

  But also more costly to train and run (needs stronger machines).

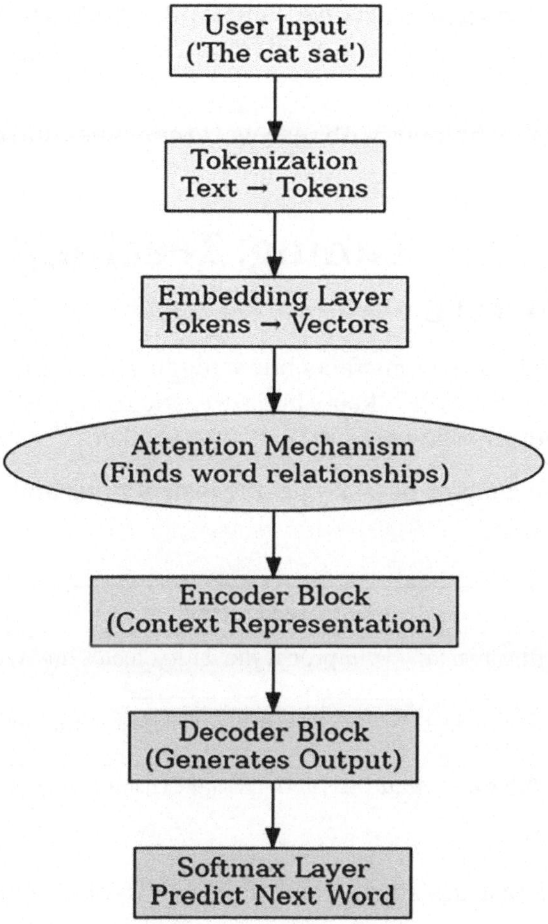

Figure 4.3: *Simple representation of a transformer*

Imagine at a logistics company, the engineering team faced a decision: "Do *we fine-tune the entire 13-billion-parameter model just to make it understand our delivery route codes? That is expensive, slow, and risky.*" Instead, they chose LoRA—a parameter-efficient fine-tuning method. A week later, their chatbot could plan and explain optimal shipping paths across 400 districts in India. Cost? Less than training a single delivery manager for a year.

Fine-tuning is not a monolith. It spans a range of strategies, each offering different trade-offs between:

- Compute cost
- Training time
- Data requirement
- Flexibility and accuracy

Depending on the business goal and constraints, you may choose from full fine-tuning, instruction tuning, or PEFT (Parameter-Efficient Fine-Tuning) approaches such as LoRA and Adapters.

Let us unpack the main techniques with real world analogies and code-friendly mental models.

Instruction Fine-Tuning: Teaching the Model to "*Follow Orders*"

Imagine a trainee who knows many facts but struggles to follow specific instructions. "*Summarize this text in 10 words.*" "*Reply in a sarcastic tone.*" Instruction fine-tuning is how we make LLMs better followers, not just smart talkers.

Fine-tuning LLMs on examples of task-specific instructions and expected outputs.

Example:

Input Instruction	**Expected Output**
"*Summarize the benefits of yoga.*"	"*Improves flexibility, focus, and reduces stress.*"
"*Respond politely to a complaint.*"	"*We are truly sorry for the inconvenience caused...*"

Table 4.1: *Input instructions and expected output*

Use Case:

- Building multi-task assistants (such as FLAN-T5 or OpenOrca models)
- Customizing model tone, instruction format, or reasoning depth

Parameter-Efficient Fine-Tuning: More with Less

If full fine-tuning is like rewriting an entire book, Parameter-Efficient Fine-Tuning (PEFT) is like adding sticky notes with changes—cheaper, faster, and more targeted.

Why PEFT:

- Full fine-tuning updates all model weights.
- PEFT updates only small subsets of parameters.
- Ideal when:
    - GPU/TPU resources are limited.
    - Frequent updates or domain shifts are expected.

- Model portability matters.

Adapter Layers: Plug-and-Play Intelligence

A content platform fine-tunes adapters to switch between "*Gen Z tone*," "*Academic tone*," and "*News tone*"—all using the same base model. Think of adapters as smart Lego blocks we can swap in and out.

Working:

1. Insert small neural layers (adapters) between transformer blocks.
2. Base model remains frozen.
3. Task-specific adapters are trained and activated as needed.

Benefits:

- **Modular**: One model, many tasks
- **Memory-efficient**: Train just a few MBs per task
- Multilingual and multi-task friendly

Low-Rank Adaptation: Elegant Efficiency

A fintech company used Low-Rank Adaptation (LoRA) to adapt a 7B model to regional taxation rules. Instead of changing the whole network, it inserted learnable low-rank matrices into key attention layers. Result: A lean, accurate assistant trained in hours.

Working:

1. LoRA injects trainable low-rank matrices **A** and **B** into the model's attention layers.
2. During training, only these matrices are updated.

   ```
   Attention weights = Attention Weight + A*B
   ```

3. Post-training, they are merged back or used during inference.

Benefits:

- Train 0.1% – 1% of parameters
- Small storage footprint
- Fast experimentation

Let us try to understand LoRA architecture using the following picture.

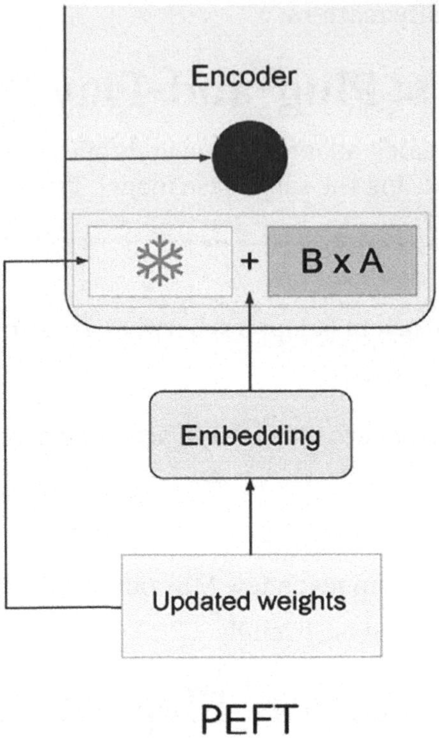

Figure 4.4: *PEFT representation*

Quantized LoRA (QLoRA)

QloRA Combines LoRA with 4-bit quantization to fine-tune large models on limited hardware. Quantization is a way to make a big, heavy AI model smaller and faster.

In simple words:

- Normally, models use big numbers (such as 32-bit floating point) to store parameters.
- Quantization shrinks these numbers into smaller versions (such as 8-bit integers).
- This means the model takes less memory, runs faster, and can fit on smaller devices (such as phones or edge hardware).

  When to Use: When we need to fine-tune very large LLMs on a single GPU.

  Pros:

  - Memory efficient
  - Maintains performance close to FP16 training

Cons: Quantization might slightly reduce accuracy.

Prompt-Tuning and Prefix-Tuning (Lightweight but Limited)

Let us understand two simple and lightweight fine-tuning techniques - Prefix-tuning, prompt-tuning, and Bitfit.

- **Prefix-Tuning:** Train a small set of input tokens ("*soft prompts*") instead of the full model.
    - For every transformer layer, attach a fixed-length prefix vector (learnable).
    - These prefixes are passed into the attention layer as additional keys and values.
    - Base model weights remain frozen.
    - The prefix conditions the model for a specific task.
    - Train only the prefix embedding.

    The "*prompt*" will become <Token1><Token2>...<Tokenn>prompt
- **Prompt-Tuning:**
    - Similar to prefix tuning, but only the embedding layer is tuned with learnable prompt vectors.
    - More lightweight than prefix tuning.

BitFit:

- Update only bias terms in the network
- Extremely lightweight (fewer parameters than LoRA)
- Works surprisingly well for classification tasks

Full Fine-Tuning - The Heavyweight Approach

Sometimes, partial measures are not enough. Full fine-tuning updates all weights of a foundation model on domain data, but training entirely from scratch is rarely practical outside frontier labs. Let us dig into more details.

Working:

1. Training or re-training all model weights on the domain data
2. Can be initialized from a foundation model or done from scratch

Downsides:

- High compute and memory requirements
- Needs careful hyperparameter tuning
- Risk of overfitting or catastrophic forgetting

When to Use:

- When extreme domain control is needed
- When LoRA/adapter methods are not enough
- For training open-weight foundational models for private use

Let us take a look at a comparison of different fine-tuning techniques:

Technique	Trainable Parameters	Storage	Speed	Ideal Use Case
Full Fine-Tuning	100%	Very High	Slow	High specialization
Instruction Tuning	100% or PEFT	High–Med	Slow–Med	Multi-task, end-user
LoRA	~0.1–1%	Low	Fast	Multi-domain adapters
Adapters	~1–3%	Low	Fast	Task modularity
Prefix Tuning	~0.01–0.1%	Very Low	Very Fast	Lightweight conditioning
Prompt Tuning	<0.01%	Very Low	Very Fast	Small task-specific shifts
BitFit	<0.01%	Very Low	Very Fast	Simple classification

Table 4.2: *Fine-tuning techniques*

Evaluation Strategies

Evaluating Large Language Models is not just about scoring them – it is about trust. Without clear, consistent metrics:

- We do not know whether our fine-tuning improved the model or made it worse.
- We risk deploying systems that sound confident but deliver misleading or irrelevant content.
- We cannot compare models across teams, versions, or vendors.

Think of metrics as the *compass* in the LLM development journey. They tell us:

- **Performance direction**: Are we heading towards better accuracy, helpfulness, or speed?
- **Trade-offs**: Is our model faster but less accurate? More creative but less factual?
- **Readiness**: Is the model safe and aligned enough for deployment in real business contexts?

While metrics are crucial, evaluating LLMs is not as straightforward as scoring a classification model.

Some key challenges include:

- **Subjectivity of "Good" Output:** Natural language is inherently flexible – two different sentences might express the same meaning, yet only one might match the "*reference*" exactly.
- **Task Diversity:** LLMs are multi-talented: summarization, reasoning, coding, dialogue... each requires different evaluation criteria.
- **Trade-off Between Automation and Insight:** Automated metrics (for example, BLEU, ROUGE) are fast but can miss nuances. Human evaluation captures subtlety but is slow and expensive.
- **Bias and Fairness:** An LLM might perform well overall but fail disproportionately for certain topics, dialects, or demographics – metrics must capture this.
- **Hallucinations and Factuality:** Models can be eloquent liars – producing false yet convincing information. Detecting and scoring this is still a research challenge.
- **Evolving Standards:** As LLMs get better, benchmarks that once separated good from bad quickly become saturated, forcing us to design harder evaluation sets.

In practice, a good evaluation framework for LLMs often combines:

- **Automatic metrics** (for example, Perplexity, BLEU, BERTScore)
- **Human evaluation** for subjective qualities
- **Domain-specific tests** (for example, TruthfulQA for factuality)
- **Safety audits** (bias and toxicity)
- **System performance tests** (latency, cost)

Let us go deeper and understand different evaluation metrics.

Text Quality Metrics (Language Modelling and Generation)

Language generation is a difficult and ambiguous task. These measure the *linguistic quality* of model outputs, independent of a specific task. Here are some well-known metrics for measuring language generation. These metrics are extremely important in measuring the final success of fine-tuning.

Metric	What It Measures	How It Works	Notes
Perplexity (PPL)	How well the model predicts the test set	Lower is better; the exponential of cross-entropy loss	Does not capture semantic accuracy
Bilingual Evaluation Understudy(BLEU)	N-gram overlap with reference	Compares exact matches of word sequences	Best for short, structured output (e.g., translations)
Recall-Oriented Understudy for Gisting Evaluation(ROUGE)	Recall-oriented n-gram overlap	Counts matching n-grams, skip-grams	Common for summarization
Metric for Evaluation of Translation with Explicit Ordering (METEOR)	Synonym-aware overlap	Considers stemming, synonyms, and word order	More semantic than BLEU
BERTScore	Semantic similarity using contextual embeddings	Compares token embeddings from BERT-like models	Good for paraphrase detection

Table 4.3: *Comparison of quality metrics*

Task-Specific Metrics

These focus on whether the model performs well on a given application. We also use different metrics for well-known tasks such as Classification (organizing the sentences into classes like sentiment). Let us take a look at the task-specific metrics.

Metric	Best For	How It Works
Accuracy	Balanced classification tasks	% of correct predictions
Precision, Recall, F1-score	Imbalanced classification	F1 is the harmonic mean of precision and recall

Exact Match (EM)	Question answering	% of answers exactly matching reference
Macro/Micro Averages	Multi-class classification	Averaging strategies for F1

Table 4.4: *Comparison of task-specific metrics*

LLM-Specific Metrics

These address challenges unique to large language models. We also need to measure LLM with respect to its fairness, consistency, truthfulness, harmlessness, and so on. Here are some well-known metrics that can help us.

TruthfulQA:	Measures how truthful model responses are (benchmark)
Hallucination Rate:	% of fabricated or incorrect facts
Toxicity Score (Perspective API):	Measures toxic language likelihood
Bias Benchmarks (e.g., BBQ, CrowS-Pairs):	Detects gender, race, and cultural bias
Jailbreak Resistance Rate:	% of successful prompt injections

Table 4.5: LLM-*specific metrics*

Example Business Case-Studies

Let us discuss some of the real use cases where the fine-tuning is implemented and which fine-tuning techniques were used.

Healthcare: Med42 – Parameter-Efficient Fine-Tuning for Medical Q&A

In healthcare, general-purpose LLMs often struggle with complex medical terminology and multi-step reasoning. A collaborative team fine-tuned Meta's Llama-2 models on a large medical Q&A corpus (StackExchange and exam questions) to create Med42, a specialized medical assistant. Using Low-Rank Adaptation (LoRA) – a parameter-efficient fine-tuning technique – they trained on in-domain instructions (medical queries and answers) while freezing most model weights. This approach injected domain knowledge without retraining the whole network. The result was a model that set a new open benchmark: Med42 achieved 72% accuracy on USMLE-style medical licensing questions. In other words, this LoRA-tuned model outperformed prior public medical LLMs. The authors note that using LoRA allowed dramatic gains at far lower cost than full fine-tuning, making it practical for hospitals and biotech.

- **Fine-tuning method**: Low-Rank Adaptation (LoRA), a PEFT approach that injects trainable rank-16 adapters into Llama-2.
- **Task**: Medical question answering (USMLE exam, clinical FAQs).
- **Results**: Med42 scored 72% on USMLE questions – a new state-of-the-art for open medical LLMs – versus ~65–68% by untuned counterparts. This substantial lift shows how domain-specific fine-tuning (especially parameter-efficient techniques) can bridge the gap.

Finance: Prefix-Tuned Summarization of Financial News

Financial analysts face an avalanche of news and sentiment; summarizing it accurately is critical. As per the paper titled "*Prefix-Tuning with Prompt Augmentation for Efficient Financial News Summarization*," researchers tackled financial news summarization by augmenting a transformer with *prefix tuning*. They built prompts that included a "sentiment label" (positive/negative market tone) and trained only the continuous prefix vectors (keeping the main model frozen). In experiments on business-news data, this prefix-tuning with sentiment augmentation delivered clear gains over ordinary fine-tuning. For example, compared to a BART model fine-tuned conventionally, the prefix-tuned model improved ROUGE scores by notable margins – roughly +0.68 ROUGE-1 and +0.86 ROUGE-L over baseline fine-tuning. It also achieved a top BERTScore-F1 of 90.52. In short, by guiding the model with sentiment-enriched prompts and tuning only prefix parameters, the team generated more focused summaries. The outcome was higher summarization accuracy and better semantic alignment, all with much lower computational cost than full fine-tuning.

- **Fine-tuning method**: Prefix tuning (a PEFT method) with prompt augmentation. A small trainable prefix vector was prepended to inputs, guiding a frozen BART model.
- **Task**: Abstractive summarization of financial news (with sentiment context).
- **Results**: The sentiment-driven prefix-tuned model outperformed both plain fine-tuning and prefix-tuning baselines. It achieved ROUGE-1/2/L scores improved by +0.68, +0.74, and +0.86, respectively, and the highest BERTScore-F1 (90.52). These gains demonstrate that prefix tuning can efficiently adapt an LLM to finance-specific summarization with real performance boosts.

Legal: LegiLM – Domain-Specific Instruction Tuning for GDPR Compliance

In the legal domain, companies face laborious compliance reviews. A recent case study in legal tech built LegiLM (*LegiLM: A Fine-Tuned Legal Language Model for Data Compliance*), an LLM fine-tuned for data-protection advice. Starting from a general LLM (SaulLM-7B), the team used a specially curated corpus: GDPR regulations, annotated data-sharing contracts, and policy documents. This domain-focused fine-tuning meant the model learned legal reasoning patterns and compliance terminology. In benchmark tests on English GDPR compliance questions, LegiLM dramatically outperformed general LLMs: it scored 68.05% accuracy (F1 68.21) versus only ~42% accuracy for GPT-4. The case study highlights that targeted legal instruction tuning – even on a smaller 7B model – can yield "sound legal justifications" and reduce manual review time. For law firms and regulators, this meant faster contract analysis and better detection of compliance gaps.

- **Fine-tuning method**: Domain-focused instruction tuning. LegiLM was trained on legal Q&A tasks and policy corpora to teach GDPR compliance reasoning.
- **Task**: Legal question answering for data protection (GDPR) cases.
- **Results**: LegiLM achieved 68.05% accuracy and F1 68.21% on a custom GDPR benchmark, significantly surpassing GPT-4 (42.35%/43.85%) and other baselines on the specific benchmarks. This specialized fine-tuning thus yielded a compliance assistant capable of much more reliable legal analysis, enabling lawyers to automate checks that previously took hours.

Customer Support: ChatGPT for Telecom Helpdesks

Verizon publicly announced a production deployment of an AI assistant (built with Google's models/Gemini integration) that helped agents reduce call time and drove measurable business KPIs. Reuters reports that Verizon's use of Google AI assistants shortened call times, freed agents to focus on sales, and was associated with a large sales uplift – the company stated a **near-40% sales increase** in the channel using those tools after rollout (and also reported reductions in handling time).

Now, we have enough motivation for fine-tuning. Let us discuss the implementation techniques.

Libraries and Implementation Strategies

Now, let us take a look at the implementation strategies from choosing the dataset to deploying the LLMs. The step-by-step implementation strategy includes:

Step 1: Identify Business Need and Task Type

a. **Define the task**: classification, summarization, Q&A, chatbot, code generation.

b. **Choose the metric** (accuracy, BLEU, ROUGE, latency, and so on).

c. **Select a base model** (for example, Llama 2, Falcon, Mistral, GPT-J) based on license, size, and speed.

Step 2: Select Fine-Tuning Method

a. Instruction Fine-Tuning for new behaviors.

b. LoRA / PEFT for domain adaptation with minimal compute.

c. Prefix Tuning for task-specific optimization.

Step 3: Prepare the Dataset

a. Clean and tokenize data.

b. Use domain-specific vocabulary when needed.

c. Follow the model's tokenizer rules (Hugging Face AutoTokenizer).

Step 4: Choose the Library

a. **Hugging Face Transformers**: Core library for loading, training, and inference

b. **Parameter Efficient Fine-Tuning (PEFT)**: Integrates LoRA, prefix tuning, and other lightweight approaches

c. **Accelerate**: Multi-GPU/TPU training without boilerplate

d. **Ollama**: Local deployment of LLMs, good for on-device serving

e. **LangChain**: For integrating LLMs into apps and APIs

f. **FastAPI**: Build lightweight, production-ready REST APIs

Step 5: Train and Evaluate

a. Implement the chosen fine-tuning method.

b. Log experiments with Weights and Biases or MLflow.

c. Evaluate using defined metrics and real-world data.

Step 6: Deploy

a. Convert to `int8` or `int4` quantized models for performance.

b. Serve via:

   - Hugging Face Inference API

- Ollama local server
- Custom FastAPI endpoint

LLM Fine-Tuning and Deployment: Best-of-Breed Stack

Now, let us take a deeper look at the implementation using the popular frameworks/ libraries.

Fine-Tuning (Hugging Face Transformers + PEFT)

Hugging Face has become the de facto platform for NLP/LLM work because of its massive model hub and easy-to-use APIs. PEFT (Parameter-Efficient Fine-Tuning) is integrated into their ecosystem, allowing fine-tuning without retraining the entire model.

Core Features:

- Supports LoRA, Prefix Tuning, Adapters
- 100,000+ pre-trained models ready for fine-tuning
- Easy dataset loading via the datasets library

The following code performs LoRA finetuning on LLM (meta-llama/Llama-2-7b-hf). The rank of the A and B matrices will be 8.

Code Example: LoRA Fine-tuning

Step 1: Import the required libraries.

```
from transformers import AutoModelForCausalLM, AutoTokenizer
from peft import LoraConfig, get_peft_model
```

Step 2: Initialize the model. We are using llama2 with 7B parameter model here.

```
model_name = "meta-llama/Llama-2-7b-hf"
```

Step 3: We need to understand the tokenization used for the tokenization.

```
tokenizer = AutoTokenizer.from_pretrained(model_name)
model = AutoModelForCausalLM.from_pretrained(model_name)
```

Step 4: Initialize the LORA now.

```
config = LoraConfig(
    r=8, //Rank
    lora_alpha=16,
    target_modules=["q_proj", "v_proj"],
```

```
        lora_dropout=0.05
    )
    model = get_peft_model(model, config)
```

When to use:

- We want to adapt an LLM to a domain-specific dataset.
- We want cost-effective training on limited hardware.

Scaling Training (Deep Speed)

A deep learning optimization library from Microsoft that makes training very large models efficient through techniques such as mixed precision, model parallelism, and ZeRO (Zero Redundancy Optimizer - to train giant models with billions of parameters) without running out of GPU memory.

Core Features:

- ZeRO optimization (splits model states across GPUs)
- Supports mixed precision (FP16/BF16) for speed
- Easily integrates with Hugging Face Trainer

Code Example: Hugging Face + DeepSpeed

```
accelerate launch --config_file deepspeed_config.yaml train.py
```

When to use:

- DeepSpeed is primarily designed for large-scale training and pretraining, not just fine-tuning. Most enterprises with >7B models prefer PEFT instead of full DeepSpeed fine-tuning.
- Distributed multi-GPU training

Inference and Deployment - Text Generation Interface

Hugging Face's official serving stack, optimized for Transformer-based models, supports multi-GPU, batching, and quantization.

Core Features:

- Streaming responses
- Auto-batching for high throughput
- Easy integration with the Transformers API

Code Example: Running TGI

```
text-generation-launcher --model-id meta-llama/Llama-2-7b-hf
```

When to use:

- Need production-grade API serving for LLMs
- Want to serve quantized models for faster response

API Layer (Fast API)

FastAPI = Fast, developer-friendly way to build APIs in Python with automatic docs and async support. Ideal for exposing fine-tuned LLMs as HTTP endpoints. Follows REST API framework. Built on top of Starlette (for web parts) and Pydantic (for data validation), making it very efficient.

Core Features:

- Async support for high performance
- Automatic docs with Swagger/OpenAPI

The following code will take a fine-tuned model and build a fast API service. We can invoke the model with a prompt through the POST command.

Code Example: Wrapping a Model in FastAPI

```
from fastapi import FastAPI
from transformers import pipeline
app = FastAPI()
generator = pipeline("text-generation", model="finetuned-model")
# implement the POST method
@app.post("/generate")
def generate_text(prompt: str):
    return generator(prompt, max_length=200)
```

When to use:

- Deploying an internal/external LLM-powered API
- Quick prototyping of AI endpoints

Monitoring (Weights and Biases - W and B)

A developer platform for tracking machine learning experiments, visualizing metrics, managing datasets/models, and collaborating on ML projects.

Core Features:

- Logs loss curves, evaluation metrics
- Tracks hyperparameters
- Compares multiple training runs

Code Example: Logging Metrics

```
import wandb
wandb.init(project="llm-finetune")
wandb.log({"loss": 0.42, "accuracy": 0.93})
```

When to use:

- Comparing fine-tuning runs
- Long-term model performance tracking

Let us visualize all the components in LLM deployment

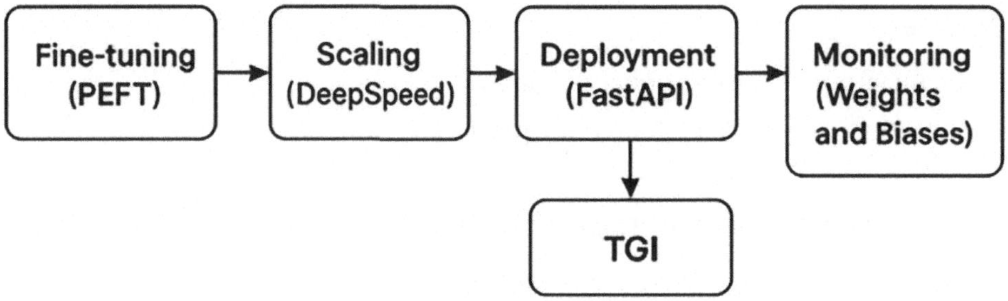

Figure 4.5: *LLM Fine-tune deployment stack*

Recommended Stack for Real-World LLM Fine-Tuning:

- Fine-tuning: Hugging Face Transformers + PEFT
- Scaling: DeepSpeed
- Serving: TGI
- API Layer: FastAPI
- Monitoring: WandB

Conclusion

Fine-tuning large language models is both an art and a science – part meticulous engineering, part creative adaptation. From instruction fine-tuning to PEFT methods such as LoRA, Adapters, and Prefix Tuning, we have seen how different approaches balance cost, speed, and performance.

The real magic lies in choosing the right technique for the task, backed by clear evaluation metrics that measure success in ways aligned with business goals.

Our journey also explored implementation tools such as Hugging Face, DeepSpeed, and Ollama – the bridges between research ideas and real-world deployments. The case studies showed that with the right tuning, LLMs can boost accuracy, productivity, and efficiency across industries – from healthcare and finance to customer support and manufacturing. These domains still require regulatory compliance, guardrails, and human oversight.

The future belongs to those who can adapt LLMs responsibly, efficiently, and creatively. The tools are here, the methods are proven, and now – the next fine-tuning breakthrough is yours to make.

In the next chapter, we will learn about building predictive machine learning algorithms from scratch for a finance domain.

References

Here is a curated set of resources you can explore to go deeper into LLM fine-tuning, evaluation, and implementation strategies:

- Hugging Face PEFT Documentation – https://huggingface.co/docs/peft/index
- LoRA Paper (Hu et al., 2021) – https://arxiv.org/abs/2106.09685
- Prefix-Tuning Paper (Li & Liang, 2021) – https://arxiv.org/abs/2101.00190
- AdapterHub Documentation – https://adapterhub.ml
- DeepSpeed Docs – https://www.deepspeed.ai
- BitsAndBytes Quantization – https://github.com/TimDettmers/bitsandbytes
- HELM Benchmark – https://crfm.stanford.edu/helm
- BIG-bench – https://github.com/google/BIG-bench
- MMLU Benchmark – https://github.com/hendrycks/test
- Hugging Face Inference Endpoints – https://huggingface.co/inference-endpoints
- Ollama – https://ollama.ai
- LangChain – https://python.langchain.com
- Customer support fine-tuning https://openai.com/blog/custom-gpt
- Google's PaLM 2 for Internal Process Automation https://ai.google/discover/palm2
- PEFT+LoRA for financial document analysis https://huggingface.co/blog/peft
- Google's T5 Adapter Fusion https://arxiv.org/abs/2005.00247
- FASTAPI Official Documentation: https://fastapi.tiangolo.com/

Fun Riddles to Test Your Understanding

1. **Riddle – Freezing Time**

   I am a method where most of my body is frozen,
   Yet two small parts are trained to keep things chosen.
   What am I?

   (**Hint**: Think about rank decomposition.)

2. **Riddle – The Disguised Prompt**

   I sneak extra tokens into a model's head,
   Not real input, but it follows what's said.
   I live inside a key-value space instead of text –
   Which fine-tuning method am I, if you guessed what's next?

   (**Hint**: Think about prefix, not suffix.)

3. **Riddle – The Speed Booster**

   I make training cheaper by splitting the load,
   Using multiple GPUs on a shared road.
   I can also handle model sharding with ease,
   Which library am I, if I aim to please?

   (**Hint**: Optimization framework.)

4. **Riddle – The Metric Matchmaker**

   I'm neither accuracy nor BLEU,
   I change depending on the task you do.
   Before you measure, you must define me –
   What am I?

   (**Hint**: Think "evaluation planning.")

5. **Riddle - The bridge**

   I serve as a bridge between a tuned LLM and an app, wrapping it in an API so that you can tap. I can run local models or call the cloud. Who am I?

   (**Hint**: I connect your tuned LLM to the real world, whether it is on your laptop or in the cloud.)

Answers

1. LoRA
2. Prefix Tuning
3. Deep Speed
4. Evaluation Metric
5. Fast API

CHAPTER 5
Designing Financial Risk Prediction Systems Using Supervised Learning

Introduction

In the modern financial landscape, risk prediction plays a crucial role in ensuring the stability and profitability of financial institutions. From credit scoring and loan default predictions to fraud detection and investment risk assessment, accurately forecasting financial risks is essential for informed decision-making. Supervised learning, a key branch of machine learning, provides powerful tools to build predictive models that can analyze historical data and generate reliable risk assessments.

Imagine a bank manager trying to decide whether to approve a loan application. They have got stacks of customer data—income, expenses, credit scores—but how do we make the call? This is where supervised learning steps in, giving us the power to make informed predictions. Supervised learning, in simple terms, is like learning from examples. Think of it as teaching a computer to predict outcomes based on patterns in historical data. Let us take a journey to see how this plays out in the real world, especially in finance and insurance.

The Risks We Are Trying to Solve

The financial and insurance worlds are full of uncertainties—risks that can make or break organizations. Let us explore a few of them:

- **Credit Risk**: Will a borrower pay back their loan?
- **Market Risk**: What if the stock market crashes?

- **Fraud Risk**: Is someone filing a fake insurance claim?
- **Underwriting Risk**: Should we issue this insurance policy?
- **Claims Risk**: Are the claims higher than expected for a policy?

This chapter explores the principles and methodologies involved in designing finance risk prediction systems using supervised learning techniques. We will delve into the core concepts of financial risk, the challenges of working with financial data, and the best practices for building machine learning models that drive actionable insights.

Structure

In this chapter, we will cover the following topics:

- Business Case Studies
- Exploratory Data Analysis
- Ethical Considerations (Explainability and Privacy)
- Introduction to Supervised Machine Learning and Algorithms
- Evaluation Criteria
- Mock Interview: Credit Risk Prediction

Figure 5.1: *Imaginative picture of a bank sanctioning a loan to a customer. Courtesy: Text to image using Canva*

Business Case Studies

Supervised learning is a type of machine learning where we feed the model labeled data. Imagine a spreadsheet: one column has customer details (age, income, credit score), and another has whether they repaid their loan (yes or no). The goal? Teach the system to predict "*yes*" or "*no*" for new customers.

Let us dive into some examples to see how supervised learning turns data into actionable insights:

- **Fraud Detection:** Picture this: someone claims their car was stolen and files an insurance claim. The details seem off, such as the time of day and the location. A supervised learning model, trained on thousands of historical claims, can spot such red flags instantly.

  Outcome: The model flags the claim for further investigation, saving the insurer from paying out to fraudsters.

- **Credit Scoring:** Let us go back to our bank manager example. Using a supervised model, you can predict whether a customer is likely to default on a loan. The system uses patterns from past loan repayments, and calculates a score.

  Outcome: You confidently approve loans, knowing the risk is calculated and manageable.

- **Claims Modeling:** Imagine an insurer trying to predict the total claims cost for the next hurricane season. By feeding the model data from past hurricanes–damage reports, costs, and locations–they get accurate estimates.

  Outcome: The company can adjust premiums and prepare financially.

- **Insurance Underwriting:** Here is another example: someone applying for health insurance. They are 45, active, and have a great medical history. A supervised model evaluates their risk and recommends a lower premium.

  Outcome: The customer gets a fair rate, and the insurer balances risk and revenue.

In finance, responsible AI is critical to ensure fairness, transparency, and trust in decision-making systems that impact credit approvals, investments, and risk assessments. By minimizing bias and ensuring accountability, responsible AI helps protect consumers while maintaining regulatory compliance and institutional integrity.

Figure 5.2: *Fun representation of the ill consequences of credit risk forecasting models*

Exploratory Data Analysis

Exploratory Data Analysis (EDA) plays a crucial role in financial analytics, where data tends to be large-scale, highly sensitive, regulated, and often noisy. EDA helps analysts understand data characteristics, uncover hidden patterns, validate assumptions, and identify potential risks before modelling. Below are the key components of EDA in financial domains.

Collecting Finance Data

Any machine learning problem starts with collecting good data.

- **Sources**: Customer transactions, credit scores, stock prices, loan applications, and market data.
- **APIs and Datasets**: Use financial APIs (such as Alpha Vantage and Bloomberg), government datasets, or scrape public data.

Storing Finance Data

The primary format of risk prediction/fraud detection models is tabular data. (Numerical data/categorical data). Hence, relational databases (RDBMS) or NoSQL data would be common ways to store the data. The data can be stored in the following ways:

- **Databases**: Use SQL databases (PostgreSQL, MySQL) or NoSQL (MongoDB) for scalability.

- **Cloud Storage**: AWS S3, Google Cloud, or Azure for large datasets.
- **Security**: Encrypt sensitive data and comply with regulations (GDPR, PCI-DSS).

Cleaning the Data

The biggest challenge that most companies face is data quality. Here are some standard ways of cleaning the data. We will learn more while doing the case study.

Handle Missing Values

One or a few columns would have missing data. The data could be missing due to unavailability/mistakes during the entry. There are several techniques, including using mean/mode imputation.

Before modelling, analysts must:

- **Quantify missingness**

  Use percentage missing by row/column, missing patterns, and missingness heatmaps.

- **Apply appropriate imputation techniques**
  - **Numerical features:** Mean/median imputation, model-based imputation.
  - **Categorical features:** Mode imputation, "*unknown*" category.

Outlier Detection

These are the data points that are either exceptional cases or mistakes during data entry. We will need to remove or cap extreme values or transform the data before using the machine learning model.

- **Statistical detection methods:** Z-score, IQR (Interquartile Range), Boxplots

Normalization or Scaling

Financial features like income, transaction amount, credit utilization, and debt-to-income ratios vary across huge ranges.

Scaling techniques:

1. **Standardization (Z-score)**

   Converts data to mean=0, variance=1
   x_scaled = (x - mean) / std

2. **Min-Max Scaling**

   Rescales to [0,1]
   Good for neural networks and bounded features.

3. **Log Transform**

   Useful for skewed distributions like income or transaction amount.

- **Categorical Encoding**: Convert categories (for example, loan type) into numerical values. We use techniques like Label encoding and Ordinal encoding for converting them to numerical values.

It is important to check the quality of data for wrong values in strings/numerical data. This is typically done by taking a sample of data and doing a manual inspection, and defining quality metrics. Some of the data quality dimensions could be correctness, completeness, consistency, and so on. We will learn in detail about these in the upcoming sections.

Labeling the Data

The important step in supervised learning is labeling the data. This is often manual and the most time-consuming task. We also need to make sure that the required features for the dataset are included. For example, in the loan default prediction, we need to identify which features are important for prediction, such as Credit Score, Loan Amount, Loan duration, Pending Loans, Defaults, and so on. This often requires strong domain understanding. Once we prepare the records, we need to label the dataset with the classes/actual values depending on classification/regression tasks. The following are some of the techniques employed in labeling the data.

- **Manual Labeling**: Hire annotators to label loan defaults, fraud cases, and so on. Often, the data scientist authors and provides the guidelines for labeling.
- **Historical Data**: Use past records with known outcomes (for example, previous loan defaults).
- **Semi-Supervised Learning**: Start with a small labeled dataset and expand with unlabeled data.
- **Crowdsourcing**: Platforms such as Amazon Mechanical Turk for bulk data labeling.
- **Synthetic Data**: Generate synthetic data using LLMs. For example, create synthetic transaction data for fraud detection.

Imbalanced datasets are a big problem with the finance datasets. For example, in the risk prediction, we would have a few examples of loan defaults compared to loan repayments. Some ML algorithms will not work well for such imbalanced datasets. Using techniques such as SMOTE to augment the missing data is one of the common approaches.

Ethical Considerations (Explainability and Privacy)

- **Data Minimization:** Only collect data that is strictly necessary for the purpose at hand. This reduces the risk of excessive data exposure and limits the potential for data breaches involving unnecessary information.
- **Anonymization and Pseudonymization:** Anonymize or pseudonymize data to reduce the likelihood of identifying individuals. This is crucial for analysis and reporting without compromising personal privacy.
- **Data Security:** Implement robust security measures, such as encryption, access controls, and regular security audits, to protect stored and transmitted data from unauthorized access or breaches.
- **Consent and Transparency:** Clearly inform customers about data collection practices, including what data is collected, how it will be used, and with whom it will be shared. Obtain explicit consent when necessary.
- **Access Control**: Limit access to financial data to only those individuals or systems that require it to perform their job functions. This includes implementing strict authentication and authorization protocols.

Compliance with GDPR and CCPA

- **General Data Protection Regulation (GDPR):** Applicable to EU citizens, GDPR requires organizations to protect personal data and uphold privacy rights.

  Key Requirements:

  - **Data Subject Rights**: Includes the right to access, delete, and rectify personal data.
  - **Data Protection Officer (DPO)**: Appoint a DPO if you process a large amount of data.
  - **Breach Notification**: Notify authorities of a data breach within 72 hours if it poses a risk to individuals.
  - **Lawful Basis for Processing**: Must have a valid legal reason to collect and process personal data.
- **California Consumer Privacy Act (CCPA):** Protects residents of California by enhancing consumer protection and privacy rights for California-based individuals.

- **Bias and Fairness:**
    - **Data Bias**: Risk prediction models can inadvertently perpetuate or amplify biases present in historical data. It is crucial to ensure that models do not unfairly disadvantage certain groups based on race, gender, or other protected characteristics. The training data needs to have data from all the races and groups.
    - **Fairness in Predictions**: Models should be evaluated for fairness, ensuring that predictions are equitable across different demographic groups.
- **Privacy and Data Protection:**
    - **Data Security**: Protecting sensitive financial and personal data used in model training and predictions is paramount. The data needs to be properly encrypted while stored in the databases. Apply privacy techniques like *differential privacy* to encrypt the data.
    - **Consent and Usage**: Ensuring that data is used in compliance with privacy laws and that individuals have consented to the use of their data for risk prediction.
- **Accountability:**
    - **Responsibility for Decisions**: Financial institutions must take responsibility for the decisions made by their models, ensuring that there are mechanisms in place to address errors or adverse outcomes.

Explainability

Machine learning algorithm explainability refers to the ability to understand and interpret the decisions made by a machine learning model. As models become more complex, especially with the rise of deep learning, understanding how they make predictions becomes crucial for trust, transparency, and compliance with regulations.

Importance of Explainability:

- **Trust**: Users are more likely to trust models whose decisions they can understand.
- **Debugging**: Helps identify and correct errors or biases in the model.
- **Compliance**: Necessary for adhering to regulations that require transparency, such as GDPR.

Good Practices of Explainability:

- **Use Appropriate Tools**: Choose the right explainability tool (for example, SHAP, LIME) based on the model and context.

- **Model Simplicity**: Prefer simpler models when possible, as they are inherently more interpretable.
- **Domain Knowledge**: Incorporate domain expertise to validate explanations and ensure they make sense in the real-world context.

SHAP (SHapley Additive exPlanations) is a powerful model interpretability technique that explains how each feature contributes to an individual prediction. In the context of a loan prediction system, SHAP values help break down why a particular applicant is approved or denied by quantifying the positive or negative impact of features such as income, credit history, loan amount, and employment status. This level of transparency is especially important in finance, where fairness, accountability, and regulatory compliance are critical. By showing applicants and regulators which factors influenced the decision, SHAP not only builds trust but also helps detect potential biases in the model.

For example, let us take a look at the SHAP dependency plot between Annual Income and Loan Approved Status.

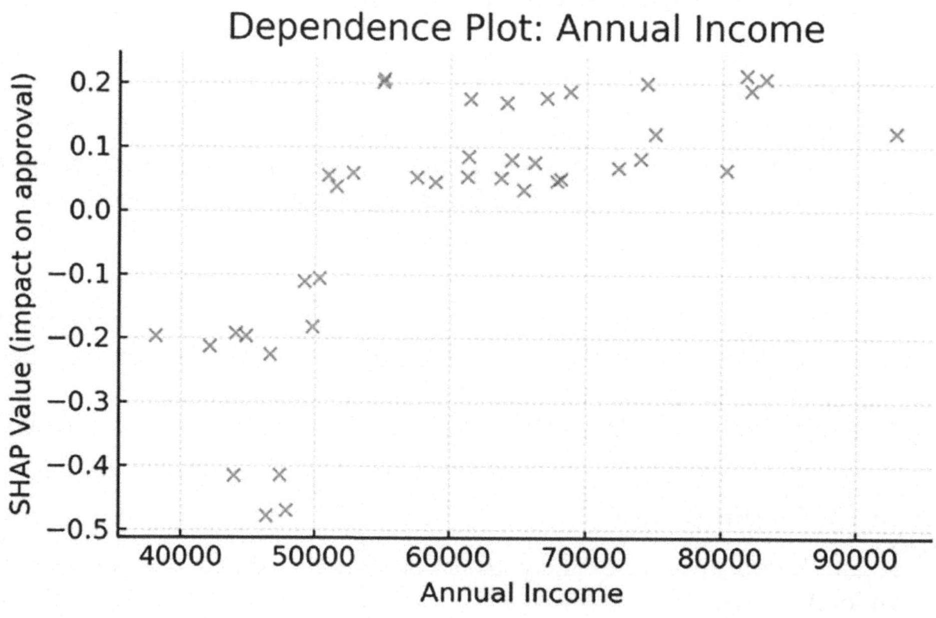

Figure 5.3: *SHAP dependency plot between annual income and impact on loan approval*

- Applicants with **higher annual income** are **more likely to be approved**.
- Applicants with **lower incomes** are **more likely to be rejected**.
- The SHAP values quantify this influence for each individual applicant.

Introduction to Supervised Machine Learning and Algorithms

Supervised machine learning is a game-changer in the financial industry. From predicting creditworthiness to identifying fraudulent transactions, these algorithms can process massive datasets and uncover patterns that are otherwise impossible to discern. In this section, we will delve deeper into supervised learning algorithms, explore the differences between regression and classification, and discuss the suitability of each for financial datasets.

Here is the basic flow:

1. **Gather Data:** Collect a dataset of inputs and corresponding correct outputs.
2. **Train the Model:** Feed this data to the model, which tries to find patterns connecting X to Y.
3. **Test and Improve:** Show the model new, unseen data and check how well it does. If it messes up, tweak it and try again.
4. **Predict:** Once the model is trained, you can let it loose on real-world data.

Regression Versus Classification

At the heart of supervised learning lies the distinction between regression and classification:

- **Regression**
    - Used when the target variable is continuous.
    - **Examples in finance**:
        - Predicting stock prices based on market trends.
        - Estimating insurance premiums.
        - Forecasting revenue or portfolio returns.
- **Classification**
    - Used when the target variable is categorical.
    - **Examples in finance**:
        - Determining whether a transaction is fraudulent (fraud detection).
        - Classifying customers into risk categories (low, medium, high).
        - Predicting loan approval (yes/no).

Choosing between regression and classification depends on the problem's nature. For instance, if you are analyzing the likelihood of loan default (for example, default or no default), we would use classification. However, if you are estimating how much loss might occur if a customer defaults, regression would be appropriate.

Key Supervised Machine Learning Algorithms

Let us explore the supervised learning algorithms in more detail, focusing on how they apply to financial datasets.

Linear Regression

Linear regression predicts a continuous target variable by finding a linear relationship between input features (X) and the output (Y). It minimizes the difference between actual and predicted values using a loss function, often Mean Squared Error (MSE).

In the following chart, we are predicting **customer risk scores** based on their **credit scores**. The relationship is pretty straightforward – **the lower the credit score, the higher the risk.**

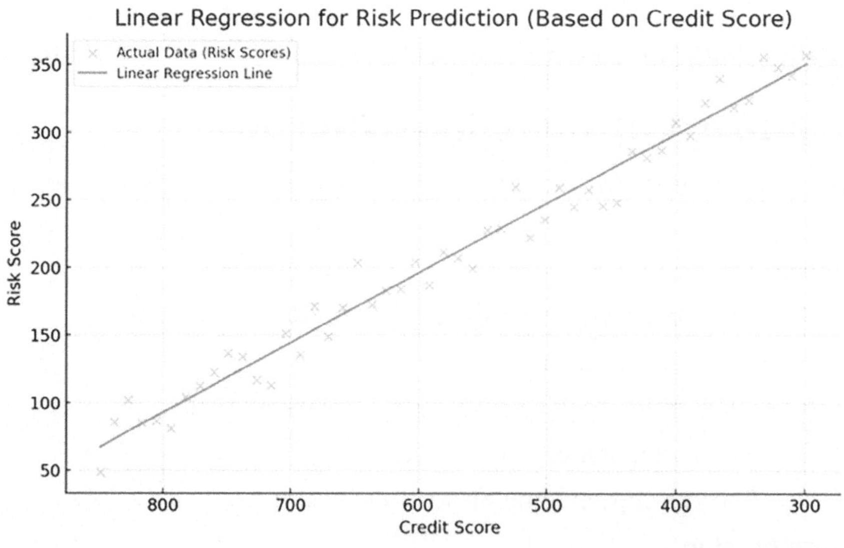

Figure 5.4: *The relationship between Credit Score and Risk Score*

The blue points you see represent **actual data** – real customer credit and risk scores. But data can be messy and scattered, so to make sense of it, we are trying to fit a straight line through these points. This line is our **linear regression model**, which aims to capture the overall trend: as credit scores increase, risk tends to decrease.

Now, not every blue point sits perfectly on this line – and that is expected. The difference between a blue point (actual value) and the point on the orange line (predicted value) is called the **error**. The model's accuracy is measured by summing up the squares of these differences – known as the **Sum of Squared Errors (SSE)**. Smaller errors mean a better fit, while larger errors suggest the model may need adjustment.

This chart helps visualize how well the model captures the relationship between credit scores and risk, giving us insights into customer profiles and potential risk levels.

Logistic Regression

Logistic regression is a classification algorithm that predicts probabilities of classes (for example, default or no default). It uses the logistic function (sigmoid) to map predictions to probabilities.

The following figure represents the logistic regression curve.

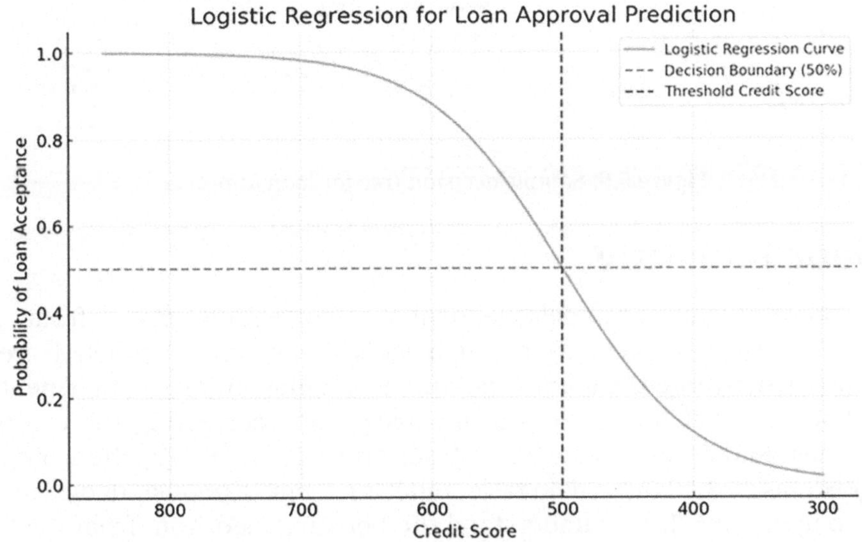

Figure 5.5: *Relation between credit score, loan approval category*

The orange line represents the probability of loan acceptance based on credit score.

The dashed horizontal line at **50%** is the decision boundary – above it, the loan is more likely to be accepted; below it, it is likely to be rejected.

The vertical dashed line marks the threshold credit score where the probability reaches 50%.

Decision Trees

Decision Trees are intuitive machine learning models that split data into hierarchical branches based on feature values. They mimic human decision-making by breaking down a complex problem into smaller, simpler decisions. Decision Trees work well with both categorical and numerical data, capture non-linear relationships effectively, and are easy to interpret and visualize. However, they can be prone to overfitting if not carefully pruned or regularized. Let us visualize a sample decision tree for a loan approval model.

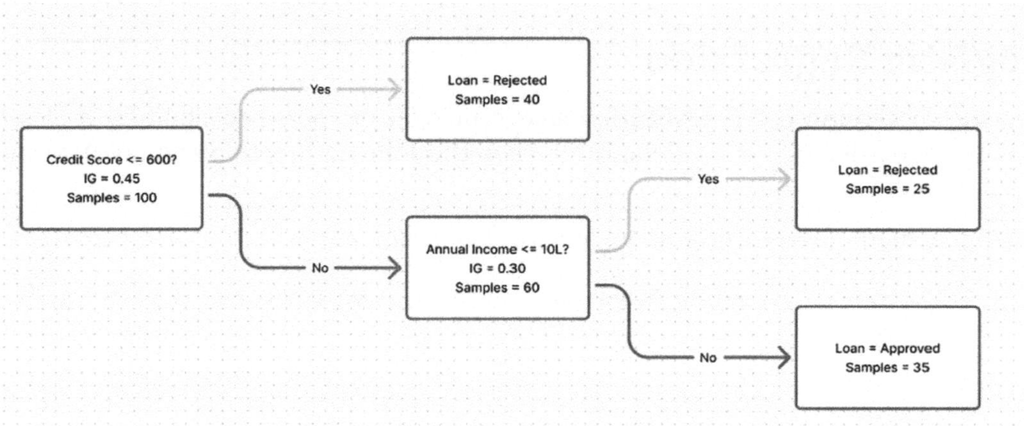

Figure 5.6: *Sample decision tree for loan approval*

Gradient Boosting

Gradient boosting builds models sequentially, correcting errors from previous iterations. Popular implementations such as XGBoost and LightGBM are widely used. **XGBoost (Extreme Gradient Boosting)** is a highly efficient implementation of gradient boosting that builds trees sequentially, each correcting the errors of the previous ones. Known for its speed and performance, XGBoost often outperforms other algorithms in structured data tasks and has become a popular choice in machine learning competitions. Let us understand the boosting algorithm from the following visual representation:

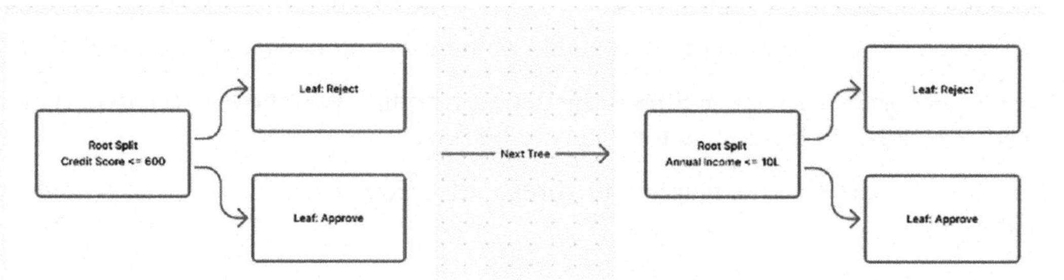

Figure 5.7: *Representation of the boosting algorithm*

Visualization:

- **Structure of Each Tree**: Each decision tree in the plot represents a weak learner. Typically, these are shallow trees (or "*stumps*"). They try to capture simple patterns from the data.

- **Sequential Learning**: The first tree is trained to predict the initial output. Each subsequent tree is trained not on the original target values but on the residual errors from the predictions of the combined former trees. This way, they function as error correctors.
- **Tree Splits**: Each node in the tree represents a decision based on one of the input features. For example, a node might split based on whether Age is greater than a certain threshold. The leaves of the tree hold the final predicted class for instances falling into that branch.

Ensemble of Trees:

- **Combining Models**: The output of the final model is a weighted sum of predictions from all individual trees. The learning rate tunes the size of the step taken to add each tree; smaller values make the learning more robust to overfitting by requiring more trees.
- **Improvement over Iterations**: With each new tree, the model's predictive performance improves. The algorithm stops adding trees either when a pre-set number of trees is reached or when additional trees fail to improve performance.

Gradient Boosting excels at capturing complex patterns, often outperforming simpler ensemble methods in competitions and real-world tasks. On the downside, gradient boosting models are more prone to overfitting if not carefully tuned, require significant hyperparameter optimization, and are computationally more intensive, which can limit their scalability on very large datasets.

Random Forest

Random Forest is an ensemble learning method that builds multiple decision trees and combines their outputs to improve accuracy and reduce overfitting. It introduces randomness in feature selection and data sampling, making the model robust and less sensitive to noise. Let us look at the visual representation of Random Forest algorithms. We see that there are two different decision trees, and the outcome is the average output/majority voting from both trees.

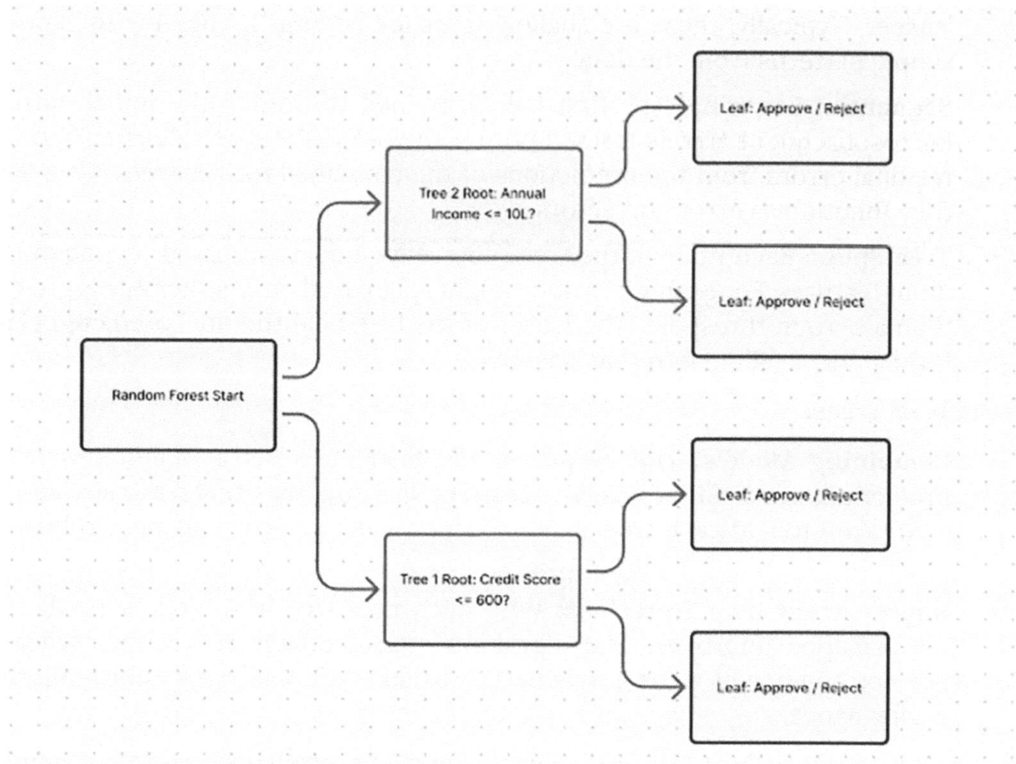

Figure 5.8: *Depicting random forest trees*

Decision Trees in Random Forest:

- **Multiple Trees**: Unlike Gradient Boosting, where trees are built sequentially, Random Forest builds multiple trees independently and in parallel. Each tree is trained on a different subset of the data.
- **Bootstrap Aggregation (Bagging)**: Each tree is trained on a random sample of the data with replacement (bootstrapping). This means some data points may be repeated in a sample, while others may be left out.
- **Random Feature Selection**: At each split in a tree, a random subset of features is considered. This randomness helps in making the trees less correlated and more diverse.

Ensemble of Trees:

- **Voting Mechanism**: For classification, each tree in the forest votes for a class, and the class with the most votes is chosen as the final prediction. This majority voting helps in reducing variance and improving accuracy.
- **Parallel Processing**: Since trees are built independently, Random Forest can be efficiently parallelized, making it scalable for large datasets.

Random Forest offers strong advantages such as robustness against overfitting, the ability to handle high-dimensional data, and resilience to noise through its bagging approach. It works well out of the box with minimal tuning and provides feature importance insights, making it easier to interpret compared to other ensemble methods. However, Random Forest can be computationally expensive with large datasets, may produce less accurate results than boosting methods in complex tasks, and its interpretability diminishes as the number of trees grows.

Support Vector Machines (SVMs)

Support Vector Machines (SVMs), on the other hand, are mathematically powerful algorithms designed to find the optimal hyperplane that separates data points belonging to different classes. They excel at handling high-dimensional spaces and complex nonlinear boundaries through the use of kernel functions. SVMs are particularly effective when the dataset has clear margins of separation and often provide high accuracy even with smaller datasets. Their main trade-off lies in higher computational cost and lower interpretability compared to Decision Trees. We can see the visual representation of SVM in the following diagram, which separates data points belonging to two different classes.

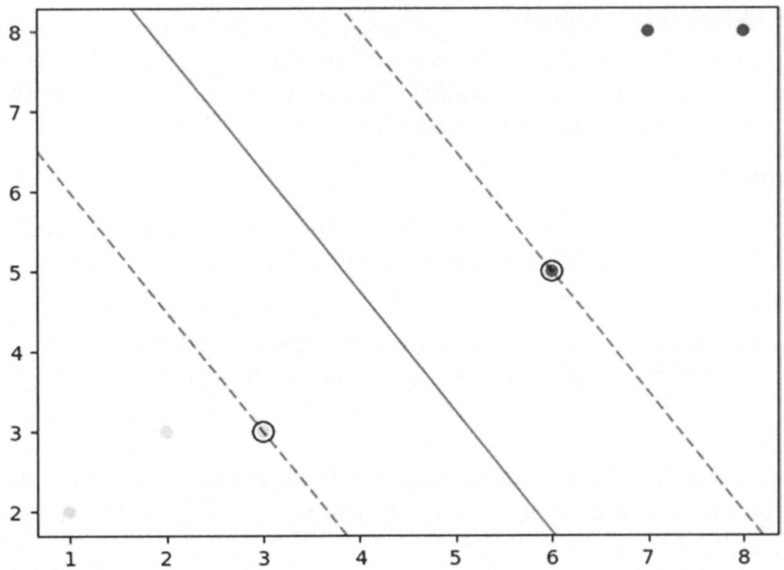

***Figure 5.9:** Sample SVM algorithm for separating blue and red points*

Here is a breakdown of the key components of the plot:

Data Points:

- Each point on the plot represents a customer, plotted based on two selected features (for example, income and purchase frequency).

- The points are colored or shaped differently to indicate different customer segments or classes. In the example, there are two classes, typically represented by two different colors.

Decision Boundary:

- The solid line in the plot is the decision boundary, which is the hyperplane that the SVM algorithm has determined to best separate the two classes.
- In a 2D space, this boundary is a straight line. The goal of SVM is to find the line that maximizes the margin between the two classes.

Support Vectors:

- These are the data points that lie closest to the decision boundary. They are critical because they define the position and orientation of the hyperplane.
- In the plot, support vectors are highlighted with a distinct marker, such as a larger size or a different edge color (for example, black circles around the points).

Margin:

- The margin is the distance between the decision boundary and the nearest data points from each class (the support vectors).
- In the plot, the margin is represented by the space between the dashed lines parallel to the decision boundary. The SVM aims to maximize this margin to ensure a robust separation between classes.

Contour Lines:

- The dashed lines on either side of the decision boundary represent the margins. These lines are equidistant from the decision boundary and pass through the support vectors.
- The area between these lines is the margin area, and the SVM tries to keep this area as wide as possible while still correctly classifying the data points.

Interpretation:

- **Separation**: The decision boundary effectively separates the two classes of customers. If the data is linearly separable, the SVM will find a clear line that divides the classes.
- **Robustness**: By maximizing the margin, the SVM model is less sensitive to small changes in the data, making it robust to overfitting.
- **Support Vectors' Role**: The support vectors are crucial as they are the only points that influence the position of the decision boundary. Other points do not affect the boundary directly.

Neural Networks

Neural networks consist of layers of interconnected neurons that process data and learn patterns through backpropagation. Let us take a look at a simple neural network architecture in the following diagram.

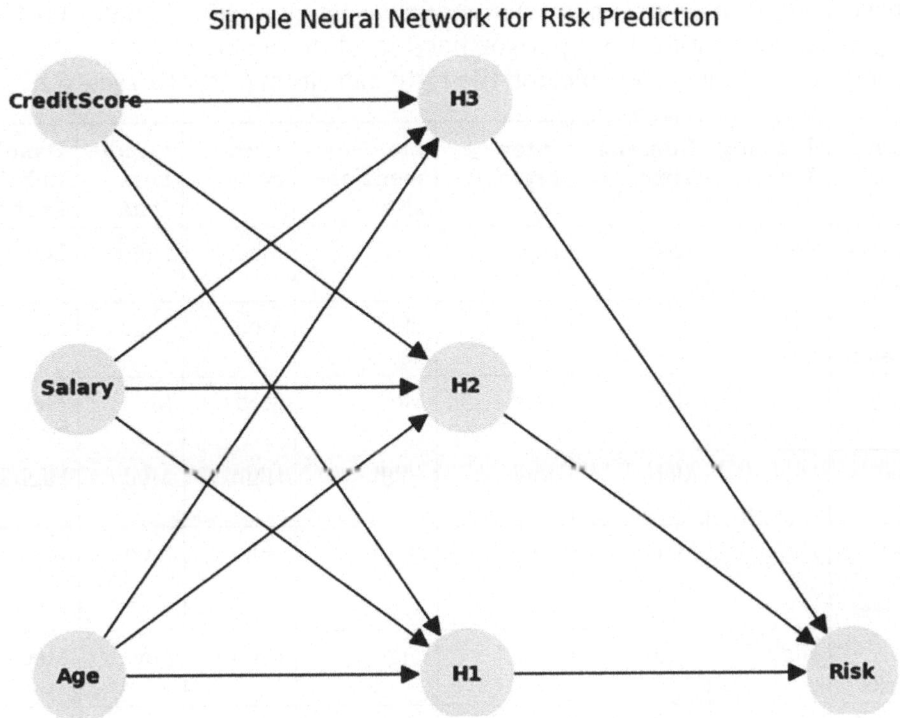

***Figure 5.10**: Simple Neural Network Representation*

Network Structure:

- **Input Layer**: Contains three nodes representing the input features: Age, Salary, and CreditScore.
- **Hidden Layer**: Contains three nodes (H1, H2, H3) for processing the inputs. The number of nodes in the hidden layer can be adjusted based on the complexity of the problem.
- **Output Layer**: Contains one node for binary classification, predicting the risk (for example, high risk or low risk). It will generate a probability score for the diabetic risk.

Edges: Directed edges connect nodes from one layer to the next, representing the flow of information through the network. The knowledge of Neural networks is represented as weights of the edges and bias values at hidden nodes and output nodes. Neural networks learns the knowledge using the Back-Propagation algorithm.

Comparison of ML Algorithms

The challenge in the supervised algorithm is to figure out which algorithm to use for the given problem definition. Often, evaluation metrics such as accuracy take the front seat in most of the documentation. In a real industry setting, every enterprise would have a different set of requirements, such as latency, explainability, cost, and so on. Here, we are presenting a comparison between different algorithms so that we can make a conscious choice while picking the right algorithm (refer to *Table 5.1*).

Algorithm	Training Time	Inference Time	Inter-pretability	Multi-dimension-ality	Accu-racy	Handle Less Data	Handles Imbal-anced Data
Linear Regression	Low	Low	High	Med	Med	High	Low
Logistic Regression	Low	Low	High	Med	Med	High	Med
Decision Trees	Med	Med	Med	Med	Med	Med	Med
Random Forest	High	Med	Low	High	High	Med	High
Support Vector Machines	High	Med	Low	High	High	Med	Med
Neural Networks	High	High	Low	High	High	Low	Med
Gradient Boosting	High	Med	Low	High	High	Med	High

Table 5.1: *Comparison of ML algorithms*

Explanation of the Table

Training Time

- **Low**: Algorithms such as Linear and Logistic Regression are generally faster to train.
- **Medium**: Decision Trees take moderate time, while Random Forests and Gradient Boosting are more computationally intensive.
- **High**: SVMs and Neural Networks often require significant time, especially with large datasets.

Inference Time

- **Low**: Linear and Logistic Regression are quick at making predictions.

- **Medium**: Decision Trees and ensemble methods such as Random Forest and Gradient Boosting are moderately fast.
- **High**: Neural Networks can be slower, especially if they are deep and complex.

Interpretability

- **High**: Linear and Logistic Regression are straightforward to interpret.
- **Medium**: Decision Trees offer some interpretability through their structure.
- **Low**: Ensemble methods, SVMs, and Neural Networks are often considered black boxes.

Multi-dimensionality

- **Medium**: Linear and Logistic Regression handle moderate feature spaces well.
- **High**: SVMs, Neural Networks, and ensemble methods excel in high-dimensional spaces.

Accuracy and F1 Score

- **Medium to High**: Most algorithms can achieve high accuracy and F1 scores, but this depends on the data and problem context.

Handle Less Data

- **High**: Linear and Logistic Regression perform well with smaller datasets.
- **Medium to Low**: More complex models, such as Neural Networks and SVMs, typically require more data to perform well.

Handles Imbalanced Data

- **Low to Medium**: Linear Regression struggles with imbalance, while Logistic Regression and Decision Trees can handle it better with techniques such as class weighting.
- **High**: Random Forest and Gradient Boosting are robust to imbalanced data, especially with techniques such as resampling or using specialized loss functions.

Evaluation Criteria

So far, we have seen how to solve different problems using Machine Learning algorithms. The main challenge is how to measure the success of the solution. The evaluation metrics differ from problem to problem. Based on the requirements, we categorize the metrics into several categories.

- **Offline metrics**: These are focused completely on the machine learning model performance. There are pre-defined metrics for classification or regression problems.

- **Online metrics**: These metrics are measured when the product involving the model runs in experimentation. These would typically be the revenue generated by the product, session engagement time spent by the user interactions such as clicks.
- **Efficiency metrics**: There are certain tangible goals for the product related to product efficiency. It measures how efficient the end product is, which includes overall cost, latency, throughput, and so on.

Offline Metrics

The offline metrics are often meant for measuring the model's performance. Sometimes they can also be used for measuring the end-to-end product performance. We are only covering classification/regression-related evaluation metrics here, as they are more relevant to the scope of this chapter.

There are several practices used to measure these criteria. Usually, a subset of the labeled data is kept aside and used for the test set. The test set could be created by the same developer and would report the model performance numbers accordingly. The test set could be collected from the real-time data. The test set can also be used as a blind test, prepared by another developer and not shown to the developer. This way, any bias in the data during model development can be fixed.

Classification Metrics

If we built a model, then how do we know that it is actually working? Here are a few key metrics that help us measure performance:

- **Accuracy (The Obvious One):**
  - **Formula:** Correct Predictions / Total Predictions.
  - **Good for:** Balanced datasets.
  - **Example:** If 90 out of 100 predictions are right, accuracy is 90%.
- **Precision (When False Positives Hurt):**
  - **Formula:** True Positives / (True Positives + False Positives).
  - **Good for:** When you care more about false alarms.
  - **Example:** In spam detection, precision matters – we do not want important emails marked as spam.
- **Recall (When Missing Positives is Bad):**
  - **Formula:** True Positives / (True Positives + False Negatives).
  - **Good for:** When missing actual positives is costly.
  - **Example:** Detecting cancer – better to catch all possible cases.

- **F1-Score (Best of Both Worlds):**
    - **Formula:** 2 * (Precision * Recall) / (Precision + Recall).
    - **Good for:** Balancing precision and recall.
- **AUC-ROC (Area Under the Receiver Operating Characteristic Curve):**
    - Measures the model's ability to distinguish between classes. A higher AUC indicates better performance.
    - Useful when class imbalance is significant.

    AUC ranges from 0 to 1:
    - **AUC = 1.0:** Perfect classifier.
    - **AUC = 0.5:** No discrimination (equivalent to random guessing).
    - **AUC < 0.5:** Worse than random guessing.
- **Gini Coefficient:** Measures inequality in prediction and is often used in credit scoring. A higher Gini means better model performance.

Regression Metrics

For measuring the regression problems, we need to find the cumulative error between the actual value and the predicted value. Some of the popular metrics include MSE, R2, SSE, and RMSE. Let us recollect their definitions once:

- **Mean Squared Error (MSE)**: Measures how far predictions are from actual values. Smaller is better.
- **Root Mean Square Error (RMSE):** Measures the average magnitude of prediction errors, penalizing larger errors more heavily by taking the square root of MSE (Mean Squared Error).
- **R-squared (Coefficient of Determination):**
    - Explains how well the model fits the data.
    - Explains the percentage of variance in credit risk that the model explains. Used for regression-based credit risk models.
- **Sum of Squared Errors (SSE):** SSE stands for Sum of Squared Errors. It is the sum of the squared differences between the observed actual outcomes and the outcomes predicted by the regression model.
    - A lower SSE indicates a better fit of the model.
    - However, SSE is sensitive to scale and outliers in the data.

Online Metrics

In supervised machine learning for finance, online metrics refer to performance measures that are monitored continuously as the model makes predictions on live, streaming, or recently incoming data, rather than only on static test sets. They help ensure the model remains reliable under changing market conditions.

Key Applications

- **Fraud Detection:** Monitor metrics such as precision, recall, and false positive rate in real-time as new transactions stream in.
- **Credit Scoring:** Track AUC, accuracy, and default prediction drift to ensure fairness and stability of loan approvals.
- **Algorithmic Trading:** Measure profit and loss (PnL), Sharpe ratio, and hit rate continuously on trades executed by the model.
- **Risk Management:** Monitor Value at Risk (VaR) violations and error distributions to ensure compliance with financial regulations.

Generally, online metrics are linked with the business objective. For the banking loan/credit card scenario, determining if the user has defaulted/skipped payments in the real world is the number one metric.

Unfortunately, measuring the recall would be difficult. (How many customers were rejected? Are they really bad customers? How much loss did it contribute to the bank?)

Efficiency Metrics

Efficiency in financial machine learning is not only about predictive accuracy but also about **resource utilization, scalability, and operational cost-effectiveness**.

1. **Compute Cost and Infrastructure Usage**
    - **GPU/CPU Utilization**: Running inference on CPU versus GPU can drastically change operational costs. Since many finance models (for example, fraud detection, credit scoring) can run efficiently on CPUs, this reduces expenses.
    - **Throughput (Predictions per Second)**: Measures how many transactions or customer profiles can be processed in real time. Critical for high-volume fraud detection or trading systems.
2. **Latency (Response Time)**
    - In finance, even milliseconds matter. Low-latency models are essential for high-frequency trading or real-time fraud blocking.
    - Metrics include average latency per prediction and tail latency (p95, p99) to ensure worst-case delays are acceptable.

3. **Scalability**
    - o Financial institutions handle millions of transactions daily. Efficiency metrics include scaling cost per 1,000 customers or transactions processed per compute unit.
    - o Measures how the system handles spikes (for example, end-of-month credit card billing).
4. **Energy Efficiency / Green AI**
    - o As sustainability becomes critical, financial organizations track energy consumption per prediction.
    - o Lower energy models reduce carbon footprint and align with ESG (Environmental, Social, Governance) mandates.
5. **Cost per Prediction / Customer**
    - o Direct metric linking operational ML costs to business value. For example, the cost of scoring one loan application versus the revenue from interest on approved loans.
    - o Useful for ROI analysis of deploying large-scale ML solutions.

Mock Interview: Building a Loan Prediction Classification System

Let us consider the problem statement: The bank has a history of records that contain the previous credit information of the customer. For any new customer (or existing customer with a new loan), we would want to decide whether the loan needs to be approved or not.

This is a typical case-study-based interview template. Imagine that the loan prediction dataset is given to the interviewer and asked to build a risk prediction model. Let us understand the step-by-step process to solve this problem.

In a typical banking scenario, let us assume that the manual records about the customer details and their loan approval status are recorded and digitized. Digitization is the first step for data collection. They might shortlist certain information about the loan amount as per the domain knowledge of the finance experts.

For example, they might record the past records of the loan approval/rejection details of a bank. Let us use the following example for the remaining part of the case study.

Consider this dataset: https://www.kaggle.com/datasets/zaurbegiev/my-dataset

The key columns in the dataset are:

- **Loan ID**: A unique Identifier for the loan information.
- **Customer ID**: A unique identifier for the customer. Customers may have more than one loan.
- **Loan Status**: A categorical variable indicating if the loan was given to this customer.
- **Current Loan Amount**: This is the loan amount that was either completely paid off or the amount that was defaulted. This data is for the previous loan.
- **Term**: A categorical variable indicating if it is a short-term or long-term loan.
- **Credit Score**: A value between 0 and 800 indicates the riskiness of the borrower's credit history.
- **Years in current job**: A categorical variable indicating how many years the customer has been in their current job.
- **Home Ownership**: Categorical variable indicating home ownership. Values are "`Rent`", "`Home Mortgage`", and "`Own`". If the value is OWN, then the customer is a homeowner with no mortgage.
- **Annual Income**: The customer's annual income.
- **Purpose**: A description of the purpose of the loan.
- **Monthly Debt**: The customer's monthly payment for their existing loans.
- **Years of Credit History**: The years since the first entry in the customer's credit history
- **Months since last delinquent**: Months since the last loan delinquent payment.
- **Number of Open Accounts**: The total number of open credit cards.
- **Number of Credit Problems**: The number of credit problems in the customer records.
- **Current Credit Balance**: The current total debt for the customer.
- **Maximum Open Credit**: The maximum credit limit for all credit sources.
- **Bankruptcies**: The number of bankruptcies.
- **Tax Liens**: The number of tax liens.

Now, we are about to start the mock interview session.

Interviewer: How to find and fix the data quality issues with the dataset?

Candidate: I approach data quality as the *foundation* of the entire ML system. In real-world financial settings, the data is rarely pristine—unlike academic datasets. So I begin with a structured triage process:

Step 1: Manual Auditing (Non-Automatable but Crucial)

Even with automation, I always take a *small sample* and manually inspect the records. I look for:

- Suspicious ranges (e.g., credit score > 1000)
- Impossible values (age = 0, income = -50, and so on.)
- Mixed formats (e.g., integer stored as string: "450" vs 450)
- Inconsistent categories ("*Home Mortgage*" vs "*HaveMortgage*")

These often arise from:

- Manual data entry errors
- ETL pipeline bugs
- Real world bugs

Step 2: Semantic Consistency Check

I check if fields *make sense* given business context.
Example:

- "*Years of Credit History* = 70" → Implies borrower is > 90 years old. Needs verification.
- Credit scores ending with a trailing zero likely indicate scaling mistakes. If all values > 800 end with 0, dividing by 10 corrects them.

Step 3: Categorical Cleanup (Merging and Normalizing)

If two categories *mean the same thing*, I merge them.

Example:

"*Have Mortgage*" and "*Home Mortgage*" can be merged.

Step 4: Imputing Missing Values

I classify missingness into three buckets:

Type	**Example**	**Treatment**
Empty	NA / blank	Mean/median for numerics
Invalid	Age = 0	Replace using domain logic
Non-standard	"N/A", "*unknown*"	Convert → standard NA, then impute

Table 5.2: *Fixing the missing values*

For numeric fields: mean, median, or KNN-based imputation
For categorical fields: mode or KNN-based imputation

If missingness > 50% → candidate for dropping **unless domain-critical**.

It could be achieved something like this:

```
from sklearn.impute import SimpleImputer
categorical_imputer = SimpleImputer(strategy='most_frequent')
data[object_col] = categorical_imputer.fit_transform(data
[object_col])

# Create an imputer to fill NaN with the mean value for numerical
columns
numerical_imputer = SimpleImputer(strategy='mean')
data[num_col] = numerical_imputer.fit_transform(data[num_col])
```

If the missing values are very high (>50%), we should consider dropping the feature.

If the feature is critical (such as a credit score), in this case, we cannot drop them. In that case, we could consider two approaches:

- Drop the records with empty values.
- Impute the remaining values and then use them.

Interviewer: Suppose some features are heavily skewed. How do you correct this?

Candidate: Most of the machine learning algorithms assume that the distribution is normal and symmetrical. The data could be skewed due to outliers. If the outliers can be removed/capped, then we fix the skewness. If we still want to retain the outliers, we might need to apply some transformations. Let us understand in detail how to fix the distribution curve.

Understanding and addressing skewed distributions is an important part of Exploratory Data Analysis (EDA) for several reasons:

- **Statistical Assumptions:** Many statistical models, such as linear regression, assume that the data follow a normal distribution. Skewed data can violate these assumptions, leading to inaccurate models and predictions.
- **Outlier Sensitivity:** Skewed distributions often indicate the presence of outliers, which can disproportionately affect the results of statistical analyses and machine learning models.
- **Interpretability:** Skewed data can make it difficult to interpret the results of analyses. For example, measures of central tendency such as the mean can be misleading if the data is heavily skewed.
- **Feature Engineering:** Understanding the distribution of your data can inform feature engineering decisions, such as transformations that can improve model performance.

To address skewed distributions, you can use several techniques:

- **Transformation**: Apply mathematical transformations to the data to reduce skewness. Common transformations include:
  - **Log Transformation**: Useful for right-skewed data. Apply it by taking the natural logarithm of the data.
  - **Box-Cox Transformation**: A more flexible transformation that can handle both left and right skewness, but it requires the data to be positive.
- **Binning**: Convert continuous variables into categorical ones by creating bins. This can help manage skewness by grouping data into intervals.
- **Outlier Treatment**: Identify and handle outliers, which can be a source of skewness. This can be done by capping, removing, or imputing outliers.
- **Data Collection**: If possible, collect more data to balance the distribution, especially if the skewness is due to a small sample size.
- **Non-parametric Methods**: Use statistical methods that do not assume a normal distribution, such as decision trees or random forests, which are less sensitive to skewed data.

Finding the Distribution Curves: We can draw a simple distribution curve using the following piece of code. For example, to find the distribution for the '**`Annual Income`**' field in the dataset, we can use the following code snippet:

```
import seaborn as sns
import pandas as pd
import matplotlib.pyplot as plt

# Sample DataFrame
# Create a violin plot
sns.kdeplot(data=data['Annual Income'], fill=True, color='blue',
alpha=0.5)

# Add titles and labels
plt.title('Distribution of Annual Income')
plt.xlabel('Annual Income')
plt.ylabel('Density')

# Show plot
plt.show()
```

We can see the graph for the column as follows:

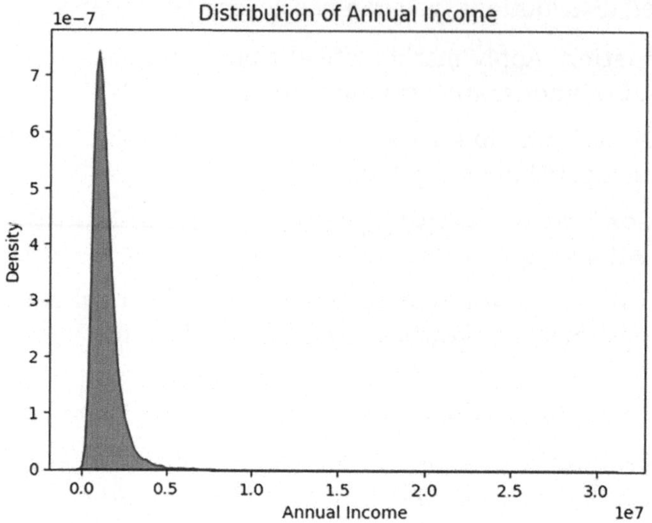

Figure 5.11: *Skewed distribution of Annual Income*

It is a normal distribution curve with slight right skewness.

Fixing the Distribution Curve: Let us try some techniques to fix the skewness in the distribution curve.

a. **Using Log Transformation**

   We can apply a simple log transformation using this single line of code:

```
data['Log Annual Income'] = np.log(data['Annual Income'])
```

   Now, the distribution curve will follow a normal distribution:

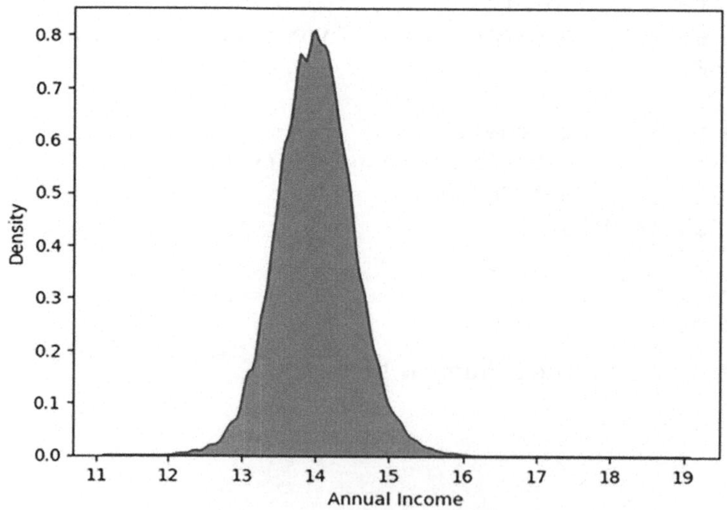

Figure 5.12: *Normalized distribution of Annual Income*

b. **Using Box-Cox transformation**

We can also use the Box-Cox transformation using the simple snippet code:

```
if (data['Annual Income'] <= 0).any():
    raise ValueError("Annual Income contains non-positive values,
which cannot be Box-Cox transformed.")

# Initialize the PowerTransformer with method='box-cox'
box_cox_transformer = PowerTransformer(method='box-cox', stan-
dardize=False)

# Reshape the data to fit the transformer
annual_income_reshaped = data['Annual Income'].values.reshape(-1,
1)

# Apply Box-Cox transformation
data['Box-Cox Annual Income'] = box_cox_transformer.fit_trans-
form(annual_income_reshaped)
```

Interviewer*: *How do we detect and treat the outliers?

***Candidate*:** Outliers are data points that differ significantly from other observations in a dataset. They can arise due to variability in the data, measurement errors, or experimental errors. Outliers can skew and mislead the results of statistical analyses and machine learning models, so it is important to identify and handle them appropriately.

Approaches to Treat Outliers:

- **Z-Score Method:** This method standardizes the data and identifies outliers as those data points that fall beyond a certain number of standard deviations from the mean. Typically, a threshold of 3 is used. For example, the '**Monthly Debt**' column is right-skewed. The outliers for this field can be removed using the following piece of code.

```
import pandas as pd
import numpy as np

# Sample DataFrame
field = 'Monthly Debt'
# Calculate Z-scores
data['Z-Score'] = (data[field] - data[field].mean()) / data[field].
std()
# Identify outliers
outliers = data[np.abs(data['Z-Score']) > 3]
# Remove outliers
data_no_outliers = data[np.abs(data['Z-Score']) <= 3]
print("\nData without outliers:\n", data_no_outliers)
```

- **IQR Method:** This method uses the interquartile range (IQR) to identify outliers. Data points that fall below Q1 - 1.5 * IQR or above Q3 + 1.5 * IQR are considered outliers.

```
field = 'Monthly Debt'
Q1 = data[field].quantile(0.25)
Q3 = data[field].quantile(0.75)
IQR = Q3 - Q1
# Identify outliers
outliers = data[(data[field] < (Q1 - 1.5 * IQR)) | (data[field] >
(Q3 + 1.5 * IQR))]
# Remove outliers
data_no_outliers = data[(data[field] >= (Q1 - 1.5 * IQR)) &
(data[field] <= (Q3 + 1.5 * IQR))]
print("\nData without outliers:\n", data_no_outliers)
```

Capping or Flooring: Instead of removing outliers, we can cap or floor them to a certain percentile. This approach is useful when we want to retain all data points but limit the influence of extreme values.

Interviewer*: *Do we really need every feature? Won't extra features slow the model?

***Candidate*:** Absolutely! We can either manually identify the importance based on the domain knowledge or use an algorithmic approach. Let us explore them in detail.

Data Quality: If the data quality is not good and the feature is not important, we can remove the feature.

Domain Knowledge: As per the domain knowledge, we can remove certain columns. For example, LoanId, `CustomerId` features and high cardinality features do not contribute to the Loan forecasting. It is safe to discard these features. Apart from this, we will discuss correlation analysis and feature importance values to filter out the important features. Similarly, based on domain knowledge, we know that the Credit Score and Loan Amount are important features for deciding whether a loan will be repaid or not.

Correlation Analysis: Correlation analysis is a simple and effective method for this purpose, especially when dealing with highly correlated features.

1. **Correlation Matrix**: Calculate the correlation matrix for the dataset to identify pairs of features that are highly correlated.

2. **Thresholding**: Set a correlation threshold (for example, 0.8 or 0.9) to identify features that are strongly correlated with each other.

3. **Feature Selection**: For each pair of highly correlated features, consider removing one of the features to reduce redundancy. The choice of which features to remove can be based on domain knowledge or further analysis.

A correlation heat map can be generated using these simple plots:

```
sns.heatmap(data.corr(), annot=True, cmap='coolwarm')
plt.title('Correlation Heatmap')
plt.show()
```

The correlation analysis for this data looks something like this:

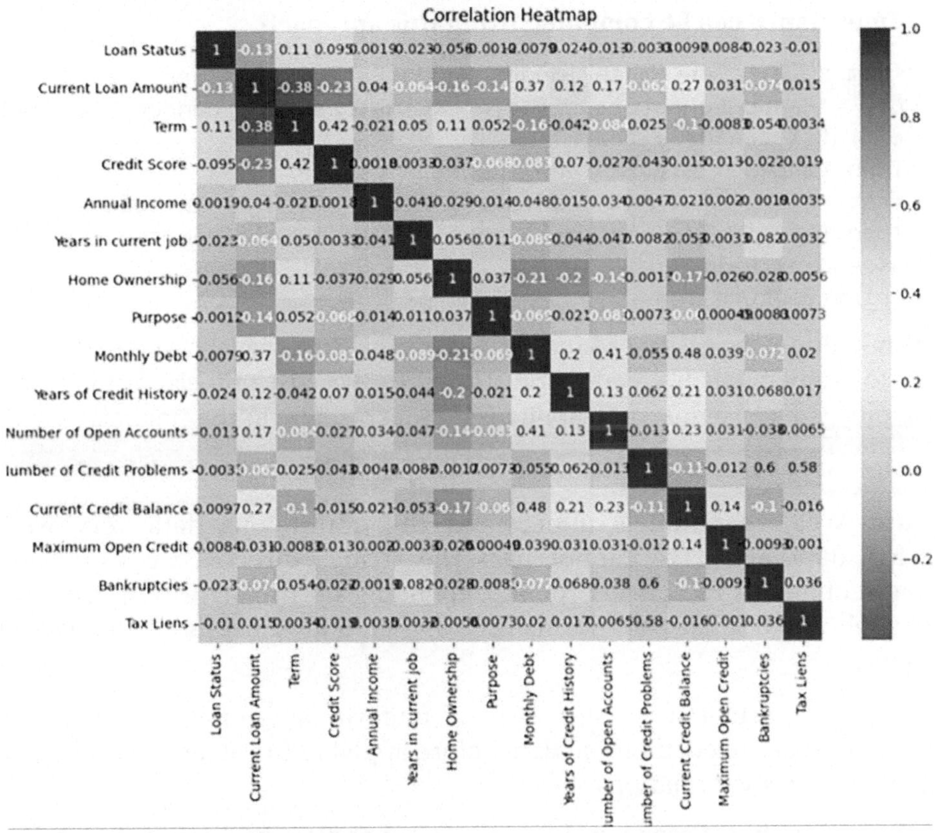

Figure 5.13: *Correlation matrix for loan prediction features*

From the preceding example, we can note that the instances '*Number of Credit Problems*' and '*Bankruptcies*' are highly correlated (~0.6). We can keep one feature and discard the other, considering the importance and data quality of the feature.

Feature Importance: Random Forest is an ensemble learning method that can be used for both classification and regression tasks. It provides a measure of feature importance, which can be used for dimensionality reduction by selecting the most important features.

Process:

1. **Train a Random Forest Model**: Fit a Random Forest model to the dataset.

2. **Feature Importance Scores**: Extract feature importance scores from the trained model. These scores indicate the contribution of each feature to the model's predictions.
3. **Feature Selection**: Select features with the highest importance scores. A common approach is to set a threshold or select the top N features.

Feature importance can be computed using this approach:

```
from sklearn.ensemble import RandomForestClassifier
clf = RandomForestClassifier(n_estimators=100, random_state=42)
clf.fit(X_train, y_train)
importances = clf.feature_importances_
feature_imp_df = pd.DataFrame({'Feature': X_train.columns, 'Gini
Importance': importances}).sort_values('Gini Importance',
ascending=False)
print(feature_imp_df)
```

Algorithmic dimensionality reduction: Algorithms such as PCA and t-SNE can also be used for dimensionality reduction. However, we are not elaborating on them because they will cause interpretability issues, especially in the financial segment.

Interviewer:* *What transformations are needed for string/numerical data?

***Candidate*:** Well, the models understand the continuous data very well. For categorical data, since we cannot pass the strings directly, we would use the encoding techniques to convert them. Depending on the algorithm used, we also need to apply standardization/normalization techniques. Let us dig deep into these techniques.

The algorithms assume the data is in a uniform and integer format. Certain transformations are needed on the data before applying the algorithms. Let us take a look at different transformations.

- **Transforming Categorical Data:** An encoding technique is needed for categorical variables. The following are some encoding techniques.
    - **Use Ordinal Encoding**: if there is sequentiality. For example, Years in the Current Job column has the following values '8 years', '10+ years', '3 years', '5 years', '< 1 year', '2 years', '4 years', '9 years', '7 years', '1 year', '6 years'. These values should be encoded using ordinal encoding.
    - **Use Label Encoding**: This is the default encoding technique, which assigns labels for the string values. This is preferred over One-hot encoding as it reduces the number of dimensions and thus model size.
- **Transforming Continuous Data:** Standardization and Normalization are two common techniques used in data preprocessing to prepare data for machine learning models.

- **Standardization** involves transforming data to have a mean of zero and a standard deviation of one. This is done by subtracting the mean of the data and dividing by the standard deviation. Standardization is useful when you want to ensure that the data follows a standard normal distribution, which can be important for algorithms that assume normally distributed data, such as linear regression or k-means clustering.
- **Normalization**, on the other hand, rescales the data to a specific range, typically between 0 and 1. This is achieved by subtracting the minimum value of the data and dividing by the range (maximum value minus minimum value). Normalization is particularly useful when you want to ensure that all features contribute equally to the distance calculations in algorithms such as k-nearest neighbors or when dealing with data that has different units or scales.

***Interviewer*: Loan defaults are rare. How do we ensure the model isn't biased?**

Candidate: Correct. We need to balance the labeled data using techniques such as SMOTE analysis. We will learn more about it in detail.

Synthetic Minority Over-sampling Technique (SMOTE) is a popular method used to address class imbalance in datasets, particularly when the target variable has significantly fewer instances of one class compared to others. This imbalance can lead to biased models that perform poorly on the minority class.

- **Synthetic Sample Generation**: SMOTE generates synthetic samples for the minority class by interpolating between existing minority class instances. It selects a minority class instance and one of its nearest neighbors, then creates a new synthetic instance along the line segment joining them.
- **Balancing the Dataset**: By adding these synthetic samples, SMOTE increases the number of minority class instances, leading to a more balanced dataset.

Here is a small code snippet for applying SMOTE on the target variable.

```
from imblearn.over_sampling import SMOTE
from sklearn.model_selection import train_test_split
from sklearn.datasets import make_classification

# Create a synthetic imbalanced dataset
X, y = make_classification(n_classes=2, class_sep=2, weights=[0.1, 
0.9], n_informative=3, n_redundant=1, flip_y=0, n_features=20, n_
clusters_per_class=1, n_samples=1000, random_state=10)
# Split the dataset into training and testing sets
X_train, X_test, y_train, y_test = train_test_split(X, y, test_
```

```
size=0.3, random_state=42)
# Apply SMOTE to the training data
smote = SMOTE(random_state=42)
X_resampled, y_resampled = smote.fit_resample(X_train, y_train)
# Check the distribution of the target variable after SMOTE
print("Original dataset shape:", y_train.value_counts())
print("Resampled dataset shape:", y_resampled.value_counts())
```

Interviewer: There are so many ML algorithms. Should we try all combinations?

Candidate: We do not need to try each and every algorithm. We can use the Grid Search approach to find the optimal solutions for the given algorithm. It will run for all the combinations and give us the optimal results.

Not only that, we can choose the algorithm depending on the business problem and the data availability. The details are as follows:

Once the data is ready, the next step is to identify the correct algorithm with the right parameters. **`GridSearchCV`** is a popular method for hyper-parameter tuning that exhaustively searches through a specified subset of the hyper-parameter space.

1. **Define Parameter Grid**: Specify the hyperparameters and the range of values to explore.

2. **Execute Search**: **`GridSearchCV`** iterates over each combination of hyper-parameter values, creating a model for each and evaluating it via cross-validation.

3. **Select Best Model**: After evaluating all combinations, **`GridSearchCV`** selects the hyper-parameter set that results in the best model performance according to the chosen scoring metric. The following code snippet shows how to implement this.

```
param_grid = {
    'n_estimators': [100, 200, 300],
    'max_depth': [5, 10, 15],
    'min_samples_split': [2, 5, 10],
    'min_samples_leaf': [1,2, 4]
rf = RandomForestClassifier(random_state=42)
grid_search = GridSearchCV(estimator=rf, param_grid=param_grid,
cv=2, scoring='accuracy', n_jobs=-1)
grid_search.fit(X_train, y_train)
# Best model
best_model = grid_search.best_estimator_
y_pred = best_model.predict(X_test)
```

***Interviewer*: What metrics would you choose for this problem?**

***Candidate*:** Choosing the evaluation metric depends on the business problem and dataset type. More details are explained in the following paragraphs.

- **Model Purpose:** If the model is used to minimize defaults, focus on Recall. If it is more important to minimize unnecessary investigations or interventions, precision might be more relevant.
- **Class Imbalance:** For imbalanced datasets, metrics such as F1 Score, ROC-AUC, or Precision-Recall AUC often provide a more meaningful evaluation than simple accuracy.
- **Regulatory and Business Requirements:** Ensure alignment with any regulatory standards or business objectives that may prioritize certain types of errors.

***Interviewer*: Once the model is trained, how do we deploy it at scale?**

***Candidate*:** We need to understand who the target customers are. If this model is only meant to be used by the bank employees, it can run in batch mode (once for all customers). If we want to make this available to individual users, then the model needs to be running in real time. Batch mode consumes fewer resources, and real-time deployment consumes more resources.

- **Model Execution:** Load the model and run predictions on the prepared data in batches. This can be done using scripts or scheduled jobs.
- **Data Pipelines:** Set up data pipelines to automate the process of feeding data into the model and storing the results. Tools such as Apache Airflow or simple cron jobs can be used for scheduling.
- **Performance Tracking:** Even in an offline setting, it is important to track the model's performance over time. This can be done by periodically evaluating the model's predictions against actual outcomes.
- **Model Updates:** Plan for regular updates to the model as new data becomes available or as business requirements change.

Conclusion

By understanding these key aspects, financial institutions can develop and deploy risk prediction models that are not only effective but also ethical and compliant with industry standards. This chapter provides a comprehensive foundation for leveraging machine learning in financial risk management, paving the way for more informed and strategic decision-making. Supervised learning, as we know, often requires significant manual effort due to its reliance on labeled data. But can we address problems where ground truth labels are unavailable? In the next chapter, we will explore how a subset of such problems can be tackled using Unsupervised Learning techniques.

Key Points

- Financial risk prediction is essential for identifying and mitigating potential financial losses. It involves using historical data and predictive models to assess the likelihood of adverse events.
- Supervised learning is a key approach in building predictive models, using labeled data to train algorithms. It includes various techniques such as regression, classification, and ensemble methods.
- High-quality, relevant data is crucial for effective model training and prediction. Challenges include data availability, quality, and the need to address class imbalances and missing values.
- Models should be evaluated using appropriate metrics such as accuracy, precision, recall, and AUC-ROC. Cross-validation and stress testing are important for assessing model robustness and generalization.
- Ethical considerations include ensuring fairness, avoiding bias, and maintaining transparency in model predictions. Privacy and data protection are critical, especially when handling sensitive financial information.
- **Case Study**: Credit Risk Prediction:
    - The case study illustrated the application of machine learning in predicting credit risk, highlighting the steps from data preparation to model evaluation.
    - It demonstrated the importance of aligning model outcomes with business objectives and regulatory requirements.

References

Han, J., Kamber, M., & Pei, J. (2011). *Data Mining: Concepts and Techniques (3rd Edition).* Morgan Kaufmann.

- A foundational book covering data preprocessing, classification, outlier detection, and evaluation metrics.

Géron, A. (2019). *Hands-On Machine Learning with Scikit-Learn, Keras, and TensorFlow (2nd Edition).* O'Reilly Media.

- Practical guide that includes implementations of grid search, encoding, scaling, and handling missing data in Python.

Research Papers and Technical References

Chawla, N. V., Bowyer, K. W., Hall, L. O., & Kegelmeyer, W. P. (2002). SMOTE: *Synthetic Minority Over-sampling Technique*. Journal of Artificial Intelligence Research, 16, 321–357. https://jair.org/index.php/jair/article/view/10302

- Original paper on the SMOTE technique used for class imbalance problems.

Scikit-learn Documentation

- Excellent official reference for GridSearchCV, LabelEncoder, StandardScaler, and RandomForestClassifier. https://scikit-learn.org/stable/user_guide.html

Chapter 6
Implementing Unsupervised Learning Systems

Introduction

Imagine a world where vast oceans of data remain uncharted, filled with hidden treasures waiting to be discovered. This is the realm of unsupervised learning—a fascinating journey into the unknown where algorithms act as explorers, uncovering patterns, structures, and insights from raw, unlabeled data. Unlike supervised learning, which relies on clearly defined instructions, unsupervised learning thrives on curiosity and adaptability, revealing the secrets buried within datasets. From identifying unique customer segments to spotting anomalies that could indicate fraud, the applications of this approach are as varied as they are impactful. In this chapter, we embark on an adventure through the methods and tools of unsupervised learning, bridging the gap between theory and real-world applications with compelling examples and hands-on case studies.

Structure

In this chapter, we will cover the following topics:

- Overview and Examples
- Embedding and Distance Algorithms
- Unsupervised Learning Techniques
- Evaluation Criteria
- Business Case Studies
- Case Study: Topic Modeling for CRM

Overview and Examples

As we observed in the previous chapter, supervised learning comes with significant costs. It requires labeled data, which is a manual and labor-intensive process, adding to the overall expense of model development. Additionally, defining labels can be challenging. For instance, when categorizing support tickets, we may not initially know the types of categories present in the data. This challenge becomes even more pronounced when dealing with large-scale datasets, such as search engine queries. In such cases, the number of categories can be vast, and due to the dynamic nature of the data, new categories continue to emerge.

In scenarios like these, supervised learning is not the most practical approach. Unsupervised learning, on the other hand, not only helps in grouping similar records but also plays a crucial role in anomaly detection. Let us explore real-world applications of unsupervised learning in more detail.

Real-Life Examples of Unsupervised Learning

- **Market Segmentation:** Picture a retail giant analyzing millions of shopping carts to uncover patterns in customer purchases. By grouping shoppers based on their buying habits, they can send personalized promotions to a "*bargain hunter*" or introduce premium products to a "*luxury seeker*."
- **Anomaly Detection:** Imagine a bank's AI system raising a red flag for a credit card transaction in a far-off country while the cardholder's phone is still at home. Such anomalies, detected through unsupervised learning, help prevent fraud before it escalates.
- **Recommendation Systems:** Ever wondered how streaming platforms always seem to know what you would love to watch or listen to next? They analyze user behaviors and group similar preferences, ensuring your playlist or watchlist always feels spot on. We will focus on recommended systems exclusively in the next chapter.
- **Image Compression:** Think of a photographer's dilemma in storing thousands of high-resolution images. Unsupervised algorithms such as K-means clustering simplify the process by reducing image colors, saving storage without compromising on the quality.
- **Customer Churn Prediction:** Telecom companies use clustering to identify signs of customer dissatisfaction, such as frequent support calls or declining usage. They can then intervene with tailored offers to retain those customers.
- **Social Network Analysis:** Social platforms delve into user connections and interactions, identifying communities of shared interests. This makes your feed more engaging by surfacing posts from groups or friends that matter most to you.

- **Healthcare:** Picture a hospital leveraging unsupervised learning to cluster patients with similar symptoms or genetic markers. This approach paves the way for more personalized treatments and better health outcomes.
- **Topic Modeling:** A news organization processes thousands of articles daily. Unsupervised learning helps uncover hidden themes–be it politics, sports, or technology–organizing content efficiently for readers.
- **Document Clustering:** Legal firms use unsupervised learning to group contracts or case files with similar language, significantly reducing the time needed for document reviews.
- **Gene Expression Analysis:** In laboratories, researchers cluster genes with similar expression patterns, unlocking insights into how they interact and their roles in diseases.

Figure 6.1: *Fun representation of side effects of unsupervised learning*

Embedding and Distance Algorithms

Imagine you are standing in a vast open field where every person around you represents a data point. Some are close to you, while others are far away. Naturally, you would assume that the people standing near you have something in common–maybe similar interests, backgrounds, or professions. That is exactly how data works in machine learning!

Every data point in a dataset exists in a mathematical space, and the distance between two points tells us how similar they are. The closer they are, the more alike they tend to be. This idea is the backbone of how we group things together–whether it is customers in a business, patients in healthcare, or even search results on Google.

Let us take a healthcare example. Suppose we have patient records with features such as Age, BMI, and Medical History. By measuring the distance between patients, we can find groups with similar health profiles, which can help doctors make better diagnoses. But how do we actually **measure** this distance?

- If we are dealing with numbers, we can use the good old **Euclidean distance** (think of it as a straight-line distance between two points). Or, if we care more about the direction of a trend, rather than the absolute numbers, **cosine similarity** is a great choice.
- If we have categories (such as `"Male"` versus `"Female"` or `"High Risk"` versus `"Low Risk"`), we measure how often they mismatch–kind of like playing a game of "spot the difference."
- For text (such as medical notes or customer reviews), raw words are not enough. Instead, we transform them into numerical representations using powerful embeddings such as **Word2Vec, GloVe, or BERT**, which capture meanings and relationships between words.
    - **BERT**: A contextual embedding model (transformer-based, bidirectional) where word meaning changes with sentence context; it also uses **segment embeddings** to distinguish sentence pairs.
    - **Word2Vec**: A static embedding model where each word has a fixed vector regardless of context, learned from local co-occurrence.
    - **GloVe**: A **static embedding** model where each word has a fixed vector, learned from global co-occurrence statistics.
- For images, pixels alone do not tell the full story. Instead, we extract unique patterns using techniques such as **HOG (Histogram of Oriented Gradients)** and **SIFT (Scale-Invariant Feature Transform)**, or we let deep learning models such as **CNNs (ResNet, VGG, and so on)** do the heavy lifting.

At the heart of all this, it is really about finding patterns–whether in people, products, or pixels. And by using the right distance measurement, we can make sense of even the most complex data and uncover hidden connections we might have never noticed otherwise.

Distance Algorithms

Choosing the right distance algorithms is very important for clustering. Let us take a look at different distance algorithms:

Hamming Distance

The Hamming distance measures the number of positions at which the corresponding symbols are different between two sequences of equal length.

Formula

For two categorical data points x and y:

```
Hamming Distance(x,y)=∑ i=n δ(xi,yi)
```

Pros of Hamming Distance

- Simplicity and Ease of Computation
- Applicability to Binary and Categorical Data
- Interpretable Results
- Non-Sensitivity to Magnitude
- Equality of Attribute Importance

Cons of Hamming Distance

- Ignores Attribute Significance (Equal Weighting)
- Not Suitable for Numerical or Ordered Data
- Equal Length Requirement
- Poor Performance with High Cardinality Variables
- Ineffective in High-Dimensional Spaces

Code Example:

```
# calculate hamming distance
def hamming_distance(a, b):
  return sum(abs(e1 - e2) for e1, e2 in zip(a, b)) / len(a)
# define data
row1 = [0, 0, 0, 0, 0, 1]
row2 = [0, 0, 0, 0, 1, 0]
# calculate distance
dist = hamming_distance(row1, row2)
print(dist)
```

Euclidean Distance

Measures the straight-line distance between two points in Euclidean space. It is the most commonly used distance metric for continuous, numeric data.

- **Formula**: if (x1,y1) and (x2,y2) are two points in vector space, `Sqrt((x2-x1)²+(y2-y1)²)`
- **Pros**:
  - Intuitive and easy to calculate.
  - Works well with continuous, numeric data.
- **Cons**:
  - Sensitive to scale; requires normalization.
  - Less effective with high-dimensional data due to the "*curse of dimensionality*."

Code Example

```
from math import sqrt
# calculate euclidean distance
def euclidean_distance(a, b):
  return sqrt(sum((e1-e2)**2 for e1, e2 in zip(a,b)))
# define data
row1 = [10, 20, 15, 10, 5]
row2 = [12, 24, 18, 8, 7]
# calculate distance
dist = euclidean_distance(row1, row2)
print(dist)
```

Manhattan Distance

Also known as "*Taxicab distance*," it calculates the distance by summing the absolute differences along each dimension. This metric is particularly useful for grid-based or categorical data.

- **Formula**: (x1,y1) and (x2.y2) are two points in vector space, then |x1-x2|+|y1-y2|
- **Pros**:
  - Handles outliers better than Euclidean distance.
  - Useful when differences along axes are more meaningful.
- **Cons**:
  - Less intuitive for non-grid-like data.

Code Example

```
# calculate manhattan distance
def manhattan_distance(a, b):
  return sum(abs(e1-e2) for e1, e2 in zip(a,b))
# define data
row1 = [10, 20, 15, 10, 5]
row2 = [12, 24, 18, 8, 7]
# calculate distance
dist = manhattan_distance(row1, row2)
print(dist)
```

Cosine Similarity

Measures the cosine of the angle between two vectors. It is often used for high-dimensional, sparse datasets, such as text or document similarity.

- **Formula**:
  - **Cosine distance**: if A and B are vectors then, $\left(\frac{|A.B|}{||A||*||B||}\right)$
- **Pros**:
  - Effective for high-dimensional sparse data (for example, text).
  - Focuses on direction rather than magnitude.
- **Cons**:
  - Not meaningful when vectors have very small magnitudes.

Code Example

```
import numpy as np
def cosine_distance(a,b):

cosine_similarity = np.dot(a, b) / (np.linalg.norm(a) *
np.linalg.norm(b))
  return (1 - cosine_similarity)
# define data
row1 = [10, 20, 15, 10, 5]
row2 = [12, 24, 18, 8, 7]
a = np.asarray(row1)
b = np.asarray(row2)
dist = cosine_distance(row1, row2)
print(dist)
```

Mahalanobis Distance

The Mahalanobis distance is a measure of the distance between a point and a distribution. It was introduced by Indian statistician Prasanta Chandra Mahalanobis in 1936. Unlike Euclidean distance, which measures the straight-line distance between two points in space, Mahalanobis distance takes into account the correlations of the dataset and is scale-invariant, meaning it is not affected by the scale of measurements.

- **Formula**: $DM(x)=(x-\mu)^T S^{-1}(x-\mu)$,

  where x= Vector representing the data point,

  μ = mean vector

  S = covariance matrix

- **Pros:**
  - Accounts for correlations between variables.
  - Scales data automatically.
- **Cons:**
  - Requires computation of the covariance matrix, which can be computationally expensive.

Code Example:

```
import numpy as np
def mahalanobis_distance(x, data):
    """
    Compute the Mahalanobis distance between each row of x and the
data.

    Parameters:
    x (ndarray): An array of data points (observations x variables).
    data (ndarray): The data set to compute the mean and covariance
matrix.

    Returns:
    distances (ndarray): Mahalanobis distances of each observation
in x.
    """
    # Calculate the mean vector
    mu = np.mean(data, axis=0)
    print(mu)

    # Calculate the covariance matrix
    cov = np.cov(data, rowvar=False)
    print(cov)
    # Compute the inverse covariance matrix
    cov_inv = np.linalg.inv(cov)
```

```
        # Center the data
        x_minus_mu = x - mu

        # Compute the Mahalanobis distance
        left_term = np.dot(x_minus_mu, cov_inv)
        distances = np.sqrt(np.sum(left_term * x_minus_mu, axis=1))

        return distances


# Example usage:
if __name__ == "__main__":
    # Sample data (10 observations of 3 variables)
    data = np.array([
        [2.5, 2.4, 1.2],
        [0.5, 0.7, 0.8],
        [2.2, 2.9, 1.1],
        [1.9, 2.2, 1.3],
        [3.1, 3.0, 1.4]
    ])
       # Points to compute the distance from
    x = data  # In this case, computing the distance of each point
to the dataset
       # Calculate Mahalanobis distances
    distances = mahalanobis_distance(x, data)
       # Print the results
    for idx, distance in enumerate(distances):
        print(f"Data point {idx}: Mahalanobis distance =
{distance:.4f}")
```

Real-World Explanation

In the real world, measuring distance is essential for understanding relationships and similarities between entities. For instance, retail companies use distance metrics to compare customer behaviors, identifying those with similar purchase patterns for personalized marketing. In healthcare, distances between patient records help group individuals with similar symptoms for targeted treatments. Social media platforms leverage these measures to recommend friends or content by analyzing user profiles and activity patterns. Each scenario relies on appropriately chosen distance metrics, tailored to the type of data and the insights sought. The Vector databases, which are used heavily these days for RAG implementation, use different distance functions to find the similarity between the strings/documents/words.

Examples Using Integers/Categorical Data for Similarity

1. **Market Basket Analysis:** Retailers analyze transactional data where product categories or IDs (integers) represent items purchased together.
2. **Student Performance Clustering:** In education, student data such as grades (integers) and categorical information (for example, subjects or majors) can help identify performance groups.
3. **User Profiling in Social Media:** Social platforms analyze user attributes such as age (integer), location (categorical), and activity levels (integer) to group similar profiles for targeted content.
4. **Health Diagnosis Clustering:** Patient data with attributes such as age (integer), blood type (categorical), and test results (integer) is clustered to identify patterns for disease diagnosis.
5. **Voting Behavior Analysis:** Political analysts group voters based on demographic data such as age (integer), education level (categorical), and income (integer).
6. **Loan Default Prediction:** Banks use clustering to group loan applicants based on credit score (integer), income bracket (categorical), and loan amount (integer).
7. **Anomaly Detection in Logistics:** Identifying irregularities in shipment data where variables such as package weight (integer) and destination type (categorical) are analyzed.

Embeddings for string Data

Word Embeddings using Word2Vec

- Word2Vec models learn vector representations of words by considering their contexts in large text corpora.
- The resulting embeddings capture semantic relationships between words.

Sentence Embeddings Using Sentence Transformers

- Sentence Transformers provide an easy way to compute embeddings for sentences and paragraphs.
- They are based on transformer models such as BERT and can capture the semantic meaning of entire sentences.

Using Pre-trained BERT for Text Embeddings

- BERT (Bidirectional Encoder Representations from Transformers) is a transformer-based model that can generate context-aware embeddings.

- Suitable for capturing nuanced meanings in text.

FastText and Glove are also popular static embedding models.

FastText is a **static embedding** model from Meta that represents words as the sum of their character n-gram embeddings, enabling it to handle rare and out-of-vocabulary words.

We briefly discussed Glove Embeddings from Google in the previous chapters, which is also a static embedding model based on global co-occurrence statistics.

Embeddings for Image data

Using raw pixel values to represent an image is not the most efficient approach. It is not only redundant but also demands a huge amount of memory and processing power. Instead, let us explore various techniques for extracting meaningful features from images.

Using HOG Features as Image Embeddings

Histogram of Oriented Gradients (HOG) is a feature descriptor used in computer vision and image processing to detect objects. The idea is to count occurrences of gradient orientation in localized portions of an image.

- **Dense Representation**: The resulting HOG feature vector is a compact representation capturing the structural information in the image.
- **Applications**: Commonly used in object detection (for example, pedestrian detection), image retrieval, and classification tasks.

Feature Extraction using Pre-trained CNNs

1. Pre-trained CNN models can be used to extract feature embeddings from images.
2. Models such as VGG16, ResNet50, and InceptionV3 are trained on large image datasets and can provide rich feature representations.

Clustering Algorithms

Clustering is an unsupervised machine learning technique used to group similar data points without predefined labels. The goal is to discover hidden patterns, natural groupings, or structure in the data. Clustering is widely used in customer segmentation, anomaly detection, image segmentation, document grouping, and recommendation systems. We will explore different clustering algorithms now.

K-Means Algorithm (Partition Algorithm)

K-means is a partitioning method that divides a dataset into K distinct, non-overlapping subsets (clusters). It aims to minimize the variance within each cluster.

Algorithm:

1. **Initialization**: The algorithm starts by selecting K initial centroids randomly from the dataset. These centroids are the initial guesses for the centers of the clusters.
2. **Assignment Step**: Each data point is assigned to the nearest centroid, forming K clusters. The distance is typically measured using Euclidean distance.
3. **Update Step**: The centroids are recalculated as the mean of all data points assigned to each cluster. This step adjusts the centroids to better fit the data.
4. **Convergence Check**: The algorithm checks if the centroids have changed significantly. If the change is below a certain tolerance level (or if a maximum number of iterations is reached), the algorithm stops.
5. **Output**: The final cluster assignments and centroids are returned.

Significance: K-means is efficient and easy to implement, making it suitable for large datasets. However, it requires specifying the number of clusters and is sensitive to initial centroid placement.

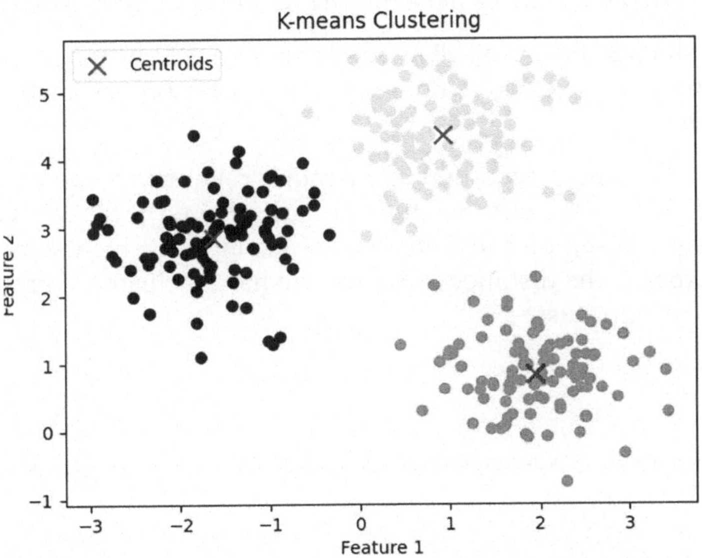

Figure 6.2: *Plotting the k-means algorithm for 3 clusters*

k-medoids is similar to the k-means algorithm. It uses medoids instead of centroids. A medoid is the most centrally located point in a cluster, minimizing the sum of dissimilarities (for example, distances) between itself and all other points in the cluster.

Hierarchical Clustering (Agglomcrativc and Divisive Methods)

Hierarchical clustering can be performed in two ways: agglomerative (bottom-up) and divisive (top-down). Here, we will focus on the agglomerative approach, which is more commonly used.

Algorithm:

1. Start with each data point as its own cluster.
   Initially, each data point is considered a separate cluster.
2. Compute the distance matrix.
   Calculate the pairwise distance between all clusters (initially, individual data points).
3. Merge the closest clusters.
   Find the pair of clusters with the smallest distance and merge them into a single cluster.
4. Update the distance matrix.
   Recalculate the distances between the new cluster and all other clusters.
5. Repeat steps 3 and 4 until all points are in a single cluster.
   Continue merging clusters until only one cluster remains, which contains all data points.

The sequence of merges is recorded in a dendrogram, which can be used to decide the number of clusters by cutting the tree at a desired level. We can choose the number of clusters based on the distance. For example, if the distance is 4 or 5, we will have 3 clusters. If the distance is 30, we will have 3 clusters. Any distance above that will have only one cluster.

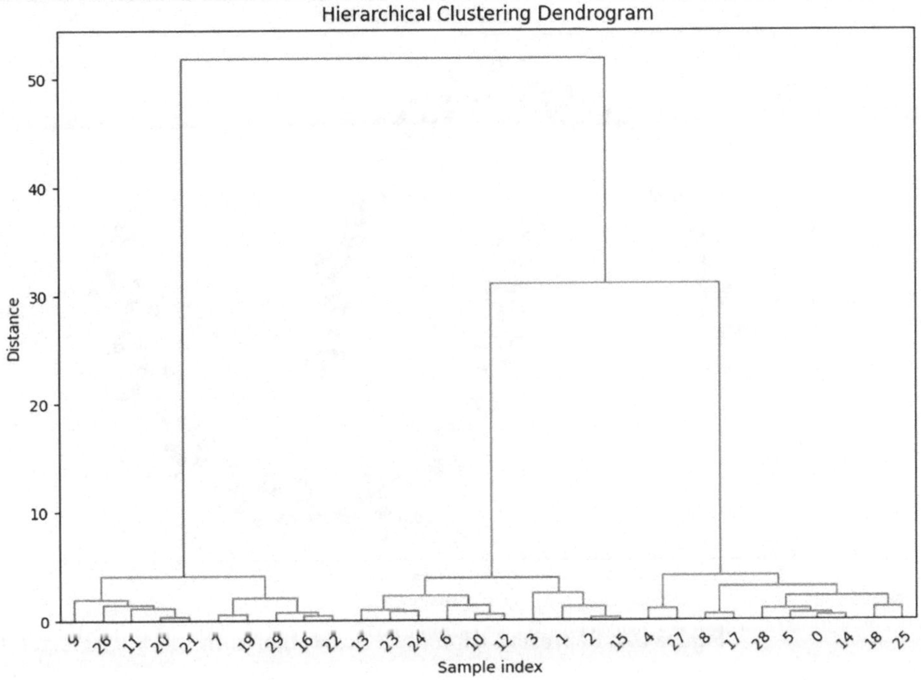

Figure 6.3: *Plotting hierarchical clustering*

Density-based Clustering: DBSCAN, OPTICS

Key Concepts:

- **Core Points**: Points that have at least a minimum number of neighboring points (MinPts) within a given radius (ε).
- **Border Points**: Points that are within the neighborhood of a core point but do not themselves have enough neighbors to be a core point.
- **Noise Points**: Points that are neither core points nor border points.

Algorithm Steps:

1. **Identify Core Points**: For each point in the dataset, count the number of points within its ε-neighborhood. If this number is greater than or equal to MinPts, mark it as a core point.
2. **Form Clusters**: For each core point, form a cluster by including all points (core and border) that are reachable from it.
3. **Mark Noise**: Any point that is not reachable from any core point is marked as noise.
4. **Repeat**: Continue until all points have been processed.

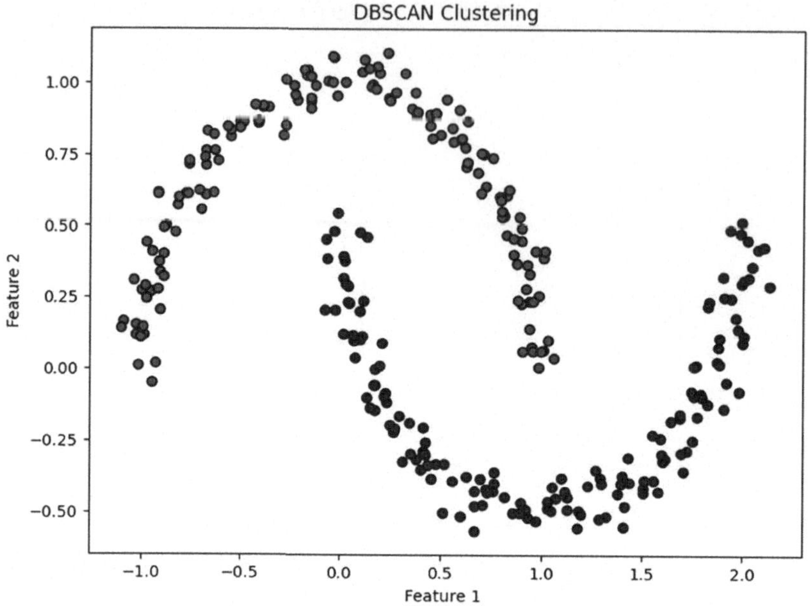

Figure 6.4: *Representation of DBScan algorithm*

Multi-dimensionality: One challenge with these algorithms would be handling multi-dimensionality. One can use one of the several dimensionality reduction techniques, such as:

- Manual dimensionality reduction techniques using domain knowledge and similar to the ones discussed in the previous chapter.
- Algorithmic dimensionality reduction techniques such as Principal Component Analysis (PCA), Linear Discriminant Analysis (LDA).
- Use architectures such as Auto Encoders for dimensionality reduction.

Gaussian Mixture Model (GMM)

The Gaussian Mixture Model (GMM) is a probabilistic model that assumes the data is generated from a mixture of several Gaussian distributions with unknown parameters. Each cluster is represented by a Gaussian distribution characterized by its mean and covariance. GMM is a powerful tool for clustering and density estimation, particularly when the clusters overlap or have non-circular shapes.

Think of GMM as trying to group your data into clusters, but instead of drawing hard boundaries like K-means, it does something smarter:

- It assumes each cluster looks like a soft, bell-shaped curve (Gaussian), not a hard circle.
- Each point belongs to every cluster with some probability, not just one.

Algorithm:

1. **Initialization – "*Guess the starting point*"**
    - You decide how many clusters (say 3).
    - The algorithm makes random guesses for:
        - The center of each cluster.
        - How spread-out each cluster is.
        - How big each cluster is compared to others.

    It is like saying:

    > "*Let us guess where each bell curve might be.*"

2. **E-Step (Expectation Step)**

    Goal: Figure out how much each point "*belongs*" to each cluster.

    For every data point, the algorithm asks:

    "Based on my current guesses, how likely is this point from each bell curve?"

    It calculates probabilities like:

    - Point A → 70% cluster 1, 20% cluster 2, 10% cluster 3
    - Point B → 5% cluster 1, 93% cluster 2, 2% cluster 3

    This is unlike K-means, where each point belongs to only one cluster.

3. **M-Step (Maximization Step)**

    Goal: Improve the cluster definitions based on the probabilities found in the E-step.

    The algorithm updates:

    - **Means**: Move the cluster centers closer to the points that belong to them more.
    - **Covariances**: Adjust the shape/spread of each cluster.
    - **Mixing coefficients**: Adjust the overall size (importance) of each cluster.

    It is like saying:

    > "*Now that I know how much each point belongs to each cluster, let me redraw the bell curves to fit better.*"

4. **Repeat E-step and M-step**

    This loop continues until:

    - The cluster shapes stop changing much.

- Or it reaches a maximum number of iterations.

This usually means:

"The algorithm is happy with the cluster shapes and positions now."

5. **Final Output**

Each data point is assigned to the cluster where it has the highest probability.

Example:

- Point A → 0.7 probability for Cluster 1 → assigned to Cluster 1
- Point B → 0.93 probability for Cluster 2 → assigned to Cluster 2

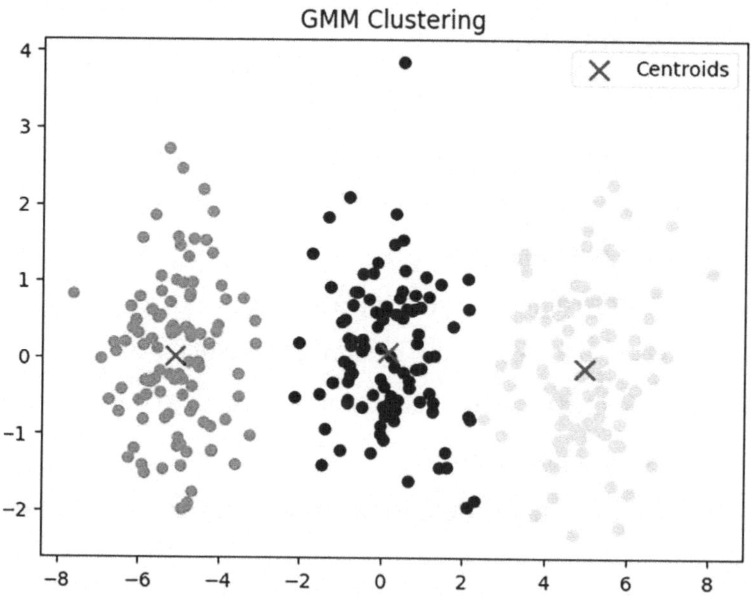

***Figure 6.5**: Representation of GMM clusters*

Latent Dirichlet Allocation (LDA)

LDA is a generative probabilistic model used to discover abstract topics within a collection of documents. It assumes that each document is a mixture of topics, and each topic is a mixture of words. LDA is widely used for topic modeling in text data.

Simple Steps of the LDA Algorithm

1. **Initialize Parameters**:

   a. Choose the number of topics K you want to discover.

   b. Initialize the topic distribution for each document and the word distribution for each topic randomly.

2. **Iterative Process**: For each document:

   For each word in the document:

   a. **Assign a Topic**: Assign a topic to the word based on the current topic distribution for the document and the word distribution for the topic.

   b. **Update Distributions**: Update the topic distribution for the document and the word distribution for the topic based on the new assignment.

3. **Repeat**: Repeat the iterative process for a fixed number of iterations or until convergence.

4. **Output**:

   After convergence, the model provides:

   a. A distribution of topics for each document.

   b. A distribution of words for each topic.

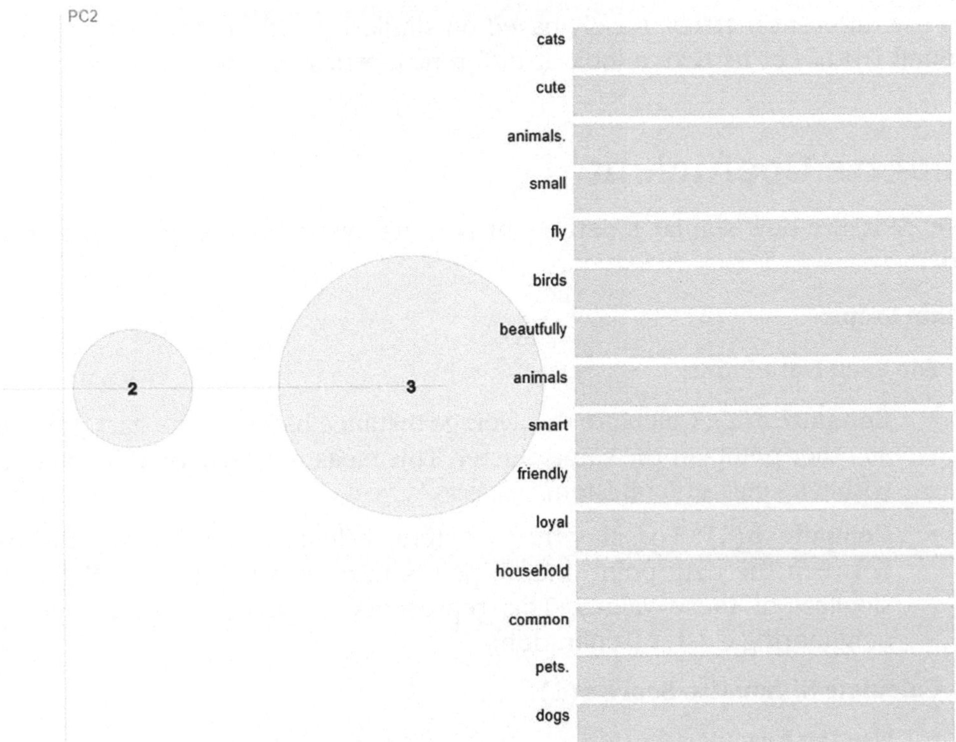

Figure 6.6: *Clustering using LDA*

Let's understand the summary of all the algorithms:

Algorithm	Type	Hard/Soft	Strengths	Weakness	Best For
K-Means	Centroid	Hard	Fast, scalable	Sensitive to outliers	Market/ customer segmentation
Hierarchical	Tree-based	Hard	Dendrogram, k not needed	Slow for large data	Biology, document grouping
DBSCAN	Density	Hard	Finds noise, arbitrary shapes	Sensitive to eps	Fraud, spatial patterns
GMM	Probabilistic	Soft	Soft clustering, flexible shapes	Gaussian assumption	Image segmentation, finance
LDA	Topic model	Soft	Multiple-topic assignment	Noisy topics	NLP topic modelling

Table 6.1: *Comparison of clustering algorithms*

Evaluation Criteria

We can use different metrics, purely based on similarity within the cluster or using the ground truth. Let us take a look at different metrics for measuring the cluster quality.

Silhouette Coefficient

Purpose: Measure how similar a data point is to its own cluster compared to other clusters.

Algorithm Steps:

1. **For Each Data Point**:
    - **Compute `a(i)`**: Calculate the average distance between the data point and all other points in the same cluster. This measures how well the point fits within its cluster (cohesion).
    - **Compute `b(i)`**: For all other clusters, calculate the average distance between the data point and all points in each other cluster. Select the smallest of these values. This represents the distance to the nearest neighboring cluster (separation).
2. **Calculate Silhouette Score `s(i)`**:
    - Use the formula:

      `s(i)=b(i)-a(i)/max{a(i),b(i)}`

- The score ranges from –1 to +1, where:
  - **+1**: The data point is well-matched to its own cluster and poorly matched to neighboring clusters.
  - **0**: The data point is on or very close to the decision boundary between two clusters.
  - **-1**: The data point may have been assigned to the wrong cluster.

3. **Compute the Average Silhouette Score**:
   - Calculate the mean of all individual silhouette scores to get an overall measure of clustering quality.

Simplified Explanation:

- For each point, see how close it is to other points in its cluster compared to points in other clusters.
- A high silhouette score means the point is well-matched to its cluster.
- Average all scores to understand how good the clustering is overall.

Coherence

The coherence metric evaluates:

- How semantically similar the items in each cluster are.
- Whether clusters represent meaningful groupings of the data.

For example:

- In topic modeling, coherence measures how related the words in a topic are.
- In general clustering, coherence measures how similar feature representations (for example, vectors) of items within a cluster are.

Step 1: Preprocess Data

a. Normalize feature vectors (for example, scale numerical data, embed textual data using techniques such as TF-IDF, Word2Vec, or BERT).

b. Remove noise or outliers to improve cluster quality.

Step 2: Compute Similarity/Distance

a. Select a similarity function.

b. **Measure intra-cluster similarity**: For all points within a cluster, calculate pairwise similarities or their distance to the cluster centroid.

Step 3: Aggregate Results

a. Compute coherence for individual clusters.

b. Aggregate cluster coherences to obtain an overall coherence score: Overall Coherence= 1/k* Sum of (coherence of individual cluster).

High coherence indicates that items in clusters are highly similar, suggesting good clustering quality.

Low coherence implies that items within clusters are dissimilar, indicating poor clustering or poorly chosen features.

Purity

Purity measures how well clusters or topics align with ground truth categories. It is a simple metric to assess clustering quality. Purity is used when we have ground truth available, even for a few samples.

Purity = $1/N \sum_{k=1,K} max(Ck \cap Cj)$

- N: Total number of data points.
- C_k: Cluster k.
- C_j: Ground truth category j.

Interpretation:

- **High purity**: Clusters mostly consist of points from one ground truth category.
- **Low purity**: Clusters are diverse and poorly aligned with categories.

Business Case Studies

Customer Relationship Management (CRM) helps businesses build relationships with customers. Artificial Intelligence (AI) has revolutionized the CRM domain by enhancing customer engagement, automating routine tasks, providing actionable insights, and personalizing customer experiences. AI technologies such as machine learning, natural language processing (NLP), and predictive analytics are integrated into CRM systems to handle vast amounts of customer data efficiently and effectively. Let us take a deeper look at the applications of unsupervised learning.

Figure 6.7: *Customer representative in the CRM world*

Topic Modeling

Topic Modeling is an unsupervised learning technique used to identify hidden themes or topics within large volumes of unstructured text data. In the CRM domain, topic modeling helps businesses analyze customer communications, such as emails, support tickets, customer feedback/queries, and social media interactions, to extract valuable insights.

Applications in CRM

- **Customer Support Analysis:**
    - **Automatic Ticket Categorization**: Classify support tickets into topics to streamline routing and prioritize issues.
    - **Identifying Common Issues**: Discover prevalent customer problems to inform product improvements and support strategies.
- **Feedback and Review Analysis:**
    - **Survey Insights**: Extract themes from open-ended survey responses to understand customer satisfaction and areas for improvement.

  - **Product Review Mining**: Analyze reviews to identify strengths and weaknesses from the customer's perspective.

Customer Segmentation

Customer Segmentation involves dividing customers into distinct groups based on shared characteristics or behaviors. This allows businesses to tailor strategies to different segments, improving marketing effectiveness and customer satisfaction.

Applications in CRM

- **Marketing Personalization:**
  - **Targeted Campaigns**: Create marketing messages that resonate with specific customer segments.
  - **Product Recommendations**: Suggest products or services that align with the preferences of each segment.
- **Customer Retention Strategies:**
  - **Identifying At-Risk Customers**: Segments that show declining engagement can be targeted with retention efforts.
  - **Loyalty Programs**: Design rewards and incentives that appeal to different customer groups.

Anomaly Detection

Anomaly Detection involves identifying unusual patterns or outliers in data that may indicate fraudulent activities or other significant events. In CRM, anomaly detection helps maintain data integrity and security.

Applications in CRM

- **Fraud Detection:**
  - **Transactional Anomalies**: Spotting unusual transaction patterns that deviate from normal customer behavior.
  - **Account Takeover Detection**: Identifying unusual login patterns, such as logins from new devices or locations.
- **Data Quality Assurance:**
  - **Detecting Data Entry Errors**: Identifying outliers in customer data that may indicate errors or inconsistencies.
  - **Monitoring System Performance**: Detecting anomalies in system logs or performance metrics that may indicate issues.

Let us walk through how topic modeling can be applied to customer support tickets and understand the complete design process.

Case Study: Topic Modeling for CRM

Analyzing large volumes of customer feedback or support tickets often involves extensive manual effort. The process typically requires first identifying the relevant product, followed by pinpointing the specific issue associated with it. At a higher level, tickets can be categorized into broad product groups, but within those groups, similar issues must be clustered at a finer level of detail. The challenge becomes even greater when entirely new issues emerge, making them harder to detect, classify, and group effectively.

Business Requirement

It is important to understand the business context to come up with a solution.

1. What is the current business objective?
    a. Enhance customer satisfaction by prioritizing and routing tickets efficiently.
    b. Provide insights for product improvement and customer service strategies.
2. What is the right granularity of the clusters? Too granular clusters would be difficult to manage, and high-level clusters often may not be significant. Depends on the organization and use-case.
3. What is the success criterion of the clustering? What is bad? Having more outliers in a cluster or missing a new cluster?

Data Curation

The following questions will help us build a right data strategy.

1. What is the form of data? What is the schema of the data? Assume the data contains details about the customer support cases, their severity, category, and so on.
2. How does the text look? Is the text short text or long-form text? Short text needs to be treated differently as they do not adhere to language semantics. Long-form text needs to be pre-processed with Lemmatization, stop word removal, and so on.
3. Do we have a golden set of data that is clustered as a reference? It is important to create a golden set of data and get it approved by the customer.

4. How to remove noise from the data? For example, removing signatures from the emails.
5. Is the text fully in English, or are mixed-language terms used? It is important to translate/transform the content into a single language.
6. Getting domain knowledge of the vocabulary. Often, the technical/business-specific terms would be used. It is important to include that knowledge, such as synonyms, abbreviations, terms connected to a specific product, and so on, and substitute them in the topic modeling.

Consider this synthetic dataset for the problem.

https://github.com/soudaminigit/TopicModelling/blob/main/windows_crm_issues.csv

Sample data looks like this:

Ticket	Issue	Description
T1	Installation Error	Unable to install CRM software on Windows.
T2	Update Issue	Windows update caused CRM to stop working.
T3	Compatibility	CRM software not compatible with the Windows version.

***Table 6.2**: Sample customer technical issue data*

- **Text Preprocessing:**
  - **Tokenization**: Split text into individual words or tokens.
  - **Stopword Removal**: Remove common words that do not contribute to topic differentiation (for example, "`the`", "`is`").
  - **Stemming/Lemmatization**: Reduce words to their base or root form.

Feature Engineering

1. What kind of vectorization to use?

   We can use Word2Vec if we use probabilistic methods such as k-means/hierarchical clustering/coherence, and so on. Alternatively, we can use word embeddings and apply dimensionality reduction techniques.

   If we plan to use a deep neural network-based / deep learning approach, then we should use high-quality embeddings such as BERT, GloVe, and so on.

2. How many fields are important in the data? Should we use only the title or fields such as category, and so on?

   Consider the 'Issue Type' column also in the additional features.

Often, we also have domain knowledge about specific technical terms, and we would want to emphasize them. In such a case, we can add those keywords as additional features.

Algorithm Selection

Algorithm selection depends on the particular business requirement. Let's evaluate two scenarios.

1. Do we run the algorithm in a one-off scenario or in real time?

   We can choose high-precision models such as BERTTopic, if the model runs once a day/week in the offline model. We can directly leverage the model for generating the results.

   BERTTopic is a very precise model for Topic modeling problems. The BERTopic model is a topic modeling technique that leverages BERT embeddings (Bidirectional Encoder Representations from Transformers) for more coherent and semantically meaningful topics. It combines transformer-based embeddings with clustering techniques to discover topics in a corpus of text.

   Here is the general architecture of BERTopic:

   - **Input**: A set of documents (text corpus).
   - **BERT Embedding**: Transform each document into a high-dimensional semantic vector using a pre-trained transformer-based model (for example, BERT).
   - **Dimensionality Reduction**: Use UMAP to reduce the dimensionality of the embeddings.
   - **Clustering**: Apply HDBSCAN to group documents into clusters based on their embeddings.
   - **Topic Representation**: Use class-based TF-IDF to identify important keywords for each cluster.
   - **Visualization**: Visualize the topics using UMAP for a low-dimensional representation and interactive plotting tools.
   - **Output**: Interpretable topics with representative keywords, cluster labels, and visualizations.

   Sample code snippet using BERTopic:

   ```
   from bertopic import BERTopic
   # Dimension reduction
   from umap import UMAP
   umap_model = UMAP(n_neighbors=10,
                     n_components=5,
   ```

```
                        min_dist=0.1,
                        metric='cosine',
                        random_state=100)
# Initiate BERTopic
topic_model = BERTopic(umap_model=umap_model, language="english",
calculate_probabilities=True)
# Run BERTopic model
topics, probabilities = topic_model.fit_transform(inci-
dents['clean_desc'])
# Get the list of topics
topic_model.get_topic_info()
```

2. When the model's semantic results are poor and demand significant domain-specific tuning and still needs a light-weight model, which algorithm do we use?

   We can possibly build a clustering algorithm that will capture the semantic understanding. The LDA algorithm is most popular for capturing semantic understanding and is also a lightweight algorithm to implement from scratch.

   Sample code snippet using LDA Algorithm:

```
#Install the required libraries

!pip install pyLDAvis
import gensim
import nltk
from gensim import corpora
from gensim.models import LdaModel
import pyLDAvis.gensim_models as gensimvis
import pyLDAvis
from nltk.corpus import stopwords
nltk.download('stopwords')
# Sample documents
documents = [
    "Cats are small and cute animals.",
    "Dogs are loyal and friendly pets.",
    "Dogs are common household pets.",
    "Cats are smart animals",
    "birds fly beautifully"
]

# Preprocess the documents
texts = [[word for word in document.lower().split()] for
document in documents]
stop_words = set(stopwords.words('english'))
texts = [[word for word in document.lower().split() if word not
in stop_words] for document in documents]
# Create a dictionary and corpus
```

```
dictionary = corpora.Dictionary(texts)
corpus = [dictionary.doc2bow(text) for text in texts]

# Train LDA model for 3 clusters
lda_model = LdaModel(corpus=corpus, id2word=dictionary,
num_topics=3, random_state=42)
# Print the topics
for idx, topic in lda_model.print_topics(-1):
    print(f"Topic {idx}: {topic}")

# Visualize the topics
lda_display = gensimvis.prepare(lda_model, corpus, dictionary,
sort_topics=False)
pyLDAvis.display(lda_display)
```

This program will take 5 sentences and display the 3 clusters based on the LDA algorithm.

While we have discussed LDA and BertTopic in detail, let us also take a look at the other competitive algorithms:

- **Non-Matrix Factorization (NMF):** Factorizes the document-term matrix into two lower-dimensional non-negative matrices, capturing hidden topics. It enforces non-negativity, making results more interpretable.
- **Latent Semantic Index (LSI):** Uses Singular Value Decomposition (SVD) to reduce dimensionality and discover latent semantic relationships in text.
- **Topic2Vector:** Uses Word2Vec-like embeddings to map documents and topics into the same vector space. Clusters documents in the semantic space, removing the need to predefine topic numbers.

Here is a quick comparison of these algorithms based on the data characteristics and business goals.

Algorithm	Approach	Strengths	Weaknesses	Best For
LDA	Probabilistic	Robust, well-separated topics, scalable	Computationally expensive, hard to interpret	Large text corpora, research papers, news articles
BERTopic	BERT + Clustering	Context-aware, great for short texts	Requires a GPU, less interpretable	Social media, chat logs, dynamic topics
NMF	Matrix Factorization	Interpretable, efficient	Sensitive to initialization, no word relationships	Business reports, document clustering

LSI	Matrix Factorization (SVD)	Captures synonyms, useful in search engines	Hard to interpret, overfits on small data	Search engines, information retrieval
Top2Vec	Word Embeddings	Auto-detects topics, no need to predefine topic count	Requires large datasets, computationally expensive	Short text, chatbot logs, customer support

***Table 6.3**: Comparison of topic-modelling algorithms*

Model Evaluation

- Use statistical metrics such as coherence score to evaluate topic quality.
- Run the algorithm on a golden set, and measure the Purity metrics.
- Select a few random samples of clusters and compute the purity score by manually labeling them.

Deployment

- **Integration:**
  - Integrate the topic modeling solution with existing CRM systems to automate ticket categorization.
  - Integrate the model in the CI/CD pipeline. As the support tickets are received, they will pass through the model and get clustered. There should be a golden set that verifies the quality of clustering for any regression changes.
  - Ensure the system can handle incoming tickets in real-time or batch mode, depending on business needs.
- **Monitoring:**
  - Set up monitoring to track model performance and detect any drift in topic distributions over time.
  - Implement feedback loops to incorporate user feedback and improve the model continuously.

Evaluation and Iteration

- **Performance Monitoring:**
  - Regularly evaluate the model's performance using new data and adjust as necessary.

- Gather feedback from customer support teams to assess the impact on response times and customer satisfaction.

- **Continuous Improvement:**
  - Update the model periodically with new data to capture emerging topics and trends.

Conclusion

And that is a wrap on our unsupervised learning adventure! We started with the basics, wandered through the land of clustering, got cozy with evaluation metrics, and even met some interesting characters such as K-Means, DBSCAN, and GMM along the way. From customer segmentation to anomaly detection, we have seen how these techniques are shaping industries and making sense of messy, unlabeled data.

Unsupervised learning is like an AI detective–uncovering hidden patterns, solving mysteries, and sometimes making a few questionable guesses. But as we refine these models and improve evaluation techniques, we get closer to extracting real value from data. The future of AI depends on making sense of vast, unstructured information, and mastering these concepts is your ticket to being part of that revolution. So, whether you are clustering customers or decoding topics in text, keep exploring–because in the world of unsupervised learning, the best discoveries are the ones you were not even looking for! We will move one step ahead and explore Recommendation Systems in the next chapter.

Multiple Choice Questions

1. What is the primary goal of unsupervised learning?
   a. To predict outcomes based on labeled data.
   b. To group data into meaningful patterns or clusters.
   c. To improve reinforcement learning models.
   d. To create supervised datasets for classification tasks.
2. Which of the following algorithms is used for density-based clustering?
   a. K-Mcans
   b. DBSCAN
   c. Gaussian Mixture Model
   d. Hierarchical Clustering

3. Which metric is most commonly used to evaluate topic models?
    a. Silhouette Coefficient
    b. Coherence
    c. Entropy
    d. Purity
4. The Silhouette Coefficient ranges from:
    a. 0 to 1
    b. -1 to 0
    c. -1 to 1
    d. 1 to ∞
5. Which clustering technique allows clusters to have elliptical shapes and varying sizes?
    a. K-Means
    b. Hierarchical Clustering
    c. Gaussian Mixture Model
    d. DBSCAN
6. Which of the following is a disadvantage of using Euclidean distance as a metric?
    a. It is sensitive to data normalization.
    b. It cannot handle sparse data.
    c. It performs poorly on categorical data.
    d. All of the above
7. Purity in clustering evaluation measures:
    a. The similarity of a point to its assigned cluster.
    b. The extent to which each cluster contains data points from a single ground-truth class.
    c. The likelihood of topics generated by a model.
    d. The randomness in a clustering result.

Answers

1. b
2. b
3. b
4. c
5. c
6. d
7. b

References

1. Bishop, C. M. (2006). *Pattern Recognition and Machine Learning*. Springer.
2. Hastie, T., Tibshirani, R., & Friedman, J. (2009). *The Elements of Statistical Learning*. Springer.
3. Pedregosa, F., Varoquaux, G., Gramfort, A., et al. (2011). Scikit-learn: Machine Learning in Python. *Journal of Machine Learning Research*.
4. Blei, D. M., Ng, A. Y., & Jordan, M. I. (2003). Latent Dirichlet Allocation. *Journal of Machine Learning Research*.

CHAPTER 7
Building Recommendation Systems for E-Commerce

Introduction

This is the power of **Recommendation Systems**—they are the invisible force behind e-commerce giants such as Amazon, Netflix, and Spotify, influencing everything from what we buy to what we watch and listen to. In the e-commerce world, where choices are overwhelming, recommendation systems act as intelligent filters, helping users discover relevant products while driving revenue for businesses. Now, imagine this experience but at the scale of millions of customers shopping online, where there is no physical assistant, yet every product recommendation feels just as personal.

However, building an effective, scalable, and responsible recommendation system is far from straightforward. In this chapter, we will explore the key components that make up a scalable recommendation system. We will start with real-life use cases, understanding how recommendation engines power different aspects of e-commerce, from product discovery to dynamic pricing. Next, we will delve into the evolution of recommendation algorithms, tracing their journey from simple rule-based approaches to advanced deep learning and graph-based methods. However, designing a successful recommendation system is not just about accuracy—it must also be ethical, explainable, and diverse. We will examine bias in AI, the importance of explainability, and methods to ensure fairness in recommendations. By the end of this chapter, we will have a deep understanding of what it takes to build and scale a recommendation system that not only improves user experience but also drives business growth in e-commerce. Let us dive in!

Structure

In this chapter, we will cover the following topics:

- Recommendation Systems and Real-Life Use-Cases
- Evolution of Recommendation Algorithms
- Measuring the Success of a Recommendation System
- Diversity, Ethical AI, and Explainability
- Experimentation, User Feedback, and Data Drifts
- Mock Interview

Recommendation Systems and Real-Life Use Cases

Imagine this: when you open Netflix after a long day, and right there on your home screen is a movie that feels like it was handpicked just for us. Or we log into Amazon, looking for a new phone, and the platform not only suggests the perfect model but also the right accessories–earbuds, a case, and a screen protector. Ever wondered how?

This is the invisible magic of **Recommendation Systems**, quietly shaping our choices, guiding our purchases, and making our digital lives smoother. But this magic is not random–it is built on carefully designed algorithms that learn from our preferences, past behavior, and even what people like us are interested in.

How Recommendation Systems Became a Game-Changer

Let us rewind to the early days of the internet. If we wanted to watch a movie, we would go to a store and pick one based on its cover or recommendations from friends. If we needed a book, we would browse through shelves, guided by bestsellers or staff picks. Then, as the digital world expanded, a new challenge emerged: Too many choices.

Suddenly, customers were not just picking from a hundred books or ten movies–they had access to millions of them. How do we help a user find what they will love without making them spend hours searching? Enter recommendation engines, the secret ingredient behind some of the world's most successful platforms.

Netflix: A $1 Billion Algorithm

Netflix's rise to global dominance was not just about streaming–it was about showing the right content to the right user at the right time. In 2006, Netflix launched a $1 million challenge to improve its recommendation algorithm by 10%. The goal? To keep users engaged longer and reduce churn.

Today, 80% of the shows watched on Netflix come from recommendations. They save 1$ billion every year due to the recommendation system. It shows the videos based on personalization rather than popularity. It helps them retain the customers and not cancel out. Their system analyzes everything–from your watch history and ratings to the time of day we watch and what similar users enjoy. If you ever felt like Netflix "*just gets you*," that is because its algorithm continuously learns and refines itself.

Figure 7.1: *Illustrative image of a salesperson offering clothing recommendations. Courtesy: Canva*

Amazon: The Master of Cross-Selling

Amazon's recommendation engine is not just about personalizing product listings–it is about driving sales. Their famous phrase, "*Customers who bought this also bought...*", is estimated to generate 35% of Amazon's total revenue.

Amazon pioneered the use of product linking, which finds connections between products and users. Amazon found that their recommendation engine worked better when they had access to users' purchase history. By using the previously bought products and product correlations, they suggest new products for the users. This approach has made Amazon the king of upselling and cross-selling, turning casual browsers into frequent buyers. Now, Amazon stores the user-item mapping using a Graph Neural Network and predicts the missing nodes for recommendations.

Spotify: Understanding Musical Tastes

Ever discovered a song on Spotify's Discover Weekly playlist and thought, "*This is exactly what I was looking for!*"? Spotify's recommendation engine uses deep learning, natural language processing, and collaborative filtering to create ultra-personalized playlists. It understands different attributes of songs, such as the singer, music director, and also includes multiple audio signals of the tune, and suggests recommendations.

It analyzes millions of songs, considers what people with similar tastes are listening to, and even examines music blogs and trends to predict the next favorite song before we even know it.

Why Recommendation Systems Matter

These examples show how recommendation systems have reshaped digital businesses, but their impact goes beyond entertainment and e-commerce.

- **Healthcare**: AI-driven recommendations help doctors identify personalized treatment options based on patient history.
- **Finance**: Banks use recommendation engines to suggest credit cards, loans, or investment plans based on customer spending behavior.
- **Education**: Platforms such as Coursera and Udemy suggest courses based on learning patterns, making online education more effective.

The Challenge: Making Recommendations Smarter and Fairer

As powerful as recommendation systems are, they are not perfect. Netflix can suggest an amazing movie, but it might also push similar content repeatedly, limiting diversity. There are thousands of movies in the Netflix corpus, but the user is still not aware of them. Amazon can drive sales, but it can also create filter bubbles, where users only see what the algorithm thinks they want, not what they might actually need.

Bias, fairness, and ethical AI have become major concerns, and companies are now working to ensure that recommendation systems do not just optimize for engagement—but also for user well-being and fairness.

Despite these concerns, recommendation systems remain one of the most impactful applications of AI in industry. They power a wide range of use cases:

- **Product Recommendations**: Personalized product suggestions (for example, Amazon's "*Customers who bought this also bought*").

- **Dynamic Pricing and Promotions**: Adjusting prices and promotions based on user behavior (for example, airline ticket prices).
- **Cross-Selling and Upselling**: Suggesting complementary items (for example, "*Complete the look*" in fashion retail).
- **Customer Retention and Churn Prevention**: Detecting users likely to churn and recommending offers to retain them.
- **Context-Aware Recommendations**: Using real-time location, device, and session-based preferences for relevant suggestions.

Figure 7.2: *Fun representation of extreme personalized recommendations. Courtesy: Supermeme.ai*

Evolution of Recommendation Algorithms

Recommendation systems are evolving faster than ever. With deep learning, reinforcement learning, and graph-based approaches, we are moving towards even smarter, more human-like AI recommendations. The future is not just about making better predictions–it is about building trust, ensuring transparency, and personalizing experiences in ways we have never seen before.

Rule-Based Systems (Early Days)

If-else conditions, expert-defined heuristics.

If a user purchases bread, then they will purchase peanut butter/jam/Nutella/similar dish. The rules can be generated based on the

- Domain knowledge
- Often implemented using association rule mining algorithms such as Apriori or FP-growth.

The user's transaction history will be analyzed to understand the association between different products.

This is a predictive solution and is simple to build. However, it is not an evolving system. One needs to keep track of the new purchase patterns and generate the patterns on a periodic basis.

Content-Based Filtering

The recommendations are suggested based on the properties of the data. For example, if a user has watched movies in the past, try to find all the properties of the movie. They will recommend new movies that will have the same properties.

- In the following picture, if the user watches "*Sleepless in Seattle*", "*You have got a mail*", both have the same lead actor, "*Tom Hanks*," and lead actress "*Meg Ryan*".

Now, there is a high probability that he watches other "*Tom Hanks*" and "*Meg Ryan*" movies also. Hence, the system recommends him "*Joe Versus the Volcano*", which features the same actors.

This approach has the advantage that we do not need user interaction data for recommendations. In this approach, we need to engineer the individual features based on the data type.

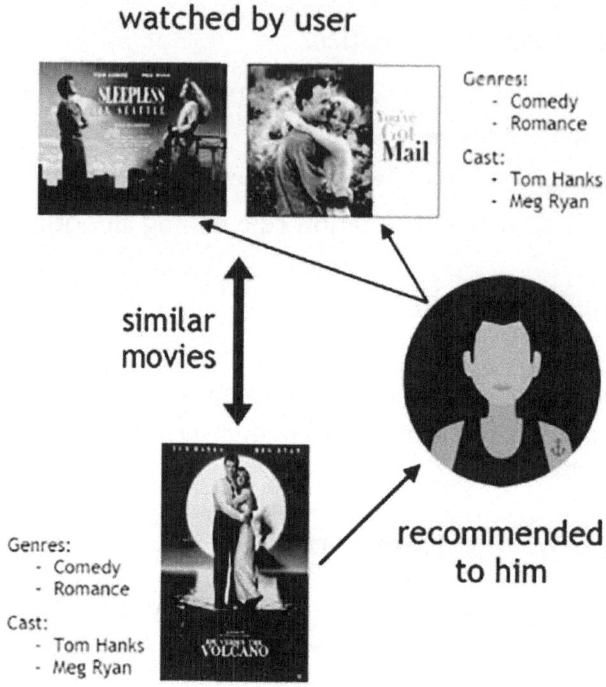

Figure 7.3: *Content-based filtering*

It is especially useful to create these rules for new products when we do not have user interaction information available.

Collaborative Filtering (User-Based and Item-Based)

Predicting user preferences based on similar users or similar items.

User-based Collaboration

Focuses on identifying users with similar behavior or preferences.

- Uses a similarity measure (for example, cosine similarity, Pearson correlation) to find users whose past ratings or interactions are similar.
- Once similar users are identified, the system recommends items that those users have liked but the target user has not interacted with.

- **Example:** If User A and User B both liked three similar movies, and User B liked a fourth movie that User A has not seen, the system recommends that movie to User A.

Challenges:

- Cold start problem (for new users with no interaction history).
- Scalability issues in large datasets (since user preferences change over time).

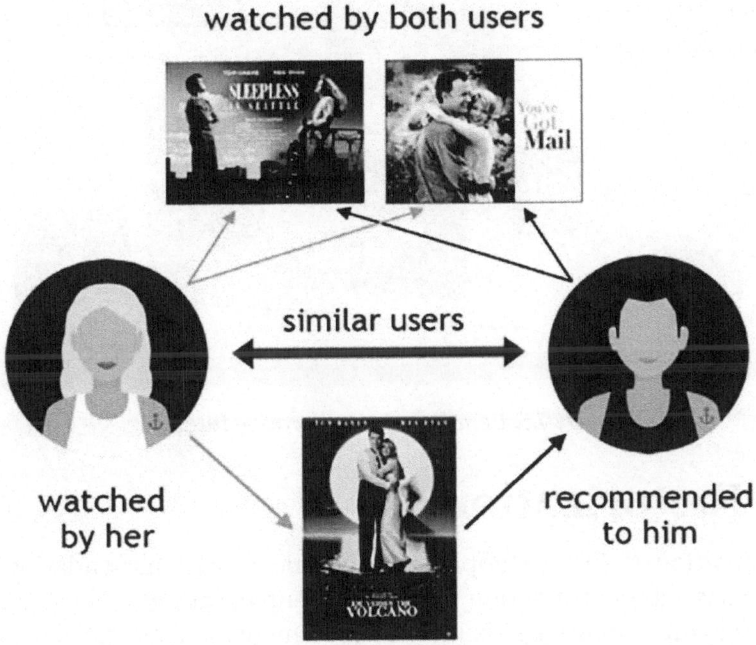

Figure 7.4: *Collaborative filtering*

Item-based Collaboration

- Focuses on identifying similarities between items rather than users.
- Computes item similarity based on user interactions (for example, ratings, clicks, purchases).
- If two items are frequently co-rated or purchased together, they are considered similar.

Example: If many users who watched Movie A also watched Movie B, then Movie B is recommended to users who watched Movie A.

Advantages:

- More stable over time since item relationships change less frequently than user preferences.

- Scales better than user-based Collaborative Filtering in large datasets.

For example, in the diagram below, User B and User D both liked the iPhone and the iPhone case. User A also liked the iPhone. Hence, the iPhone case is recommended to User A.

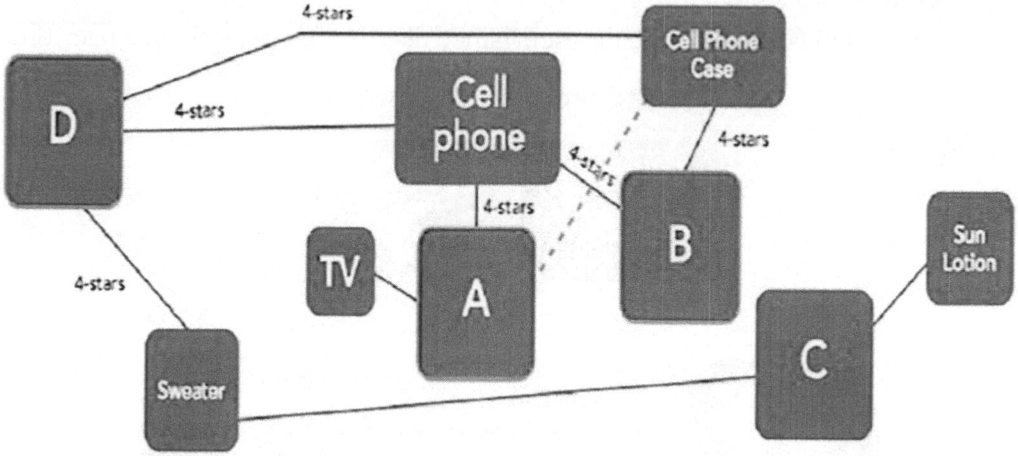

***Figure* 7.5:** *Item-based collaborative filtering*

Matrix Factorization

Matrix Factorization (MF) is a popular technique in recommendation systems to handle sparse user-item interaction data (for example, ratings, clicks). It decomposes a large user-item interaction matrix into lower-dimensional matrices to reveal hidden patterns and relationships.

Example:

- In a **user–item rating matrix**, we do not explicitly know *why* a user likes a movie.
- Matrix factorization learns **latent features** such as:
    - F1 = "*preference for action versus romance*"
    - F2 = "preference for popular versus niche content"
- Each user and item is mapped into this **latent space**.
- A user and an item are considered a good match if their latent vectors are close/aligned.

So even though we never directly labeled "*action*" or "*romance*," the system discovered these hidden factors automatically.

Given a user-item matrix R, where R,I represents the rating given by user *u* to item *i*,

MF decomposes it into two lower-dimensional matrices using different factorization techniques:

- **User matrix** U (Users × Latent Factors)
- **Item matrix** V (Items × Latent Factors)

These matrices capture latent features (for example, user preferences and item characteristics). The predicted rating is obtained as:

$$R=U * V^T$$

Original User-Item Matrix

This table represents the original interaction matrix, where each row corresponds to a user and each column to an item. The entries capture explicit ratings (for example, 1–5 stars), while the missing values (?) denote unknown preferences that the model aims to predict.

Users	**Item1**	**Item2**	**Item3**	**Item4**
User1	5	?	3	1
User2	?	4	?	2
User3	2	1	4	?
User4	?	3	5	4

Table 7.1: *User item interaction table*

Let us understand how to split the user-item matrix into U (User) and V (item) matrices.

Popular Matrix Factorization Techniques

- **Singular Value Decomposition (SVD):** Decomposes the matrix using linear algebra methods.
- **Non-Negative Matrix Factorization (NMF):** Enforces non-negative constraints for better interpretability.
- **Alternating Least Squares (ALS):** Optimizes U and V iteratively by minimizing error.

User Matrix (U)

The user feature matrix is derived from matrix factorization. Each user is represented as a vector of latent features (F1, F2), capturing hidden patterns in their preferences that cannot be observed directly.

Users	F1	F2
User1	0.8	0.5
User2	0.6	0.7
User3	0.3	0.9
User4	0.9	0.2

Table 7.2: *User feature table*

Item Matrix (V)

This matrix encodes items in the same latent feature space as users. Each item is represented by feature values (F1, F2), enabling similarity comparisons and user-item matching.

Items	F1	F2
Item1	0.9	0.6
Item2	0.5	0.8
Item3	0.7	0.4
Item4	0.2	0.9

Table 7.3: *Item feature matrix*

Predicted User-Item Ratings Matrix

Using the dot product of the user and item feature matrices, this table shows the predicted ratings for each user-item pair. These estimates fill in the missing entries from the original matrix (*Table 7.1*) and form the basis for generating recommendations.

User	Item1	Item2	Item3	Item4
User1	4.9	3.6	3.1	1.2
User2	3.1	4.2	3.5	2.1
User3	2.2	1.1	4.0	2.5
User4	2.7	3.0	4.8	3.9

Table 7.4: *User-item rating matrix*

The ratings matrix can be enhanced to a feedback matrix, which could include user explicit feedback/implicit feedback, such as user clicks, ratings, and so on.

Advantages

- Captures hidden patterns in user-item interactions.
- Scales well for large datasets using optimization techniques.
- Provides better recommendations by reducing sparsity issues.

Limitations

- Struggles with cold start problems (new users or items).
- Computationally expensive for very large matrices.

Matrix factorization is widely used in recommendation systems such as Netflix, Amazon, and Spotify, often combined with deep learning for enhanced predictions.

Two-Tower Network

A Two-Tower Neural Network (TTNN) is a deep learning architecture commonly used in recommendation systems, retrieval tasks, and representation learning. It consists of two separate neural networks (or "*towers*") that process different types of input data and learn meaningful representations. The specialty of Two-Tower Networks is that they enable large-scale, efficient, and flexible recommendation by separately encoding users and items into the same latent space, making it possible to retrieve the most relevant items via vector similarity search.

Traditional **matrix factorization** learns a fixed user–item embedding table (limited to known users/items).

Two-Tower networks learn functions (neural encoders) that can handle new users/items using their features. That is why Google describes it as the backbone of large-scale recommenders (for example, YouTube retrieval, Play Store, Ads).

Architecture Overview

The two towers typically represent:

- **User Tower**: Encodes user-related features (for example, user ID, demographics, past interactions).
- **Item Tower**: Encodes item-related features (for example, product ID, description, category).

Each tower projects its input into a shared latent space using deep neural networks. The final output embeddings from both towers are compared using a similarity function (for example, dot product, cosine similarity).

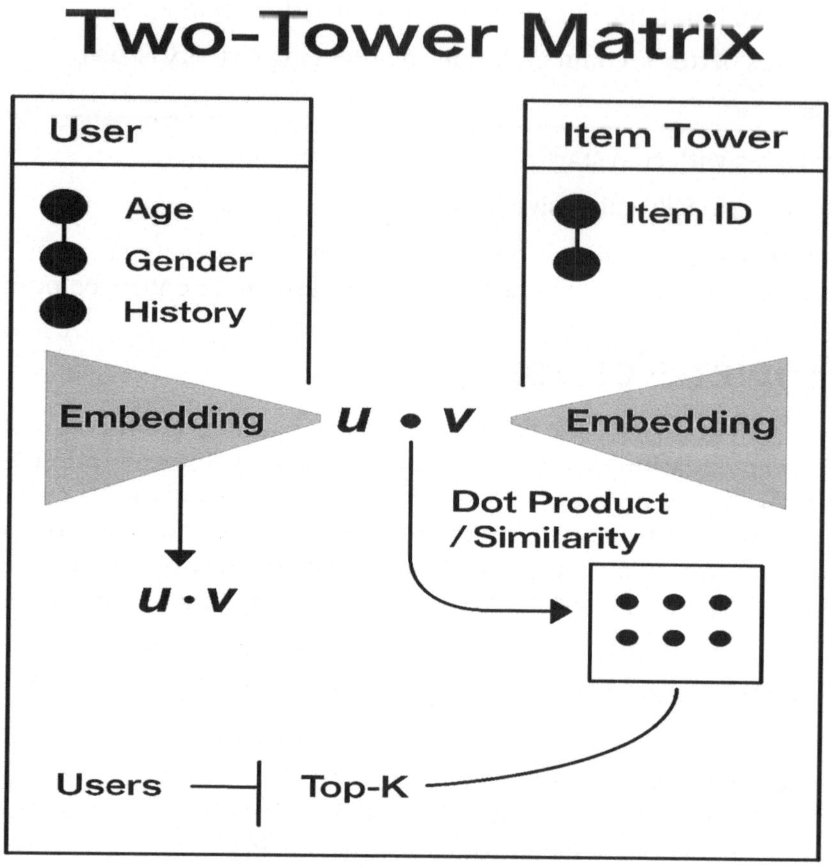

***Figure 7.6**: Two-Tower network*

Workflow

1. **Input Processing**:
   - The User Tower receives user-related features and processes them through a neural network.
   - The Item Tower receives item-related features and processes them similarly.
2. **Embedding Learning**: Each tower outputs an embedding (vector representation) for its input.
3. **Similarity Computation**: The embeddings from both towers are combined using a dot product or cosine similarity to measure relevance.

4. **Training**:
    - o The network is trained using contrastive loss (for example, softmax cross-entropy, triplet loss) with positive and negative samples.
    - o The goal is to maximize similarity for relevant pairs and minimize it for irrelevant pairs.

Deep Learning-Based Approaches

As the scale of the user and product data is increasing, deep neural network-based approaches are gaining momentum. Let us take a look at some of the popular techniques.

Neural Collaborative Filtering

Neural Collaborative Filtering (NCF) is an advanced deep learning approach for recommendation systems that extends traditional Matrix Factorization (MF) by replacing dot product interactions with neural networks.

- Uses two separate embedding layers for users and items.
- Combines Generalized Matrix Factorization (GMF) and Multi-Layer Perceptron (MLP) to learn complex, non-linear relationships.
- **Example**: NeuMF (Neural Matrix Factorization) integrates both GMF and MLP.
- Suitable for implicit feedback (for example, clicks, purchases).
- It is similar to a two-tower network, but it learns the interactions using a neural network.

Autoencoders for Latent Representation Learning

Autoencoders are a type of neural network used for unsupervised learning. They learn efficient representations (encodings) of data by trying to reconstruct the input at the output.

Architecture: Consists of two main parts:

- **Encoder:** Compresses input data into a lower-dimensional latent representation.
- **Decoder:** Reconstructs the original data from this latent representation.

Training Objective: Minimize reconstruction error (difference between input and output).

Autoencoders learn compressed representations (latent factors) of user-item interactions using an encoder-decoder structure.

Use in Recommendation Systems

- **Dimensionality Reduction:** Autoencoders reduce high-dimensional user-item interaction data into compact latent vectors, capturing hidden patterns and preferences.
- **Collaborative Filtering:** Instead of relying on explicit ratings, autoencoders learn latent features of users and items, similar to matrix factorization.
- **Handling Sparsity:** User-item rating matrices are often sparse (many missing ratings). Autoencoders can effectively learn from incomplete data and predict missing values.
- **Cold Start Mitigation:** By integrating side information (for example, user profiles, item attributes), autoencoders help make better recommendations for new users/items.
- **Scalability:** Deep autoencoders can handle very large datasets, making them suitable for platforms such as Netflix or Amazon.

Example: Netflix can use autoencoders on its user-movie rating matrix. The encoder learns compressed user preference vectors, while the decoder predicts how much a user would like unrated movies—enabling personalized recommendations.

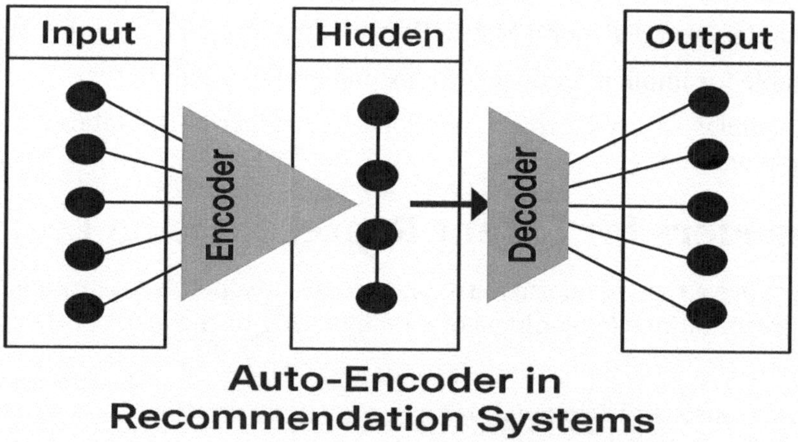

Figure 7.7: *Auto Encoders for recommendation systems*

Transformer-Based Models (BERT4Rec)

Transformer-based models leverage self-attention mechanisms to model sequential user behavior.

- **BERT4Rec** (based on BERT) is trained using a bidirectional Transformer to capture user-item dependencies.

- Excellent for sequential recommendation tasks (for example, predicting the next movie a user will watch).
- **Example**: Used in e-commerce and streaming platforms such as Amazon and Netflix.

Graph Neural Networks for Recommendations

It uses graph-based user-item relationships for enhanced performance.

One of the most powerful techniques behind these smart recommendations is Graph Neural Networks (GNNs)! This is the latest technology powering Amazon recommendations.

Why? Because user-item interactions naturally form a graph! Think of users as nodes, items as nodes, and their interactions (likes, purchases, clicks) as edges connecting them. GNNs allow recommendation systems to make smarter, deeper connections between users and items beyond direct interactions.

Pinterest used Pinsage (a GNN) for web-scale recommendations.

Architecture

Graph Representation

- Users and items are nodes in a bipartite graph.
- An edge represents an interaction—if you watched a movie, there is a link!
- Extra information such as user preferences or item categories? They can be features in the graph!

Message Passing = Learning Smarter Embeddings

- Each node learns from its neighbors (users learn from items they are engaged with, and vice versa).
- Multi-hop aggregation captures indirect connections—just like how your friend's favorite movie might also be relevant to you!

Popular GNN Techniques for Recommendations

- **Graph Convolutional Network (GCN-CF)**: Learns from direct and indirect connections in a graph.
- **Graph Attention Networks (GAT)**: Uses attention mechanisms to focus on the most relevant neighbors.

Graph Neural Networks are used for three types of predictions:

- **Node-level prediction:** These involve analyzing individual customers, products, or sellers. Applications include predicting customer churn, categorizing products into appropriate categories, detecting fake reviews, and identifying high-value customers for personalized marketing.

In the example below, Yash uses mobile and desktop from Hyderabad and purchases using a credit card. It is observed that another user, Saket, who logged in from Hyderabad, is using a different mobile and accessing the same credit card. Saket can be identified as a potentially malicious user.

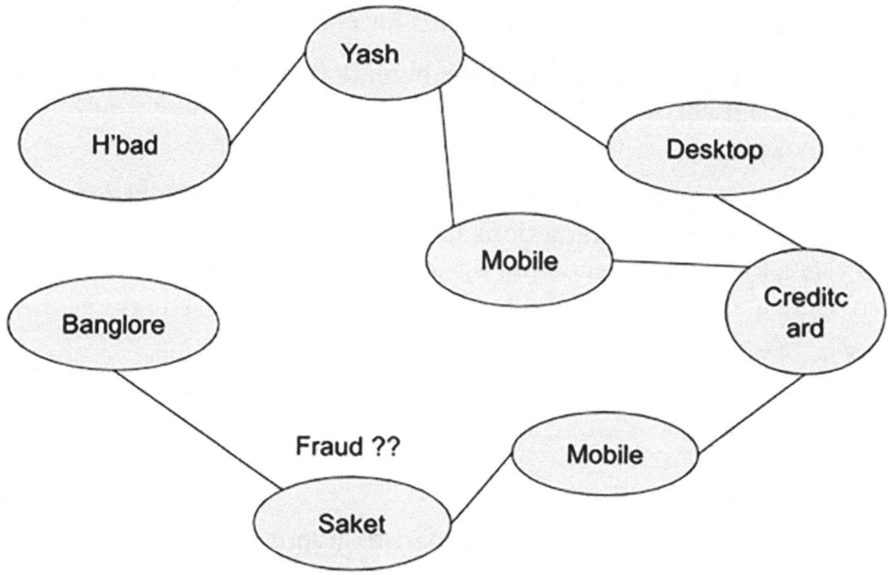

Figure 7.8: *Node-level prediction*

- **Edge-level prediction:** These focus on relationships between entities in an e-commerce platform. Examples include predicting whether a customer will purchase a recommended product (link prediction), estimating the likelihood of a user returning to a seller (repeat purchase probability), or detecting fraudulent transactions between buyers and sellers.

  In the example below, Jatin bought a laptop and external memory, rated them 5*. Teja bought the same laptop and rated 5*. Teja also bought a webcam and only rated 4*. Now, if Jatin buys the webcam, what would be his rating? The item would be recommended to him after predicting the rating.

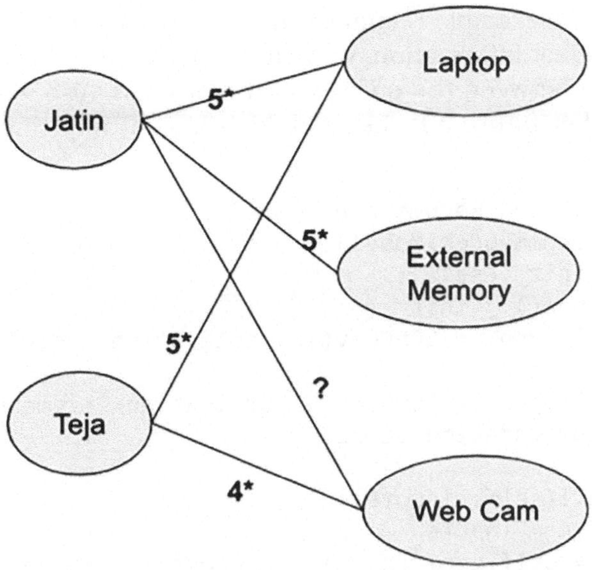

Figure 7.9: *Edge-level prediction*

- **Graph-level prediction**: This technique looks at the entire e-commerce network to derive insights. Examples include analyzing shopping behavior trends across a marketplace, detecting anomalies in seller-buyer interactions, or predicting the success of a new product based on historical patterns in the platform. In the example below, nodes represent the product categories and edges represent the weights of their transitions. For example, people transition between Beauty and Fashion categories a lot. By analyzing the patterns, we will be able to predict future product category trends.

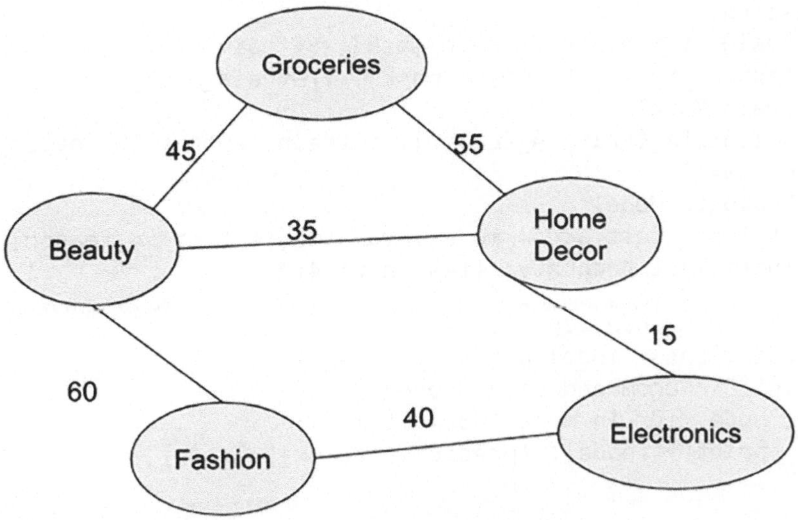

Figure 7.10: *Graph-level prediction*

These are some of the example recommendation systems based on GNNs. Based on the user query, product information, we can predict the product types. We can find the semantic match between the query and the product. Also, based on the past ad clicks, we can predict future ads. Let us take a look at implementing the GNN for sample users and items.

```
#Define GCN-Based Recommender Model
class GCNRecommender(Model):
    def __init__(self):
        super().__init__()
        self.gcn1 = GCNConv(16, activation="relu")  # First Graph
Convolution Layer
        self.gcn2 = GCNConv(1, activation="sigmoid")  # Output
Layer (Recommendation Score)

    def call(self, inputs):
        X, A = inputs
        H = self.gcn1([X, A])  # First GCN Layer
        H = self.gcn2([H, A])  # Output GCN Layer
        return H

#Train the Model
model = GCNRecommender()
model.compile(optimizer="adam", loss="binary_crossentropy",
metrics=["accuracy"])
# Convert adjacency matrix to Tensor
A_tensor = tf.convert_to_tensor(A.todense(), dtype=tf.float32)
# Train/Test Split
train_mask = np.random.rand(num_nodes) < 0.8  # 80% training, 20%
testing
X_train, Y_train = X[train_mask], Y[train_mask]
X_test, Y_test = X[~train_mask], Y[~train_mask]
# Train Model
model.fit([X_train, A_tensor], Y_train, epochs=50, batch_size=1,
verbose=1)
# Evaluate Model
test_loss, test_acc = model.evaluate([X_test, A_tensor], Y_test)
print(f"Test Accuracy: {test_acc:.4f}")

#Get Recommendation Scores
predictions = model.predict([X, A_tensor])
print("\nRecommendation Scores:")
for node, idx in node_index.items():
    print(f"{node}: {predictions[idx][0]:.4f}")
```

Defining the GCN Model

Uses Graph Convolutional Networks (GCNs) to learn node representations.

- Two-layer GCN architecture:
  - The first layer captures local user-item interactions.
  - The second layer predicts recommendation scores (sigmoid output).

Training and Evaluating the Model

- Uses binary cross-entropy loss for classification.
- Splits the data into train/test subsets.
- After training, the model assigns recommendation scores to items.

Measuring the Success of a Recommendation System

To truly understand how well a recommendation system performs, we need to measure its effectiveness through various metrics. A great recommendation system does not just suggest items–it drives user engagement, improves business outcomes, and adapts to real-world challenges.

Accuracy-Based Metrics

Precision measures how many of the recommended items are truly relevant to the user. A high precision score means fewer irrelevant suggestions. However, relevance is subjective–how do we define the "*right*" recommendations? The answer lies in business objectives.

For instance, if the goal is to maximize order value, the system should prioritize recommendations that encourage higher spending, rather than just showing cheaper alternatives.

Recall

Recall assesses how many of the relevant products were successfully recommended. Imagine a user is interested in gaming laptops, but your system only suggests headphones–this would result in a low recall score.

Measuring recall in recommendation systems is challenging because of the vast product catalog. With millions of items, manually identifying what was "*missed*" in the recommendations is not practical.

F1-Score: Finding the Right Balance

The **F1-score** balances precision and recall, ensuring the system is not overly optimized for one at the expense of the other. A holistic evaluation often involves an end-to-end approach, rather than just analyzing algorithmic output. This may require manual assessments with clear evaluation guidelines.

At the algorithmic level, we can measure recommendations against ground truth data, but this approach has limitations. Static catalog evaluations do not consider dynamic factors such as user interactions, which play a crucial role in real-world recommendation systems.

Precision@K

- Measures the fraction of recommended items in the top K that are relevant.
- **Formula**: k-precision = (number of relevant items in top K) / K.
- **Example**: If a user clicks or purchases 3 out of the top 6 recommended products, the k-precision@6 is 50%.

The choice of **K** is critical—too high, and less relevant items may dilute precision; too low, and the system may miss valuable suggestions. The optimal K depends on factors such as user scrolling behavior and the number of visible products on the first page.

Normalized Discounted Cumulative Gain (NDCG): Prioritizing Highly Relevant Items

NDCG ensures that the most relevant products appear at the top of the recommendation list. It uses a logarithmic discounting approach, giving higher weight to top-ranked items while penalizing those that appear lower. This aligns with real-world user behavior—most users engage more with items positioned at the top.

By leveraging these metrics, we can fine-tune recommendation engines to deliver personalized, engaging, and business-aligned suggestions—ultimately driving better user experiences and higher conversions.

Suppose the top-3 recommended items for a user have relevance scores: **[3, 2, 0]**:

- If the system ranks them as [3, 0, 2] → high relevance is present but poorly ordered.
- If the system ranks them as [3, 2, 0] → perfect order, NDCG = 1.
- If the system ranks [0, 2, 3] → relevant items are at the bottom, so NDCG is much lower.

This shows NDCG punishes bad ranking order even if relevant items exist.

The main advantage of NDCG over simpler metrics (Precision, Recall, MAP) is that it captures both the graded relevance of items and their rank position, reflecting user satisfaction more realistically.

Engagement Metrics

A recommendation engine is not just about accuracy–it is about engagement. You can recommend the right product, but if no one clicks, it is useless. Engagement metrics help measure this:

- **Click-Through Rate (CTR)**: The percentage of recommended items that users actually click on. A low CTR may indicate irrelevant or poorly positioned recommendations.
- **Conversion Rate**: Tracks the percentage of recommendations that lead to purchases. Even if users click, are they buying?
- **Session Duration**: Measures how much time users spend interacting with recommended content. Longer engagement often indicates better recommendations.

Business KPIs

Beyond engagement, recommendations should align with business objectives. Here is how to measure their impact:

- **Revenue Impact**: Tracks how much additional revenue is generated by recommendation-driven purchases.
- **Average Order Value (AOV)**: Measures how much a user spends per order when influenced by recommendations.
- **Customer Lifetime Value (CLV)**: Estimates the long-term value of a customer who interacts with personalized recommendations.

Cold Start Problem Handling

One of the biggest challenges in recommendation systems is the cold start problem–how do you recommend items when you have little to no user data?

New Users: Personalization without History

The challenge is that a new user has no interaction data, making it difficult to recommend items. Some solutions:

- **Rule-based systems**: Use predefined rules such as recommending popular or trending items, or using business logic (for example, "*new users get introductory offers*").

- **Content-based filtering**: Ask users for explicit preferences at sign-up (for example, movie genres, favorite artists) and recommend based on those.
- **Demographic-based models**: Cluster users by shared characteristics (for example, location, and so on) and provide recommendations based on what similar users liked.
- **Implicit feedback**: Use early interactions (for example, clicks, time spent on items) to quickly adjust recommendations.

New Items: No Interaction Data Available

A brand-new item will not have a user interaction history, so traditional collaborative filtering fails. Solutions:

- **Metadata-based recommendations**: Recommend based on item attributes (for example, recommend a new sci-fi book to users who liked other sci-fi books).
- **Hybrid models**: Combine collaborative filtering with metadata-based recommendations, so even if there is no interaction data, recommendations can be made based on content similarity.
- **Exploiting early interactions**: Track clicks, wishlists, or even how often an item appears in search results to gauge interest.

Cross-Domain Knowledge Transfer

When data is limited, one way to improve recommendations is by leveraging data from similar platforms or domains:

- **Transfer learning**: If a user has interactions in one domain (for example, movies), use that to predict preferences in another domain (for example, TV shows).
- **Shared embeddings**: Use multi-domain embeddings where items from different platforms are mapped to a common feature space, allowing knowledge transfer.

Promotions: Leveraging Engagement Data

Promoted items can be introduced into recommendations, but their effectiveness must be validated:

- **Controlled exposure**: Show promoted items to a limited audience and track engagement metrics such as click-through rates.

- **Reinforcement learning**: Algorithms such as the Multi-Armed Bandit can dynamically adjust the exposure of promoted items based on user response.
- **Blending with organic recommendations**: Instead of forcefully pushing promoted content, mix it with personalized recommendations to maintain user trust.

Diversity, Ethical AI, and Explainability

- Diversity exposes users to a broader range of content, products, or perspectives rather than reinforcing past behaviors. A diverse recommendation system enhances user experience, promotes discovery, and supports business goals by preventing stagnation.
- Ethical AI ensures fairness, minimizes biases, and prevents unintended consequences such as discrimination or misinformation. Ethical considerations help build trust and align recommendations with user well-being rather than just maximizing engagement.
- Explainability makes recommendations transparent, allowing users and businesses to understand why certain items are suggested. This fosters trust, improves system debugging, and enables regulatory compliance in sensitive domains such as finance and healthcare.

Diversity and Serendipity: Avoiding Filter Bubbles

Many recommendation systems tend to reinforce a user's existing preferences, leading to a filter bubble where they only see content similar to what they have previously engaged with. This can reduce engagement over time and limit exposure to new items.

The first question is, what do we mean by diversity?

Diversity means how different the recommended items are to the user. The diversity should exist between two different users as well. Two users should get two different results for the same item.

How do we ensure that the same user sees different results every time?

Novelty means how different the recommended items shown to the user are from the previously seen results.

What is serendipity?

Serendipity means the unexpectedness, surprise, and usefulness as perceived by the user.

The good and popular recommendations will usually be diverse, novel, and unexpected at the same time. In some categories, this is more important than others. For example, in grocery websites, users might show onions, potatoes with every purchase because they are common and repetitive purchases. For Myntra/ Nykaa websites, which are meant for fashion clothing, novelty and diversity become more important.

Let us compare these attributes across different known e-commerce platforms.

Platform	Serendipity (Unexpected but useful)	Diversity (Varied content)	Novelty (Previously unseen items)
Amazon ·	*Low*: Focuses on frequently bought items rather than surprising suggestions.	*Moderate*: Shows different brands/ categories, but mostly related to previous purchases.	*High*: Highlights newly launched products in recommendations.
Netflix ·	*Moderate*: Occasionally suggests lesser-known content outside the user's usual preferences.	*Low*: Tends to recommend content similar to what the user watches.	*Moderate*: Recommends new shows but also re-promotes older content.
Spotify ·	*High*: Discover Weekly & Release Radar introduce unexpected yet relevant music.	*High*: Provides genre-based diversity in playlists.	*High*: Highlights new releases and emerging artists.
YouTube ·	*Low*: Prioritizes familiar content, reinforcing filter bubbles.	*Moderate*: Shows some variety but mostly within the user's niche.	*Moderate*: Pushes trending videos and new channels occasionally.

Table 7.5: *Comparison of different e-commerce platforms*

Solutions:

- **Diversity-aware recommendations**: Ensure recommendations include a variety of styles, brands, colors, genres, or categories.

  Example: Instead of only recommending black sneakers to a user who bought black sneakers, suggest a mix of white, blue, or patterned options.

- **Pairwise similarity metrics**: Calculate the similarity between recommended items and introduce diversity constraints to avoid recommending only near-identical products.

  Example: If an item is too similar (based on cosine similarity, Jaccard index, and so on), replace it with a more diverse option.

- **Serendipity-focused algorithms**: Inject novel recommendations that are outside the user's typical choices but still relevant.

  Example: A music recommender could suggest a niche indie song that shares features with a user's favorite mainstream artist.

Fairness and Bias Mitigation: Addressing Algorithmic Bias

Recommendation systems can unintentionally reinforce social biases, such as gender, ethnicity, or socioeconomic bias.

Example: A job recommendation engine may show high-paying roles more often to men than to women due to historical biases in training data.

Some real-world examples:

- **Amazon:** Prioritizes Amazon-branded products in search results.
- **Alibaba**: New sellers struggle to compete due to popularity bias, limiting their reach.

Let us take a look at different types of biases in e-commerce systems.

Bias Type	Description	Example in E-commerce
Popularity Bias	Recommends already popular items more frequently, reducing diversity.	Amazon recommends only bestsellers, ignoring new products.
Exposure Bias	Items that appear in top positions get more visibility.	The first few products on Flipkart's homepage get most clicks.
Demographic Bias	Recommendations favor specific user groups.	Women see more fashion ads, while men see more electronics.
Data Bias	Historical purchase data is skewed towards specific behaviors.	Past high sales of certain brands lead to biased future recommendations.
Selection Bias	Only users with prior interactions influence recommendations.	New users get poor recommendations (cold start problem).
Seller Bias	Large sellers dominate due to algorithmic preferences.	Amazon promotes its own products over third-party sellers.

***Table 7.6**: Explanation of different biases in recommendation systems*

But how do we solve them?

- **Debiasing training data**: Ensure datasets are representative of different user groups.
- **Fairness-aware algorithms**: Adjust ranking models to prevent over-representing or under-representing certain categories.

  Example: In job recommendations, ensure equal visibility for male and female candidates.

- **Counterfactual fairness modeling**: Test if a recommendation would be different if a user's demographic attributes were changed.

Let us take a look at all the algorithms in detail.

Method	How It Works	Example
Re-ranking Algorithms	Adjusts ranking to promote fairness.	Ensures small businesses appear alongside top brands.
Fairness-aware Loss Functions	Modifies optimization objectives to reduce bias.	Penalizes models if they overly favor one group.
Graph Neural Networks (GNNs)	Captures user-item relationships in a fairer way.	Reduces popularity bias by exploring multi-hop connections.
Diversity Constraints	Forces recommendations to include less popular items.	Ensures new product discovery (for example, niche books on Amazon).
Counterfactual Analysis	Checks if different user groups receive similar recommendations.	Ensures fairness in gender-based product suggestions.

Table 7.7: *Comparison of different bias-removal algorithms*

Explainability: Making Recommendation Logic Transparent

Problem: Many AI-based recommendation systems work as **black boxes**, making it hard for users and businesses to understand why certain items are recommended. This can reduce trust.

Solutions:

- **Feature attribution methods**: Use techniques such as SHAP (Shapley Additive Explanations) or LIME (Local Interpretable Model-Agnostic Explanations) to explain which factors influenced a recommendation.

  Example: If a movie is recommended, the system could highlight:

  - *"Because you liked Inception (similar genre)"*
  - *"Highly rated by users with similar preferences"*

We can use the following code snippet to explain the model output:

```
explainer = shap.Explainer(model, X_train)
shap_values = explainer(X_test)
# Visualize SHAP values for a single recommendation (first test
sample)
shap.initjs()
shap.force_plot(explainer.expected_value, shap_values[0].values,
X_test.iloc[0])
```

The output graph visualization looks like this:

Figure 7.11: *SHAP plot for feature importance*

This can be converted into an explanation such as "*You got this recommendation because you are 30 years old, prefer Sci-Fi, and rated similar movies highly.*"

- **Base value = 4.107** (global average prediction).
- Contributions (from SHAP values):
  - **`User_Age = 30`** → pushed prediction up slightly.
  - **`Movie_Popularity = 55, Movie_Genre = 2`** → pushed prediction down.
- Final predicted score = **3.63**.
- **Interactive explanations**: Allow users to refine recommendations by selecting preferences.

  Example: "*Would you like more thriller recommendations?*"
- **Business-facing explanations**: Help content creators and sellers understand why their items are or are not being recommended.

Privacy and Security Considerations: Handling User Data Responsibly

Problem: Recommender systems process large amounts of personal data, making them a target for misuse or regulatory violations (for example, GDPR, CCPA).

Solutions:

Technique	**How It Works**	**Example Use Case**
Differential Privacy	Adds controlled noise to data, ensuring individual users cannot be identified.	Apple's iOS collects usage stats without revealing individual user behavior.
Federated Learning	Trains models **locally on user devices**, sending only model updates, not raw data.	Google Keyboard (Gboard) improves word predictions while protecting personal text data.

Anonymization and Encryption	Removes or encrypts personally identifiable data before processing.	Netflix anonymizes user data before running collaborative filtering algorithms.
User Control and Consent	Allows users to opt out of data collection or specify what data they share.	Amazon lets users manage ad preferences and personalized recommendations.
Regulatory Compliance (GDPR, CCPA)	Ensures data collection is transparent and aligns with legal frameworks.	Facebook must provide users with access to their collected data under GDPR.

Table 7.8: *Privacy solutions for recommendation systems*

- Google uses Federated Learning (FL) to train models locally on users' devices. Instead of collecting raw text, each device trains a model and only sends model updates (gradients), not actual data, to Google's servers.
- Netflix released anonymized user rating data for the Netflix Prize competition (to improve movie recommendations). However, researchers de-anonymized users by cross-referencing IMDb ratings.
- Netflix now applies Differential Privacy (DP), adding random noise to individual user data while preserving overall recommendation accuracy.

Experimentation, User Feedback, and Data Drifts

Recommendations are a dynamic feature, and hence, experimentation and user feedback are essential.

- **Running A/B tests**: Comparing different recommendation algorithms by showing different suggestions to different user groups. We will measure key metrics such as CTR, conversion rates, user session time, and revenue growth in experimental settings. We have discussed key business metrics such as Average Order Value earlier. We need to measure them during the experimentation period.
- **Using adaptive techniques**: The Multi-Armed Bandit (MAB) problem is a reinforcement learning approach where a system dynamically explores and exploits different options to maximize rewards. Multi-armed bandits help optimize recommendations dynamically by prioritizing what works best in real time.
- **User Feedback Loop**: Integrating explicit and implicit feedback for system improvement. User likes/dislikes can be monitored regularly. After the dislikes reach a certain threshold, we can use the recommendations to re-train the models. The user could be giving verbal feedback. We can run sentiment

analysis and pattern recognition on user feedback to identify key missing patterns and re-train the model.

- **Handling Data Drifts**: Addressing changes in user behavior and market trends using online learning models. For example, if we are building a clothing recommendation system, the fashion choices change per region and per season. The model needs to be retrained depending on user behavior shifts and seasonality/trends.

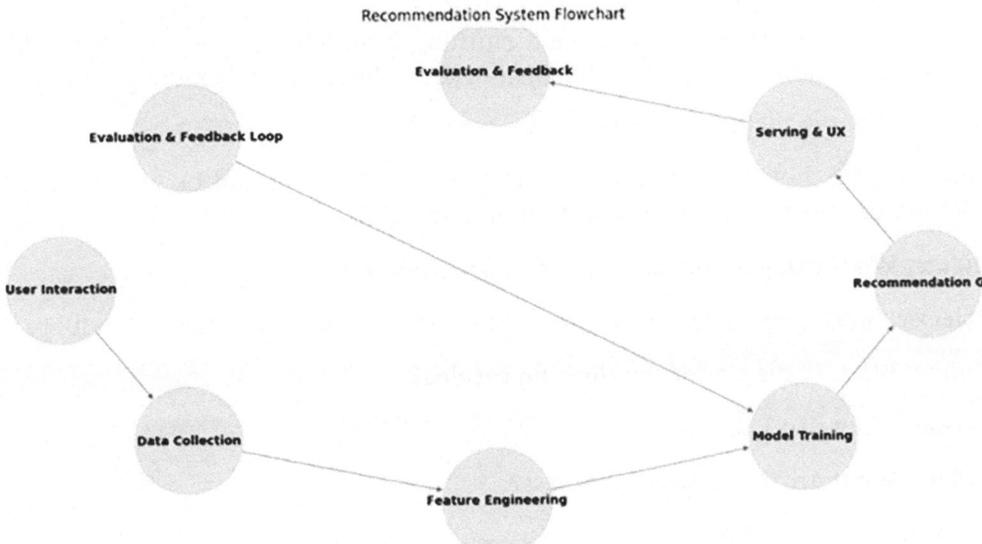

***Figure 7.12**: Flow chart of recommendation system*

Mock Interview Example

Scenario-Based Question: ***"Design a complementary recommendation system for a new e-commerce clothing brand that has a huge catalog of data."***

It is a cold-start problem. Ask all the questions as an interviewee to get clarity on the business scenario.

This time, we will make the Candidate proactive by asking the right set of questions upfront.

Business Requirements

Candidate: What is the goal of the recommendation system?

Interviewer:

- To add more visibility to all categories of products.

- To increase the average order value of the customer.

Candidate: What is the end-user scenario? Are there similar or complementary recommendations?

Interviewer:

- Similar recommendations will improve visibility of the basic categories. We are looking to increase order value also. We are looking for complementary recommendations.
- When a user tries to purchase a clothing item (shirts/dresses), they will be recommended with pants, shoes/sneakers/flats, Socks, Handbags, and Belts.

Candidate: What is the latency expected by the end user?

Interviewer: The moment the user selects the item, they should be able to see the complementary products will have minimum latency (assume <500 ms).

Candidate: What category of clothing items are present?

Interviewer: Shirts, Pants, Dresses, Shoes, Sneakers, Flats, Socks, Belts, Handbags

Candidate: What is the size of the clothing catalog?

Interviewer: Close to 1 TerraByte

Candidate: What are the targeted markets?

Interviewer: All en-* markets

Candidate: How many recommendations are shown per product?

Interviewer: 4 complimentary products are shown for each product.

Candidate: What should be the algorithm for complementary suggestions? Because we do not have purchase patterns?

Interviewer: Choose the right products as per fashion recommendations.

Now that the candidate have understood the problem statement, he will explain the end-to-end design like the following:

Data Collection and Labelling

- Ensure all clothing items are correctly categorized by type, gender, size, and style.
- Standardize attributes such as color, material, and pattern to maintain consistency.
- Remove duplicate or incorrect entries from the catalog to avoid misleading recommendations.

Knowledge Graph Construction

1. Create a **Fashion Knowledge Graph** that defines complementary relationships between clothing items.
2. Use **fashion experts** to annotate a sampled catalog dataset for initial relationships.
3. Cover diverse styles, colors, and country-specific fashion trends (for example, regional preferences in en-* markets).
4. Define category-based restrictions (for example, handbags are recommended only for female clothing).
5. Ensure periodic updates to reflect changing fashion trends and new catalog entries.

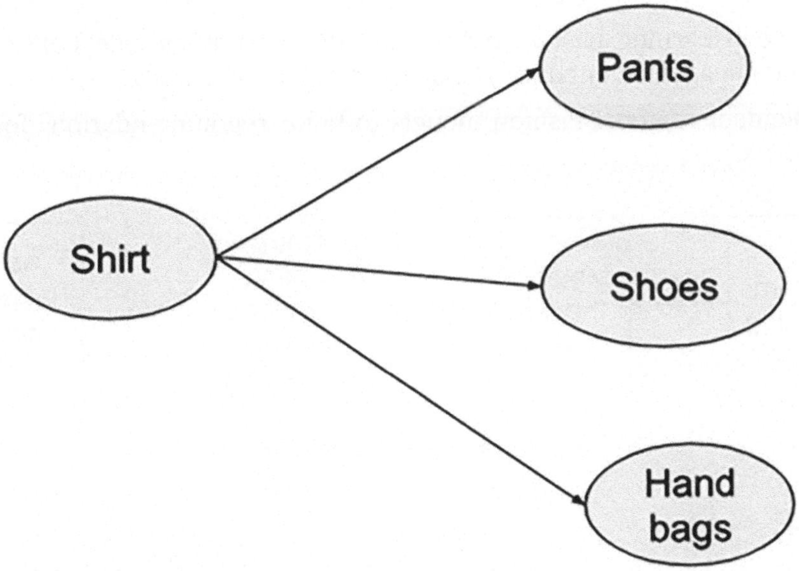

Figure 7.13: *Fashion knowledge graph*

Algorithm

Since this is a **cold-start problem** (no prior user data), recommendations are purely knowledge-driven.

Matching Process:

1. If the selected clothing item exists in the fashion knowledge graph, retrieve its predefined complementary items.

2. If the item is not in the graph, use a nearest-neighbor algorithm to find the most similar clothing item from the graph and retrieve its complementary products.
3. Map the retrieved items to currently available products in the catalog.
4. Introduce diversity and serendipity by selecting visually similar but distinct items rather, than exact matches.

Ensuring Attribute Consistency:

- **Gender Matching:** Female clothing items should only be paired with female-specific complementary items.
- **Size Matching:** An XL-sized shirt should be matched with XL-sized pants.
- **Category Constraints:** Handbags are recommended only with female clothing.

Improving Matching Accuracy:

- Use deep learning-based clothing embeddings (for example, CNNs trained on fashion images) to enhance the nearest-neighbor search.
- Implement regional fashion models to tailor recommendations for different markets.

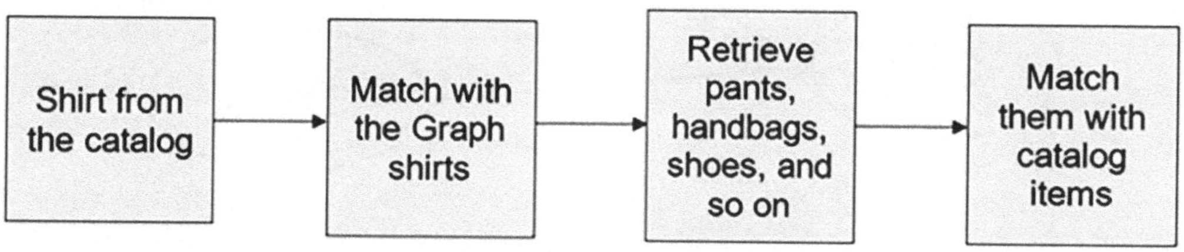

Figure 7.14: *Matching algorithm*

Ranking

Initially, ranking is static, but as user interaction data is collected, dynamic personalization is introduced.

Static Ranking Factors:

- **Image and Catalog Quality**: High-quality images and well-documented catalog entries rank higher.
- **Similarity to Catalog Item**: Items closer in style, color, and fit receive priority.
- **Brand Reputation**: Well-known brands are ranked higher. Make sure that it is balanced with fairness, such that small brands also get exposure.

- **Price Sensitivity**: Recommendations should align with the price range of the original selection.
- **Item Popularity**: Clothing with high engagement (clicks, purchases, reviews) is prioritized.

Dynamic Personalization (Post User Data Collection):

- **User Browsing and Purchase History**: Personalize rankings based on past interactions.
- **A/B Testing for Model Refinement**: Optimize ranking algorithms based on real-time user feedback.

Ranking Algorithm Choices:

- **Gradient Boosting (for example, XGBoost, LightGBM)**: Captures non-linear relationships for better ranking.
- **DeepFM (Deep Factorization Machines)**: Combines deep learning and supervised machine learning for personalized ranking.

Deployment and Architecture:

1. A user selects an item from the catalog.
2. The system identifies complementary products based on the **Fashion Knowledge Graph** and nearest neighbor search.
3. Recommendations are ranked and displayed to the user within **<500 ms latency**.

Offline Processing (Precomputed Features and Matching)

Performed in batch mode to reduce real-time computational costs.

Feature Extraction and Storage:

- Compute feature embeddings for all clothing items and store them in a Vector Database.
- Create an embedding table that maps original clothing items to their complementary products using the **Fashion Knowledge Graph**.

Precomputed Matching (Optimization for Latency and Cost):

- Compute the complementary product embeddings for all the products in the catalog using the product embeddings and fashion knowledge graph computed above.

- Perform pre-ranking based on nearness, popularity, and product quality.
- Store precomputed product mappings (product ID → recommended products) in an online lookup table.

Advantages:

- **Optimized for cost:** Reduces the need for expensive real-time computations.
- **Scalability:** Works well for large catalogs without affecting response time.

Limitations:

- Recommendations may not adapt instantly to new arrivals or changing user preferences.

User flow: When the user selects the item from the catalog, select the recommended product IDs from the online lookup table and show them.

Online Processing (Real-Time Inference and Ranking)

Executed in real time for dynamic recommendations.

Steps:

1. **Feature Computation:** Compute the feature vector for the selected product using a deep learning model in production.
2. **Nearest-Neighbor Search:** Query the Vector Database to retrieve the closest match from the Fashion Knowledge Graph.
3. **Complementary Product Retrieval:**
    - Fetch precomputed complementary product embeddings from the graph.
    - Match them against available products in the catalog.
4. **Quality and Consistency Checks:** Ensure correct gender, size, and category mapping.
5. **Real-Time Ranking:** Rank products based on similarity, popularity, and quality.
6. **Display Recommendations:** Show ranked recommendations to the end user within **<500 ms latency**.

Advantages:

- **Personalized and Adaptive:** Can dynamically adjust based on real-time inventory changes.
- **Better coverage:** Includes new arrivals that may not have been available during offline processing.

Limitations:

- **Computationally expensive:** Requires high-performance hardware for real-time inference.
- **Increased latency risk:** Due to online database queries and deep learning model execution.

Choosing the Right Approach

Aspect	Offline Processing	Online Processing
Latency	Fast (Precomputed)	Higher (Real-time)
Computational Cost	Lower	Higher (Requires GPU/TPU)
Adaptability to New Data	Slower (Batch Updates)	Adaptive (Live updates)
Scalability for Large Catalogs	Efficient for large datasets	Expensive for large-scale inference
Personalization	Limited	Real-time personalized ranking

***Table 7.9**: Online versus offline processing*

Hybrid Approach (Balanced Trade-Off)

A **hybrid approach** can help balance cost, latency, and accuracy:

1. Use offline precomputed recommendations for most users.
2. Run online inference selectively for:
    - New arrivals in the catalog.
    - Trending or personalized recommendations.

To optimize deployment without sacrificing accuracy, consider:

Efficient Model Serving:

- Use ONNX/TensorRT to optimize deep learning models for fast inference.
- Deploy models using serverless inference (for example, AWS Lambda, Google Cloud Run) for cost-effective scaling.

Database and Storage Optimization:

- Use Approximate Nearest Neighbor (ANN) algorithms (for example, FAISS, ScaNN) to speed up similarity searches.
- Cache precomputed recommendations for frequent queries to reduce database load.

Incremental Updates for Catalog Changes:

- Instead of full batch updates, refresh embeddings only for new arrivals.
- Use an event-driven pipeline (Kafka, AWS Kinesis) to trigger updates dynamically.

Evaluation Metrics

- We will use NDCG and precision for measuring the quality of the complementary item in the catalog.
- Use A/B testing and compare the user engagement metrics, such as CTR and session rate. We also need to measure business metrics such as AOV and revenue.
- Post the experimentation, we would get real user feedback in terms of engagement metrics, which can be used to measure the success of this feature.
- We also need to measure the diversity of each category of product. It should not be recommending the same product every day to the same user.
- We also need to ensure that it is gender-aware and provides gender-specific recommendations.

Conclusion

In this chapter, we explored the foundations, methodologies, and challenges of building scalable recommendation systems that power real-world applications across e-commerce, streaming platforms, and personalized services.

We began by examining real-life use cases, understanding how recommendation engines drive engagement and business growth. We then delved into content-based filtering and collaborative filtering, the two classical approaches that form the backbone of many recommendation systems. Moving beyond traditional methods, we explored two-tower networks and Graph Neural Networks (GNNs), which leverage deep learning and graph-based representations to improve recommendation accuracy and scalability.

However, effectiveness alone is not enough. A well-rounded recommendation system must also prioritize diversity, ethical AI, and explainability—ensuring fairness, mitigating biases, and providing transparency in how recommendations are generated. Evaluation plays a crucial role, and we covered key metrics such as precision, recall, F1-score, MAP@K, and NDCG, which help assess system performance.

Finally, we reinforced these concepts through a mock interview, preparing you to articulate your knowledge and problem-solving skills in real-world scenarios.

Building a scalable recommendation system requires a balance of technical depth, responsible AI practices, and business alignment. By combining these elements, we can create recommendation engines that not only enhance user experience but also drive meaningful impact at scale.

In the next chapter, we will learn about another important system design aspect - building image classification systems for edge devices. We will learn how to design optimal models for low-performance systems.

Multiple Choice Questions

1. Which of the following best describes a collaborative filtering recommendation system?
   a. Recommends items based on past user interactions and attributes.
   b. Uses item properties such as genre, brand, or price to recommend items.
   c. Suggests items by identifying similar users or behaviors.
   d. Randomly selects items to test user engagement.
2. What is the purpose of A/B testing in recommendation systems?
   a. To compare two recommendation strategies and measure user engagement.
   b. To collect labeled data for training supervised learning models.
   c. To ensure data privacy compliance in recommendations.
   d. To generate random recommendations for new users.
3. What is the primary goal of explainability in recommendation systems?
   a. To increase user engagement by generating random recommendations.
   b. To provide users with transparency about why a recommendation was made.
   c. To improve model performance without considering ethical concerns.
   d. To replace collaborative filtering with content-based filtering.
4. What is a sign that data drift has occurred in a recommendation system?
   a. Increased model accuracy over time.
   b. The recommendation model starts showing irrelevant suggestions.

   c. The system consistently recommends only high-rated products.
   d. The number of user interactions remains constant.

5. How can bias be reduced in recommendation systems?
   a. By training models only on historical user preferences.
   b. By ensuring diverse datasets and applying fairness constraints.
   c. By recommending only the most popular items.
   d. By excluding user feedback from model training.

Answers

1. c
2. a
3. b
4. b
5. b

References

- https://www.amazon.science/the-history-of-amazons-recommendation-algorithm
- https://www.music-tomorrow.com/blog/how-spotify-recommendation-system-works-a-complete-guide-2022
- https://medium.com/pinterest-engineering/pinsage-a-new-graph-convolutional-neural-network-for-web-scale-recommender-systems-88795a107f48#:~:text=To%20achieve%20our%20goal%20of%20generating%20high-quality%20embeddings%2C,of%20nodes%20and%20tens%20of%20billions%20of%20edges.
- https://link.springer.com/article/10.1007/s00607-018-0687-5
- https://www.alibabacloud.com/blog/getting-started-with-recommendation-system_597740

CHAPTER 8
Building Image Classification Models for Edge Devices

Introduction

Imagine a farmer walking through his vast fields at sunrise, examining crops for signs of pest infestations. In the past, this process relied heavily on experience and manual inspection–time-consuming, error-prone, and often too late to prevent significant losses. Now, picture the same farmer holding a smartphone, capturing an image of a leaf, and instantly receiving an AI-powered diagnosis, identifying the pest and suggesting the best course of action.

This is the power of image classification on edge devices–AI models deployed on mobile phones, drones, and IoT sensors that provide real-time intelligence without relying on cloud connectivity. From precision agriculture and autonomous vehicles to security cameras and medical diagnostics, edge AI is transforming industries by enabling fast, localized decision making in environments where speed and privacy matter.

But deploying machine learning models on edge devices comes with challenges. Unlike cloud-based systems with vast computational power, edge devices have limited resources, battery constraints, and real-time performance requirements. How do we design AI models that are not just accurate but also lightweight and efficient? How do we optimize them for smartphones, Raspberry Pi, or even low-power microcontrollers?

In this chapter, we will unravel the journey of building image classification models tailored for edge devices–from understanding the basics of image classification to optimizing deep learning architectures and deploying them in real-world applications. Along the way, we will explore the evolution of model architectures, the trade-offs between latency and accuracy, and strategies for deploying AI on mobile and embedded systems.

By the end of this chapter, you will be well-equipped with the knowledge to build AI models that do not just stay in research labs but are ready for deployment—whether it is identifying pests in a field, detecting defects in manufacturing, or enabling smart surveillance in cities. The future of AI is not just in the cloud—it is in our pocket, on our wrist, and embedded in the world around us. Let us dive in.

Figure 8.1: *Farmer inspecting the crops for pests and diseases*

Structure

In this chapter, we will cover the following topics:

- Introduction to Image Classification
- Image Annotation Techniques
- Architecture Evolution
- Real-Life Case Studies
- Tradeoffs between Latency and Performance
- Model Optimization and Deployment Strategies for Edge/Mobile Devices
- Mock Interview

Introduction to Image Classification

Image classification is a fundamental task in computer vision where an algorithm assigns a label or category to an input image. It enables machines to recognize patterns and understand visual data, much like humans do. From face recognition in smartphones to medical diagnosis from X-ray scans, image classification is widely used across industries.

At its core, image classification involves feature extraction and classification:

- **Feature Extraction:** Identifying key characteristics in an image, such as edges, textures, and shapes.
- **Classification:** Assigning the image to a predefined category based on extracted features.

We often hear the related terms image classification, image recognition, image localization, and image segmentation. Let us understand the similarities and differences between all of these.

Feature	Image Recognition	Image Classification	Image Localization	Image Segmentation
Definition	Identifies objects or patterns in an image but does not specify location.	Assigns a single label to an entire image.	Identifies and locates objects by drawing bounding boxes.	Assigns a label to each pixel to segment different objects.
Output	Object label(s) (for example, "*Dog, Tree*").	A single label for the whole image (for example, "*Dog*").	A bounding box with an object label (for example, "*Dog*" + box around it).	A pixel-wise segmentation mask highlighting object regions.
Example Use Case	Recognizing whether an image contains a person, animal, or object.	Classifying an image as "*cat*" or "*dog*".	Identifying and marking where a cat is in the image.	Identifying and segmenting different objects (for example, separating cats from the background).
Complexity	Low to moderate.	Low.	Moderate to high.	High (requires pixel-level accuracy).
Common Models	ResNet, VGG, Inception.	MobileNet, EfficientNet.	YOLO, Faster R-CNN.	U-Net, Mask R-CNN, DeepLab.
Edge Device Suitability	Moderate – Can be optimized.	High – Suitable for lightweight models.	Moderate – Needs more computation.	Low – Computationally expensive for real-time edge inference.

***Table 8.1:** Comparison between image problems*

We will focus on only image classification in this chapter.

Types of Image Classification

- **Binary Classification**
  - The simplest form, where an image is classified into one of two categories.
  - **Example**: Identifying whether an X-ray scan is normal or abnormal.
- **Multi-Class Classification**
  - Each image is assigned to one of multiple predefined classes.
  - **Example**: Recognizing different types of animal species from images.
- **Multi-Label Classification**
  - An image can belong to multiple categories simultaneously.
  - **Example**: Multi-label classification means an image might be tagged with several labels—for example, a photo tagged with '*beach*', '*sunset*', and '*people*'.
- **Hierarchical Classification**
  - Classification follows a structured hierarchy, where categories are grouped into broader parent classes.
  - **Example**: Classifying a vehicle as a car → sedan/SUV/truck.

Designing an Image Classification Model

Let us understand the process of designing an image classification model.

1. **Data Collection and Preprocessing**
   - Gathering diverse datasets to ensure model generalization.
   - Data augmentation (flipping, rotation, brightness changes) to increase robustness.
   - Normalization and resizing to standardize input images.
2. **Model Selection**
   - Traditional Machine Learning (for example, SVM, Random Forest) for simple tasks with handcrafted features.
   - Deep Learning with CNNs (Convolutional Neural Networks) and Vision Transformers for complex visual patterns.
   - We will need to specifically focus on lightweight models that can be deployed in low-resource devices.

3. **Training the Model**
   - Defining the architecture (layers, activation functions, optimizers).
   - Loss function selection (cross-entropy for classification tasks).
   - Using transfer learning to leverage pre-trained models such as ResNet and MobileNet.
   - Apply model optimization techniques to reduce the model size.
4. **Performance Evaluation**
   - Accuracy, Precision, Recall, and F1-score for balanced datasets.
   - Confusion Matrix to analyze misclassifications.
   - Performance evaluation also involves meeting latency and throughput constraints.

***Figure 8.2:** Fun interpretation of fitting large models on small devices* **credits**: *supermeme.ai*

Image Annotation Techniques

In the world of machine learning, data is the foundation on which models are built. For image classification tasks, having a well-labeled dataset is crucial for training robust models. Image annotation is the process of labeling images with appropriate class labels so that machine learning models can learn to classify new, unseen images accurately.

In this chapter, we will explore different image annotation techniques specific to image classification, the challenges associated with annotation, commonly used annotation tools, and strategies to reduce annotation time without compromising accuracy.

Challenges in Image Annotation

Annotating images/assigning labels for classification comes with several challenges:

Time and Cost Constraints

- Manually labeling large datasets is resource-intensive and expensive.
- Annotation requires domain experts for specialized tasks (for example, medical images, satellite imagery).

Subjectivity and Labeling Errors

- Different annotators may classify the same image differently.
- Misclassifications lead to poor model performance.

Data Imbalance: Some classes may have significantly fewer labeled images than others, leading to biased models.

Scalability Issues: Large datasets require efficient annotation workflows to maintain quality at scale.

Annotation Tools for Image Classification

To simplify and accelerate the annotation process, several tools are available:

Open-Source Tools

- **LabelImg**: Common for bounding boxes, but can be adapted for classification.
- **VGG Image Annotator (VIA)**: Simple and web-based for classification tasks.
- **Computer Vision Annotation Tool (CVAT)**: Supports classification and can handle large datasets.

Cloud-Based Tools

- **Labelbox**: Provides AI-assisted labeling workflows.
- **Supervisely**: Collaborative annotation platform with automation.
- **Amazon SageMaker Ground Truth**: Scalable annotation with active learning integration.
- **Azure ML Data Labeling**: Integrated into the Azure ecosystem, supports AI-assisted classification annotation, and offers automation to speed up labeling.

AI-Assisted and Automated Annotation Tools

- **Google's AutoML Vision**: Automatically labels datasets using a pre-trained AI model.
- **Roboflow**: Automates annotation and preprocessing for ML pipelines.

- **Scale AI**: Enterprise-level annotation with AI assistance.

Techniques to Reduce Annotation Time

To make the annotation process more efficient, several strategies can be used:

Active Learning

- Instead of labeling the entire dataset, a model selects the most uncertain samples for human review.
- Reduces manual effort, while improving model accuracy.

Pre-Annotating with AI

- Uses a pre-trained model to generate initial labels, which humans then verify.
- Speeds up the process, while maintaining accuracy.

Crowdsourcing with Consensus Labels

- Multiple annotators label the same image, and the final label is based on majority voting.
- Ensures higher accuracy while distributing workload.

Data Augmentation

- Generates additional labeled images using transformations such as rotation, flipping, and scaling.
- Reduces the need for excessive manual labeling.

Transfer Learning and Synthetic Data

- Uses models trained on similar datasets to reduce manual annotation.
- Synthetic data generation techniques (GANs, domain adaptation, and so on) help fill gaps in datasets.

Architecture Evolution

Image classification has undergone a remarkable transformation over the years, evolving from traditional machine learning approaches to modern deep learning architectures like **CNNs** and **Vision Transformers (ViTs)**. Initially, models relied on manually crafted features and classical algorithms, but deep learning revolutionized the field by enabling automated feature extraction and hierarchical learning. More recently, ViTs have introduced self-attention mechanisms that outperform CNNs in specific applications. This chapter explores the evolution of these architectures, highlighting key milestones and their significance for efficient image classification.

Classical Machine Learning for Image Classification

Before the rise of deep learning, image classification relied on extracting handcrafted features and using conventional machine learning models to classify images. The process typically involved:

Feature Extraction Techniques

Handcrafted feature extraction played a critical role in classical image classification. Some of the widely used techniques include:

- **SIFT (Scale-Invariant Feature Transform):** Detects and describes local image features that remain robust under scaling and rotation.
- **HOG (Histogram of Oriented Gradients):** Captures edge direction patterns, commonly used for object detection and recognition.
- **LBP (Local Binary Patterns):** Efficient texture descriptor used in face recognition and other classification tasks.

Traditional Machine Learning Models

Once features were extracted, they were fed into classical machine learning models such as:

- **Support Vector Machines (SVMs):** Find the optimal hyperplane for separating different image categories.
- **Decision Trees and Random Forests:** Tree-based models that classify images based on learned hierarchical rules.
- **k-Nearest Neighbors (k-NN):** A distance-based algorithm that classifies an image based on its similarity to labeled examples.

While these methods achieved reasonable performance on small datasets, they suffered from:

- **Manual feature engineering:** Requires domain expertise and extensive experimentation.
- **Scalability issues:** Struggles with high-dimensional data and large-scale image classification.
- **Limited adaptability:** Features may not generalize well across diverse image categories.

Convolutional Neural Networks (CNNs)

Deep learning, particularly CNNs, marked a paradigm shift in image classification by eliminating the need for manual feature extraction. CNNs automatically learn hierarchical patterns directly from raw image pixels, leading to improved accuracy and generalization.

CNNs Overview

CNNs are a type of deep learning model designed mainly for image and video data. They automatically learn spatial features (such as edges, textures, shapes) from raw input, making them powerful for computer vision tasks.

Core Components of CNN Architecture

1. **Input Layer:** Accepts raw data (for example, an image with pixel values).
2. **Convolutional Layer:** Applies filters (kernels) that slide over the image to detect local patterns (edges, corners, colors). Each filter learns a specific feature.
3. **Activation Function (ReLU):** Adds non-linearity, allowing CNNs to learn complex patterns.
4. **Pooling Layer:** Reduces spatial size (for example, max pooling takes the maximum value in a region). This lowers computation and helps the model focus on important features.
5. **Fully Connected Layer (Dense):** Flattens extracted features into a vector and combines them to make predictions.
6. **Output Layer:** Produces the final result, such as class probabilities in image classification.

Key Characteristics

- **Local connectivity:** Each filter looks at small parts of the input at a time.
- **Weight sharing:** The same filter is applied across the image, reducing parameters.
- **Hierarchy of features:** Early layers learn edges, middle layers detect shapes, and deeper layers capture objects.

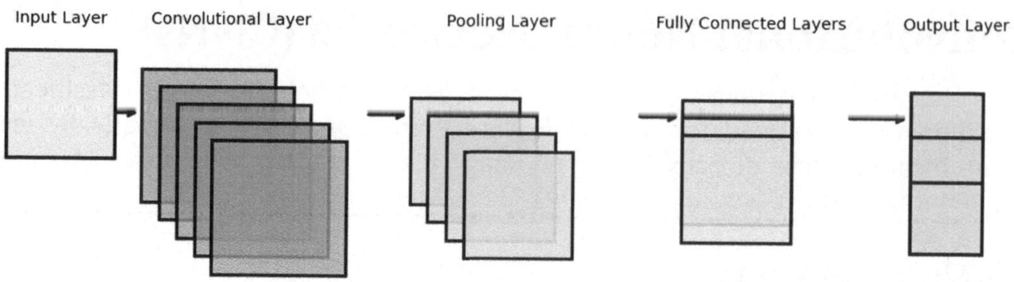

Figure 8.3: *Pictorial representation of CNNs*

Key CNN Architectures

Several landmark CNN architectures have shaped the evolution of image classification:

- **LeNet-5 (1998):** One of the earliest CNNs, designed for handwritten digit recognition.
- **AlexNet (2012):** Popularized deep CNNs by winning the ImageNet challenge, introducing ReLU activations and dropouts.
- **VGGNet (2014):** Deepened CNNs to 16-19 layers, improving hierarchical feature learning.
- **ResNet (2015):** Introduced residual connections or skip connections to combat vanishing gradients (gradients becoming vanished after some layers in the CNN), enabling the training of extremely deep networks.

Lightweight CNN Variants for Edge Deployment

As CNNs grew in complexity, the need for efficient architectures became evident, especially for deployment on resource-constrained edge devices. Some notable lightweight CNNs include:

- **MobileNet:** A lightweight model designed for mobile devices. It uses a special type of convolution (called *depthwise separable convolution*) to make calculations faster while still keeping good accuracy.
- **EfficientNet:** Focuses on getting the best performance with the least resources. It scales the model's width, depth, and resolution in a balanced way so it runs efficiently without losing accuracy.
- **SqueezeNet:** A very small model that reduces the number of parameters by using many **1×1 filters** (tiny convolutions). Despite being small, it still performs well on image recognition tasks.

Vision Transformers (ViTs) and Modern Approaches

While CNNs have dominated image classification for years, Vision Transformers (ViTs) have recently emerged as a powerful alternative. Unlike CNNs, which rely on convolutional operations, ViTs use self-attention mechanisms to capture global dependencies within an image.

Introduction to Vision Transformers

ViTs treat an image as a sequence of non-overlapping patches, similar to tokens in natural language processing. Key innovations include:

- **Self-Attention Mechanism:** Enables the model to focus on important regions dynamically.
- **Positional Encoding:** Retains spatial relationships between patches.
- **Multi-Head Attention:** Enhances feature extraction across multiple perspectives.

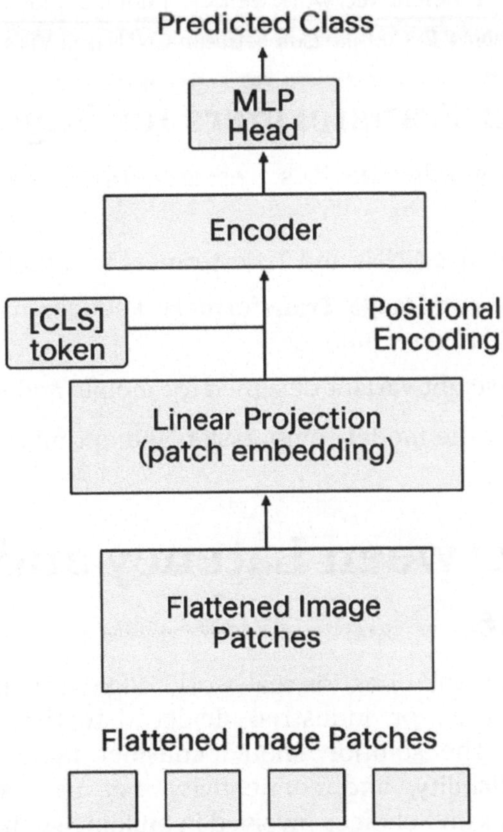

***Figure 8.4:** ViT architecture*

CNN versus Vision Transformers for Image Classification:

Feature	CNNs	Vision Transformers (ViTs)
Feature Extraction	Uses convolutional kernels to detect spatial patterns	Uses self-attention to model global dependencies
Computational Cost	Efficient for small/ medium datasets	Requires large-scale pre-training for best results
Data Efficiency	Works well with limited data	Needs more data to generalize effectively
Training Complexity	Easier to train on smaller datasets	Computationally expensive, requires transformers' optimization techniques
Interpretability	Feature maps provide visual insights	Attention maps highlight relevant image regions
Suitability for Edge Devices	Optimized versions (for example, MobileNet, EfficientNet) work well	Requires lightweight variants (for example, MobileViT, TinyViT) for edge deployment

Table 8.2: *Comparison between CNNs and ViTs*

Efficient Vision Transformers for Edge Deployment

To make ViTs viable for edge devices, researchers have introduced optimized variants:

- **MobileViT:** Combines CNNs and Transformers for efficiency and accuracy.
- **DeiT (Data-Efficient Image Transformer):** Reduces data dependency using knowledge distillation techniques.
- **TinyViT:** A lightweight variant designed for mobile and edge applications.

We will learn more about the model compression and optimization techniques in the subsequent sections.

Tradeoffs between Latency and Performance

When designing AI-based solutions for real-world edge scenarios such as precision farming, medical diagnosis, or industrial defect detection, choosing the right architecture is crucial. The solution should consider factors such as data size, processing latency, reliability, and connectivity. Let us walk through the key architectural components and choices involved in building such intelligent systems.

Data Processing Architectures: Edge versus Cloud versus Hybrid

Edge-Only Processing (On-Device AI Inference)

- In this architecture, all AI models run directly on edge devices, such as smartphones, embedded sensors, or industrial IoT devices.
- Used when real-time decisions are critical, and network connectivity is unreliable or expensive.
- **Example**: A pest classification model on a farmer's mobile device that works without the internet.
- **Pros**:
  - Ultra-low latency.
  - Privacy-preserving (data does not leave the device).
  - Cost-effective when the network cost is high.
- **Cons**:
  - Limited computational power.
  - Complex models may need to be heavily compressed or quantized.

Cloud-Only Processing (Centralized AI Inference)

- Here, edge devices act as data collectors, sending raw data (such as images, audio, sensor streams) to cloud services where AI models process it.
- Used when high accuracy is required, large models are necessary, and stable connectivity is available.
- **Example**: High-resolution medical imaging sent to the cloud for diagnosis.
- **Pros**:
  - Leverage large, powerful AI models.
  - Easier to update and manage AI models centrally.
- **Cons**:
  - High latency.
  - Dependence on network connectivity.
  - Possible privacy concerns (sending sensitive data).

Hybrid Edge-Cloud Architecture

- **Combination**: Light AI inference on-device for real-time feedback, with detailed analysis offloaded to the cloud.

- Used when some decisions are time-sensitive, while others can be analyzed in-depth later.
- **Example**: A sensor detecting abnormal machine vibration locally and sending aggregated trends to the cloud for deeper failure prediction.
- **Pros**:
  - Balance between performance and complexity.
  - Reduced bandwidth usage (send only summaries).
  - Scalable and flexible.
- **Cons:**
  - Requires careful design to split tasks.

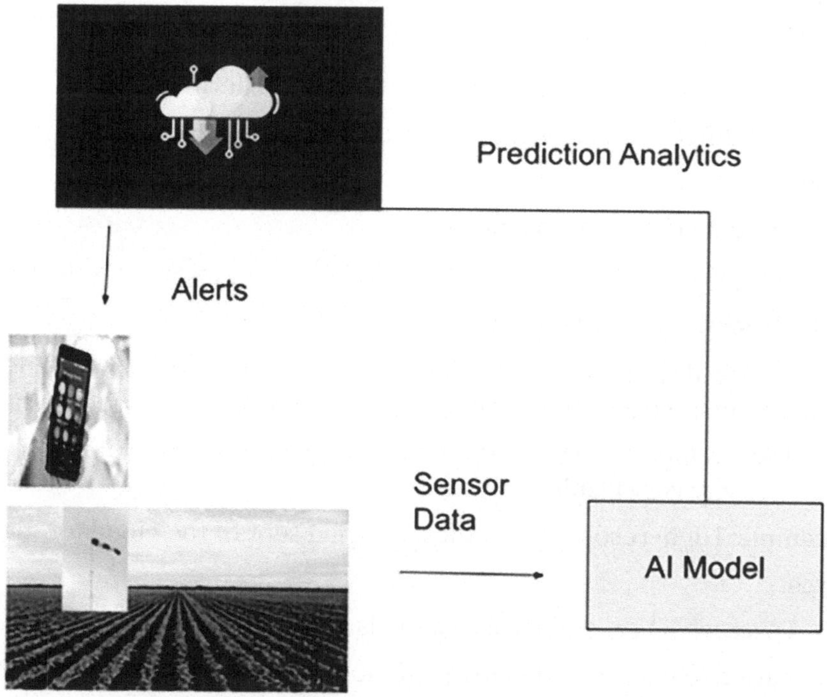

Figure 8.5: *Sample architecture for precision farming*

Architectural Components: End-to-End Flow

Now, let us understand the end-to-end flow for designing a system for supporting a system such as precision farming.

Data Collection Layer (Sensors and Cameras)

- Sensors (for temperature, humidity, soil pH in farming, medical sensors, industrial vibration).

- Cameras (for pest images, defect detection, medical scans).

Edge AI Layer (On-Device AI Processing)

- Lightweight AI models (for example, MobileNet, EfficientNet, TinyML models).
- **Devices**: Smartphones, Raspberry Pi, Nvidia Jetson, Google Coral.
- **Tasks**:
    - Immediate classification (for example, pest identification, early anomaly alerts).
    - Preprocessing: filtering noise, data compression.

Edge Gateway / Edge Server Layer

- **Role**: Aggregates data from multiple sensors, runs moderate AI models, and manages secure communication.
- **Example**: Local farm edge gateway, factory floor hub.
- Supports batching, anomaly detection, and alert generation.

Cloud and Data Center Layer

- For heavy AI models (for example, transformer-based models, federated learning aggregation).
- Long-term data storage, analytics, and dashboard visualization.
- Scalable cloud platforms: AWS, Azure, Google Cloud, and Private Clouds.
- **Functions**:
    - Historical data analysis.
    - Training/updating AI models.
    - Federated model aggregation.

Depending on the application and requirement, we choose the right layers. However, we have three popular deployment strategies - Edge-only, Cloud-only, and Hybrid. Let us compare the three strategies.

Criteria	**Edge-Only**	**Cloud-Only**	**Hybrid**
Latency	Very Low	High	Low for real-time, high for deep analytics
Model Complexity	Simple (compressed)	Complex (large)	Mix
Connectivity Dependence	Low	High	Medium
Privacy	High	Low	Medium

Scalability	Limited to device capabilities	Highly scalable	Scalable with trade-offs

***Table 8.3:** Comparison between different deployments*

Model Optimization and Deployment Strategies

The key aspect in edge/mobile deployment is to reduce the model size. It requires processing the data and model under a highly resource-constrained environment. Let us understand different techniques for data optimization and model optimization in edge/mobile devices.

Data Optimization Techniques

Before digging into model optimization techniques, let us also understand some techniques to load the big data in an efficient way. Let us understand some techniques in data loading.

- **Lazy loading**: Load only necessary data rather than loading everything into memory. For example, Python generators and PyTorch IterableDataset.
- **Memory mapping**: Directly map files into memory, allowing efficient access, for example, **`numpy.memap`**, **`torch.from_file()`**
- **Efficient DataFormats:** Using TFRecord, RecordIO, HDF5, Parquet.
- **Batch loading and Prefixing**: Batch load data into memory and prepare the next batches asynchronously.
- **Prefetch:** Load the next batch while the current batch is being processed. Using the PyTorch **`DataLoader`** class.

Let us take a look at the implementation details to understand more:

```
from torch.utils.data import DataLoader
# Custom Dataset
class MyDataset(torch.utils.data.Dataset):
    def __init__(self, file_paths):
        self.file_paths = file_paths
    def __getitem__(self, index):
        data = load_and_process(self.file_paths[index])  # Lazy
load per item
        return data

    def __len__(self):
        return len(self.file_paths)
# Optimized DataLoader
```

```
train_loader = DataLoader(
    MyDataset(list_of_large_files),
    batch_size=64,
    shuffle=True,
    num_workers=8,      # Parallel data loading
    pin_memory=True,   # Faster transfer to GPU
    prefetch_factor=2  # Prefetch batches to avoid bottlenecks
)
```

Quantization

Imagine trying to carry a big suitcase full of books on a small scooter. That is what deploying a large AI model on a tiny device such as a smartphone or a Raspberry Pi feels like. Quantization is the magic that makes the suitcase lighter – by compressing those books without losing too much information.

Quantization as a concept emerged from signal processing and hardware design, but AI researchers adopted it when they saw deep learning models growing too big for embedded devices. Early adopters included engineers at Google (TensorFlow Lite) and Facebook (PyTorch Mobile) who wanted to run AI on phones.

Who uses it

- Google Pixel's on-device AI for image enhancement.
- Smart cameras that recognize faces without sending data to the cloud.
- Voice assistants, such as Alexa and Siri, run on constrained chips.

Functionality

Instead of storing numbers (weights and activations) in 32-bit floating-point, quantization uses 8-bit integers. Imagine replacing "3.1415926535" with just "3"–you lose some precision, but the world keeps spinning. Modern techniques even let models simulate quantization during training, so they learn to deal with lower precision (Quantization Aware Training).

Sample Code Snippet:

```
# TensorFlow Lite Quantization
import tensorflow as tf
converter = tf.lite.TFLiteConverter.from_saved_model('model_dir')
converter.optimizations = [tf.lite.Optimize.DEFAULT]
tflite_model = converter.convert()

# PyTorch Dynamic Quantization
import torch
import torch.quantization
model = torch.load('model.pth')
```

```
quantized_model = torch.quantization.quantize_dynamic(
    model, {torch.nn.Linear}, dtype=torch.qint8
)
```

Mixed Precision

Imagine using a fine brush for detailed painting and a big brush for broad strokes. Mixed precision uses different numerical precision (for example, FP16, INT8) depending on where it is needed.

Who uses it:

- NVIDIA Tensor Cores.
- Modern AI on smartphones with GPU/TPU/Neural Engines.

Functionality

- Critical parts of the model use high precision, while others can safely use lower precision – balancing speed and accuracy.
- Heavy computations (matrix multiplications) are done in FP16.
- Critical operations (such as loss calculation, batch norm) stay in FP32 to avoid numerical instability.
- Automatically handled via frameworks such as AMP (Automatic Mixed Precision) in PyTorch or TensorFlow.

Pytorch uses **GradScaler** as a smart adjuster that scales up the loss and gradients during backpropagation so that they do not vanish when represented in FP16. Once scaled, gradients are computed normally, and before updating model weights, GradScaler rescales them back down, ensuring that the update is correct.

PyTorch code snippet using GradeScaler:

```
from torch.cuda.amp import autocast, GradScaler
scaler = GradScaler()
# Training loop
for data, target in trainloader:
    optimizer.zero_grad()
    with autocast():
        output = model(data)
        loss = criterion(output, target)
    scaler.scale(loss).backward()
    scaler.step(optimizer)
    scaler.update()
In Tensorflow, its achieved using global policy.
from tensorflow.keras import mixed_precision
mixed_precision.set_global_policy('mixed_float16')
```

Pruning

Think of a tree in your backyard growing wildly. Some branches are weak or unnecessary. Pruning means trimming these branches so that the tree grows stronger and healthier – and that is exactly what AI scientists do to models!

Pruning was first proposed back in 1990 in the seminal paper "*Optimal Brain Damage*" by Yann LeCun, one of the godfathers of deep learning. The idea: remove weights that do not contribute much to the output.

Who uses it:

- Manufacturers using edge AI to detect defects – their models need to be fast.
- Healthcare devices that scan for anomalies in real-time but cannot afford bulky models.
- Autonomous drones where every millisecond counts.

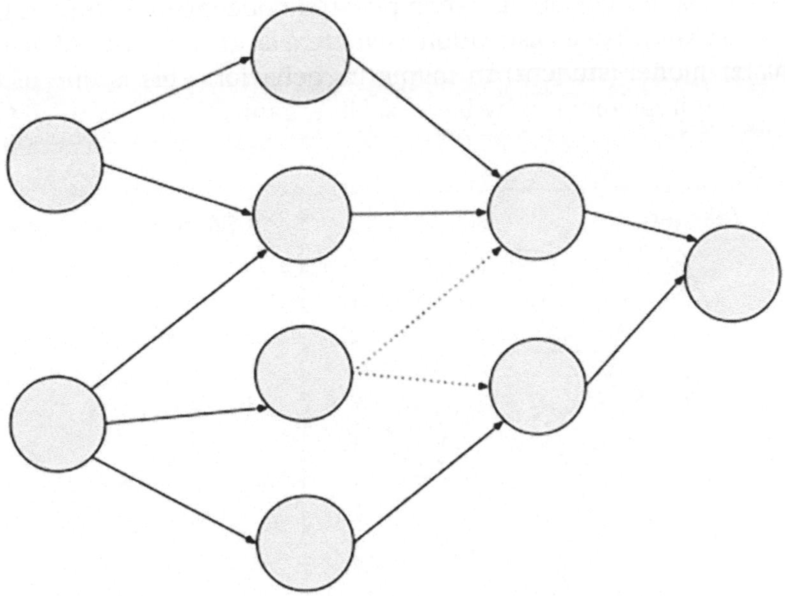

Figure 8.6: *Pictorial representation of pruning*

Functionality

AI models are like giant spider webs with thousands of connections. Pruning snips away the weak links–those weights close to zero–shrinking the model. What is left is a leaner, faster network that retains almost the same brainpower.

Let us understand the implementation using a small code snippet. We will loop in every convolutional layer and apply pruning.

Let us apply L1 unstructured pruning to the weight tensor of each Conv2D layer.

L1 refers to using the L1 norm (absolute value) to decide which weights are less important. Smaller absolute values are seen as less important.

Unstructured means it does not care where the weights are located – it will just zero out 30% of the smallest-magnitude weights across the whole filter matrix.

`amount=0.3` means prune (remove) 30% of the weights in that layer!

```
import torch.nn.utils.prune as prune
for module in model.modules():
    if isinstance(module, nn.Conv2d):
        prune.l1_unstructured(module, name='weight', amount=0.3)
torch.save(model.state_dict(), 'prune_model.pth')
```

Knowledge Distillation

Imagine a wise teacher explaining a complicated concept to a student using simple language. That is Knowledge Distillation – where a large, powerful AI model (teacher) trains a smaller model (student) to mimic its behavior. This is one of the popular techniques, being implemented by large-scale organizations. Let us dig deeper into this one.

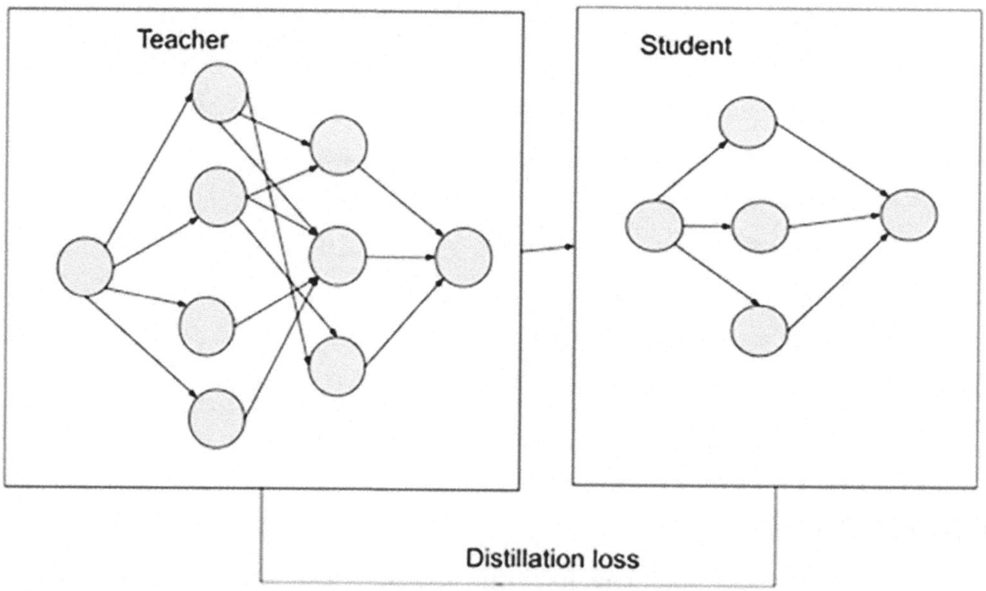

Figure 8.7: *Knowledge distillation*

How it started: Introduced by Geoffrey Hinton and his team in 2015, they realized that instead of training a small model from scratch, it could learn from the softened outputs of a big model – a concept similar to how students learn from a teacher's summarized notes.

Who uses it:

- Google Assistant uses distilled models for speech recognition.
- Mobile NLP apps such as Grammarly for grammar checking on phones.
- Surveillance systems for real-time face and object recognition.

How it works: **DistillBERT**, for instance, is a student model of BERT.

- DistilBERT is approximately 40% smaller than BERT.
- But it retains approximately 97% of the BERT's capabilities.

The teacher model gives "*hints*" – not just right or wrong answers but probabilities over all classes. The student watches, learns patterns, and becomes an expert in its own right – but much smaller and faster. One of the popular techniques in knowledge distillation is response-based knowledge distillation. In this technique, the focus is on matching the output responses (predictions) of the teacher model and the student model.

```
Simple implementation of knowledge Distillation:
import torch
import torch.nn.functional as F
import torch.optim as optim
# ------------------------------
# 1. Define the Teacher and Student Models
# ------------------------------
# Assume 'model' is a pre-trained teacher model
teacher = model  # Pre-trained, larger, more accurate model
(teacher)
# Define a smaller student model that we want to train using
distillation
student = SimpleCNN().to(device)  # Student model learns from
teacher
student.train()  # Set student model to training mode
# ------------------------------
# 2. Define the Distillation Loss Function
# ------------------------------
def distillation_loss(student_output, teacher_output,
temperature=3):
    """
    Computes Kullback-Leibler divergence between the softened
outputs
    of teacher and student models.

    Args:
```

```
        student_output: Output logits from student model
        teacher_output: Output logits from teacher model
        temperature: Controls softness of probabilities; higher
temp => softer

    Returns:
        KL divergence loss (scalar)
    """
    # Softmax with temperature smoothens the outputs
    # Soft targets from teacher vs student predictions
    teacher_probs = F.softmax(teacher_output / temperature,
dim=1)
    student_log_probs = F.log_softmax(student_output / temperature,
dim=1)

    # KL divergence measures how close student is to teacher's
distribution
    return F.kl_div(student_log_probs, teacher_probs, reduction
='batchmean') * (temperature ** 2)
# ------------------------------
# 3. Setup Optimizer
# ------------------------------
# Adam optimizer for updating student model parameters
optimizer = optim.Adam(student.parameters(), lr=0.001)
# ------------------------------
# 4. Distillation Training Loop
# ------------------------------
# Number of epochs for training
num_epochs = 3
# Loop over epochs
for epoch in range(num_epochs):
    running_loss = 0.0  # To track total loss
    for batch_idx, (inputs, _) in enumerate(trainloader):
  # Iterate over data loader
        inputs = inputs.to(device)  # Move input data to device
(GPU/CPU)
        # ------------------------------
        # Forward pass
        # ------------------------------
        optimizer.zero_grad()  # Clear gradients for this step
        with torch.no_grad():  # No gradient calculation for
teacher (frozen model)
            teacher_output = teacher(inputs)  # Teacher's
predictions (soft targets)
        student_output = student(inputs)  # Student's predictions
        # ------------------------------
```

```
            # Compute distillation loss
            # --------------------------------
            loss = distillation_loss(student_output, teacher_output,
    temperature=3)
            # --------------------------------
            # Backpropagation and Optimization
            # --------------------------------
            loss.backward()  # Backpropagate the loss
            optimizer.step()  # Update student model's weights
            running_loss += loss.item()  # Accumulate batch loss
        # --------------------------------
        # Logging for Each Epoch
        # --------------------------------
        print(f"Epoch [{epoch+1}/{num_epochs}], Loss: {running_loss/
    len(trainloader):.4f}")
    print("\nDistillation training completed! Student model trained
    to mimic teacher.")
```

This code demonstrates **knowledge distillation**, where a smaller **student model** is trained to mimic a larger pre-trained **teacher model**. Instead of using hard class labels, the student learns from the teacher's **soft probability outputs**, generated using a temperature-scaled softmax. The training loop computes the **distillation loss** (KL divergence between teacher and student distributions), backpropagates it, and updates the student's weights using the Adam optimizer. Over multiple epochs, the student gradually learns to approximate the teacher's behavior while being lighter and faster.

Lightweight Model Design

Sometimes, instead of shrinking a big AI model, why not design a small one from the start? That is the philosophy behind MobileNet, EfficientNet-Lite, Tiny-YOLO – architectures built to be efficient.

The Google Brain team introduced **MobileNet** in 2017 as a response to growing demands for on-device AI, using depth-wise separable convolutions–a way to split big math operations into smaller, and faster ones.

Who uses it:

- Plantix app for pest recognition in fields.
- Smartphones for real-time photo processing.
- IoT security cameras to identify faces or track motion.

How it works: Instead of doing massive matrix multiplications, these models break computations into tiny pieces, focusing only on the essentials. It splits the convolutions into depth-wise convolutions and pointwise convolutions, which reduce the convolution operations and thus require less *Compute*.

MobileNet can be loaded as the pretrained model.

Hardware Aware Training

Imagine buying a suit. Off-the-rack may not fit perfectly, but tailoring makes it just right. Hardware-aware training means training AI models specifically optimized for the target hardware, such as a Jetson Nano, Edge TPU, or Apple Neural Engine.

Hardware-aware training is a strategy in machine learning where models are trained with awareness of the hardware constraints they will eventually run on.

Instead of training a model purely for accuracy and then struggling to deploy it, hardware-aware training incorporates deployment constraints (such as memory, compute, latency, or power usage) directly into the training process.

Who uses it:

- NVIDIA Jetson-powered robots.
- Coral EdgeTPU-based sensors for smart farms.
- iPhones running CoreML models for on-device AI.

How it works: AI models are trained or compiled knowing their final home. If a model is destined for Jetson Nano, it avoids layers or operations that Jetson cannot run fast. Specialized compilers such as TensorRT or Edge TPU compiler do this magic.

Hardware-aware training ensures that the model's **architecture, precision, and export format** are chosen to match the deployment hardware (for example, Jetson Nano with TensorRT or Coral TPU with Edge TPU compiler), so the final system runs efficiently in the real world. Saving or exporting the model in ONNX format is useful for hardware such as NVIDIA Jetson (via TensorRT) or mobile.

If a model is going to run on **Jetson Nano**:

1. During training → use hardware-friendly ops (avoid exotic layers).
2. During export → save as ONNX.
3. During deployment → use TensorRT to optimize for Jetson (layer fusion, quantization, GPU kernels).
4. Result → smaller, faster, hardware-efficient model with little accuracy loss.

Sparsity and Low-Rank Approximations

Think of a library – most shelves are full, but some are half-empty. If a model has many zero weights (sparse), it does not need to store or compute them. Also, some large weight matrices can be approximated with smaller ones (low-rank).

Large models (Transformers, CNNs) have huge weight matrices in fully connected layers and attention layers. Many of these matrices are redundant – they can be well-approximated by lower-rank representations.

Who uses it:

- Speech recognition on embedded devices.
- Object detection in tiny drones.

How it works: Any matrix with rank k can be decomposed into a long and a short matrix. The purpose of this algorithm is to find the best approximation of the two matrices.

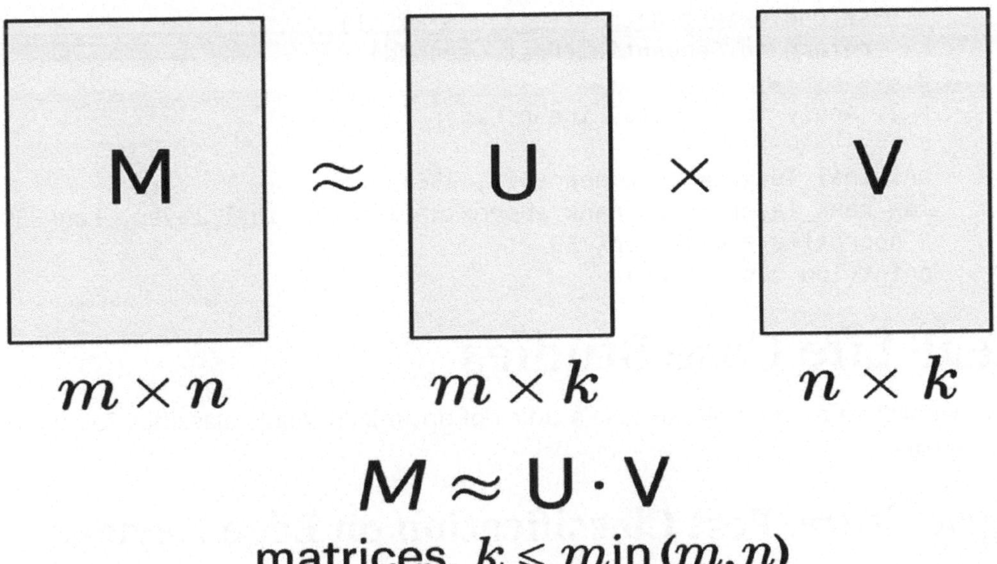

Figure 8.8: *Low rank approximation algorithm*

By recognizing and exploiting redundancy in the model, we can make AI lighter and faster, without a significant loss in intelligence.

This is a classical low-rank factorization method. Modern variation to the algorithm LoRA (Low-Rank Adaptation is discussed in LLM Finetuning techniques in *Chapter 4, Enhancing Systems through LLM Fine-tuning*).

Sample code snippet for implementing low-rank to an existing neural network:

```
import torch.nn as nn
# ---------------------------
# 1. Function for Low-Rank Approximation
# ---------------------------
def low_rank_approximation(layer, rank):
    """Decompose Linear layer using SVD and approximate with
low-rank"""
    W = layer.weight.data
    U, S, V = torch.svd(W)
    U_k = U[:, :rank]
    S_k = S[:rank]
    V_k = V[:, :rank]
    # Create approximated layers
    first = nn.Linear(V_k.shape[0], rank, bias=False)
    second = nn.Linear(rank, U_k.shape[0], bias=True)
    # Set weights
    first.weight.data = V_k.t()
    second.weight.data = (U_k * S_k).t()
    return nn.Sequential(first, second)
# ---------------------------
# 2. Apply to Example Linear Layer
# ---------------------------
original_layer = nn.Linear(512, 256)
low_rank_layer = low_rank_approximation(original_layer, rank=50)
# Approximate with rank 50
print(low_rank_layer)
```

Real-Life Case Studies

Now, we will study the real life case studies of optimized image classification usage in key sectors.

Agriculture: Pest Classification on Edge Devices

Imagine a farmer walking through their field early in the morning, only to notice leaves of their crops eaten away and strange insects crawling on them. Now, identifying the pest accurately is crucial–using the wrong pesticide could harm the crops or be completely ineffective. But this farmer does not need to wait for an agricultural expert to visit, which might take days. Instead, they pull out a smartphone, click a picture of the pest, and within seconds, an app such as Plantix analyzes the image and identifies the pest species. Not only that, it also provides actionable advice–what kind of pesticide to use, and how to apply it safely.

Behind this seamless experience lies a lightweight CNN model, such as MobileNet, running directly on the phone. To make this possible in rural areas with limited connectivity, the model is quantized and converted into **TensorFlow Lite** (TFLite), so it can work offline. However, it is not without challenges–imagine trying to capture a good image when pests are tiny, the lighting is poor, or when farmers grow crops that are not in the training dataset. These variations make building a robust AI system tough, but the reward–empowering farmers with instant, expert advice–is immense.

Agriculture: Precision Farming

Picture a farmer standing at the edge of a vast field, looking at the sky to predict whether it will rain or shine. But modern agriculture has moved beyond guesswork. With precision farming, farmers are equipped with sensors embedded in their farms–sensors that monitor soil moisture, pH levels, and even the micro-climate around the plants. These devices work together to analyze real-time data and give personalized advice: when to sow, how much fertilizer to use, and when to irrigate. While the models run offline, the data is collected periodically by connecting to the cloud.

Systems such as Microsoft's Farm Beats take this to another level by combining AI models with sensor data. A lightweight CNN, optimized to run on small, battery-powered devices, processes this data right in the field. Farmers receive updates on their smartphones without ever needing a reliable internet connection. The system helps make critical decisions that could mean the difference between a failed harvest and a bumper crop. Still, farmers in remote areas face challenges such as intermittent power, poor connectivity, and highly localized farming conditions that can vary significantly even within a few kilometers. Overcoming these constraints makes precision farming a game-changer for sustainable agriculture.

Remote Medical Diagnosis: Detecting Diabetic Retinopathy

In many rural and underdeveloped parts of the world, access to specialized healthcare is a luxury. Consider a patient in a small town in India, suffering from diabetes, but unaware that they are also at risk of diabetic retinopathy–a condition that could lead to blindness if left undiagnosed. Traditionally, they would need to travel miles to reach a city hospital for a retinal scan. But now, imagine a scenario where a mobile device with an attached camera takes a retinal image, and within seconds, an **EfficientNet** or MobileNet-based AI model analyzes it, and gives a diagnosis.

The magic here is that the model runs locally on the device–no need to upload sensitive data to the cloud, ensuring privacy. The system can instantly flag high-risk patients and recommend a visit to an ophthalmologist, potentially saving their vision. But deploying such a system requires extreme precision–there is no room for error in medical diagnosis. The AI model must be tiny yet accurate, a combination that challenges even the best engineers. But for patients and doctors alike, it becomes a life-changing tool.

Industrial Defect Detection and Predictive Maintenance

Step inside a massive manufacturing plant. Hundreds of products roll off conveyor belts every minute—everything from car parts to electronics. Traditionally, workers would need to inspect each product by hand to catch defects, but this is slow and prone to errors. Now, high-speed cameras scan each item as it moves, and edge AI models classify defects in real-time—scratches, misalignments, missing components—anything that deviates from perfection.

But that is not all. The same system can "*listen*" to the machines, using vibration, temperature, and acoustic sensors to sense subtle signs of wear and tear. An edge AI model, running locally, learns what "*normal*" looks like and raises alarms when it detects the slightest anomaly. It might notice a motor vibrating slightly more than usual—an early sign that the bearing is failing. Fixing it then, rather than after it breaks down, saves thousands of dollars in downtime.

These predictive maintenance systems use CNNs optimized for edge devices, and since they operate in noisy industrial settings with limited connectivity, local real-time analysis is crucial. It is like giving the factory its own nervous system—constantly sensing, analyzing, and reacting to stay efficient and safe.

Wildlife Conservation: Species Identification in Remote Forests

Deep inside a dense forest, a motion-activated camera trap silently clicks photos of animals that pass by. For conservationists working to protect endangered species, these images are priceless. But manually sifting through thousands of pictures to identify species is a monumental task. Now, imagine if these camera traps were equipped with edge AI models—lightweight CNNs trained to recognize animals.

When a tiger, elephant, or rare bird walks by, the system identifies the species instantly, tags the image, and stores it. If needed, it sends just the metadata back to researchers via satellite link, saving bandwidth. This allows researchers to track animal populations, understand their movements, and detect poaching threats, all without human presence.

Challenges? Oh, plenty! Poor lighting at night, animals partially hidden behind bushes, and the sheer diversity of species. Yet, such systems are revolutionizing wildlife conservation—helping save species that might otherwise vanish unnoticed.

Mock Interview

Design a pest detection system similar to Plantix. The farmer takes their Android phone, takes a picture of the plant condition, and it should identify the pest/disease and provide recommendations.

Requirements Gathering

Now again our smart interviewer gets proactive and asks the right questions.

Candidate: What are the end business metrics here?

Interviewer: Ability to display the correct pest/disease and recommendations. Farmer satisfaction is the key.

The success metrics:

- Number of apps downloaded
- Number of farmers using
- Number of images scanned for pests /diseases

Candidate: Is there any farmer feedback loop?

Interviewer: *Farmers can report incorrect diagnoses.*

Candidate: What are the latency/bandwidth requirements?

Interviewer: *Should work with 3G network with communication providers. The latency should be < 5 sec.*

Candidate: What is the user scale?

Interviewer: *It should be accessible to all Indian farmers, including house gardening. The scale is expected to be 1 billion.*

Candidate: What are the throughput requirements?

Interviewer: *Many farmers could simultaneously log in to the app. The simultaneous users can be in the order of lakhs.*

Candidate: What is the revenue model?

Interviewer: *Once the recommendations are provided, users will be given links to buy the specific pesticides/treatment products, which are monetizable.*

Candidate: What models of phones need to be supported?

Interviewer: *It is an Indian farmer's scenario and hence should be supported as an Android app.*

***Candidate*: How many crops/pests need to be supported?**

***Interviewer*:** *All major crops, including cotton, paddy, sugarcane, and so on, and all vegetables/fruits are to be supported.*

***Candidate*: Which markets are targeted?**

***Interviewer*:** *Target only the en-in market for now.*

***Candidate*: Which languages need support?**

***Interviewer*:** *Support recommendations in nationally recognized Indian languages.*

Now that the candidate understood the problem, he will be able to answer the end-to-end system design questions.

Data Collection

***Interviewer*: How do we create the dataset?**

***Candidate*:** We need high-quality images of the pests and crops. We need the images to be annotated with the right pests/diseases. If the data is not captured for the Indian market, we need to get the annotation done. We can either use open source tools, such as VIA, or cloud-based tools, such as Azure ML, to get the annotation done. The IP102 Dataset is a good dataset for pest classification. Plant Village is another popular dataset.

***Interviewer*: How do we ensure completeness of the dataset?**

***Candidate*:** Since the same pest can live in multiple stages, including larva and moth, we need the pest image in all the phases to be included. Also, the pests/diseases are not visible on the crop. The crop effect can be captured by the farmer, but not the exact pest. Our dataset should also include examples of just crop (without the pest). For example, images of eaten leaves/stems with white powder kind of disease should be included. Start with important crops and pests, and slowly increase the scale.

***Interviewer*: How do we increase the dataset size?**

***Candidate*:** Once the data is collected, the data needs to be augmented with different angles, rotations, and different lighting conditions (considering how a farmer would capture the pictures). We can also use GANs and Stable Diffusion to create similar examples and increase the dataset. When using GANs or Stable Diffusion, always have experts validate synthetic samples to avoid introducing misleading training data.

***Interviewer*: Is the dataset balanced?**

***Candidate*:** Some pests are rare, and some are popular. We would need to balance the dataset using image augmentation techniques and the SMOTE technique in feature space. SMOTE in feature space involves extracting embeddings using a pretrained CNN, applying SMOTE on embeddings to oversample.

Model Selection

Interviewer: Which model would be selected for the training?

Candidate: For this task, we need a lightweight yet efficient deep learning model, as it will be deployed on edge devices with limited computational resources. Transfer learning models such as MobileNet, EfficientNet, and SqueezeNet are ideal candidates due to their compact size and high accuracy.

Additionally, model optimization techniques such as quantization and pruning can be applied to further reduce the model's footprint, making it suitable for deployment on resource-constrained environments while maintaining performance.

Interviewer: How many models do we need?

Candidate: The number of models depends on how we structure our classification approach:

One Model for All Pests/Diseases:

- A single, large model trained to classify multiple pests and diseases.
- While this approach simplifies deployment, it may require a substantial amount of labeled data and a larger model size, making it harder to deploy on edge devices.

One Model Per Pest/Disease:

- Each pest or disease has its own dedicated model.
- This keeps the model architecture smaller and more specialized, improving accuracy for individual cases.
- At inference time, when a user uploads an image, multiple models can be executed either in parallel or sequentially to determine the best match.

Hybrid Approach (Grouped Models for Similar Pests/Diseases):

- Instead of training a separate model for each pest, we can group similar pests and diseases into clusters and train a dedicated model for each group.
- This balances accuracy and efficiency by reducing the total number of models while ensuring pests with similar visual characteristics are properly classified.
- Additional contextual information, such as crop type, geographic location, and seasonality, can be incorporated to further refine predictions.

Evaluation Metrics

- **Type of problem**: Multi-class classification (identifying pest type from image/sensor data).
- **Data Imbalance**: Some pests may be rarer than others, causing class imbalance.
- **Business Impact**: Misclassifying a harmful pest as harmless (false negative) may be costly in real-world agriculture.

Interviewer: How do we know which metrics are important?

Candidate:

Metric	Why Use It?	When Important?
Accuracy	General model performance	If the dataset is balanced
Precision	Avoid false pest alarms	If false positives are costly
Recall	Catch all harmful pests	If false negatives are costly
F1-Score	Balance precision & recall	Imbalanced dataset
Class-wise Precision/Recall/F1	Handle imbalance, focus on rare pests	If some pests are rare and critical
Confusion Matrix	Visual error analysis	Diagnostic tool
ROC-AUC	Probability-based ranking	If considering threshold tuning
Latency	Time taken per prediction (ms)	(ms) When deploying on edge devices or real-time detection
Throughput	Number of predictions per second	When handling large-scale or high-frequency pest monitoring

Deployment Considerations

Interviewer: What is the right deployment approach? Edge/cloud?

***Candidate:* On-Device Deployment (Edge AI)**

- For real-time inference without internet dependency.
- Requires quantized and pruned models.
- **Example**: TensorFlow Lite, OpenVINO, NVIDIA Jetson Nano.

Cloud Deployment

- Higher accuracy, but requires an internet connection.
- **Example**: AWS Lambda, Google Cloud AI, Azure ML.

Hybrid Approach

- Use on-device inference for quick detection.
- Send uncertain images to the cloud for high-accuracy verification.

Interviewer: What are the steps involved in deploying on an edge device?

Candidate:

Step 1: Convert Model to Edge-Compatible Format

a. Convert PyTorch model to ONNX → TensorRT for NVIDIA Jetson.

b. Convert TensorFlow model to TensorFlow Lite for mobile devices.

Step 2: Deploy on Mobile Device

Install TensorFlow Lite Interpreter or TorchScript runtime.

Step 3: Run Inference on Edge

Interviewer: *How do we detect concept drift, and how would we retrain the model?*

Candidate: Concept drift occurs when the relationship between input data and output labels changes over time, reducing model accuracy.

Types of Concept Drift:

- **Sudden Drift**: A new pest appears due to climate change, making old labels invalid.
- **Gradual Drift**: Pest appearance varies seasonally, making past training data obsolete.
- **Incremental Drift**: Slowly evolving pest traits (for example, different wing patterns).

Interviewer: How to Detect Drift?

Candidate:

- **Monitor Prediction Confidence**: If confidence scores start dropping over time, drift may be occurring.
- **Compare Distribution Shifts**: Use statistical tests (for example, KL Divergence, Wasserstein Distance) to compare old vs. new data distributions.
- **Monitor Accuracy Trends**: A sudden drop in accuracy is a sign of drift.

- **Out-of-Distribution (OOD) Detection**: Flag images that look very different from the training data.

Interviewer: How to Handle Drift?

Candidate:

- **Regular Model Updates**: Fine-tune on new data samples.
- **Re-label Drifted Samples**: Create a human-in-the-loop mechanism.
- **Dynamic Model Selection**: Maintain multiple models, and choose the best one based on current conditions

Flow chart summarizing the design:

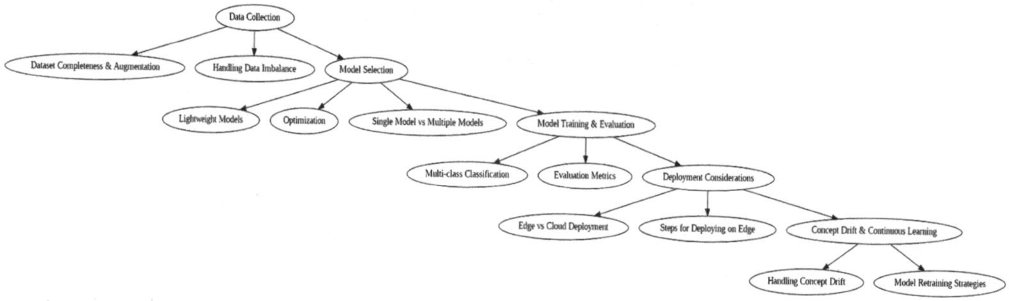

Figure 8.9: *Flowchart for designing pest classification system*

Conclusion

Building image classification models for edge devices presents unique challenges and opportunities. Unlike traditional cloud-based AI systems, edge AI requires models to be optimized for efficiency, operating with limited computational power, memory, and battery life. Throughout this chapter, we explored various techniques to make models lightweight while maintaining high accuracy.

We began by understanding the architecture choices available for edge devices and how different deep learning models, such as CNNs and Vision Transformers, can be adapted for deployment on low-power hardware. We then explored optimization techniques, including quantization, pruning, knowledge distillation, and mixed precision, all of which help reduce model size and inference latency. Hardware-aware training and efficient data loading strategies further enhance performance when deploying models on devices such as mobile phones, Raspberry Pi, or custom AI accelerators such as EdgeTPUs.

Real-world case studies demonstrated how these techniques are applied in critical domains such as agriculture, healthcare, industry, and wildlife conservation. Whether it is detecting pests on crops, diagnosing diseases from medical scans, identifying defective products in factories, or recognizing animal species in remote locations, edge AI is transforming the way we interact with intelligent systems.

One of the key aspects of deploying models on edge devices is ensuring their continued accuracy over time. We discussed the importance of continuous learning, detecting concept drift, and incorporating user feedback to refine models. With the right infrastructure, edge AI systems can evolve dynamically, improving their predictions as new data becomes available.

The future of image classification on edge devices is promising. Advances in self-supervised learning, federated learning, and neural architecture search will continue to push the boundaries of what is possible. As hardware improves and AI techniques become more efficient, we can expect even more powerful models to run directly on edge devices, enabling faster, smarter, and more autonomous decision-making across industries.

References

- Bag of Tricks for Image Classification with Convolutional Neural Networks
  - **Paper**: arXiv:1812.01187
- MobileViT: Light-weight, General-purpose, and Mobile-friendly Vision Transformer
  - **Paper**: arXiv:2110.02178
- Data efficient transformers: **Paper**: arXiv:2012.12877
- Vision Transformers: **Paper**: arXiv:2010.11929
- Low rank approximations: https://homes.cs.washington.edu/~jrl/cse422wi24/notes/svd.pdf
- IP102 Dataset for Pest Classification: https://arxiv.org/abs/1905.05141
- Edge AI for Smart Agriculture: https://ieeexplore.ieee.org/document/9207957
- Model Optimization Techniques (Pruning, Quantization, Distillation) https://pytorch.org/tutorials/advanced/static_quantization_tutorial.html

CHAPTER 9
Designing Sequence-to-Sequence Systems

Introduction

Consider the task of reading a lengthy legal contract and wishing for an immediate plain-language summary, speaking in one's native language and receiving fluent real-time translation, or dictating a report during a morning walk and obtaining an accurate transcription shortly thereafter. At the foundation of these capabilities lies a common computational framework: the sequence-to-sequence (seq2seq) model. These models underpin applications such as Google Translate, Siri, text summarization systems, and customer support agents, and they have become integral to the ways in which individuals interact with digital technologies.

The effectiveness of seq2seq models is contingent upon the availability of large, high-quality datasets. Constructing such resources poses significant challenges, whether sourcing parallel corpora for machine translation, generating transcriptions for automatic speech recognition, or collecting document–summary pairs for text summarization. These processes are often complicated by noise, incompleteness, or imbalance within the data. Addressing these issues is essential for developing models that generalize effectively. In parallel, the architectures themselves have undergone a notable evolution: from recurrent neural networks (RNNs) and long short-term memory networks (LSTMs), to the introduction of attention mechanisms, and ultimately to the Transformer architecture, which has redefined the state of the art in Natural Language Processing (NLP).

With this theoretical foundation established, the focus turns to practice. The design of Transformer-based seq2seq models will be examined in detail, including the encoder and decoder components, self-attention, positional encoding, and cross-attention. Implementation will be reinforced through both conceptual explanation and PyTorch code. Evaluation methodologies will then be considered, with particular attention to metrics such as BLEU, ROUGE, METEOR, and BERTScore, as well as the circumstances in which human assessment remains indispensable. The discussion culminates in a practical case study: the development of a text summarization engine utilizing a pre-trained BART model, encompassing dataset preprocessing, fine-tuning, evaluation, and opportunities for further extension.

Structure

In this chapter, we will cover the following topics:

- Applications of Sequence-to-Sequence Models
- Data Creation Annotation Challenges
- Architecture Evolution
- Designing an Encoder and a Decoder for Transformers
- Evaluation Strategies
- Case Study of Building a Summarization Engine

Applications of Sequence-to-Sequence Models

At its heart, a seq2seq model is a storyteller. It reads a sequence – whether it is text, speech, or structured data – and transforms it into another sequence, one that captures the essence of the original but repackages it in a new form. This transformation has revolutionized countless domains. Let us step into the lives of professionals, students, and everyday users to understand just how far-reaching these models have become.

Machine Translation

Imagine a French-speaking tourist trying to order food in India, or a team of researchers from India and Germany collaborating on a scientific paper. None of this would be seamless without machine translation – one of the earliest and most iconic applications of seq2seq modeling.

When Google replaced its rule-based translation engine with a neural seq2seq system in 2016, fluency levels improved dramatically. The system did not just translate – it understood context. Today, these models help businesses expand into international markets, let travelers navigate foreign lands, and empower NGOs to communicate across continents – all by turning one language sequence into another.

Speech Transcription

"*Hey Siri, schedule a meeting at 3.*" A command as simple as this belies the sophistication beneath it. **Speech recognition** (converting spoken words into text) – is a classic seq2seq task, and one that powers a wave of voice-first interfaces.

Whether it is Amazon Alexa running our smart home, a telemedicine app transcribing doctor-patient conversations, or a hands-free assistant helping a driver send messages, seq2seq models are bridging the gap between human speech and machine understanding. Microsoft reached human-level transcription accuracy in 2017 using these models – a breakthrough that is now embedded in call centers, meeting assistants, and accessibility tools.

Summarization in Media and Research

In today's media-saturated world, attention spans are short and deadlines are tighter. Journalists, editors, and readers alike rely on automatic summarization to keep up. A seq2seq model, when trained on news articles and highlights, learns to compress complex narratives into bite-sized summaries.

Media outlets use summarizers to build real-time news digests. Research platforms such as **Semantic Scholar** offer plain-English summaries of academic papers. In healthcare, these models condense electronic medical records into digestible overviews for clinicians. In law, they help lawyers skim through long case files. And for the everyday user? Tools such as **Notion AI** summarize meeting notes and **Grammarly** rewrites bulky paragraphs – enhanced their functionality by seq2seq learning.

From Questions to Insight

Now, picture a high schooler studying biology. She types, "*How does photosynthesis work?*" into an AI tutor, and gets an articulate, accurate answer – not a link, but an explanation. Or imagine a customer reaching out to a telecom company asking, "*Why is my bill higher this month?*" and a bot instantly provides a detailed response.

Question Answering (QA) systems are yet another frontier where seq2seq models thrive. These systems do not just fetch data; they generate answers from context, whether it is Wikipedia articles or internal company FAQs. In education, this means a personalized tutoring assistant. In business, they can assist with the technical support calls.

Machines That Talk Back

Gone are the days when chatbots responded with rigid, robotic phrases. Today's dialogue systems feel more like talking to a helpful friend. Whether it is OpenAI's ChatGPT carrying on a nuanced conversation or a mental health app providing supportive talk therapy, seq2seq models are behind the scenes – listening, interpreting, and generating.

In customer service, chatbots trained on historical conversations can cluster and summarize the issue types. In gaming, characters respond dynamically to player actions. These models do not just answer questions – they hold conversations, adapting their language to context and tone.

The Pattern behind the Magic

Across these domains – media, education, healthcare, business – one pattern holds: transforming one form of sequential input into another meaningful output. Whether it is a paragraph turned into a summary, a voice command turned into text, or a question turned into an answer, the seq2seq model sits at the core.

Technically, these systems share a common structure: an encoder reads and understands the input sequence, and a decoder generates the new sequence, word by word, token by token, using statistical context learned during training.

As we move forward in this chapter, we will uncover how to gather the data to train such systems, how these architectures evolved, and how to evaluate and build them, culminating in a hands-on project where you will bring a summarization engine to life.

Figure 9.1: *Media person preparing the news summary (Courtesy: Sora (OpenAI))*

Data Creation and Annotation Challenges

Training powerful seq2seq models requires large amounts of parallel data (input-output pairs), which can be hard to obtain. Let us delve into how training data is created for tasks such as translation, speech recognition, and others, and the common annotation challenges:

- **Collecting Parallel Corpora:** For machine translation, a "*parallel corpus*" is a set of sentences in language A paired with their translations in language B. Creating such corpora is labor-intensive. Some are extracted from official sources (for example, European Parliament proceedings are translated into many languages, providing millions of parallel sentences). Others come from the web – for instance, crawling websites that offer content in multiple languages and aligning the matching texts. Automatic alignment is not perfect and can introduce errors (sentences misaligned or mistranslated). In low-resource languages, parallel data might be scarce, so researchers resort to crowdsourcing translations. Crowdsourcing has been shown to be a reliable way to get translations and even speech transcripts for NLP tasks. Projects have used online platforms where bilingual speakers translate sentences or transcribe audio for a modest fee. Still, ensuring quality is a challenge, and hence, one must filter out incorrect or inconsistent annotations.
- **Speech Data and Transcription:** For speech recognition, the parallel data is audio paired with text transcripts. Creating this means recording hours of speech and manually transcribing it – a tedious job. Datasets such as **LibriSpeech** (1000 hours of read English speech) were developed with significant effort. Crowdsourcing can help here, too (for example, having crowd workers transcribe short audio clips). But transcribers can make mistakes, especially with homophones or proper nouns. Also, the audio needs labeling of speaker segments, which can be complex if there are multiple speakers. Alignment issues appear here as well: the timing of words in audio versus text can be off. To train seq2seq Automated Speech Recognition (ASR), we typically need audio broken into manageable segments with accurate transcripts. Rich annotations (such as punctuation, casing) may be lost, since many ASR corpora only have lowercase words without punctuation. All these issues make speech data prep a big endeavor.
- **Summarization and Dialogue Data:** For summarization, creating a parallel corpus can be tricky because a summary is not uniquely defined. A common approach is to use naturally occurring pairs – for example, news articles and their professionally written "*highlights*" (as in the CNN/DailyMail dataset), or movie reviews and a one-line summary. These give us (article → summary) pairs. However, these "*found*" datasets often have inconsistencies: the summary might assume knowledge not in the article, or the article might

have multiple equally valid summaries. For dialogue, a large corpus of human-human conversations (such as movie subtitles or chat logs) has been used to train chatbots. But these often need cleaning (removing personally identifiable info, profanity, and so on), and the dialogues might be short question-and-answer rather than free-form conversation. An annotation for dialogue might involve labeling dialog acts or intents, which is another layer of complexity.

- **Ambiguity and Multiple References:** A core challenge in seq2seq tasks is that there may be multiple correct outputs for a given input. A sentence in English can be translated into French in several equally valid ways. An article summary could highlight different aspects. This ambiguity makes training and evaluating tricky. If the training data only contains one reference translation or summary, the model might consider other valid outputs as "*errors*" during learning. Similarly, for question answering, there might be several phrasings of the correct answer. Dataset creators try to mitigate this by providing multiple reference outputs when possible (for example, some QA datasets have multiple correct answers listed, and translation tests often have 4 reference translations). Most systems use a single reference per example, though multiple-reference training methods are an active research area.
- **Domain and Distribution Mismatch:** Another issue is that the domain of training data might differ from where you deploy the model. For example, a translation model trained on formal news text might struggle with casual conversational language or slang. A speech model trained on read audio might falter on spontaneous, accented speech. Creating domain-specific parallel data is costly, so often we have to make do with what is available and then apply techniques such as fine-tuning on a smaller in-domain dataset later. Annotation complexity grows with domain: transcribing medical conversations requires understanding medical jargon, and translating poetry requires cultural nuance.

Solutions to Annotation Challenges

Once raw data is collected, the annotation process comes into play, especially when the desired output sequence is not directly available and needs to be created or refined. This is where human expertise often becomes indispensable, and a new set of challenges emerges:

- **Defining Clear Annotation Guidelines:** Ambiguous or poorly defined guidelines can lead to inconsistent annotations, undermining the quality of the training data. Annotators need clear instructions on how to handle various linguistic phenomena, edge cases, and subjective aspects (for example, what constitutes a good summary).
- **Ensuring Consistency and Reliability:** Different annotators might interpret guidelines differently, leading to variations in annotations. Implementing

measures such as inter-annotator agreement (measuring the consistency between multiple annotators) and providing feedback are crucial for maintaining reliability.

- **Quality Control and Cleaning:** Before training, parallel data often go through cleaning pipelines. This might include removing obviously misaligned pairs (for example, a sentence paired with a completely unrelated sentence), filtering out pairs that are too long or too short (to avoid noisy examples such as a one-word summary of a page of text), and standardizing formats. In translation, filtering methods use language identification and simple bilingual dictionaries to make sure a supposed French-English pair is truly French and English and rough translations of each other. In summarization, one might remove examples where the "*summary*" is longer than the article (which signals a problem). This cleaning can dramatically improve the quality of the final model.
- **Handling Subjectivity:** Tasks such as text summarization or generating creative text inherently involve a degree of subjectivity. Capturing the nuances and variations in human judgment during annotation is challenging.
- **The Cost and Time of Annotation:** High-quality annotation, especially for complex tasks or large datasets, can be expensive and time-consuming. This often becomes a bottleneck in the development cycle.
- **Annotation Tooling and Infrastructure:** Efficient annotation requires appropriate tools and infrastructure that support various data formats, annotation schemes, and quality control processes.
- **Ethical Considerations:** Depending on the data being annotated (for example, speech with personal information, text containing sensitive content), ethical considerations regarding privacy, bias, and responsible data handling must be carefully addressed.

In addition to data annotation, we can use the following techniques to increase the dataset size.

- **Data Augmentation:** Augmentation techniques involve transforming existing training examples in minor ways to create new examples. For text and speech: for speech recognition, we can speed up or slow down audio clips, add background noise or reverberation, or splice audio segments – the transcript stays the same, so you have effectively created a new (noisier) training example. This helps models become noise-robust. In NLP tasks, augmentation could mean paraphrasing input sequences (using thesaurus synonyms, or back-translating a sentence to another language and back to get a variant) so that the model does not overly depend on exact wording. For dialogue, one might swap in equivalent phrases ("*hello*" versus "*hi*") in training data to teach diversity. Augmentation can also involve splitting or merging sequences (for instance, in summarization, maybe splitting a long article into chunks with corresponding sub-summaries). All these techniques aim to increase the diversity of training data without new manual annotations.

- **Crowdsourcing and Community Contribution:** As mentioned, involving humans via crowd platforms or volunteer communities (such as Wikipedia translators, or projects such as Mozilla Common Voice for speech) can expand the dataset. While quality can vary, careful curation and verification (for example, having multiple annotators per example and using majority votes or expert review) can help. Crowdsourcing has enabled corpora for languages and domains that commercial interests had not covered by tapping into the knowledge of many people online.
- **Synthetic Data Generation:** A clever approach to boost parallel data is to generate it automatically. In translation, a popular method is *back-translation*: take a large collection of monolingual text in the target language, use a preliminary model to translate it backwards into the source language, and then you have synthetic source-target pairs to augment training. For example, to improve French-to-English translation, translate a lot of English text into French with a rough model, then train the French→English model on this synthetic data plus real data. This was shown to significantly improve quality. In speech, one can use text-to-speech (TTS) systems to generate spoken audio from text, producing synthetic audio transcripts to train an ASR model. Or apply noise and distortions to existing audio to teach the model to handle variability. In summarization, people have tried generating artificial summaries by using templates or rule-based compressions of text to pre-train a model, and then fine-tuning on real pairs. Synthetic data helps fill data gaps but should be validated to avoid systematic errors or bias.

In summary, creating training data for seq2seq is a big part of the iceberg that users do not see when they enjoy a translated webpage or a voice assistant. Behind the scenes, it requires assembling parallel examples and dealing with alignment errors, ambiguities, and biases. Through crowdsourcing, synthetic augmentation, and careful curation, researchers have been able to feed seq2seq models the data they need to learn. With data in hand, the next step is to consider how the model architectures themselves have evolved to better handle sequences, which we will explore next.

Here are some annotation frameworks for sequence-to-sequence models:

Doccano

Best for: Text-to-text annotation tasks such as translation, summarization, and paraphrasing. Ideal for NLP datasets and want a quick, reliable web interface.

- Out-of-the-box support for seq2seq
- Simple UI, ideal for both individuals and teams

- Easy export formats (JSONL)
- Actively maintained open-source project

Use cases:

- Machine translation
- Headline generation
- Text simplification

Label Studio

Best for: Multi-modal seq2seq annotation (text, audio, video) with deep customization. Ideal for projects that span multiple data types or require model-in-the-loop workflows.

- Highly flexible annotation templates
- Supports audio-to-text, text-to-text, and structured data
- Integration with machine learning models for pre-labeling
- Scalable for enterprise projects

Use cases:

- Speech recognition
- Text summarization
- Video captioning

Prodigy (Commercial)

Best for: Fast, scriptable, and active learning-powered annotation workflows. Ideal for research teams and startups that value automation and iterative labeling.

- Python-native interface for automation
- Powerful active learning loop for rapid labeling
- Great for prototyping and fine-tuning NLP tasks

Use cases:

- Generative QA
- Summarization
- Chatbot training

LightTag (Commercial)

Best for: Team-oriented annotation with built-in QA and review mechanisms

- Collaborative annotation dashboards
- Annotation assignment and progress tracking
- Excellent for large team management

Use cases:

- Multi-annotator translation projects
- Summarization with human-in-the-loop QA
- Ideal for enterprises or agencies managing large teams of annotators.

ELAN

Best for: Audio/video-based seq2seq annotations

- Professional-grade multi-layer annotation for speech and video
- Time-aligned transcription and translation
- Widely used in linguistics and ASR research

Use cases:

- Speech transcription
- Spoken language translation
- Sign language annotation
- Ideal for academic or research projects involving spoken or visual language.

When choosing the annotation tools, consider privacy, scalability, and cost aspects.

Architecture Evolution

Not long ago, the idea of a machine summarizing a novel, translating a political speech, or holding a semi-coherent conversation seemed out of reach. The core limitation? Teaching machines how to generate sequences, not just recognize patterns, but *respond in kind*. The journey to today's powerful sequence-to-sequence models did not happen overnight. It evolved through years of innovation, trial and error, and a deepening understanding of how context, memory, and attention matter in language.

Let us trace the story from the early architectures that sparked the revolution to the models that power everything from Google Translate to ChatGPT today.

The Recurrent Neural Networks Era (2014)

Recurrent Neural Networks (RNNs) try to mimic this process in a neural network. They process a sequence of inputs step by step, and they have a kind of "memory" that allows them to keep track of information from earlier in the sequence. This memory is represented by the hidden state.

RNN Architecture:

- **Input**: Each token in the sentence.
- **Hidden State**: A mental summary we build up as we read the sentence. When we read a new word, we update our mental summary based on the current word and our previous understanding.
- **Output**: Maybe we are trying to predict the next word in the sentence, or classify the overall sentiment of the sentence. Our prediction or classification will be based on our current mental summary.

RNN Functionality:

1. **Process the First Input**: The first word goes into the RNN. It uses some initial "*memory*" (usually just zeros) and the first word to create a new "*memory*" (the first hidden state).
2. **Process the Second Input**: The second word goes in. Now, the RNN uses the *second* word *and* the "*memory*" it created after reading the first word to create a *new* "*memory*" (the second hidden state).
3. **Continue**: This process repeats for each word in the sentence. The "*memory*" at each step is influenced by all the words seen so far.
4. **Generate Output**: At each step, or the end of the sequence, the RNN can use its current "*memory*" to produce an output, such as predicting the next word or making a classification.

The Problem with Simple RNNs: Forgetting the Distant Past

Imagine a very long sentence. By the time you reach the end, our initial mental summary might have faded, and we might not remember the very first words as clearly. Simple RNNs face a similar issue called the vanishing gradient problem. During training, it becomes difficult for the network to learn how earlier parts of a long sequence influence later parts. The "*memory*" fades away.

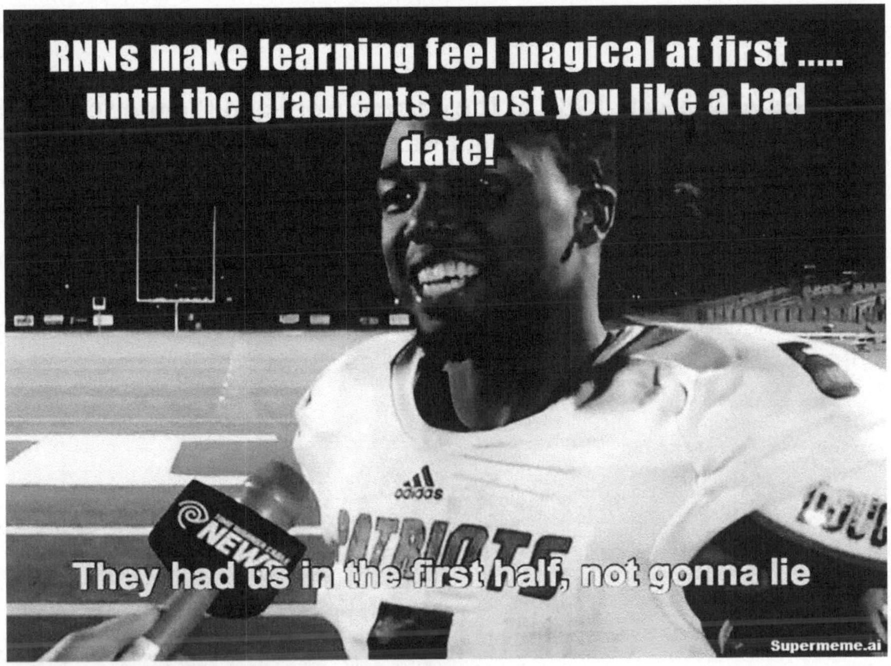

Figure 9.2: *Fun representation of vanishing gradients*

Long Short-Term Memory Networks

Long Short-Term Memories (LSTMs) are like smarter RNNs with a much better way of remembering information over long sequences. They have a more sophisticated "*memory*" called the LSTM cell state, and they use "*gates*" to control what information is stored, what is forgotten, and what is passed on.

Instead of just one memory, you now have two:

- **Hidden State (Short-Term Memory)**: Our immediate understanding of the current part of the sentence.
- **Cell State (Long-Term Memory)**: A separate, more persistent memory that can carry important information from the very beginning of the sentence all the way through.

The "*Gates*" - Deciding What to Remember and Forget:

LSTMs have three main "*gates*" that act like filters for the information flowing through them:

- **Forget Gate**: This gate looks at the current token and the previous short-term memory and decides what information in the *long-term memory (cell state)* is no longer relevant and should be discarded. It is like deciding what details from the beginning of the sentence are no longer important for understanding the current part.

- **Input Gate**: This gate looks at the current word and the previous short-term memory and decides what new information from the current word should be added to the *long-term memory (cell state)*. It also decides how much of this new information is important.
- **Output Gate**: This gate looks at the current short-term memory and the *updated long-term memory (cell state)* and decides what information should be outputted as the new *short-term memory (hidden state)* for the next step. This output is also used to make predictions.

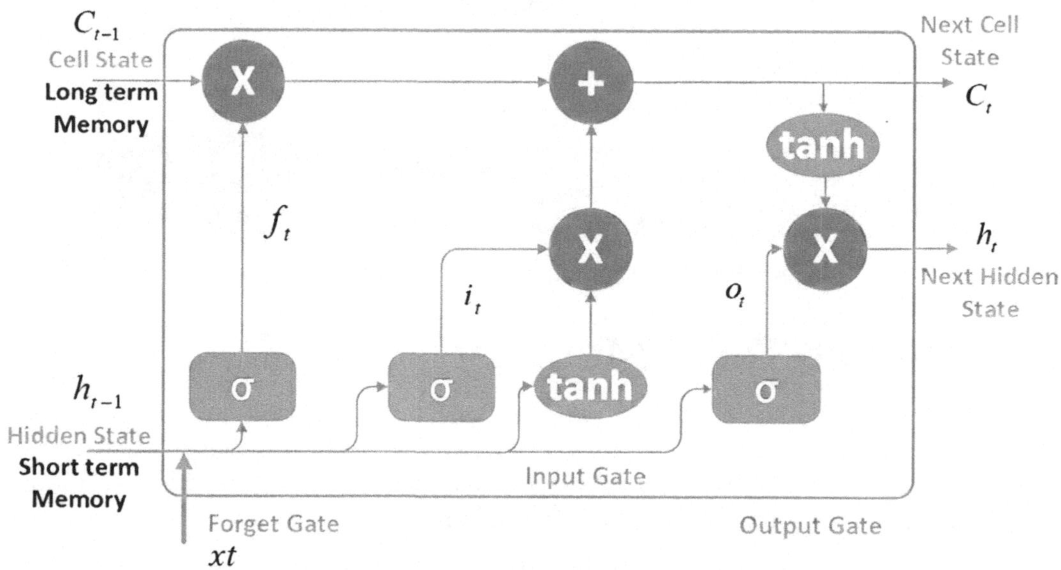

Figure 9.3: *LSTM architecture*

X_i is the input value, and H_{t-1} is the previous hidden state. H_t carries the short-term memory, and Ct carries the long-term memory. Forget gate, Input gate, and Output gate are also represented in the picture.

Functionality:

1. **Receive Input**: The LSTM receives the current word, and the previous short-term memory as well as the long-term memory.
2. **Decide What to Forget**: The forget gate decides what to throw away from the long-term memory.

3. **Decide What to Add**: The input gate decides what new information to add to the long-term memory.
4. **Update Long-Term Memory**: The long-term memory is updated by forgetting some old information and adding some new information.
5. **Decide What to Output**: The output gate decides what information from the updated long-term memory should be used to create the new short-term memory (which is also the output of the LSTM cell for this step).
6. **Pass On**: The new short-term memory and the updated long-term memory are passed on to the next step in the sequence.

LSTMs are Better for Long Sequences

The cell state and the gating mechanisms allow LSTMs to selectively remember important information over long periods. The forget gate helps to get rid of irrelevant information, while the input gate helps to incorporate new, important information. The output gate controls what information is exposed at each step. This makes LSTMs much better at capturing long-range dependencies compared to simple RNNs.

In 2014, a major shift occurred. At Google, a group of researchers – Ilya Sutskever, Oriol Vinyals, and Quoc Le – proposed something deceptively simple but incredibly effective: what if we used two recurrent neural networks, one to read an input sequence and the other to generate an output?

This became the encoder-decoder RNN architecture, the first true sequence-to-sequence model. The encoder read an input – say, an English sentence – one word at a time and condensed it into a single latent vector, a fixed-length representation that (hopefully) captured its meaning. The decoder then took that vector and produced the translated sentence in, say, French – again, word by word.

This design was a revelation. For the first time, machines were not relying on hand-crafted rules or statistical phrases. They were learning, from data, how to translate, summarize, or respond. And it worked – sort of.

But beneath this success was a structural flaw: the fixed-length bottleneck. No matter how complex the sentence, the encoder had to cram it into a single vector of fixed size, often just 512 dimensions. That is like trying to compress an entire novel into a single sentence and expecting perfect recall. For short sentences, it was passable. For longer inputs – such as a paragraph of legal text or a dense scientific explanation – important details got lost. The decoder was essentially flying blind past the first few tokens.

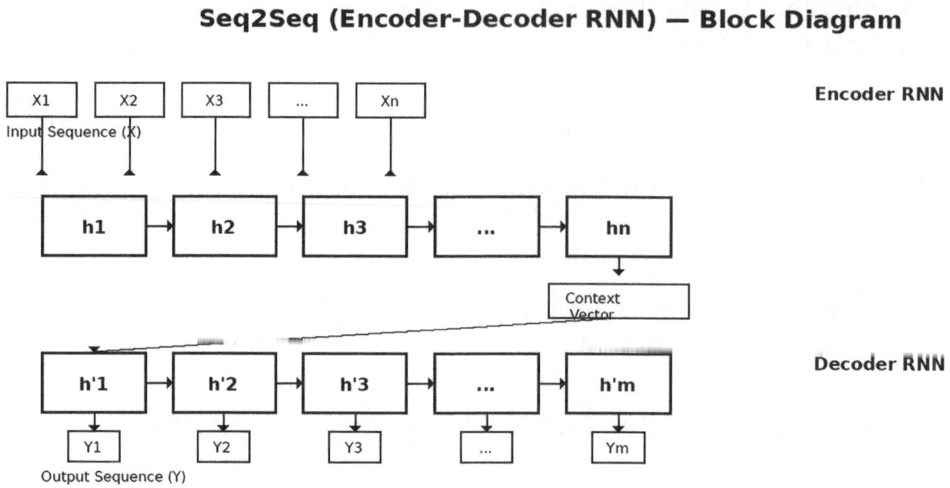

Figure 9.4: RNN *encoder-decoder representation*

Moreover, RNNs struggled with long-term dependencies. By the time they reached the end of a sequence, they had often forgotten what came at the beginning. To fix this, researchers turned to **Long Short-Term Memory networks (LSTMs)** – a variant of RNNs that could "*remember*" key information across longer spans of input. LSTMs, and their simpler cousin **GRU**s, gave the model the ability to preserve and forget information selectively, much like a human choosing what to focus on.

This innovation improved translation and summarization for moderate-length inputs, but the core problem remained: the model was still trying to compress everything into one fragile vector. It needed a better way to "*look back*" – and that is when attention came in.

Learning to Focus: The Rise of Attention (2015)

What if, instead of stuffing everything into a single memory cell, the model could glance back at the input whenever it needed?

That is the idea behind the attention mechanism, introduced in 2015 by Bahdanau, Cho, and Bengio. Rather than feeding the decoder just one context vector, attention allowed the decoder to dynamically focus on different parts of the input at each step of output generation.

Here is how it works: the encoder no longer produces one vector, but a sequence of vectors, one for each input token. These vectors collectively represent the entire input in context. When the decoder generates a new word, it computes a set of attention weights that decide *how much it should care about each input token*. This weighted sum becomes the new context vector for that step.

The result? The decoder does not just remember – it actively chooses where to look. This mechanism mimics how a human translator aligns source and target words – focusing on one clause, then another, as needed. In practice, this means better translations, more accurate summaries, and much better handling of longer texts.

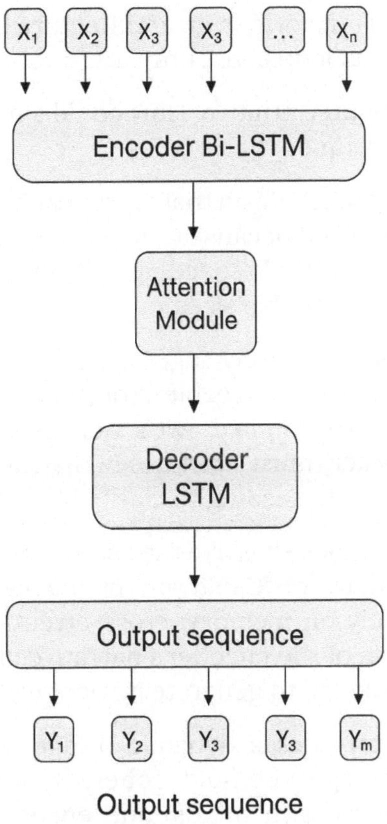

Figure 9.5: *LSTM with attention*

Attention turned out to be a breakthrough not only for translation but across domains:

- In speech recognition, it helped align segments of audio to words or characters.
- In image captioning, it lets the model focus on different parts of an image while generating a sentence.
- In text-to-speech, it allowed smooth, aligned synthesis of audio from text inputs.

By 2016, attention was no longer a side feature – it had become the main lens through which seq2seq models were understood and generated. But researchers were not done. They asked a bold question: if attention is so powerful, why not make it the *only* thing that matters?

The Transformer Revolution: Attention is All You Need (2017)

In 2017, a paper titled "*Attention* Is *All You Need*" redefined everything. The authors – Vaswani et al. – proposed the Transformer, an architecture that eliminated recurrence entirely. No RNNs. No sequential loops. Just pure attention, applied at scale.

At first glance, this seemed counterintuitive. How could a model process a sentence if it did not read it one token at a time?

The trick was self-attention – a mechanism that allows each token in a sequence to look at every other token, all at once. And because there is no recurrence, this computation could be fully parallelized – dramatically speeding up training and making it feasible to scale models to previously unimaginable sizes.

Imagine two companions working closely together on a complicated task: one is an attentive listener, the other a knowledgeable storyteller. The storyteller (encoder) carefully narrates a detailed story filled with rich context, facts, and nuances. Meanwhile, the listener (decoder) must craft a new narrative or summary based on what they have heard, occasionally needing to clarify important details.

This is where cross-attention shines—it is like the listener stopping occasionally to ask, "*Wait, what did you say about that?*" or "*Could you remind me exactly how this character felt?*" Rather than relying solely on memory, cross-attention allows the decoder to selectively revisit specific parts of the encoder's narrative at each step, gathering just the right amount of context needed to generate its next word or sentence.

In essence, cross-attention provides a dynamic bridge between the encoder and decoder, allowing the storytelling to be fluid, coherent, and context-aware. It is the careful exchange between these two minds—one encoding knowledge, the other decoding and creating—that makes modern sequence-to-sequence tasks such as translation, summarization, and dialogue generation feel so remarkably human.

Each Transformer has an encoder-decoder architecture:

- The encoder processes the input using stacked layers of multi-head self-attention (where each attention head captures a different kind of relationship, such as grammar, co-reference, or topic), followed by feedforward networks.
- The decoder does the same for the output, but with two attention layers: one that looks at the previously generated tokens (with a mask to avoid peeking ahead), and one that attends to the encoder's output.

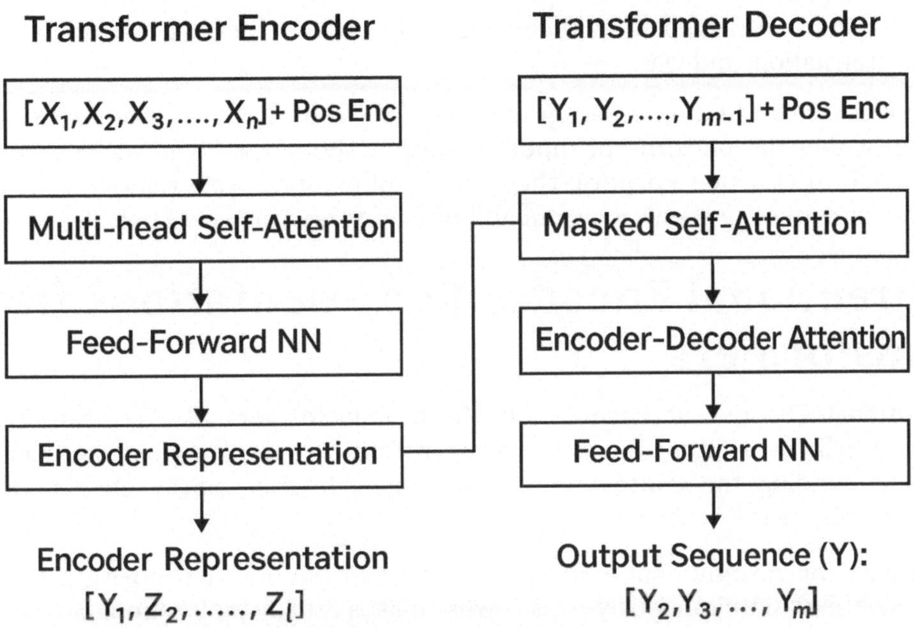

Figure 9.6: *Transformer architecture*

To retain word order, since Transformers do not process input sequentially like RNNs, positional encodings are added to input embeddings. These provide a sense of token position in the sequence, enabling the model to distinguish "*the cat sat*" from "*sat the cat*."

The Transformer was more than just faster – it was better. It captured long-range dependencies effortlessly, adapted to various sequence lengths, and generalized across tasks. Within a year, it dethroned LSTMs across benchmarks in translation, summarization, question answering, and beyond.

And it opened the floodgates to pretrained language models.

Pretraining and the Modern Seq2Seq Renaissance

With the Transformer's parallelism and capacity, researchers began training massive models on massive datasets. These models were not trained for one task – they learned language itself, then were fine-tuned for specific applications.

This gave birth to a new class of seq2seq models:

- BERT (2018) learned representations of text through masked language modeling, but only had an encoder.

- BART and T5 (2019) brought back the full encoder-decoder Transformer, trained on corrupt-and-reconstruct objectives – perfect for summarization, translation, and QA.

These models can take in a paragraph, distill it, translate it, or even continue it – all by learning the patterns of input-to-output sequences. And because they are pretrained on vast text corpora, they can be fine-tuned with relatively little task-specific data, making them powerful and efficient for real-world use.

Bidirectional Encoder Representations from Transformers

Bidirectional Encoder Representations from Transformers (BERT), introduced by Google (Devlin et al., 2018), is a powerful Transformer-based language model focused on understanding the context of words deeply. It is primarily an encoder-only architecture.

Core Idea: Unlike traditional models, BERT learns from both left-to-right and right-to-left contexts simultaneously–this is what makes it truly bidirectional.

BERT Highlights

- **Masked Language Modeling (MLM):** BERT is trained by masking out some tokens in a sentence and asking the model to predict them, forcing it to understand context deeply.
- **Next Sentence Prediction (NSP):** It also learns sentence-level understanding by predicting whether two given sentences follow each other logically.

Applications:

- Text classification (sentiment analysis)
- Named entity recognition (NER)
- Question answering
- Textual entailment

BERT revolutionized NLP by allowing easy fine-tuning for a wide range of language tasks.

Bidirectional and Auto-Regressive Transformers

Bidirectional and Auto-Regressive Transformers (BART) (Lewis et al., 2019) builds on the strengths of models such as BERT but provides a full encoder-decoder Transformer architecture, ideal for generating coherent text.

Core Idea: BART combines bidirectional encoding (like BERT) with an auto-regressive decoder (like GPT), effectively bridging understanding (encoding) and generation (decoding).

Auto-regressive Transformers are a special class of Transformer models that generate sequences token-by-token, predicting each next token based only on the previously generated tokens. These models excel at tasks involving text generation and modeling complex language structures.

BART Highlights:

- **Corruption and Reconstruction:** BART's pre-training involves corrupting text (by masking, rearranging, or deleting words) and then reconstructing it, enabling the model to learn contextual understanding and generation simultaneously.
- The encoder processes corrupted input bidirectionally, and the decoder auto-regressively generates the original, uncorrupted sequence.

Applications:

- Text summarization (extractive and abstractive)
- Machine translation
- Creative text generation (storytelling, content creation)
- Question answering and dialogue systems

BART excels particularly at tasks requiring fluent text generation and summarization.

Designing Encoders and Decoders for Transformers

Choosing and designing the encoder and decoder for sequence-to-sequence (seq2seq) tasks is critical, and depends on factors such as:

- Task complexity
- Input and output data modality
- Sequence length
- Computational constraints
- Desired interpretability and accuracy

Let us understand different seq2seq problems, and what are the different modalities involved in each task.

Task	Input	Output	Examples
Machine Translation	Text	Text	English → French
Summarization	Long Text	Short Text	Article → Summary
Speech Recognition (ASR)	Audio	Text	Audio recording → Transcript
Dialogue Systems	Text	Text	Conversation history → Next response
Text-to-Speech (TTS)	Text	Audio	Text → Spoken audio
Video Captioning	Video/Frames	Text	Video → Text description

Table 9.1: *Sequence-to-sequence task examples*

Common Encoder Architectures

Let us understand different types of encoder architectures and their suitable task association.

- **RNN/LSTM Encoder (Sequential):**
  - **Strength:** Good for short sequences; captures sequential patterns naturally.
  - **Weakness:** Struggles with very long sequences; computational bottlenecks.
  - **Suitable for:** Short sentence translation, small-scale dialogue systems.
- **CNN-based Encoder (Convolutional):**
  - **Strength:** Efficient and parallelizable; good for tasks with spatial structure (for example, audio or images).
  - **Weakness:** Limited context range without deep stacking.
  - **Suitable for:** Speech recognition, text-to-speech, and video captioning.
- **Transformer-based Encoder (Attention-based):**
  - **Strength:** Captures long-range context effectively; parallelizable and scalable.
  - **Weakness:** Computationally expensive without optimization; less efficient for extremely long inputs.
  - **Suitable for:** Translation, summarization, dialogue, and large-scale language tasks.

Quick Recommendations:

- **Textual tasks (Translation/Summarization):** Transformer Encoder.
- **Short sequences/simple tasks:** RNN/LSTM Encoder.

- **Audio/Image/Video sequences:** CNN or hybrid CNN-Transformer Encoder.

Choosing the Right Decoder

Now, let us understand different types of decoders.

- **RNN/LSTM Decoder:**
  - **Suitable for:** Moderate-length generation (short dialogues, simple summarization).
- **Transformer-based Decoder:**
  - **Suitable for:** Complex summarization, conversational agents, and high-quality translations.
- **CNN-based Decoder (rarely used alone):**
  - **Suitable for:** Hybrid setups or TTS/audio generation systems.

Quick Recommendations:

- **Text generation (Translation, Summarization, Dialogue):** Transformer Decoder.
- **Audio synthesis (TTS, voice cloning):** Hybrid CNN + RNN/Transformer Decoders.

Task-Specific Architecture

- **Summarization:** Use Transformers such as **BART or T5** (encoder-decoder models specifically trained for summarization tasks).
- **Machine Translation:** Pre-trained Transformer encoder-decoder (for example, MarianMT, T5) fine-tuned on parallel text data.
- **Dialogue Systems:** Transformer decoders trained auto-regressively (for example, GPT-based models). Auto-regression is a modeling approach where the next value in a sequence is predicted based on its own past values.
- **Speech Recognition (ASR):** Hybrid CNN encoders with Transformer decoders or specialized models (Conformer, Whisper).
- **Text-to-Speech (TTS):** Encoder-decoder with CNN/RNN encoders and Transformer decoders (for example, Tacotron, and FastSpeech).

Choosing the Right Tokenizer

Tokenizer is the first step for Natural Language data. Splitting the data into words or characters is a simple tokenization model. When we handle a large corpus of data, we need optimal ways to tokenize the data for pre-training and the actual training process. Let us understand different types of tokenizers and their explanation.

Type	Explanation	Pros	Cons	When to Use
Word-level	Splits text into words based on whitespace/ punctuation	Simple to interpret	Large vocabulary, poor handling of out-of-vocabulary (OOV) words	Small, clean corpora
Character-level	Splits text into individual characters	Very small vocabulary, no OOV issues	Long sequences, difficult modelling	Multilingual or morphologically rich languages
Byte-Pair Encoding (BPE)	Learns to merge frequent character pairs, balancing vocabulary size and tokenization granularity	Moderate vocabulary, efficient, handles OOV well	Slightly less interpretable	General-purpose, most Transformer models GPT-2, RoBERTa, BART)
WordPiece	Similar to BPE but based on frequency and likelihood; optimized for sub-word units	Efficient vocabulary, handles unknown words well	Less interpretable	BERT-based models, multilingual tasks
SentencePiece (Unigram)	Unigram language model-based subword tokenizer	Robust multilingual support, no explicit OOV	Less intuitive	Multilingual tasks, tasks involving diverse languages

***Table 9.2**: Choosing the right tokenizer*

Practical Recommendations:

- **Small-scale and simple tasks:** Word-level tokenizer
- **General NLP** - BPE/Wordpiece
- **Multilingual NLP** – SentencePiece

Choosing the Right Positional Encoding

Positional encoding will help provide the sequence information to the encoder/ decoder. Let us understand different types of popular positional encoding techniques.

Positional Encoding Type	Description	Applications
Sinusoidal	General Seq2seq tasks	Variable sequence lengths, translation, and summarization.
Learned Positional Embedding	Learned during training, requires positional embedding for each position in the input sequence.	Tasks with limited, consistent sequence lengths; pre-trained models such as BERT, GPT, and BART typically use learned positional embeddings.
Relative Positional Encoding	Captures relative distances between tokens, enhancing performance on tasks needing strong positional awareness.	Complex tasks, long sequences, language modeling, and question answering (used in models such as T5, Transformer-XL).
Rotary Positional Encoding (RoPE)	Encodes positions as rotations in embedding space, providing better extrapolation to longer sequences.	Long-context models, large-scale language modeling, and retrieval augmented generation (RoPE used in GPT-NeoX, LLaMA).

Table 9.3: *Explanation of different positional encoding techniques*

Practical recommendations for using positional encoding:

- Default: Sinusoidal (Transformer original paper)
- Long sequences (512+ tokens): Rotary or Relative positional encoding
- Pre-trained models (GPT, BERT, BART): Use their learned embeddings

Choosing the Correct Attention Mechanism

Attention is a core component of modern Transformer architectures that allows models to dynamically focus on different parts of the input when generating output. Instead of processing sequences strictly left-to-right (such as RNNs), attention mechanisms enable models to weigh the relevance of all tokens in the sequence, helping them capture long-range dependencies and contextual relationships.

There are two main types of attention used in seq2seq systems:

- **Self-Attention**: Each token in a sequence attends to all other tokens in the same sequence. It helps the model understand context and relationships within a sentence (for example, resolving pronouns or dependencies). This helps the encoder build contextual representations of the input.

- **Example**: In a translation task, "*bank*" in "*He sat on the bank*" will attend to "*sat*" and "*river*" to figure out that it means riverbank, not a financial bank.

Masked Self-attention

- Masked Self-attention layer is present in the decoder block. Tokens in the output sequence attend only to earlier positions, not future ones. This ensures predictions are generated **autoregressively** (left-to-right).
- **Cross-attention:** Used in encoder-decoder architectures, where the decoder attends to the encoder outputs. It allows the model to align generated tokens with specific parts of the input sequence, crucial for tasks such as translation or summarization.

Let us explore different types of attention mechanisms.

Attention Type	Explanation	Strengths	Weaknesses	Ideal Applications
Additive (Bahdanau) Attention	Computes alignment weights using a feed-forward network; combines encoder and decoder states.	Flexible, good with RNNs/ LSTMs	Computationally expensive for large sequences	RNN/ LSTM-based translation, speech recognition
Multiplicative (Luong/Dot-Product)	Calculates attention by dot product between the encoder and decoder hidden states.	Efficient, simpler, faster than additive	Less flexible, needs similar encoder/ decoder dimensions	Translation, summarization with RNN/ LSTM, Transformers
Scaled Dot-Product Attention (Transformer)	Dot-product attention scaled by the square root of the key dimension, used in Transformers.	Highly parallelizable, efficient, and easy computation	Requires positional encoding, intensive memory use	General seq2seq tasks (translation, summarization, dialogue, generation)
Self-Attention (Transformer)	Attention mechanism applied to a single sequence itself (inputs interacting internally).	Great for context modeling, fully parallelizable	Computationally intensive for very long sequences	Language modeling, summarization, and long-context reasoning

Cross-Attention (Encoder-Decoder Attention)	Decoder attends to encoder outputs; commonly used in Transformer decoders.	Efficiently captures relationships between source and target sequences	Requires careful optimization for speed	Translation, summarization, dialogue systems
Local/Global Attention	"*Local*": Decoder attends to the limited window of encoder inputs. "*Global*": Decoder attends to all encoder inputs.	Local reduces computational cost, Global provides richer context	Local may miss important distant contexts; global is computationally heavy	Document summarization (local), general translation (global)
Sparse Attention (Longformer, BigBird)	Attends selectively, ignoring many irrelevant interactions, efficient for long sequences.	Handles very long sequences efficiently	May miss complex long-range interactions	Long document modeling, summarization, and QA
Multi-head Attention	Multiple attention "*heads*" attend in parallel, each capturing different aspects of relationships.	Richer representation, parallel and diverse modeling	More parameters, more computational cost	General-purpose seq2seq tasks, standard in Transformers

Table 9.4: *Exploring attention mechanisms*

Let us understand the different attention mechanisms used in popular architectures. Multi-head attention is more popular in language generation tasks. For long sequences, computing the attention would be a challenge. Hence, longformer (which can handle long sequences) uses sparse attention mechanisms.

Architecture	**Attention Type**	**Ideal Use Case**
Transformer	Scaled Dot-Product, Multi-head Self and Cross-attention	General seq2seq, summarization, translation
GPT Models	Multi-head Self-Attention (auto-regressive)	Language modeling, dialogue, and generation
BERT	Multi-head Self-Attention (bidirectional)	Classification, NER, QA, embeddings
Longformer/BigBird	Sparse/Sliding Window Attention	Long-document summarization, QA

Bahdanau (2015)	Additive Attention (original paper)	RNN/LSTM-based translation, TTS, ASR
Luong Attention (2015)	Multiplicative (dot-product) Attention	RNN-based Translation

Table 9.5: *Attention mechanisms*

Evaluation Strategies

Seq2seq models generate complete outputs–translations, summaries, captions, and even conversations–where there can be multiple correct responses. As a result, evaluation must go far beyond simple accuracy. We need to assess qualities such as fluency, clarity, relevance, and semantic correctness. Automating these assessments is challenging, especially because we are not looking for exact word matches. In many cases, even manual evaluation is subjective and non-trivial. For example, in translation, we often ask: *How close is this output to the intended meaning*? To address this, researchers have developed a range of evaluation strategies tailored for sequence generation. Let us explore these in detail.

Automatic Metrics

These are the spellcheckers of the seq2seq world – quick, objective, and consistent. They measure how close your model's output is to one or more reference outputs created by humans.

Bilingual Evaluation Understudy (BLEU)

Bilingual Evaluation Understudy (BLEU) scores how many n-grams (phrases of n words) from your model's output match the reference. For example, if your model says "*The cat sleeps*" and the reference is "*The cat is sleeping,*" you might get partial credit.

- Good for Machine translation
- Not suitable for creative tasks such as summarization or dialogue, where multiple valid outputs exist
- It cares too much about exact matches and not enough about meaning.

Recall-Oriented Understudy for Gisting Evaluation (ROUGE)

Recall-Oriented Understudy for Gisting Evaluation (ROUGE) flips BLEU's focus: it checks how much of the **reference** your model has captured.

- **ROUGE-N** checks for n-gram overlap (such as BLEU)

- **ROUGE-L** focuses on the longest common subsequence
- Suitable for summarization, headline generation, and paraphrasing
- It rewards verbosity and does not check if the summary is accurate

METEOR: The More Thoughtful Cousin

METEOR tries to go deeper than BLEU and ROUGE. It not only checks exact matches but also considers synonyms, stemming (for example, *run*, *running*), and paraphrasing.

- Closer to human judgment
- Suitable for translation, paraphrasing tasks
- Slower, less widely adopted in benchmarks

BERTScore: The Context-Aware Evaluator

What if we judged based on meaning, not just word overlap? That is what BERTScore does. It uses embeddings from a pre-trained language model, such as BERT, to see how semantically close your output is to the reference.

- Excellent for QA, summarization, and any task where wording may vary but meaning should match.
- It actually *understands* the sentence.
- Computationally heavier.

Embedding-Based and Learned Metrics

As we moved from rule-based systems to learned models, evaluation evolved too. Newer metrics use deep language models fine-tuned to predict how a human might score a generated sentence.

BLEURT (Bilingual Evaluation Understudy with Representations from Transformers)

Fine-tuned on human judgment data, BLEURT (from Google) is like having a trained editor read your model's output and score its fluency and accuracy.

- Suitable for summarization, translation
- Captures nuance and fluency better than string-based metrics

COMET (Crosslingual Optimized Metric for Evaluation of Translation)

Trained on human-labeled translation scores, COMET goes further by learning how *humans* evaluate translations.

- Suitable for translation tasks at a professional quality level

- Designed for *cross-lingual understanding*

Human Evaluation

Just like a wine tasting – only humans can truly tell if something is flavorful, smooth, or subtly wrong. Automatic metrics are fast, but humans judge nuance.

Judge Criteria:

- **Fluency**: Does the output read naturally, like a human wrote it?
- **Adequacy**: Does it capture all the important information from the input?
- **Faithfulness**: Is it factually correct and true to the source?
- **Relevance**: Is it appropriate and contextually useful?
- **Coherence**: Does the output logically flow from start to finish?
- **Diversity**: Are the outputs varied across different prompts?

Methods:

- **Likert Rating** (1 to 5): "*How good is this summary?*"
- **A/B Testing**: "*Which one do you prefer, Model A or Model B?*"
- **Error Annotation**: Spot issues such as grammar mistakes, hallucinations, or omissions

Strategic Recommendations

Goal	Strategy
During model development	Use ROUGE and BERTScore for fast feedback.
For research comparison	Combine automatic metrics with human evaluation.
Before deployment	Do qualitative error analysis and task-specific tests.
When model outputs vary	Use multiple references and semantic metrics (BERTScore, BLEURT).

Table 9.6: *Evaluation metrics for different tasks*

Case Study of Building a Summarization Engine

To solidify our understanding, let us create a text summarization system using PyTorch. We will use a Transformer-based model (specifically, we can fine-tune a pre-trained **BART** model) on a popular dataset, CNN/DailyMail, which contains news articles and their summaries (often called "*highlights*"). The goal is to take a news article as input and generate a concise summary.

Dataset and Setup

CNN/DailyMail is a widely used summarization dataset with on the order of ~300k articles for training. Each article comes with a few bullet-point highlights that serve as the reference summary. We will use the Hugging Face "*datasets*" library to load it easily. We also use the Hugging Face transformers library to get a pre-trained BART model. BART is an excellent choice here: it is a Transformer encoder-decoder pre-trained on a large corpus (with a denoising objective) and then further fine-tuned by Facebook on CNN/DailyMail to create the **`bart-large-cnn`** variant. We could fine-tune it ourselves quickly for demonstration, or even use the already fine-tuned weights for inference (since those are publicly available).

Let us start by loading the dataset and a tokenizer:

```
!pip install datasets transformers sacrebleu  # ensure required
packages are installed
from datasets import load_dataset
from transformers import BartTokenizer, BartForConditional
Generation

# Load CNN/DailyMail dataset (3.0.0 is a specific version)
dataset = load_dataset("cnn_dailymail", "3.0.0")
print(dataset.keys())  # should show 'train', 'validation',
'test' splits

tokenizer = BartTokenizer.from_pretrained("facebook/bart-large-
cnn")
model = BartForConditionalGeneration.from_pretrained("facebook/
bart-large-cnn")
```

When we run this, it will download the dataset (which is a bit large, ~1GB for the train split) and the BART model. For our purposes, let us assume we have a subset, or just focus on how to process a batch. The tokenizer will handle converting text to subword token ids that BART expects, and adding special tokens such as **<s>** (start of sequence) and **</s>** (end of sequence).

Data Preprocessing

We need to prepare the data for training. Each example in CNN/DailyMail has an article (the news story) and highlights (the summary). We will tokenize both. BART was trained with a specific maximum input length (1024 tokens for the article) and typically generates around 56 tokens for the summary (but we can allow up to, say, 128). We will truncate the article to 512 or 1024 tokens to fit memory.

Using the datasets library, we can map a preprocessing function over the dataset:

```
max_input_length = 512   # truncate article to 512 tokens
max_output_length = 128  # truncate summary to 128 tokens

def preprocess_function(batch):
    inputs = batch["article"]
    targets = batch["highlights"]

    # Tokenize inputs
    model_inputs = tokenizer(
        inputs,
        max_length=max_input_length,
        truncation=True,
        padding="max_length"
    )

    # Tokenize targets
    labels = tokenizer(
        text_target=targets,
        max_length=max_output_length,
        truncation=True,
        padding="max_length"
    )
    model_inputs["labels"] = labels["input_ids"]
    return model_inputs

# Use the dataset.map to apply preprocessing in batches
train_dataset = dataset["train"].map(preprocess_function,
batched=True, remove_columns=["article", "highlights", "id"])
val_dataset = dataset["validation"].map(preprocess_function,
batched=True, remove_columns=["article", "highlights", "id"])
```

This will produce a **`train_dataset`** where each entry has **`input_id`**s, **`attention_mask`**, and labels (which are the token IDs of the summary). We remove original text columns to save memory. Padding is done to the **`max_length`** we specified for efficient batching (so every input is 512 tokens, padded if shorter).

A *note on labels*: In seq2seq training with "**`BartForConditionalGeneration`**," the labels serve as the target sequence. The model will automatically shift them by one inside (so that at position **`t`** it is predicting **`label[t]`**, given that **`label[t-1]`** was the input at **`t`**). The loss is computed as cross-entropy against these labels. The **`attention_mask`** covers the input, and the model also internally creates a causal mask for the decoder. Padding tokens in labels are usually ignored by setting them to -100 (which Transformers does by default), so they do not count in the loss.

Fine-Tuning the Model

Now, we can fine-tune the model on the training set. This is basically training the model to generate the reference summary given the article input. Hugging Face's `Trainer` API makes this fairly straightforward, handling the training loop, evaluation, and saving. For the sake of brevity, we will outline the training setup:

```
from transformers import TrainingArguments, Trainer

training_args = TrainingArguments(
    output_dir="bart-summarizer",
    num_train_epochs=1,
    per_device_train_batch_size=2,
    per_device_eval_batch_size=2,
    gradient_accumulation_steps=4,  # to simulate larger batch
    learning_rate=3e-5,
    logging_steps=100,
    evaluation_strategy="epoch",
    save_strategy="epoch",
    save_total_limit=2,
    predict_with_generate=True,  # let Trainer handle generation
for eval
)

trainer = Trainer(
    model=model,
    args=training_args,
    train_dataset=train_dataset,
    eval_dataset=val_dataset,
)
trainer.train()
```

We set a small batch size (2) for illustration; in practice, one might use 8 or 16 per GPU if memory allows. We accumulate gradients to simulate a bigger batch (2 * 4 = 8). The learning rate 3e-5 is typical for fine-tuning a large model such as BART. We enable **`predict_with_generate=True`** so that during evaluation, the Trainer will perform generation on the validation set to compute metrics such as ROUGE easily.

Training a single epoch on the full dataset may still take a long time (hours) on a GPU, so for our purposes, imagine we train for 1 epoch and the model starts to learn to copy some phrases from article to summary (with pre-training, actually, one epoch might already yield decent summaries). This is full fine-tuning. We can also apply techniques like **LORA** which we learnt in the early chapters.

After training, one could evaluate on the test set. The Trainer can use a **compute_metrics** function with **sacrebleu** or **rouge_score** libraries to calculate **ROUGE** or **BLEU** on the outputs. For example:

```
# Define compute_metrics for ROUGE
from datasets import load_metric
rouge_metric = load_metric("rouge")

def compute_metrics(eval_pred):
    preds, labels = eval_pred
    # Decode predictions and references
    decoded_preds = tokenizer.batch_decode(preds, skip_special_
tokens=True)
    # Replace -100 in the labels as they are ignored (convert to
pad token id before decode)
    labels = labels.astype(int)
    labels[labels == -100] = tokenizer.pad_token_id
    decoded_labels = tokenizer.batch_decode(labels, skip_special_
tokens=True)
    # Compute ROUGE
    result = rouge_metric.compute(predictions=decoded_preds, ref-
erences=decoded_labels, use_stemmer=True)
    # Take average ROUGE-L
    result = {key: value.mid.fmeasure * 100 for key, value in re-
sult.items()}
    return result

# Re-instantiate Trainer with compute_metrics
trainer = Trainer(
    model=model,
    args=training_args,
    train_dataset=train_dataset,
    eval_dataset=val_dataset,
    compute_metrics=compute_metrics
)
```

If we then call "**trainer.evaluate()**", it would generate summaries for the validation set and compute ROUGE-1,2,L (the preceding code computes all by default). A well-fine-tuned BART on CNN/DailyMail typically gets around ROUGE-2 of 21 and ROUGE-L of 40+. (Those are decent scores, indicating the summary overlaps quite a bit with the reference.)

Testing the Summarization Model

Let us manually test the model on a couple of articles to see the output. We can pick an article from the dataset or use a custom one. For brevity, suppose we have an example article:

```
article_text = dataset["test"][0]["article"][:500]  # first 500
chars of a test article for demo
print("Article snippet:\n", article_text)

# Run generation
inputs = tokenizer(article_text, return_tensors="pt",
truncation=True, max_length=512)
summary_ids = model.generate(inputs["input_ids"], attention_
mask=inputs["attention_mask"], max_length=100, num_beams=4,
length_penalty=2.0, early_stopping=True)
generated_summary = tokenizer.decode(summary_ids[0], skip_spe-
cial_tokens=True)
print("\nGenerated Summary:\n", generated_summary)
```

We use the **`model.generate`**, which handles the autoregressive generation. Here we set **`num_beams=4`** for beam search to potentially get a better outcome than greedy, and a **`length_penalty`** to encourage brevity (since in summarization you want shorter than the input). The output is a token ID sequence, which we decode to get the summary text.

For example, if the article was about a political event, the generated summary might look like: "*The government passed a new law on Tuesday that aims to improve education. The law received bipartisan support and is expected to benefit millions of students, officials said.*" This is hopefully a concise version of the key facts.

We can also compare it to the reference summary:

```
print("\nReference Summary:\n", dataset["test"][0]["highlights"])
```

This allows us to qualitatively see if the model is capturing the important points. With BART, usually the outputs are quite fluent and often capture the gist, though sometimes they might omit a detail or include a slight distortion (for example, misstating a number).

Serving and Deployment

Once we have trained and evaluated our summarization engine, the next step is to make it accessible (serving) and ensure that it runs reliably and efficiently in production (monitoring). A well-trained model is only as useful as its deployment strategy. Let us walk through both aspects.

Model Serving with FastAPI

We can wrap our trained (or pre-trained) BART summarizer into a simple REST API.

This allows external systems (a web app, mobile app, or pipeline) to send text articles and receive summaries on demand. Save the file as **app.py**

```
!pip install fastapi uvicorn transformers torch
from fastapi import FastAPI
from pydantic import BaseModel
from transformers import BartTokenizer, BartForConditional
Generation

# Load model and tokenizer (can be your fine-tuned checkpoint
instead)
tokenizer = BartTokenizer.from_pretrained("facebook/bart-large-
cnn")
model = BartForConditionalGeneration.from_pretrained("facebook/
bart-large-cnn")

# Define request schema
class Article(BaseModel):
    text: str
    max_length: int = 100
    min_length: int = 30

# Create API
app = FastAPI(title="Summarization API")

@app.post("/summarize")
def summarize(article: Article):
    inputs = tokenizer(article.text, return_tensors="pt",
truncation=True, max_length=512)
    summary_ids = model.generate(
        inputs["input_ids"],
        attention_mask=inputs["attention_mask"],
        max_length=article.max_length,
        min_length=article.min_length,
        num_beams=4,
        length_penalty=2.0,
        early_stopping=True
    )
    summary = tokenizer.decode(summary_ids[0], skip_special_to-
kens=True)
    return {"summary": summary}
```

Run the server:

```
uvicorn app:app --reload --port 8000
```

Now, you can send a POST request:

```
curl -X POST "http://127.0.0.1:8000/summarize" \
     -H "Content-Type: application/json" \
     -d '{"text": "The government passed a new law today aiming
to improve education across the country."}'
```

Also, we can use the small code snippet to call it.

```
import requests
res = requests.post("http://127.0.0.1:8000/summarize",
              json={"text": "The government has passed a new law
today which is aiming to improve education sector"})

print("Response:", res.json())
```

Scaling and Optimization for Serving

For production, consider:

- Batching requests to improve throughput (**`transformers.pipeline`** supports batching).
- Quantization (for example, **`int8`** inference with **`bitsandbytes`**) to reduce latency.
- Model export to ONNX/TensorRT for hardware acceleration.
- Containerization with Docker and orchestration using Kubernetes or Ray Serve for auto-scaling.

Monitoring the Summarization Service

Monitoring ensures that the system is not only live but also performing well.

- **System Metrics**: CPU/GPU utilization, memory, and latency per request.
- **Model Metrics**: Quality of summaries (ROUGE/BERTScore drift over time).
- **Usage Analytics**: Number of requests, input length distribution, and response sizes.
- **Error Logging**: Detect malformed inputs, excessively long requests, or decoding errors.

Prometheus is an open-source monitoring and alerting system widely used in modern infrastructure and ML deployments. Originally developed at SoundCloud and later donated to the Cloud Native Computing Foundation (CNCF), it has become the de facto standard for monitoring in cloud-native environments (such as Kubernetes).

Here is a lightweight example of adding Prometheus-style metrics via **prometheus_client**:

```
!pip install prometheus-client
from prometheus_client import Counter, Histogram, generate_latest
from fastapi.responses import PlainTextResponse
import time

# Metrics
REQUEST_COUNT = Counter("request_count", "Number of requests")
REQUEST_LATENCY = Histogram("request_latency_seconds", "Request
latency")
@app.post("/summarize")
def summarize(article: Article):
    start_time = time.time()
    REQUEST_COUNT.inc()
    inputs = tokenizer(article.text, return_tensors="pt",
truncation=True, max_length=512)
    summary_ids = model.generate(
        inputs["input_ids"],
        attention_mask=inputs["attention_mask"],
        max_length=article.max_length,
        min_length=article.min_length,
        num_beams=4,
        length_penalty=2.0,
        early_stopping=True
    )
    summary = tokenizer.decode(summary_ids[0], skip_special_
tokens=True)
    REQUEST_LATENCY.observe(time.time() - start_time)
    return {"summary": summary}

# Endpoint to expose metrics
@app.get("/metrics")
def metrics():
    return PlainTextResponse(generate_latest().decode("utf-8"))
```

Example in Our Context

In the summarization engine:

- Every time the **/summarize** endpoint is called, Prometheus tracks:
  - How many times it was called (**request_count**).
  - How long it took (**request_latency_seconds**).

- These metrics can then be scraped by a Prometheus server and visualized in Grafana, allowing us to monitor whether the summarization API is:
    - o Handling increasing loads.
    - o Slowing down due to longer inputs.
    - o Failing more often over time.

With this, you can scrape *http://localhost:8000/metrics* to get live system statistics. In production, these metrics can be visualized with Grafana for monitoring.

With serving and monitoring in place, the summarization engine becomes a production-ready system rather than just a research prototype. It can now reliably deliver summaries at scale, with observability ensuring that both performance and quality remain consistent over time.

Real-World Effectiveness

Our fine-tuned model can now be used to summarize any news article (within the domain it knows). For instance, if you feed it a CNN article about a sports game, it should output a few sentences covering the final score and key moments. That is pretty powerful – it is like having an AI news editor. One must be careful: these models can occasionally hallucinate information (that is, output facts not in the source). BART is generally good at staying grounded, but it might rephrase in a way that slightly changes emphasis. However, LLMs might hallucinate, especially if they are trained on data that is not grounded. So in practice, generated summaries might be reviewed by humans in critical settings.

To ensure effectiveness, we could evaluate with metrics (as above) and also test on a variety of inputs. Suppose we feed a completely unrelated sentence, such as "*The sky is green*." The model, since it was trained on news, might produce something like "*Scientists discover why the sky is green*," or just repeat it. It is always interesting to probe such models.

Tips for Further Improvement

In a production or research setting, there are many ways to improve summarization beyond this basic fine-tuning:

- Use a larger model or the latest architectures (such as PEGASUS, which was specifically pre-trained for summarization by masking out sentences).
- Perform hyperparameter tuning (learning rate, beam size, length penalty) to maximize ROUGE or whatever metric correlates with quality.
- If multiple references per article are available, consider using them or consensus scoring.

- Integrate a factuality check to ensure the summary does not say things that are not in the article (a common issue in abstractive summarization).
- Try prompting or few-shot techniques if using extremely large models (such as prompting GPT-3 or GPT-4 with "*Summarize this:*" could yield good summaries without fine-tuning at all).
- Use the simple fine-tuning techniques, such as PEFT and Prompt tuning, which were discussed in the earlier chapters.
- Evaluate with humans for qualitative aspects: Is the summary clear and correct?

Wrapping Up the Case Study

We have walked through building a summarization engine using PyTorch. Starting from the seq2seq design, we chose a Transformer model (BART), prepared data, fine-tuned the model, and generated sample summaries. This exercise highlights several takeaways:

- Modern seq2seq tasks heavily leverage pre-trained models to achieve strong performance with relatively little task-specific data. (BART was trained on a huge generic corpus before we fine-tuned it on a news dataset.)
- PyTorch and its ecosystem provide high-level tools (`datasets`, `transformers`) that abstract away a lot of boilerplate, allowing us to focus on the core modeling. We did not have to manually code backpropagation or worry about teacher forcing – the library handled it.
- The principles from earlier sections come together: the model's encoder-decoder architecture with attention is what makes it able to compress an article and expand it into a summary.
- Evaluation with metrics such as ROUGE gives a quick sense of average performance, but reading a few examples of model summaries versus reference really gives intuition. We recommend always looking at outputs qualitatively when developing such models.

Trivia

1. I take in the tokens, but do not speak a word,
   I process and pass them, but my voice is not heard.
   From layer to layer, I polish the sense,
   Without me, translation would be quite dense.
   What am I?

2. I build the response, but need some clues,
   From the past and present, I carefully choose.
   I peek at the source through an aligned view,

Then, word by word, create something new.
What am I?

3. I focus on parts of my own kind,
Seeking the patterns I am meant to find.
With keys and queries, I search and see,
The most important parts of me.
What am I?

4. I do not look within, I look beyond,
To another's message, I form a bond.
The encoder whispers, I listen with care,
To shape a reply from what's hidden there.
What am I?

5. I wear many hats and look many ways,
Catching all patterns and their secret plays.
Though I am one at heart, I split my sight,
To understand the world just right.
What am I?

6. Words come in lines, but I give them place,
A rhythm, a sequence, a step in the race.
Though all sounds are static to those who hear,
I whisper the order that makes it clear.
What am I?

Answers

1. Encoder
2. Decoder
3. Self-attention
4. Cross-attention
5. Multi-head attention
6. Positional Embedding

Conclusion

Designing sequence-to-sequence (seq2seq) systems is both a creative and technical pursuit, requiring choices about encoders, decoders, and attention mechanisms, as well as an understanding of domains, input-output structures, and task-specific trade-offs. The evolution from RNNs with memory bottlenecks to Transformer-based architectures has transformed the field, enabling models that scale, attend globally, and generate with fluency. Along the way, considerations such as tokenization, positional encoding, and richer evaluation metrics beyond accuracy–focusing on meaning, coherence, and user experience–have become essential.

Whether for translation, chatbots, summarization, or voice assistants, seq2seq systems provide the flexibility to capture and generate complex sequences in human-like ways. The field continues to advance with pre-trained models, sparse attention techniques, and agent-driven workflows, pushing the boundaries. This chapter highlighted not just how seq2seq models operate, but also their applications, design principles, and practical implementation. Equipped with PyTorch tools and evaluation strategies, you now have the foundation to build, fine-tune, and assess seq2seq systems in real-world scenarios.

In the next chapter, we will discuss Transformers in depth.

References

1. Sutskever, I., Vinyals, O., & Le, Q. V. (2014). **Sequence to Sequence Learning with Neural Networks**. *Advances in Neural Information Processing Systems* (NeurIPS). https://arxiv.org/abs/1409.3215
2. Bahdanau, D., Cho, K., & Bengio, Y. (2015). **Neural Machine Translation by Jointly Learning to Align and Translate**. *International Conference on Learning Representations* (ICLR). https://arxiv.org/abs/1409.0473
3. Vaswani, A., Shazeer, N., Parmar, N., et al. (2017). **Attention is All You Need**. *Advances in Neural Information Processing Systems* (NeurIPS). https://arxiv.org/abs/1706.03762
4. Devlin, J., Chang, M. W., Lee, K., & Toutanova, K. (2018). **BERT: Pre-training of Deep Bidirectional Transformers for Language Understanding**. NAACL-HLT. https://arxiv.org/abs/1810.04805
5. Lewis, M., Liu, Y., Goyal, N., et al. (2019). **BART: Denoising Sequence-to-Sequence Pre-training for Natural Language Generation, Translation, and Comprehension**. ACL 2020. https://arxiv.org/abs/1910.13461
6. Raffel, C., Shazeer, N., Roberts, A., et al. (2020). **Exploring the Limits of Transfer Learning with a Unified Text-to-Text Transformer (T5)**. *Journal of Machine Learning Research*. https://arxiv.org/abs/1910.10683
7. Papineni, K., Roukos, S., Ward, T., & Zhu, W. J. (2002). **BLEU: a Method for Automatic Evaluation of Machine Translation**. ACL 2002.

8. Lin, C. Y. (2004). **ROUGE: A Package for Automatic Evaluation of Summaries**. *Workshop on Text Summarization Branches Out.*
9. Zhang, T., Kishore, V., Wu, F., et al. (2020). **BERTScore: Evaluating Text Generation with BERT**. ICLR 2020. https://arxiv.org/abs/1904.09675
10. Sellam, T., Das, D., & Parikh, A. (2020). **BLEURT: Learning Robust Metrics for Text Generation**. ACL 2020. https://arxiv.org/abs/2004.04696

CHAPTER 10
Building Domain-Specific LLMs from Scratch

Introduction

"*Code is law.*" – Lawrence Lessig
"*And sometimes the law needs better code.*" – every junior associate who has ever searched 200 pages of precedent at 2 a.m.

In the previous chapter, we fine-tuned an existing transformer model for summarization and saw promising results. Now, we take a bold step further: building a domain-specific Large Language Model (LLM) from scratch for the legal domain. This chapter follows an educational journey–an LLM that understands court rulings and statutes. We will accompany them from gathering a corpus of legal documents to designing a custom transformer, training it on powerful hardware, and finally evaluating and deploying the model in the real world. Along the way, we will delve deeper into the transformer's architecture and learn practical tips for tackling the challenges unique to legal language. By the end of this chapter, we will know how to design and train a transformer from scratch, tailor it for long legal documents, and ensure it performs well on specialized legal tasks.

Training a LLM from scratch for a specific domain can be a major undertaking, but it offers unique benefits in certain situations where fine-tuning a general model might not suffice. Building an LLM from scratch is highly impractical as it is a very costly approach. We are building it for educational purposes here. Here are key motivations for building a domain-specific LLM from the ground up:

- Deeper coverage of specific knowledge
- Custom architectures, size, and accuracy
- When fine-tuning is not enough
- The data is too specialized and requires privacy

Structure

In this chapter, we will cover the following topics:

- Data Creation
- Transformer Architecture in Depth
- Distributed Training
- Evaluation and Deployment
- Case Study: Building a legal LLM from Scratch

Data Creation

Building a domain-specific LLM starts with the right data. The quality, relevance, and volume of your domain text data directly affect how well the model will understand specialized content. This section covers how to source and prepare domain-specific datasets across fields such as medicine, finance, law, and technology. We will explore strategies for gathering data, preprocessing techniques to clean and normalize it, tokenization for domain terminology, creating labeled data for fine-tuning, and important privacy and ethical considerations. By the end, we should grasp general data preparation methods that apply to any domain.

Figure 10.1: *Imaginary picture of a legal LLM. Credits:* SORA

Sourcing Domain-Specific Data

Collecting a high-quality corpus is the first step. Depending on your domain, you may draw from a mix of public and private sources:

- **Public Corpora and Open Datasets:** Leverage openly available text collections related to any field. For example, scientific and medical models can use research papers and journals (for example, PubMed articles), finance models might use stock reports or economic news, and tech models might use documentation or forum posts. Public resources such as websites, online books, research repositories, and even Wikipedia are commonly tapped for LLM training. Many organizations release curated datasets (on platforms such as Kaggle or Hugging Face) covering domain-specific content. Using diverse sources (news, forums, academic papers) helps ensure a varied data distribution.
- **APIs and Open Data Sources:** In some cases, data can be gathered via APIs. For instance, a healthcare LLM might pull medical articles using the PubMed API, or a finance LLM could fetch historical market data through financial APIs. Likewise, social media or community platforms often provide APIs to access text (for example, Twitter's API for finance sentiment, Stack Exchange data dumps for technical Q&A). Using APIs can simplify collecting up-to-date information in structured formats (JSON, XML, and so on) without manual scraping.
- **Web Scraping:** For domains with rich web content but no single dataset, web scraping is a powerful approach. This involves writing scripts to crawl and extract text from relevant websites (with permission). For example, we might scrape legal opinions from court websites, product reviews for retail, or technical blog posts for programming. Tools such as BeautifulSoup, Scrapy, or Selenium can automate this process by parsing HTML and collecting the raw text. It is important to structure the scraped data (for example, saving it as CSV or JSON) and respect web ethics and legality – always check the site's terms of service and robots.txt, and avoid overloading servers. Web scraping yields large volumes of domain text quickly, but be prepared to clean the data afterward (removing navigation menus, ads, HTML tags, and so on).
- **Institutional and Proprietary Data**: In specialized domains, the most valuable data may come from private sources or partnerships. This includes internal documents, databases, or data shared by domain experts. For example, a medical LLM can benefit from anonymized electronic health records or hospital clinical notes, a legal LLM might use a firm's brief archives, and a finance LLM could incorporate transaction logs or analyst reports. Collaborating with institutions (hospitals, law firms, banks, and so on) or data providers can grant access to such datasets. Always ensure you have permission or data-sharing agreements in place. The data would be highly sensitive and would require

formal review board approvals and strict agreements, and compliance. The goal is to expose the model to the real jargon, workflows, and edge cases of the domain - including internal knowledge (such as product manuals, support chat transcripts, or customer emails) that general web data will not contain. While these sources may require extra effort (NDAs, licensing fees, and so on), they can make your model truly industry-grade.

Collecting data is an iterative process. We might start with public data to get a base corpus and then augment with more specific or proprietary texts. Always prioritize quality over sheer quantity - a smaller curated set of relevant texts is often more potent than a huge dump of unrelated or noisy data. Once we have the raw data, the next step is to preprocess it for training.

A smaller model trained on carefully-filtered, textbook-quality text (Phi) can match—or even beat—larger models trained on huge but noisy web dumps (GPT-2).

GPT-2 is trained with 8 million webpages (~40 GB) chosen chiefly for popularity, not pedagogical value. It is great at general next-word prediction and fluent prose, but it still "*under-fits WebText*" (the authors' words), and struggles on structure-heavy tasks, such as code generation or formal reasoning.

Microsoft Phi is an LLM pre-screened raw web document, keeping only ones that read like step-by-step explanations, tutorials, or worked examples ("textbook-quality"). Anything off-topic, repetitive, or low-signal was discarded. 7 B tokens are tiny compared with WebText, yet every token teaches something explicit (a definition, an example, a solved exercise). With 20 × fewer tokens than GPT-2, Phi-1 still outruns GPT-2-sized models on HumanEval and MBPP coding tests—benchmarks that reward logical consistency rather than surface fluency. The emphasis on data quality wins over the quantity of data!

Figure 10.2: *Fun interpretation of GPT-2 versus Microsoft Phi. Credits:* SORA

Preprocessing and Normalization

Raw text from the wild is rarely ready for direct use. Preprocessing turns this raw corpus into clean, consistent, and machine-readable text. Common challenges include different file formats, noise and errors in text, duplicate entries, and preserving important structure. A typical data processing pipeline for LLMs might include several steps (as illustrated in the following paragraphs) before the data is ready for training.

Format Normalization

Domain data comes in various formats – HTML web pages, PDFs, Word documents, spreadsheets, and so on. The first task is to convert these to plain text in a consistent encoding (for example, UTF-8). For web pages, this means stripping out HTML tags and scripts; for PDFs or scans, using OCR if needed to extract text. Libraries such as BeautifulSoup (for HTML/XML) or PDF parsers (for example, PyPDF or pdfplumber) help automate this conversion. You should also standardize things such as newline usage, punctuation, and case if appropriate (some models train on all-lowercase text). For instance, you might want to remove markup artifacts (HTML entities such as ` ` or LaTeX commands in research papers). Normalizing the text format ensures later steps deal with text and not binary data or layout.

Noise Removal and Filtering

Real-world text is noisy. This step removes irrelevant or low-quality content that could confuse the model. Examples of noise include advertisements or navigation text on web pages, boilerplate legal disclaimers, broken characters from OCR errors, and text in other languages that may have slipped in. We might filter out non-domain content (for example, exclude a news article in a medical corpus that is not actually medical). Some filtering can be automated by rules or simple models – for example, removing lines that are too short or filled with symbols, or using language detection to drop texts not in the desired language. Quality filtering is crucial because bad data (garbage in) will lead to a poorer model (garbage out). In fact, large-scale LLM projects often apply heuristic or classifier-based filters to eliminate low-quality text. Heuristic filters might remove content with lots of profanity, weird formatting, or unrelated keywords, while classifier-based filters use a smaller ML model to classify text as high versus low quality. At a minimum, remove obvious junk and standardized filler content. If working with OCR'd domain documents, invest time in fixing OCR mistakes (for example, "O" versus "0", random punctuation) because domain terms need to be spelled correctly to be learned.

Deduplication

Redundant data appears often, such as the same article copied on multiple websites or repeated sections in logs. Duplicate passages can hurt an LLM's training, causing it to overweigh those examples, and possibly overfit or simply waste computation. Therefore, it is standard practice to deduplicate the corpus at some level. This can be done at the exact string match level or using hashing algorithms to catch near-duplicates. For example, one might remove duplicate lines or paragraphs, or use a shingling algorithm to detect mostly-similar documents. Deduplication can be computationally heavy for very large corpora, but it pays off by increasing the effective diversity of your training set. In domain data, be mindful: if a certain important document (such as a legal statute or medical guideline) is duplicated verbatim, you may keep one copy but do not need it many times. The goal is to ensure that each training example adds new information.

Preserving Structural Markers

Unlike general web text, domain-specific documents often have meaningful structure – sections, lists, formulas, code blocks, and so on. During preprocessing, we must decide how to handle these. In some cases, we will remove the structure (for example, strip out all XML tags or section headings if they are not needed). In other cases, preserving structure can provide context to the model. For instance, keeping Markdown formatting for technical documentation (such as code fences around code snippets, or bold for important terms) might help the model identify them. In a medical dataset, headings such as "*Diagnosis*:" or bullet lists of symptoms are valuable cues. We can choose to insert special tokens or markers to indicate these structures instead of raw symbols. For example, we might replace each section title with [SECTION: title] to let the model know it is a heading, or use a token such as `<TABLE>` to denote where a table was removed. If your domain text has metadata (timestamps, speaker IDs, and so on, such as in clinical dialogues or legal transcripts), we may incorporate those as tokens as well, or remove them if not needed. The key is consistency: decide on a scheme for representing structure and apply it uniformly. That way, the model can learn from it. On the other hand, extraneous structures that do not aid understanding should be cleaned out. It is a balance between simplifying the text and keeping domain-specific cues. A good practice is to manually inspect a few samples of processed text to ensure that it still "reads" logically and contains the critical information, minus the clutter.

Best Practices in Tokenization

Tokenization is the process of breaking text into pieces (tokens) that the model actually sees. Modern LLMs use subword tokenization – instead of splitting only on spaces or using full words, they break text into subtokens (often using Byte Pair Encoding or similar algorithms). For domain-specific data, careful tokenization ensures that specialized terms are encoded in a sensible way that the model can learn.

Off-the-shelf tokenizers (such as the one used for GPT-2 or BERT) are trained on general text, so they may split a domain word into awkward pieces. For instance, the medical term "*hyperglycemia*" might get split into tokens such as "*hyper*", "*gly*", and "*cemia*" by a generic tokenizer. This makes it harder for the model to recognize the term as a single concept. One best practice is to customize the tokenizer with domain vocabulary. There are a couple of ways to do this:

- **Train a new tokenizer on the corpus:** Libraries such as SentencePiece or Hugging Face's tokenizers can learn a new subword vocabulary from the domain data. Recent LLM projects often build custom tokenizers with SentencePiece. This ensures common domain terms (for example, chemical names, legal phrases) become single tokens or a small number of tokens, preserving meaning. For example, if the corpus has many instances of "neural network," the tokenizer might create a single token for "*neural*" and "*network*" each, rather than letter chunks. Byte-level BPE is popular for robustness (it can handle rare characters by breaking into bytes without losing information).
- **Extend an existing tokenizer's vocabulary:** If we fine-tune from a base model, we can take its tokenizer and add new tokens for terms frequently found in the domain. This way, we can leverage what the model already knows and only introduce a few hundred or thousands of new tokens. Most transformer libraries allow adding tokens and then resizing the model's embedding layer to accommodate them. For example, with Hugging Face Transformers.

Choosing whether to retrain a tokenizer or extend existing ones can depend on data size and how different your domain is from generic text. Training a new tokenizer from scratch requires a sizable corpus but gives full control over tokenization. Adding tokens is simpler and works well if only a moderate number of new terms are needed.

Another consideration is tokenizer normalization. Many tokenizers apply Unicode normalization (such as NFKC) or lowercasing. In domains such as biomedical or legal, case and special characters might carry meaning (gene symbols are case-sensitive, "*Section* §5" has a symbol). Aggressive normalization can distort domain text (the Labeller guide notes that NFKC normalization sometimes hurts tokenization for complex corpora). It can be beneficial to turn off lowercasing or certain normalizations when training a tokenizer on domain data so that "MRI" and "*mri*" are not conflated if that matters.

Step	What It Is	Why It Matters	Key Techniques / Tools	Notes and Examples
1. Format Normalization	Converting heterogeneous raw files into consistent plain text (UTF-8).	Models can only learn from clean, uniform text – not raw HTML, PDF layout, or binary content.	BeautifulSoup (HTML), pdfplumber, PyPDF, OCR, text cleaning rules.	Strip HTML tags, remove scripts, normalize punctuation, remove LaTeX markup, fix newline inconsistencies.

2. Noise Removal and Filtering	Removing irrelevant, low-quality, or non-domain content.	Bad text → bad model ("*garbage in, garbage out*"). Reduces confusion in domain learning.	Heuristic filters, regex rules, profanity filters, language detection, small ML-quality classifiers.	Remove ads, menus, boilerplate, OCR errors, unrelated topics, strange characters, or extremely short/garbled lines.
3. Deduplication	Eliminating repeated text at the line, paragraph, or document level.	Prevents overfitting, reduces wasted compute, increases dataset diversity.	Exact match hashing, near-duplicate detection (shingling, MinHash).	Keep **one** copy of important repeated documents (legal statutes, guidelines). Remove copied articles across websites.
4. Preserving Structural Markers	Handling or adding structure markers like headings, lists, code blocks, formulas.	Structure often provides domain meaning (e.g., "*Diagnosis:*" or bullet lists).	Insert special tokens, keep Markdown, consistent formatting rules.	Use [SECTION: *Diagnosis*], <TABLE>, code fences, or metadata tokens. Remove irrelevant structure; keep meaningful cues.
5. Best Practices in Tokenization	Splitting text into subword units the model uses.	Subword modeling allows LLMs to learn domain terms without exploding vocabulary size.	BPE, SentencePiece, HuggingFace Tokenizers, byte-level BPE.	Generic tokenizers may split domain terms poorly – e.g., *hyperglycemia* → *hyper* + *gly* + *cemia*.
6. Custom Tokenizer Training	Training a tokenizer from scratch on domain corpus.	Creates domain-aware tokens representing full terms (chemical names, medical/law phrases).	SentencePiece training, Unigram/BPE models.	Ensures common terms (e.g., "*neural*", "*network*") become stable subwords instead of random fragments.

7. Extending Existing Tokenizers	Adding new vocabulary to a base model's tokenizer instead of training from scratch.	Leverages pre-trained embedding space while adapting to domain terminology.	HuggingFace `tokenizer.add_tokens()`, resizing embedding matrices.	Add only hundreds–thousands of tokens; faster than retraining entire tokenizer.
8. Tokenizer Normalization Choices	Deciding whether to apply Unicode normalization, lowercasing, etc.	Over-normalization may destroy meaning in domains where case/symbols matter.	Adjust tokenizer config: disable lowercasing, disable NFKC if needed.	For example, "MRI" ≠ "mri" in biomedical text; "§5" is meaningful in legal documents.

Table 10.1: *Summary of data processing techniques*

Supervised Learning

So far, we have discussed gathering text for unsupervised pre-training (where the model learns from raw text alone). In many cases, you will also want to fine-tune our LLM on supervised data – that is, examples with input-output pairs or labels, specific to tasks in your domain. Creating this annotated data is often the most labor-intensive part, but it is crucial for tasks such as question-answering, classification, or dialog in a specialized field.

Some common strategies for data annotation are as follows:

- Manual Annotation by Domain Expert
- Trained Annotators and Crowd Sourcing
- Human in the Loop and Iterative Enhancement
- Data Augmentation and Synthetic Labels

These techniques are discussed in detail in previous chapters; hence, we are not elaborating on them further.

Privacy, Licensing, and Ethical Considerations

Working with domain-specific data brings responsibilities to handle sensitive information and legal considerations properly. It is critical to address these from the start:

Privacy and PII Removal

Domains such as healthcare and law often involve personal or confidential data. Any personally identifiable information **(PII)** (names, addresses, phone numbers, patient IDs, and so on) should be removed or anonymized in the training data. This process is sometimes called privacy redaction. Simple methods include using regex or keyword lists to redact obvious PII (for example, replace names with `[NAME]`). More advanced approaches use NLP models to detect PII entities (such as a named entity recognizer trained to find person names, SSNs, and so on). Removing PII not only protects individuals but also reduces the risk of the model memorizing and regurgitating sensitive facts. In fact, duplicate occurrences of PII in the corpus can increase privacy leakage risk, so deduplication (mentioned earlier) also helps mitigate that. Always follow regulations such as HIPAA (for medical data) or GDPR (for any personal data of EU citizens), which mandate strict data handling and anonymization. If you must use sensitive data, consider techniques such as data pseudonymization (replacing real identifiers with fake but consistent ones) or federated learning (where data stays on-premise and only model updates are shared, reducing raw data transfer).

Licensing and Copyright

Not all text on the internet is free to use. Public domain data (for example, works published by the government, or very old texts) is generally safe and straightforward – it is free for anyone to use. However, many valuable texts (scientific papers, books, news articles) are under copyright. Using them for training without permission could violate laws. Companies building serious domain LLMs often license datasets or subscribe to data services. For example, a legal LLM might license a database of court cases, or a finance LLM might pay for access to a news archive. Licensing ensures we have rights to the data and often comes with quality guarantees. It can be costly, but for specialized domains, it may be the only way to get sufficient high-quality data legally. The benefit is that licensed data often comes directly from the source (for example, a medical research firm providing clinical trial text), and those providers might help with anonymization or curation as part of the agreement.

Ethical Use and Bias

Domain-specific data can reflect biases or ethical pitfalls that need mitigation. For instance, historical medical notes might under-represent certain groups, or legal texts might contain biased language. It is important to review the dataset for bias – are all demographics fairly represented? Does the data contain stigmatizing language or out-of-date terminology? If so, consider balancing the data or injecting more diverse perspectives if possible. Ethically, the outputs of a domain LLM should not reinforce harmful stereotypes or incorrect practices. Another aspect is hallucinations and accuracy in high-stakes domains (medical advice, legal interpretations); an LLM making up information can be dangerous. While this is more about model training and deployment, the data creation stage can help by providing ample factual content and by possibly annotating or removing known false statements in training data. Additionally, be transparent about the data sources when possible. Having documentation for the dataset (a datasheet) is a good ethical practice – it informs users what the model was trained on, highlighting any limitations.

Compliance and Legal Constraints

Depending on the domain, there may be laws governing data. Financial data usage could fall under regulations against insider information if it is very recent or proprietary. Government or military domain data might be classified or export-controlled. Always ensure that by creating and using the dataset, the organization complies with all relevant laws. If collaborating with an institution (say, a hospital or bank), data sharing agreements must specify allowed uses and compliance measures (such as encryption at rest, who can access the raw data, and so on). As an additional safeguard, maintain audit logs of how data was collected and processed. Version control the dataset so we know exactly what went into model training. This helps in auditing and is useful if a privacy issue arises and you need to trace it.

Open Source vs Proprietary Considerations

If we plan to open-source the domain model or dataset, we must ensure none of the data has licenses that forbid that (for example, we cannot release text from a copyrighted journal article). In such cases, only release derived models if allowed, and never the raw text. Even releasing only weights can expose copyright risks if the training corpus was protected. If the model could potentially output large chunks verbatim from training data (a risk if data were limited or repetitive), it is another reason to avoid including any passages we are not allowed to redistribute. Some teams address this by transforming the text (paraphrasing it) before training, but that can be complex and is not foolproof. The safest route is to curate data that we have full rights to use for the intended purpose.

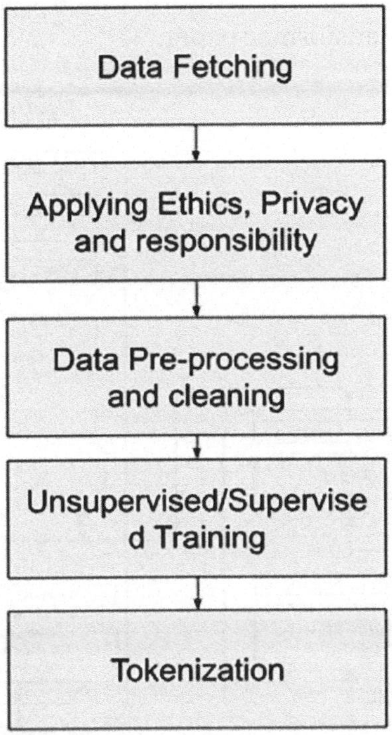

Figure 10.3: *Flow chart for data creation*

Transformer Architecture in Depth

This section shows how to implement both halves of the original Transformer—the encoder and the decoder—so we can assemble the exact architecture the domain-specific LLM needs. In the previous chapter, we introduced the transformer concepts for designing the sequence-to-sequence problems. In this chapter, we focus on practical implementation, design choices, and architectural variants that matter when the domain is narrow and the data precious.

Building a Transformer from scratch involves designing the core architecture choices that underpin any domain-specific large language model. In this section, we describe how to construct encoder-only, decoder-only, and encoder-decoder Transformers in a domain-agnostic way. We will walk through the key architectural components - from multi-head attention (self-attention and cross-attention) to feed-forward networks and positional encodings - and discuss design decisions such as the number of layers, attention heads, and hidden dimensions. We also provide guidance on balancing model accuracy with computational efficiency (for example, model size versus memory usage and training speed), and include PyTorch code examples for custom encoder/decoder modules and a full model skeleton. Finally, we compare these architecture variants and their suitability for different use cases in a summary table.

Take a look at the transformer architecture which consists of both encoder and decoder from the original transformer paper.

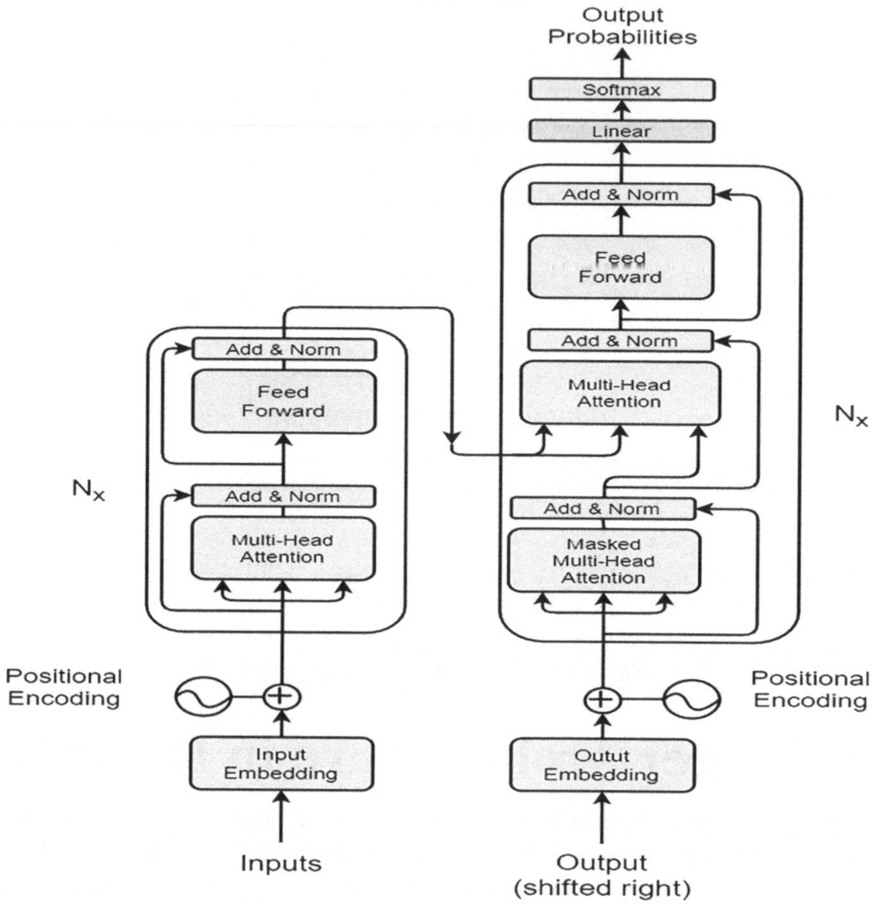

***Figure 10.4**: Transformer architecture from original paper*

Encoder and Decoder: Decoded

Transformers process sequences by attending to different positions of the input and transforming representations through stacked layers. A Transformer can include an encoder component, a decoder component, or both, depending on the use case. Encoder-only models (also known as autoencoding transformers) consist solely of the encoder stack, enabling bidirectional self-attention over an input sequence. Encoder-only models are not used for generation tasks but are used for context understanding, embeddings, and classification (for example, BERT). Decoder-only models (autoregressive transformers) consist solely of the decoder stack and use only causal (one-directional) self-attention to generate outputs sequentially. Decoder-only models are the backbone for today's larger LLMs, such as GPT models. Encoder-decoder models (sequence-to-sequence transformers) combine both: an encoder that first processes the input sequence, and a decoder that generates an output sequence while attending to encoder outputs (via cross-attention).

A standard Transformer architecture, with an encoder and decoder. The encoder stack comprises layers of multi-headed self-attention and feed-forward networks, while the decoder stack contains masked self-attention and cross-attention sublayers in addition to feed-forward networks. Residual connections (➕) and layer normalization (Norm) are applied at each sublayer. In encoder-decoder models, the decoder's cross-attention allows it to attend to the encoder's final outputs, whereas in decoder-only models, this cross-attention is omitted.

Let us understand the difference between three (3) different transformer architecture models: encoder-only, decoder-only, and encoder-decoder.

Aspect	**Encoder-only**	**Decoder-only**	**Encoder-Decoder**
Architecture	Stack of encoder blocks	Stack of decoder blocks	Encoders + Decoders
Input Type	Full input sequence	Partial input (auto-regressive)	Source (encoder) + Target (decoder)
Masking in Self-Attention	No masking (bidirectional attention)	Causal masking (prevents peeking)	Encoder: No masking Decoder: Causal masking
Cross-Attention	(not needed)	(not needed)	Decoder attends to encoder outputs
Pretraining Objective	Masked Language Modeling (MLM)	Causal Language Modeling (CLM)	Sequence-to-sequence tasks (for example, translation)
Common Use Cases	Text classification, embedding tasks, and retrieval	Text generation (chatbots, story writing, code)	Machine translation, summarization, and question answering
Popular Models	BERT, RoBERTa, DistilBERT	GPT-2, GPT-3, LLaMA, Falcon	T5, BART, mT5, ProphetNet
Advantages	Better contextual understanding	Efficient for generation tasks	Handles input-output pairs effectively
Limitations	Not suitable for generation	Lacks bidirectional context	More complex and slower to train

Table 10.2: *Comparison of different transformer architectures*

Recommendation: Start with encoder-only if the tasks are "*read and understand*," decoder-only if we just need fluent domain text, and full encoder-decoder when we must transform one sequence into another (for example, statute → plain-language).

Multi-Head Self-Attention (Shared by Encoder and Decoder)

An attention model is a mechanism in deep learning that enables a network to selectively focus on the most relevant parts of the input when making predictions, rather than treating all information equally. Originally introduced in sequence-to-sequence models for machine translation, attention computes a weighted combination of input features, where the weights (attention scores) indicate the importance of each element relative to the current task. This allows the model to capture long-range dependencies, handle variable-length inputs, and improve interpretability by showing which parts of the input influenced the output most.

Multi-head attention is a key component of the Transformer architecture that allows the model to focus on different parts of the input sequence simultaneously. Instead of performing a single attention operation, the model splits the input embeddings into multiple smaller "*heads*." Each head projects the inputs (queries, keys, and values) into lower-dimensional spaces and computes attention independently. This enables the model to capture diverse relationships, such as short-term dependencies in one head and long-range dependencies in another, making the representation more expressive. After each head computes its attention outputs, these results are concatenated and projected back into the original embedding dimension.

The following PyTorch code illustrates a single Transformer encoder layer. It applies multi-head self-attention to the input `x` (allowing the token at every position to attend to all others), then a feed-forward network, with residual connections and layer normalization around each sub-layer output (often called post-norm configuration). A mask can be optionally provided to the attention function (for example, to ignore padding tokens). This basic structure can be stacked **`N`** times to form the full encoder module.

Multi-head attention allows the model to jointly attend to information from different representation subspaces. Formally, it is defined as:

$$\text{Multihead}(Q,K,V) = \text{Concat}(\text{head}_1, \text{head}_2, \ldots, \text{head}_h)W^{\theta}$$

where each attention head is calculated as:

$$\text{head}_i = \text{Attention}(QW_i^{Q}, KW_i^{K}, VW_i^{V})$$

and the scaled dot-product attention is calculated as:

$$\text{Attention}(Q,K,V) = \text{softmax}(QK^{T}/\text{Sqrt}(d_k))\ V$$

Here:

- Q, K, and V are the Query, Key, and Value matrices, respectively.
- W_i^{Q}, W_i^{K}, and W_i^{V} are learnable parameters.

- W^0 is the output linear transformation matrix.

First, let us understand how we can implement the multi-head attention.

This class implements multi-head self-attention (or cross-attention) using PyTorch, a core component of Transformer models. It can operate in both encoder (self-attention) and decoder (cross-attention + optional causal masking) modes. Replace **`nn.MultiheadAttention`** with Flash-Attention or **`xFormers`** for speed once prototypes work.

```
class MultiHeadSelfAttention(nn.Module):
    def __init__(self, d_model: int, n_heads: int, causal: bool = 
False):
tokens (used in decoders).
#d_model: total dimension of input embeddings (e.g., 512 or 768).
#n_heads: number of attention heads to split the model into.
#causal: if True, applies a causal mask to prevent attending to 
future
        super().__init__()
        assert d_model % n_heads == 0
        self.head_dim = d_model // n_heads
        self.n_heads = n_heads
        self.causal = causal
        self.qkv = nn.Linear(d_model, 3 * d_model)    # Projects 
input into queries (Q), keys (K), and values (V) in a single 
linear operation.
        self.out = nn.Linear(d_model, d_model)

    def forward(self, x, kv=None, mask=None):
        #If kv is provided, it's used for cross-attention (e.g., 
decoder attends to encoder output). Otherwise, it's 
self-attention.
        k_in = v_in = kv if kv is not None else x
        B, T, _ = x.size()
        q, k, v = self.qkv(x), self.qkv(k_in), self.qkv(v_in)
        q, k, v = [t.view(B, -1, self.n_heads, self.head_dim).
transpose(1, 2)
                   for t in (q, k, v)]     # Computes query, key, 
and value vectors for all tokens.
  # Computes scaled dot-product attention scores.
        scores = (q @ k.transpose(-2, -1)) / self.head_dim**0.5

        if self.causal:
            # Applies causal mask to prevent attention to future 
tokens (decoder mode).
            causal_mask = torch.tril(torch.ones(T, T, device=x.
device, dtype=torch.bool))
```

```
            scores = scores.masked_fill(~causal_mask, float
('-inf'))
        if mask is not None:                    # optional
padding mask
            scores = scores.masked_fill(mask == 0, float('-inf'))
        attn = torch.softmax(scores, dim=-1)
        #Applies attention weights to value vectors.
        context = attn @ v
        context = context.transpose(1, 2).contiguous().view(B, T,
-1)
        return self.out(context)
```

Encoder and Decoder Layers

The Encoder class represents one layer of the Transformer encoder, combining self-attention and feed-forward sublayers.

- Applies LayerNorm → Multi-head Self-Attention → Dropout → Residual connection.
- Then applies LayerNorm → FeedForward → Dropout → Residual connection.
- Residual connections allow better gradient flow and faster convergence.

The Decoder class represents one layer of the Transformer decoder, which includes causal self-attention, encoder-decoder cross-attention, and a feed-forward network.

- **Causal Self-Attention** over target (x): prevents peeking at future tokens
- **Cross-Attention** with encoder output (**enc_out**).
- **Feed-Forward** network.

```
class EncoderLayer(nn.Module):
# d_model: Dimension of input tokens.
# n_heads: Number of attention heads.
# d_ff: Dimension of the feed-forward network's hidden layer.
# dropout: Dropout probability for regularization.

#Key Components:
#self.attn: Multi-head self-attention layer.
# self.ffn: Position-wise feed-forward network.
# self.norm1, self.norm2: Layer normalization to stabilize
training.
# self.drop: Dropout for regularization after each sublayer.
    def __init__(self, d_model, n_heads, d_ff, dropout=0.1):
        super().__init__()
        self.attn = MultiHeadSelfAttention(d_model, n_heads)
        self.ffn  = FeedForward(d_model, d_ff)
```

```
        self.norm1, self.norm2 = nn.LayerNorm(d_model), nn.Layer-
Norm(d_model)
        self.drop = nn.Dropout(dropout)

    def forward(self, x, mask=None):
        x = x + self.drop(self.attn(self.norm1(x), mask=mask))
        x = x + self.drop(self.ffn(self.norm2(x)))
        return x

# Decoder Layer inputs are same as encoder
class DecoderLayer(nn.Module):
    def __init__(self, d_model, n_heads, d_ff, dropout=0.1):
        super().__init__()
        self.self_attn   = MultiHeadSelfAttention(d_model, n_
heads, causal=True)
        self.cross_attn  = MultiHeadSelfAttention(d_model, n_
heads, causal=False)
        self.ffn         = FeedForward(d_model, d_ff)
        self.norm1 = nn.LayerNorm(d_model)
        self.norm2 = nn.LayerNorm(d_model)
        self.norm3 = nn.LayerNorm(d_model)
        self.drop  = nn.Dropout(dropout)

    def forward(self, x, enc_out, src_mask=None, tgt_mask=None):
        x = x + self.drop(self.self_attn(self.norm1(x),
mask=tgt_mask))
        x = x + self.drop(self.cross_attn(self.norm2(x), kv=enc_
out, mask=src_mask))
        x = x + self.drop(self.ffn(self.norm3(x)))
        return x
```

Full Transformer (encoder-decoder)

Now, let us combine all the pieces and nail down the transformer architecture.

This class defines a complete Transformer model combining an encoder-decoder architecture for tasks such as sequence-to-sequence modeling, language translation, summarization, and domain-specific LLM training.

```
class Transformer(nn.Module):
    def __init__(self, vocab, d_model=768, n_layers=12,
                 n_heads=12, d_ff=3072, max_len=1024,
tied_embeddings=True):
        super().__init__()

        # Token embedding lookup table: maps token IDs → d_model
vectors
```

```
        self.token_emb = nn.Embedding(vocab, d_model)

        # Positional embedding table: adds position information
to each token
        self.pos_emb   = nn.Embedding(max_len, d_model)

        # Encoder: stack of N encoder layers (Multi-head
attention + FFN)
        self.encoder = nn.ModuleList([
            EncoderLayer(d_model, n_heads, d_ff)
            for   in range(n layers)
        ])

        # Decoder: stack of N decoder layers (Masked attention +
Cross-attention + FFN)
        self.decoder = nn.ModuleList([
            DecoderLayer(d_model, n_heads, d_ff)
            for _ in range(n_layers)
        ])

        # Final linear projection from hidden state → vocabulary
logits
        self.lm_head = nn.Linear(d_model, vocab, bias=False)

        # Weight tying: share embedding + output projection
weights
        # This improves generalization and reduces parameters
        if tied_embeddings:
            self.lm_head.weight = self.token_emb.weight

    def _add_pos(self, x):
        """
        Adds token embeddings + positional embeddings.
        x: [B, T] token IDs
        Returns: [B, T, d_model]
        """
        B, T = x.size()

        # Create position indices [0, 1, ..., T-1]
        pos = torch.arange(T, device=x.device).unsqueeze(0)

        # Embed tokens and positions, then sum them
        return self.token_emb(x) + self.pos_emb(pos)

    def forward(self, src_ids, tgt_ids, src_mask=None,
tgt_mask=None):
        """
```

```
        Runs the full Transformer forward pass.
        src_ids: [B, T_src] input sequence tokens
        tgt_ids: [B, T_tgt] output sequence tokens (shifted right
during training)
        src_mask: optional padding mask for encoder
        tgt_mask: causal mask to prevent attending to future
tokens
        """

        # ----- ENCODER -----
        # Add embeddings + positions
        enc = self._add_pos(src_ids)

        # Pass through all encoder layers
        for layer in self.encoder:
            enc = layer(enc, mask=src_mask)

        # ----- DECODER -----
        # Add embeddings + positions
        dec = self._add_pos(tgt_ids)

        # Pass through decoder layers (with encoder output =
cross-attention keys/values)
        for layer in self.decoder:
            dec = layer(dec, enc, src_mask, tgt_mask)


        # Final logits for next-token prediction
        return self.lm_head(dec)
```

Model Size: Layers, Heads, and Hidden Dimensions

- **Number of Layers (Depth):** The depth of the encoder and decoder (number of Transformer blocks) is a primary factor in model capacity. More layers allow the model to learn more complex transformations and higher-level abstractions. For instance, small Transformers might use 2–6 layers, moderate ones 6–12, and very large models use dozens of layers (GPT-3 has 96 decoder layers; some models exceed 100 layers). Increasing layers generally improves accuracy, provided we have enough training data and computational budget to train them properly. However, deeper models are harder to optimize (they benefit from techniques such as learning rate warmup and careful initialization) and, of course, slower. A trade-off: if the domain data is limited, a very deep model might overfit or not yield proportional benefit. Often it is better to start with a reasonable number (for example, 6 or 12) and increase if needed.

For the encoder-decoder, we can choose different depths for each. Some tasks might require a heavier encoder (if input needs a lot of processing) and a lighter decoder, or vice versa. The original Transformer had equal numbers (6 each). BART-large uses 12 encoder layers + 12 decoder layers. T5-large uses 24 + 24. We could also experiment with asymmetric designs (for example, 6 encoder + 3 decoder for a task where generating text is relatively easy once input is understood, which saves parameters on the decoder side).

- **Hidden Size (`d_model`):** This is the dimensionality of token embeddings and the model's layers. Common values range from 128 to 2048 or more in very large models. Larger **`d_model`** means each token's representation carries more features, which usually improves model expressiveness. It also directly increases the size of the weight matrices. In practice, choosing **`d_model`** is about balancing model capacity with memory/compute. Many NLP models use 768 (BERT-base) or 1024 (BERT-large, T5-base) or 2048 (T5-3B), and so on. Vision Transformers often use 768 or 1024 as well. If the domain has very complex inputs or you aim for high accuracy, lean towards a larger dimension; if you need something lightweight for fast inference, lean smaller. Keep in mind that **`d_model`** must be divisible by the number of heads.
- **Number of Attention Heads:** As discussed, more heads can allow the model to attend to different types of information. Typical choices: 8 heads for moderate models (up to 512d or 768d), 12 heads for 768d (as in BERT), 16 heads for 1024d, 32 heads for 2048d, and so on. There is no exact formula, but ensuring each head has at least 32 or 64 dimensions is a good practice (so if you want 64 heads, you would better have a huge model dimension to support it). Too few heads might bottleneck the model's ability to focus on multiple things; too many heads with too few dimensions might make each head underpowered. Generally, sticking to powers of 2 up to 16 or 32 is common. If in doubt, you can start with 8 or 12 for smaller models, and maybe 16 for larger.
- **Feed-Forward Dimension (`d_ff`):** As mentioned, a common default is 4 times **`d_textmodel`**. This was the case in the original Transformer (for example, 2048 FF for 512 model size) and in many derivatives. This ratio has been empirically successful. Increasing **`d_ff`** will linearly increase parameters and computation in that sublayer. If the model seems underfitting or lacking capacity, boosting **`d_ff`** might help it store more information. Conversely, if we need to reduce model size, you could try reducing **`d_ff`** at the cost of some expressiveness.
- **Dropout and Regularization:** Transformers often include dropout layers – typically dropout is applied after attention (on **`attn_out`**) and after the FFN (on **`ff_out`**) before adding to the residual. A dropout rate such as 0.1 is standard. If training data is abundant and the model is not overfitting, dropout may be less critical, but it is generally good to include it as a safety against overfitting, especially when training from scratch on not-so-massive data. Besides dropout,

other regularizers include weight decay (common in transformer training, decaying weights of matrices slightly) and label smoothing for classification tasks.

- **Parameter Initialization:** When building from scratch, ensure we use a good initialization scheme. PyTorch's default for linear layers (Kaiming uniform) is usually fine. The original Transformer used a custom initialization and also an increase in the learning rate for the first few thousand steps (*learning rate warmup*) to help training. Warmup followed by decay is now a common strategy for transformer training.

Design Recommendations for Domain-Specific LLMs

- **Depth versus Width**
  - Rule of thumb: `d_ff ≈ 4 × d_model`, `n_heads = d_model / 64`.
  - **Small/medium corpora** (≤20 GB) often saturate beyond 12 encoder + 12 decoder layers at 768 dims; training deeper may overfit.
  - For jargon-dense domains (chemical patents, legal contracts), consider wider embeddings (1024–1280) rather than more layers; this helps store rare terms in the vector space.
- **Attention Variants**: Increasing the context length will raise the memory and compute costs. We have a couple of attention choices for long sequence lengths.
  - **Relative or rotary positional embeddings** reduce extrapolation errors when sequence length grows beyond pre-training length.
  - **Sparse/local attention** (Longformer, BigBird) scales to 4 k+ tokens; swap MultiHeadSelfAttention for a sparse version when your domain documents are huge (for example, whole technical manuals).
- **Cross-attention Tricks**
  - Tie key/value projections between self and cross-attention to cut parameters (used in T5). This will reduce the parameter count but might impact flexibility on certain tasks.
  - For retrieval-augmented setups, feed encoder outputs from selected context passages and let the decoder attend to them (RAG). Keep the encoder frozen if memory-constrained.
- **Normalization Style**
  - *Pre-Norm* (LayerNorm before sublayer, as in our code) is more stable for deep stacks.

    - *Post-Norm* (original 2017 paper) can slightly improve convergence speed on shallow networks but is less stable for >24 layers.
- **Domain-aware Initialization**
    - Initialize **`token_emb`** with general pretrained vectors for low compute scenarios; else start from scratch but scale residuals by $1/\sqrt{N}$ (where N = number of layers) to prevent gradient blow-up in deep nets.
- **Memory Footprint Hacks**
    - **Gradient checkpointing** (**`torch.utils.checkpoint`**) halves the memory cost at ~30 % more compute.
    - **Mixed precision** (bfloat16/FP16) is almost mandatory beyond 1 B parameters; pair with **`torch.cuda.amp.autocast()`**.
- **Encoder-Only Shortcut:** If we decide the decoder is not needed, strip the DecoderLayer stack and keep only the encoder. Replace the LM head with a softmax over vocabulary for masked-LM pre-training *or* attach task-specific heads (classification, regression). Embeddings and tokenization should be adapted to new tasks/contexts.

We have built an encoder-decoder Transformer from scratch, engineered it for the domain, and generated output with greedy decoding. Swap in beam-search or nucleus sampling for higher quality text.

Distributed Training

As language models scale into the realm of billions of parameters, conventional training on a single GPU becomes a bottleneck. Memory limitations, compute constraints, and data throughput all impose practical challenges when training these transformer-based architectures. Distributed training strategies are essential tools that enable researchers and engineers to scale model development to modern industrial and research-grade demands.

In this section, we explore the core paradigms of distributed training, analyze their respective strengths and limitations, and provide guidance on selecting an appropriate strategy based on model size, resource availability, and training objectives.

Data Parallelism

Data parallelism is the most widely adopted and conceptually straightforward form of distributed training. In this approach, multiple copies of the model are instantiated across different GPUs. Each model replica processes a unique subset of the training data during each iteration. After computing the gradients independently, the gradients are aggregated and averaged across devices, ensuring that all model copies remain synchronized.

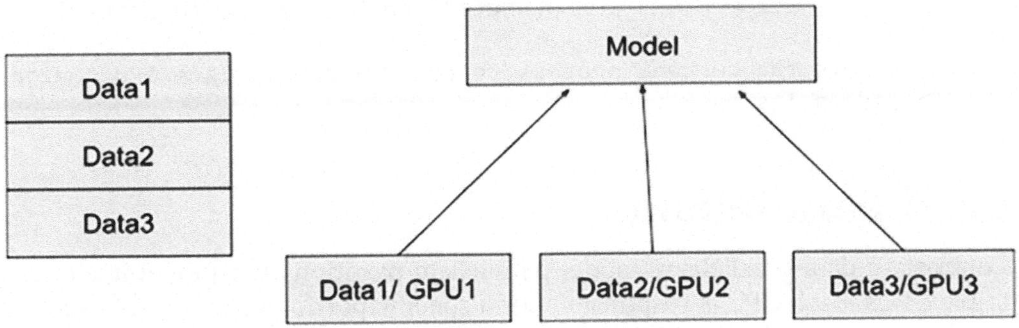

Figure 10.5: *Data parallelism*

Functionality:

- The same model is replicated on all GPUs.
- Each GPU receives a different batch of training data.
- Gradients are calculated locally, then averaged and applied across all replicas.

Advantages:

- Straightforward to implement using frameworks such as PyTorch's **`DistributedDataParallel`** or Hugging Face Accelerate.
- Scales efficiently with increasing GPU count, especially when the model fits within the memory of each GPU.
- Allows for larger batch sizes, which can stabilize training and improve convergence rates.

Limitations:

- Each GPU must maintain a complete copy of the model, which can be a limiting factor for very large models.
- Gradient synchronization introduces communication overhead, especially with many GPUs.

Sample code snippet for PyTorch distributed training

```
import torch
import torch.nn as nn
import torch.distributed as dist
from torch.nn.parallel import DistributedDataParallel as DDP
def setup(rank, world_size):
    # Initializes the default process group for distributed
training.
    # 'nccl' is the backend optimized for multi-GPU communication
on NVIDIA hardware.
```

```
    dist.init_process_group("nccl", rank=rank, world_size=world_
size)
   # Sets the current process to use the appropriate GPU device
(based on its rank).
    torch.cuda.set_device(rank)
```

Model Parallelism

In contrast to data parallelism, model parallelism partitions the model itself across multiple GPUs. Each GPU is responsible for a specific portion of the model, such as a group of transformer layers. This makes it possible to train models that are too large to fit on a single GPU.

Functionality:

- Layers are divided across GPUs.
- The input passes through these layers sequentially, moving between GPUs during computation.

Advantages:

- Allows training of models that would otherwise exceed single-device memory limits.
- Can be implemented without modifying the model architecture significantly.

Limitations:

- Sequential execution across devices may cause some GPUs to remain idle while waiting for input from previous stages.
- Less efficient GPU utilization due to these idle periods.
- Implementation requires careful management of inter-device communication and model partitioning.

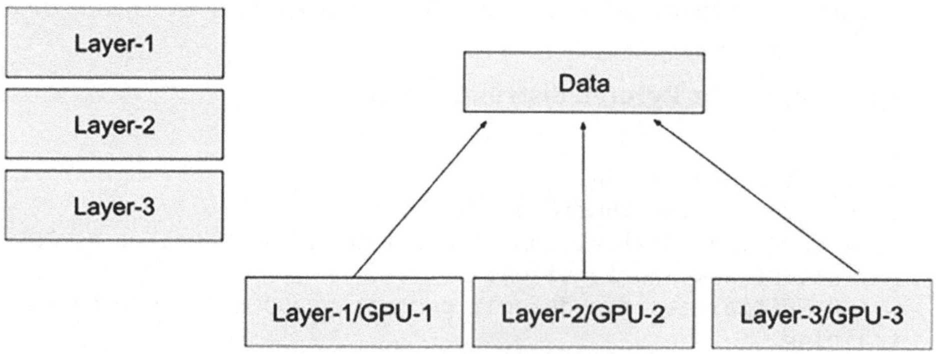

Figure 10.6: *Model parallelization*

Sample code snippet for model parallelization

```
# Define a Transformer model that uses model parallelism across
two GPUs
class ModelParallelTransformer(nn.Module):
    def __init__(self):
        super().__init__()

        # Instantiate the first transformer block and place it on
GPU 0
        self.layer1 = TransformerBlock().to('cuda:0')
        # Instantiate the second transformer block and place it
on GPU 1
        self.layer2 = TransformerBlock().to('cuda:1')

    def forward(self, x):
        # Move the input tensor to GPU 0 and pass it through the
first layer
        x = self.layer1(x.to('cuda:0'))
        # Move the output from GPU 0 to GPU 1 and pass it through
the second layer
        x = self.layer2(x.to('cuda:1'))
 # The output is now on GPU 1
        return x
```

Pipeline Parallelism

Pipeline parallelism enhances model parallelism by addressing its inefficiencies. Here, the model is again divided into stages across multiple GPUs. However, rather than processing entire batches at once, the training data is divided into micro-batches that flow through the pipeline in a staggered manner. This ensures that all GPUs are utilized concurrently for most of the training cycle.

Functionality:

- The model is segmented across GPUs.
- Input batches are split into micro-batches.
- Micro-batches flow through the model pipeline in a staggered, overlapping sequence.

Advantages:

- Reduces GPU idle time.
- Maintains the benefit of training larger models.

Limitations:

- Pipeline fill and drain times introduce latency.
- Not ideal for models with complex or non-sequential topologies.
- Requires batching infrastructure and careful scheduling of micro-batches.

Tensor Parallelism

Tensor parallelism enables fine-grained model partitioning by dividing individual weight matrices across GPUs. This is particularly useful in transformer architectures with very large feedforward or attention layers.

Functionality:

- A large matrix (for example, the weight matrix in a dense layer) is split into submatrices across GPUs.
- Each GPU computes a portion of the matrix operation.
- The results are aggregated to produce the final output.

Advantages:

- Provides significant memory savings for large layers.
- Ideal for horizontally scaling massive transformer blocks.

Limitations:

- Implementation complexity increases due to the need for custom parallelized operations.
- High inter-GPU communication overhead, especially for synchronizing activations and gradients.

ZeRO and Sharded Optimizers

One of the more recent and powerful advancements in distributed training comes from the family of Zero Redundancy Optimizers (ZeRO). Implemented in frameworks such as DeepSpeed and FairScale, ZeRO introduces a novel sharding technique that allows the distribution of not just model parameters, but also optimizer states and gradients.

ZeRO is typically described in three stages:

- **Stage 1**: Shards optimizer states across GPUs.
- **Stage 2**: Adds sharding of gradients.
- **Stage 3**: Adds sharding of model parameters themselves, so no GPU holds the full model.

Advantages:

- Dramatically reduces memory footprint.
- Makes it possible to train models that would otherwise require prohibitively large hardware resources.
- Compatible with data parallelism, often used in hybrid configurations.

Limitations:

- Increased system complexity.
- Higher learning curve and more sophisticated checkpointing mechanisms.
- Potential bottlenecks if not tuned properly for communication and computation.

Strategic Considerations and Trade-offs

Choosing the right distributed training strategy requires a deep understanding of the computational constraints and model requirements. The table below summarizes the trade-offs among different strategies:

Strategy	Memory Efficiency	GPU Utilization	Implementation Complexity	Ideal Model Size
Data Parallelism	Low	High	Low	Small to Medium
Model Parallelism	High	Low to Medium	Medium	Medium to Large
Pipeline Parallelism	High	High	Medium to High	Large
Tensor Parallelism	Very High	High	High	Very Large
ZeRO (Stage 3)	Extremely High	High	Very High	Extremely Large

Table 10.3: *Comparison of distributed training techniques*

In practice, many production-grade systems employ a hybrid of these techniques. For instance, models such as GPT-3 combine data, model, and tensor parallelism, often orchestrated with frameworks such as *DeepSpeed* or *Megatron*-LM. Understanding the core principles of each strategy allows practitioners to make informed trade-offs between training efficiency, hardware usage, and development complexity.

Frameworks

- **PyTorch DDP (DistributedDataParallel)**: For multi-GPU data parallel training.

- **DeepSpeed**: For advanced features such as ZeRO optimization to handle large models and increase batch sizes by sharding memory load.
- **FSDP (Fully Sharded Data Parallel):** A PyTorch feature to shard model parameters across GPUs, achieving similar goals to DeepSpeed. Useful for very large models.
- **Hugging Face Accelerate:** A high-level tool to manage device placement and distributed setup with minimal code changes.
- **PyTorch Lightning/Fast.ai**: Frameworks that can simplify training loops and multi-GPU training by abstracting the boilerplate.
- **TensorBoard or Weights & Biases (W&B):** Logging tools to track training progress (loss curves, perplexity) and compare runs. The team uses W&B to monitor how training proceeds over epochs, which is vital for debugging and ensuring the model learns.

Hardware Accelerators:

- **GPUs**: NVIDIA GPUs with sufficient VRAM (the team uses 4 × RTX 3090, each 24GB, for example) or cloud equivalents on AWS, GCP, and so on.
- **TPUs**: Google's TPUs (v3-8, v4) are accessible via Google Cloud or the TFRC program, offering very fast matrix computation. Requires using XLA-compatible code (TensorFlow or JAX, or PyTorch with some limitations).
- **High-memory instances**: For preprocessing large corpora or hosting the final model, having plenty of RAM and disk is useful. The corpus (12GB text) is processed on a machine with enough disk and maybe 64GB+ RAM to comfortably handle data pipelines.

Evaluation and Deployment

Evaluating domain-specific Large Language Models (LLMs) requires a combination of general-purpose language benchmarks and domain-relevant tasks. Standard metrics such as BLEU, ROUGE, and perplexity provide surface-level insights, while custom task-specific evaluation reveals deeper model understanding in the domain.

General Metrics

- **Perplexity**: Measures how well the model predicts text. Lower perplexity indicates better performance.
- **BLEU/ROUGE**: Useful for comparing generated text against reference summaries or translations.
- **Accuracy/F1 Score**: Useful for classification-oriented outputs (for example, legal clause classification).

Designing evaluation tasks grounded in real-world domain objectives is key. For example, a legal LLM may be evaluated on its ability to identify statutes relevant to a query or to summarize case judgments. Evaluation must align with domain priorities such as correctness, precision, explainability, or logical structure.

LLM Evaluation Frameworks

- **LM Evaluation Harness (EleutherAI)**: A popular benchmark suite to evaluate LLMs on diverse tasks.
- **HELM and BigBench**: Provide broad multilingual and reasoning-oriented evaluation tasks.
- **RAGAS, TruLens, and LangSmith**: Focus on evaluating RAG (Retrieval-Augmented Generation) systems.

Human evaluation remains vital in high-stakes or nuanced domains such as law, medicine, or finance. Expert review of model outputs helps uncover subtleties that automatic metrics may miss. Evaluation forms may include Likert scale assessments, ranking comparisons, or checklists.

Deployment Strategies

Deploying a domain-specific LLM efficiently and reliably is critical to ensuring its practical value. Considerations include latency, scalability, memory footprint, and secure API exposure.

- **vLLM**: Offers fast and memory-efficient inference with continuous batching support.
- **Text Generation Inference (TGI)**: Hugging Face's optimized serving stack for LLMs.
- **Triton Inference Server**: Production-grade multi-framework server by NVIDIA.
- **TorchServe**: Easy-to-use PyTorch model deployment tool with REST API support.

Containerize the LLM and serve it using REST/gRPC endpoints. Tools such as Docker, Kubernetes, and BentoML help with packaging and scaling. Load balancers and autoscaling mechanisms ensure availability during demand surges.

MLflow and WandB are used to track model predictions, input drift, and errors.

PromptLayer and LangSmith capture LLM behavior and prompt flows in production.

Case Study: Building a Legal LLM from Scratch

To illustrate the concepts in this chapter, we present a case study based on real-world efforts to build a legal domain LLM. One prominent example is the creation of LEGAL-BERT by Chalkidis et al. (2020), a family of transformer models trained on legal corpora. We will walk through their process, which closely mirrors what our fictional team did, and highlight key takeaways.

In 2019, NLP researchers noticed that general-purpose models such as BERT were not performing as well on legal text tasks because of vocabulary gaps and domain-specific language. The goal was to create a transformer-based language model specialized for law that could be used for tasks such as legal document classification and QA. The motivation was clear: improve accuracy on legal NLP tasks by providing the model with legal knowledge through pretraining on law data.

Data Collection and Preparation

The LEGAL-BERT team gathered a large corpus of English legal texts (~12 GB in total). These came from multiple sources reflecting different subdomains of law:

- **EU Legislation (Eur-Lex)**: 61.8k documents
- **UK Legislation**: 19.8k documents
- **European Court of Justice Cases**: ~20k cases
- **European Court of Human Rights Cases**: 12.5k cases
- **U.S. Court Cases**: 164k cases from the Case Law Project
- **U.S. Contracts**: 76k contract documents from SEC EDGAR filings

All these sources (except the U.S. case law, which required special access) were open access. They had to parse different formats (HTML, PDF, XML) to extract plain text. They paid attention to removing non-text elements and anonymizing as needed. The diversity of sources ensured the model was not biased to one jurisdiction's style.

Importantly, they trained a tokenizer on this corpus, building a vocabulary that captures legal jargon. They used an uncased WordPiece tokenizer (since legal text often is not case-sensitive for meaning, and this also simplifies things). The final vocab included many legal terms and was likely similar in size to BERT's (around 30k tokens). Some legal/medical terms are case-sensitive; emphasize that casing choice should match both data distribution and downstream use cases.

Model Design

The team decided to use the proven BERT architecture as their base. Specifically, they took the BERT-Base config: 12 layers, hidden size 768, 12 attention heads (110M parameters). This was a bidirectional encoder (unlike the GPT-style decoder we built in our example). They chose BERT so that the model could be easily fine-tuned for classification or sequence labeling tasks, which are common in legal NLP.

They also experimented with a smaller model, about 1/3 the size of BERT (which they call Legal-BERT-Small), to see if a lightweight model could achieve similar results. This smaller model was faster and had less environmental training cost, yet was reported to have competitive performance. This is a valuable lesson: bigger is not always necessary if your data is domain-specific enough.

One twist in BERT training is the objective: they used Masked Language Modeling (MLM), where the model learns to predict masked-out words in sentences, and possibly the Next Sentence Prediction (NSP) objective (original BERT used it to help understand sentence relationships). MLM is well-suited to an encoder model and forces the model to build bidirectional context understanding.

Training Process

Training was conducted on a single Cloud TPU v3-8 (which has 8 cores, analogous to 8 TPUs working in data parallel). They followed the original BERT training recipe:

- Steps: 1,000,000 training steps (which is a lot – they effectively passed through their 12GB corpus many times).
- Batch size: 256 sequences per step (each sequence 512 tokens). On a v3-8 TPU, that means each core might handle 32 sequences, for example.
- Learning rate: around 1e-4 with warmup, decayed over the course of training.
- Optimizer: Adam with weight decay.

The training likely took a few days to a week. The result was a set of pretrained weights for Legal-BERT (and the smaller variant). The model had essentially learned the patterns of legal language from all those documents.

Evaluation

The researchers evaluated Legal-BERT on several downstream legal tasks to verify that pretraining on legal data gave an edge:

- **Case law text classification**: for example, predicting which article of law was violated in a human rights case. Legal-BERT outperformed a generic BERT that had not seen legal text, especially on rare categories.

- **Contract clause classification**: determining the clause type from its text. Again, the domain-tuned model showed higher accuracy.
- **Legal QA**: In some Q&A tasks, Legal-BERT (after fine-tuning) was better at understanding the question context when it was phrased in legal terms, compared to baseline models.

They found that further pretraining a general model on legal data versus training from scratch on legal data both gave improvements, but training from scratch had a slight edge for certain tasks. This justified the effort to build a domain-specific model from the ground up.

For example, on a dataset of EU legal case judgment predictions, Legal-BERT from scratch achieved higher F1 scores than a model that was just fine-tuned from general BERT. This underscores that the model picked up nuances of the domain.

Deployment and Usage

Legal-BERT was released to the public via the Hugging Face Model Hub. This means researchers and developers can directly use it with the Transformers library, making deployment easier for various tasks.

For instance, a legal tech startup could take Legal-BERT and fine-tune it on their in-house dataset of, say, contract risk classifications, then deploy that model in their product. The availability of the model accelerated adoption – it became a building block for legal NLP applications.

Moreover, the case study highlighted efficiency: their smaller Legal-BERT-Small model, which was 33% the size of BERT, achieved comparable performance to BERT-base on many tasks. That model would be much cheaper to host in production (uses less memory and CPU/GPU) and faster, which is valuable for deployment at scale.

Conclusion

In this chapter, we stepped beyond the realm of fine-tuning general-purpose models and embraced the challenge of designing Large Language Models (LLMs) from scratch for specialized domains. Fields such as healthcare, law, finance, and science demand more than surface-level fluency—they require systems that are built from domain data, shaped for domain tasks, and measured through domain-specific benchmarks. We began by grounding this process in data creation, underscoring that the quality and relevance of a domain corpus often outweigh sheer size. Through methods such as synthetic augmentation and careful preprocessing, we laid the foundation for models capable of capturing subtle context. Revisiting the transformer architecture, we dissected components such as self-attention, feed-forward layers, and positional encoding, emphasizing how architectural control allows us to adapt and optimize models for domain-driven needs. Distributed training strategies, from model sharding to memory-efficient backpropagation, were introduced as the practical machinery that scales experimentation into billion-parameter territory, made accessible through open-source tools such as DeepSpeed and Hugging Face Accelerate.

Yet building such models is only half the journey—the real test lies in how they are evaluated and deployed. The question, then, is not simply how to build domain-specific LLMs, but why. In sensitive and regulated contexts, fine-tuned general models often fall short, carrying risks of hallucination, imprecision, or misinterpretation. Purpose-built LLMs, by contrast, embody accuracy, trustworthiness, and responsibility, making them more than just fluent—they become expert voices within their domains, bridging foundational AI principles with the critical realities of the world they serve.

In the next chapter, we will learn about multi-modal transformers.

References

1. Sutskever, I., Vinyals, O., & Le, Q. V. (2014). **Sequence to Sequence Learning with Neural Networks**. *Advances in Neural Information Processing Systems* (NeurIPS). https://arxiv.org/abs/1409.3215

2. Bahdanau, D., Cho, K., & Bengio, Y. (2015). **Neural Machine Translation by Jointly Learning to Align and Translate**. *International Conference on Learning Representations* (ICLR). https://arxiv.org/abs/1409.0473

3. Vaswani, A., Shazeer, N., Parmar, N., et al. (2017). **Attention is All You Need**. *Advances in Neural Information Processing Systems* (NeurIPS). https://arxiv.org/abs/1706.03762

4. Devlin, J., Chang, M. W., Lee, K., & Toutanova, K. (2018). **BERT: Pre-training of Deep Bidirectional Transformers for Language Understanding**. NAACL-HLT. https://arxiv.org/abs/1810.04805

5. Lewis, M., Liu, Y., Goyal, N., et al. (2019). **BART: Denoising Sequence-to-Sequence Pre-training for Natural Language Generation, Translation, and Comprehension**. ACL 2020. https://arxiv.org/abs/1910.13461

6. Raffel, C., Shazeer, N., Roberts, A., et al. (2020). **Exploring the Limits of Transfer Learning with a Unified Text-to-Text Transformer (T5)**. *Journal of Machine Learning Research*. https://arxiv.org/abs/1910.10683

7. Papineni, K., Roukos, S., Ward, T., & Zhu, W. J. (2002). **BLEU: a Method for Automatic Evaluation of Machine Translation**. ACL 2002.

8. Lin, C. Y. (2004). **ROUGE: A Package for Automatic Evaluation of Summaries**. *Workshop on Text Summarization Branches Out.*

9. Zhang, T., Kishore, V., Wu, F., et al. (2020). **BERTScore: Evaluating Text Generation with BERT**. ICLR 2020. https://arxiv.org/abs/1904.09675

10. Sellam, T., Das, D., & Parikh, A. (2020). **BLEURT: Learning Robust Metrics for Text Generation**. ACL 2020. https://arxiv.org/abs/2004.04696

11. Legal BERT **arXiv Preprint**: https://arxiv.org/abs/2010.02559

CHAPTER 11
Building Multimodal Applications for Healthcare

Introduction

In recent years, multimodal transformers have revolutionized the way artificial intelligence systems perceive and understand the world by integrating multiple data modalities—such as text, images, audio, and structured data—into a unified framework. This chapter takes a deep dive into building multimodal applications, with a particular emphasis on the healthcare domain. By harnessing the power of multimodal architectures, we can unlock richer insights from diverse healthcare data, paving the way for smarter clinical decision support, improved patient care, and accelerated medical research.

We begin with the essential foundations of multimodal dataset preparation, highlighting best practices in collecting, curating, and aligning heterogeneous data sources such as medical records, diagnostic images, and patient narratives. Next, we explore multimodal embeddings and alignment, detailing how transformers learn to integrate diverse modalities seamlessly through joint representations. We then unpack various multimodal architectures, from early fusion to cross-attention mechanisms, illustrating how they enable powerful reasoning across modalities.

Recognizing the importance of rigorous validation, we discuss evaluation strategies tailored to multimodal systems in healthcare, including benchmarks, metrics, and scenario-specific considerations. To bridge the gap between research and practice, we present business case studies demonstrating real-world applications in healthcare—such as disease prediction, medical imaging, and patient triage—and their impact on operational efficiency and patient outcomes.

We also tackle the deployment trade-offs inherent in multimodal systems: balancing privacy concerns, computational costs, and latency requirements in resource-constrained healthcare environments. To conclude, we include a mock interview designed to help readers consolidate their understanding and prepare for roles involving multimodal transformer systems.

By the end of this chapter, readers will gain a comprehensive understanding of the end-to-end process of building, evaluating, and deploying multimodal transformer applications, along with the critical nuances of applying them in the healthcare sector.

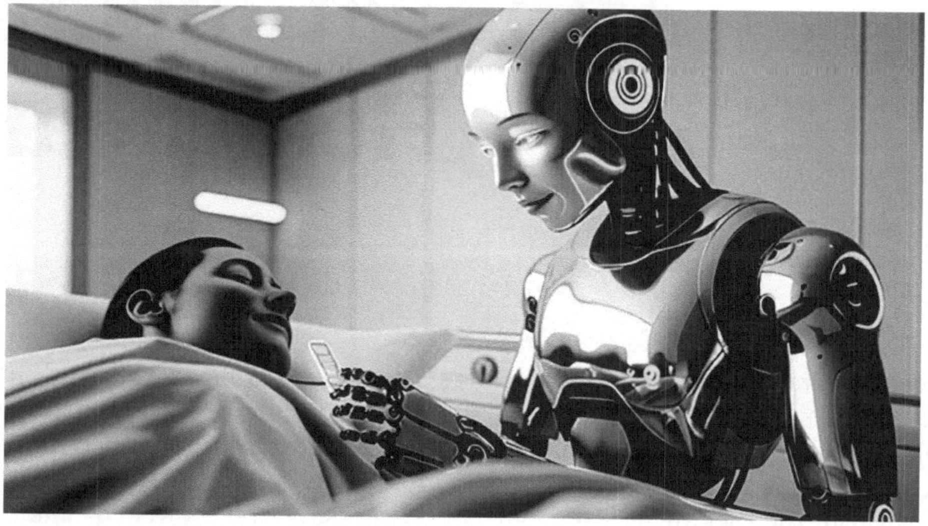

Figure 11.1: *AI Robot that checks the patient and collects the diagnostic information*

Structure

In this chapter, we will cover the following topics:

- Multimodal Dataset Preparation
- Multi-modal embeddings and alignment
- Multi-modal architectures
- Evaluation Strategies
- Business case studies in Healthcare segment
- Deployment trade-offs
- Mock interview

Multimodal Dataset Preparation

In our increasingly interconnected digital world, data comes in diverse forms—text, images, audio, video, and even structured sensor readings. This diversity fuels innovation, enabling more sophisticated and human-like artificial intelligence (AI) systems. Multimodal data—data that spans multiple modalities—provides richer context, deeper insights, and more robust performance than single-modal data alone. This chapter explores why multimodal data is crucial, how it empowers AI models (especially multimodal transformers), and how to process it effectively for real-world applications.

Multimodal data refers to data that combines two or more different types of information sources. Common modalities include:

- **Text:** Natural language descriptions, captions, or metadata.
- **Images/Videos:** Visual context, scenes, or object interactions.
- **Audio:** Speech, environmental sounds, or music.
- **Structured Data:** Sensor readings, tabular records, or metadata.

For example, an e-commerce application might have product images (visual), descriptions (text), and user reviews (textual sentiment). Healthcare datasets may include MRI scans (visual), doctor notes (text), and lab test results (tabular). The agriculture segment may have image data from satellite images and customer support call transcripts, which are text. Harnessing all these modalities together can dramatically improve model accuracy and reasoning capabilities.

Combining text and images allows AI systems to understand complex relationships. For example, interpreting a medical report alongside an X-ray provides richer and more personalized diagnostic capabilities.

Models trained on multimodal data are often more robust to noise or missing data. If one modality is corrupted, the model can leverage others to maintain performance.

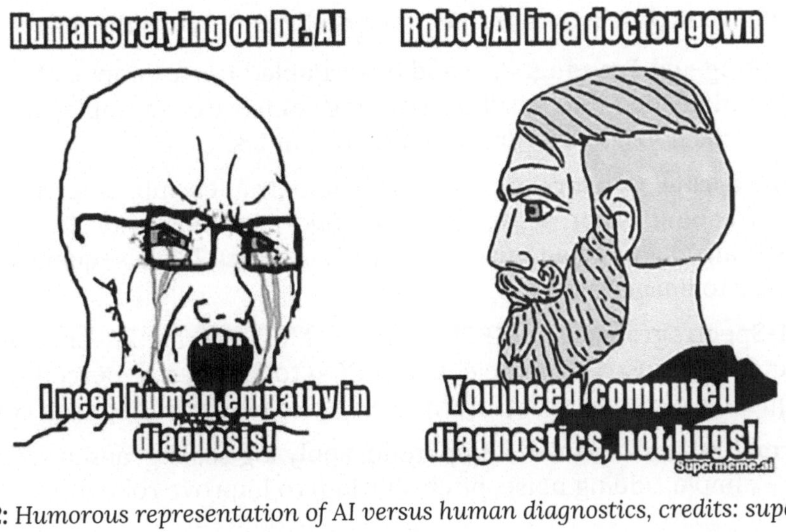

Figure 11.2: *Humorous representation of AI versus human diagnostics, credits: supermeme.ai*

Data Preprocessing

Structured Data Processing: We have covered structured data processing intensively in the previous chapters. Exploratory data analysis, data cleaning/ normalization are applied.

- **Normalization:** Scale numerical features.
- **Embedding:** Embed categorical variables using embedding layers.

Text Processing: We have covered natural language text processing techniques such as lemmatization in the previous chapters.

- **Tokenization:** Use subword tokenizers (for example, Byte-Pair Encoding or WordPiece).
- **Normalization:** Lowercase, remove stop words (if needed), or apply stemming/ lemmatization (task-dependent).

Image Processing: Image augmentation techniques, image cleaning techniques are covered in the previous chapters.

- **Preprocessing:** Resize, normalize pixel values, and apply data augmentation.
- **Feature Extraction:** Use pre-trained vision models (CNNs, Vision Transformers) to generate embeddings.

Audio Processing

Audio data is a rich and dynamic modality, conveying information such as speech, music, ambient sounds, and emotional tone. We will elaborate on the processing steps for audio data, as it has not been covered earlier.

Before feeding audio into a transformer, it typically undergoes the following steps:

- **Sampling and Framing:** Raw audio is sampled (for example, at 16 kHz or 44.1 kHz) and divided into small overlapping frames (for example, 25 ms windows with 10 ms hops) to capture temporal dynamics.
- **Spectrogram Conversion:** Convert audio frames into spectrograms (a 2D time-frequency representation) using Short-Time Fourier Transform (STFT). This is analogous to an image and can be treated like a sequence of "*patches*" (similar to images).
- **Mel-Spectrograms or MFCCs:** Apply Mel filterbanks or compute Mel-Frequency Cepstral Coefficients (MFCCs) to emphasize perceptually relevant frequencies, compressing information while preserving speech content.
- **Normalization:** Normalize amplitude, apply log scaling, and possibly augment (for example, adding noise, pitch shifting) to improve robustness.

Pre-trained audio encoders can transform these representations into embeddings:

- **Wav2Vec 2.0:** Self-supervised learning on raw waveforms, producing powerful contextual embeddings.
- **HuBERT:** Another self-supervised model that clusters and predicts masked audio segments.
- **VGGish or YAMNet:** CNN-based feature extractors pre-trained on large-scale audio datasets (for example, AudioSet).

The output can then be treated as a sequence of audio tokens or patches for integration into a transformer.

Video Data and Multimodal Representations

Video data is inherently multimodal, blending visual, audio, and temporal information. Transformers designed for video must handle not just sequences but sequences of sequences.

Decomposing Video into Modalities

Visual Stream: Each video is composed of frames. Processing involves:

- **Frame Sampling:** Extract key frames (uniformly or using keypoint detectors) to reduce computational cost.
- **Frame Preprocessing:** Resize, normalize, and apply augmentation similar to images.
- **Patch Extraction:** Use Vision Transformers (ViTs) to tokenize frames into patches for embedding.

Audio Stream: Many videos have an accompanying audio track.

- Extract audio as described above, aligning it with the corresponding video frames.

Textual Metadata or Subtitles: Videos often come with:

- **Captions/Subtitles:** Dialogue aligned to timestamps.
- **Metadata:** Titles, tags, or descriptions.

Multimodal Embeddings and Alignment

Multimodal embedding alignment aims to combine information from different modalities—such as text, images, audio, and video—into a unified representation space. This enables seamless cross-modal tasks such as image captioning, video question answering, and cross-modal retrieval.

Early Fusion

Definition: Early fusion refers to concatenating raw or low-level features from different modalities at the input level before feeding them into a shared network for joint learning.

Use Case: Audio-visual speech recognition, where spectrograms and video frames are concatenated to capture lip movements and audio cues simultaneously.

Example Diagram:

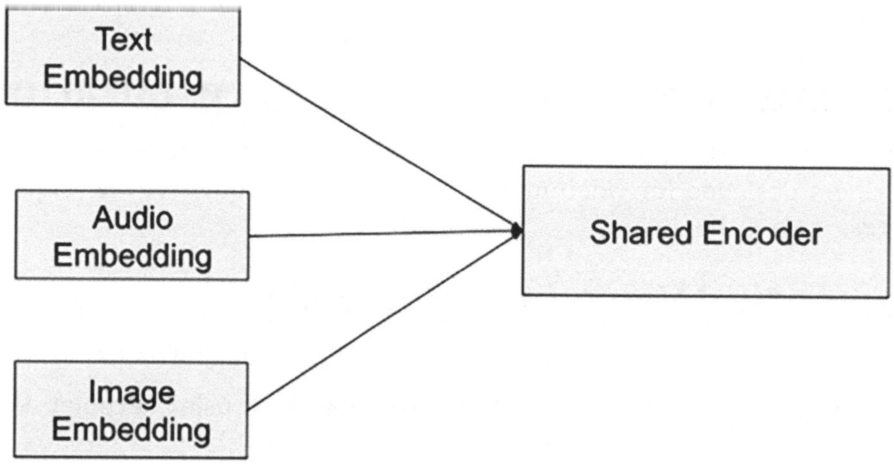

Figure 11.3: *Representing early fusion*

Code Snippet:

```
import torch
import torch.nn as nn

class EarlyFusionModel(nn.Module):
    def __init__(self, text_dim, image_dim, audio_dim, hidden_
dim, output_dim):
        super(EarlyFusionModel, self).__init__()
        self.fusion = nn.Linear(text_dim + image_dim + audio_dim,
hidden_dim)
        self.output_layer = nn.Linear(hidden_dim, output_dim)

    def forward(self, text_emb, image_emb, audio_emb):
        # Concatenate along the feature dimension
        fused = torch.cat((text_emb, image_emb, audio_emb),
dim=1)
        hidden = torch.relu(self.fusion(fused))
        output = self.output_layer(hidden)
        return output
```

Pros:

- Simple to implement.
- Allows immediate interaction between modalities.

Cons:

- Modalities might dominate or overshadow each other (for example, visual features overshadow textual ones).
- Difficult to handle different sequence lengths (for example, audio and text).

Late Fusion

Definition: Late fusion processes each modality independently and combines the outputs (for example, logits or embeddings) at the decision stage.

Use Case: Sentiment analysis with text and audio processed separately before combining their predictions.

Example Diagram:

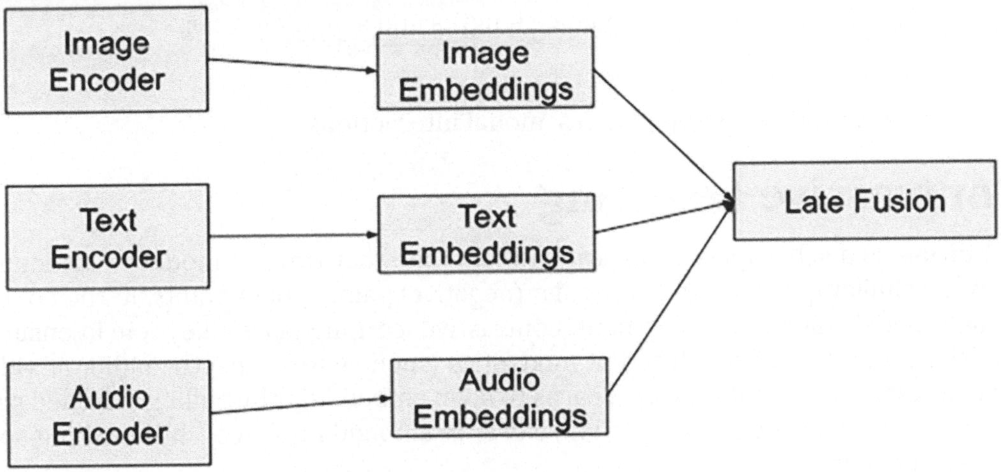

***Figure 11.4**: Representation of late fusion*

Code Snippet:

```
import torch
import torch.nn as nn

class LateFusionModel(nn.Module):
    def __init__(self, input_dims, hidden_dim, output_dim):
        super(LateFusionModel, self).__init__()
        self.text_encoder = nn.Linear(input_dims['text'],
hidden_dim)
```

```
        self.image_encoder = nn.Linear(input_dims['image'],
hidden_dim)
        self.audio_encoder = nn.Linear(input_dims['audio'],
hidden_dim)
        self.output_layer = nn.Linear(hidden_dim * 3, output_dim)

      # Get the individual feature outputs and then concatenate
them.

    def forward(self, text_emb, image_emb, audio_emb):
        text_feat = torch.relu(self.text_encoder(text_emb))
        image_feat = torch.relu(self.image_encoder(image_emb))
        audio_feat = torch.relu(self.audio_encoder(audio_emb))
        fused = torch.cat((text_feat, image_feat, audio_feat),
dim=1)
        output = self.output_layer(fused)
        return output
```

Pros:

- Modalities can have separate architectures tailored to their nature.
- Flexible with different sequence lengths and sampling rates.

Cons:

- Might miss fine-grained cross-modal interactions.

Contrastive Learning

Definition: is a self-supervised learning technique that trains a model to distinguish between similar (positive) and dissimilar (negative) pairs of data points. In the context of multimodal embedding alignment, contrastive learning plays a key role in ensuring that representations from different modalities (such as text, images, audio, or video) share a common semantic space. Learns to align embeddings by pulling matched pairs (for example, an image and its caption) closer in embedding space while pushing apart unmatched pairs.

How does it work?

1. **Data Sampling**:
    - **Construct positive pairs**: For example, an image and its actual caption, an audio clip and its transcript.
    - **Construct negative pairs**: For example, an image with a mismatched caption or an audio clip with a different transcript.

2. **Embedding Extraction**:
   - Each modality is processed through its dedicated encoder (for example, a CNN for images, a Transformer for text).
   - Each encoder produces a fixed-size embedding.
3. **Contrastive Loss (for example, InfoNCE)**:
   - The model is trained using a contrastive loss function such as InfoNCE or NT-Xent.
   - The loss encourages the distance between positive pairs to be minimized and the distance between negative pairs to be maximized in the embedding space.

Diagram:

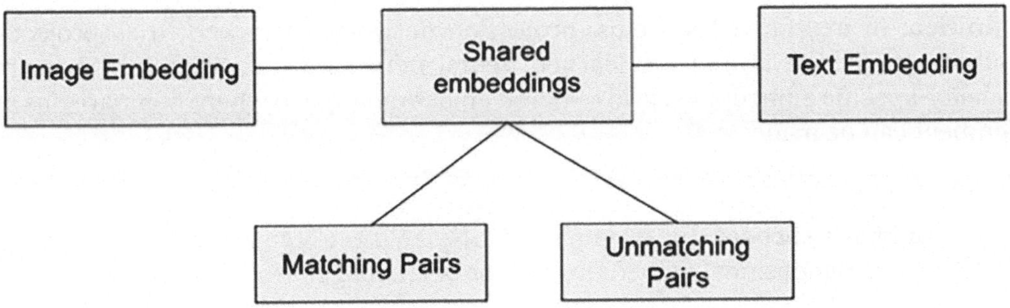

Figure 11.5: *Contrastive learning*

Code Snippet:

```
import torch.nn.functional as F
def contrastive_loss(image_emb, text_emb, temperature=0.07):
    # Normalize embeddings so they lie on the unit sphere.
    # This makes cosine similarity equivalent to dot-product
similarity.
    image_emb = F.normalize(image_emb, dim=1)
    text_emb  = F.normalize(text_emb, dim=1)

    # Compute pairwise similarity matrix:
    # logits[i, j] = similarity between image i and text j
    # Dividing by temperature sharpens the distribution (lower
temp -> stronger peaks)
    logits = torch.matmul(image_emb, text_emb.T) / temperature

    # Labels are [0, 1, 2, ..., batch_size-1]
    # Each image should match with the text at the same index
    labels = torch.arange(len(image_emb)).to(image_emb.device)
```

```
    # Image-to-Text loss:
    # For each image, the correct text is the one with the same
index.
    loss_i2t = F.cross_entropy(logits, labels)

    # Text-to-Image loss:
    # Same idea but reverse: for each text, the correct image is
the same index.
    loss_t2i = F.cross_entropy(logits.T, labels)

    # Final loss is symmetric: average of both directions.
    return (loss_i2t + loss_t2i) / 2
```

Projection Networks

Definition: In multimodal systems, projection networks (also known as projection heads or projection layers) are learned neural network layers that transform raw modality-specific embeddings into a shared embedding space where comparisons and alignment can be made.

Imagine you have:

- **An image encoder** (for example, a CNN or Vision Transformer) that produces a high-dimensional embedding vector of an image.
- **A text encoder** (for example, a BERT-like Transformer) that produces a different high-dimensional embedding vector for a caption.

These raw embeddings often have different distributions and scales because they come from different modalities. To make them comparable (so that a caption embedding is close to its corresponding image embedding), we project both embeddings into a common embedding space.

Diagram:

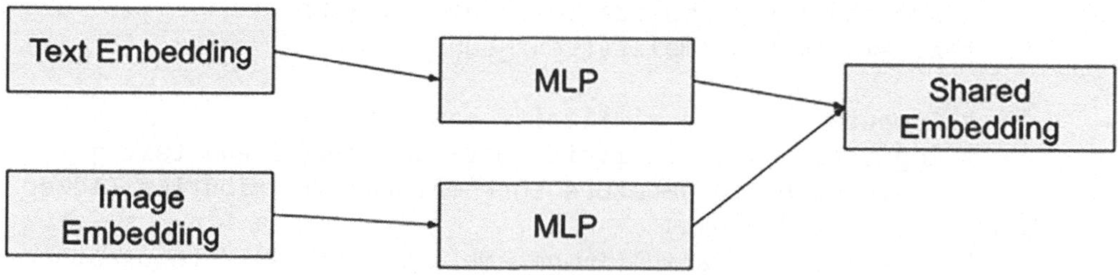

***Figure 11.6:** Projection networks*

Code Snippet:

```
import torch.nn as nn
class ProjectionNetwork(nn.Module):
    def __init__(self, input_dim, hidden_dim, output_dim):
        super().__init__()

        # A simple 2-layer MLP used to project embeddings or
feature vectors
        # into a new representation space (often used in
contrastive learning,
        # multimodal alignment, or latent space transformations).
        self.projection = nn.Sequential(
            nn.Linear(input_dim, hidden_dim),  # First linear
layer: input → hidden
            nn.ReLU(),                         # Non-linear
activation
            nn.Linear(hidden_dim, output_dim)  # Second linear
layer: hidden → output
        )

    def forward(self, x):
        # Pass input through the projection MLP
        return self.projection(x)
```

Cross-Modal Attention

Cross-modal attention is a neural mechanism that allows a model to dynamically focus on relevant features of one modality while processing information from another modality. In simpler terms, it lets one modality query another to decide which parts are important for a given task.

For example:

- In VQA, a question (text) can use cross-modal attention to decide which parts of an image are relevant to answer the question.
- In video-language tasks, a caption might attend to different video frames to generate a coherent description.

Dynamic alignment: Unlike simple concatenation or late fusion, cross-modal attention allows a model to learn task-specific alignments between modalities.

Context-aware representation: The model can focus on different regions of the input dynamically depending on the query (for example, the question in VQA).

Fine-grained interactions: Especially important when modalities are complex or high-dimensional, like in images (multiple objects) or videos (temporal information).

Diagram:

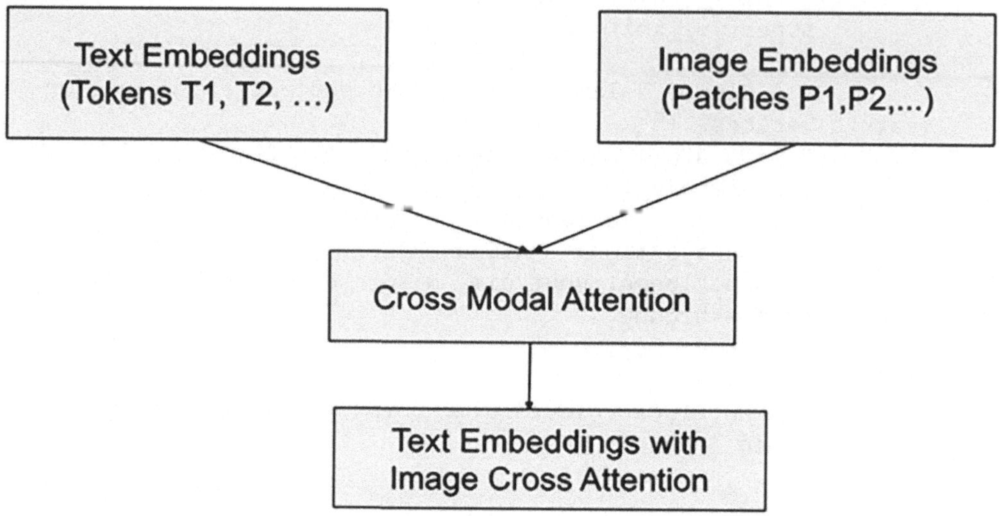

Figure 11.7: *Cross-modal attention*

Comparison between different techniques

Technique	Key Idea	Pros	Cons
Early Fusion	Concatenate features early	Simple, immediate interaction	Can struggle with sequence length differences
Late Fusion	Combine outputs at the decision stage	Flexible, separate networks	May miss fine-grained interactions
Contrastive Learning	Pull matched pairs, push apart	Learns strong alignment	Requires careful negative sampling
Projection Networks	Map into shared space	Flexible with architectures	May not fully capture modality interactions
Cross-Modal Attention	Attention across modalities	Captures interactions dynamically	Computationally intensive

Table 11.1: *Comparison between multimodality architectures*

Multimodal Architectures

Multimodal architectures are designed to handle data from multiple modalities–such as text, images, audio, or video–enabling applications such as cross-modal retrieval, captioning, and understanding. Below are some of the most prominent architectures:

Model Architectures

- **Unified Models**: Models such as Perceiver IO can handle various modalities through a shared architecture.
- **Encoder-Decoder Models**: Utilizing separate encoders for each modality and a shared decoder for task-specific outputs.
- **Attention Mechanisms**: Implementing cross-modal attention to allow the model to focus on relevant features across modalities.

We will learn about the popular multimodal architectures in the coming sections.

Contrastive Language–Image Pre-training (CLIP)

Developed by OpenAI, CLIP aligns images and their textual descriptions into a shared embedding space using **contrastive learning**.

CLIP is a dual-encoder model that jointly learns image and text representations from a large set of (image, text) pairs. It uses a 12-layer Transformer to encode text and a ResNet or Vision Transformer (ViT) to encode images, projecting both modalities into a shared 512-dimensional embedding space. CLIP is trained with a contrastive loss on ~400M noisy image-text pairs, teaching the encoders to pull matching images and captions together and push non-matching pairs apart. This enables strong zero-shot performance: at inference, CLIP can classify or retrieve images by simply comparing the similarity between image embeddings and text description embeddings. In practice, CLIP powers zero-shot image classification (for example, ImageNet labels from text) and content-based image search (text-to-image and image-to-text retrieval.

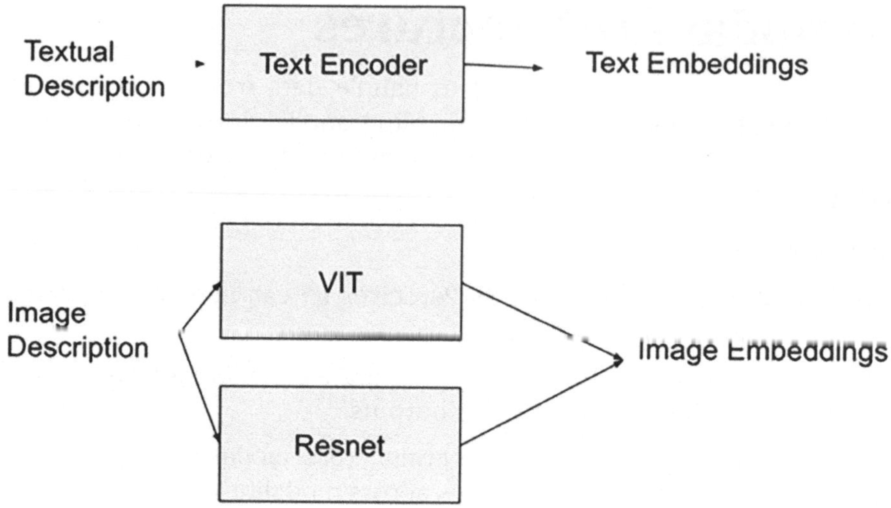

Figure 11.8: *Architectural diagram of CLIP*

Architecture:

- **Image Encoder:** Vision Transformer (ViT) or ResNet, which processes images into fixed-size embeddings.
- **Text Encoder:** Transformer-based language model that encodes captions into embeddings.
- **Training:**
    - **Contrastive Loss (InfoNCE):** Encourages correct image-caption pairs to have higher similarity while pushing apart incorrect pairs.
    - The loss is computed across large batches to improve generalization.

Key Features:

- Learns zero-shot capabilities (for example, classify images with text prompts such as "*a photo of a cat*").
- Can be fine-tuned for downstream tasks such as image classification or retrieval.

Weekly Supervised Speech Recognition (Whisper)

Also from OpenAI, Whisper is a multi-lingual, multi-task model for speech processing. While not strictly "*multimodal*" in the sense of combining different inputs (such as images and text), it does combine audio with text in its training.

Whisper is an end-to-end encoder-decoder Transformer model for speech-to-text and speech translation. It is trained on 680,000+ hours of diverse multilingual and multitask audio data, which gives it strong robustness to accents, background noise, and technical vocabulary. Whisper's architecture is simple: input audio is converted into log-Mel spectrograms (30-second windows) and fed to a Transformer encoder; the decoder is an autoregressive Transformer that emits text tokens. Special tokens in the output sequence tell the model to perform tasks such as language identification, timestamping, transcription, or translation. By training on vast multi-lingual data (about one-third non-English audio) and mixed objectives (transcription versus translation), Whisper can both transcribe speech in many languages and translate them to English in one model.

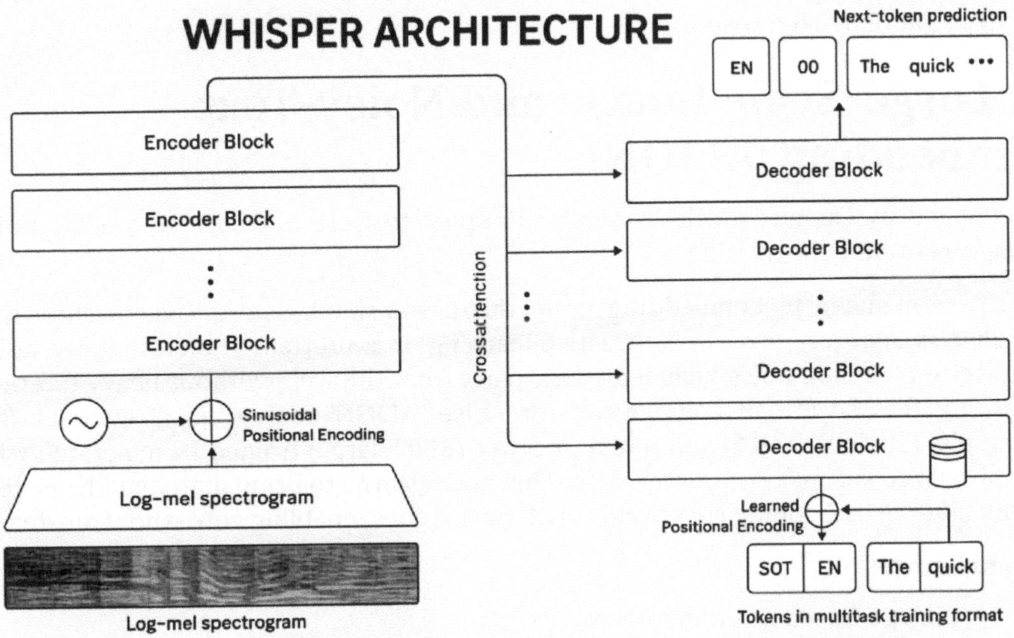

Figure 11.9: *Whisper architecture from OpenAI documentation*

Architecture:

- **Audio Encoder:** Convolutional front-end converts raw audio (for example, waveforms) into spectrogram-like features.
- **Transformer Encoder-Decoder:**
  - o Encoder processes the audio features.
  - o Decoder generates text tokens (transcription) or performs other tasks (such as language identification).
- **Training:**
  - o Uses supervised training with transcribed speech.
  - o Can handle multiple tasks (transcription, translation, language detection).

Key Features:

- Handles multiple languages.
- Supports speech translation and detection.
- Robust to noisy audio inputs.

Use Cases:

- Automatic speech recognition (ASR).
- Speech-to-text translation.
- Multilingual transcription.

A Large-Scale ImaGe and Noisy-Text Embedding (ALIGN)

Developed by Google, ALIGN is similar in spirit to CLIP but uses web-scale noisy image-text pairs for training.

ALIGN is an image-text embedding model that uses a *simple dual-encoder architecture* to align images and text via contrastive learning. It is pretrained on a massive noisy dataset (~1.8 billion noisy image–alt-text pairs from the web) without heavy filtering, showing that scale can compensate for noise. ALIGN uses a visual encoder (for example, EfficientNet-L2) and a text encoder (BERT-large) trained from scratch with a normalized softmax contrastive loss. The model learns to bring matched image-text pairs close in embedding space and repel mismatches, enabling zero-shot transfer.

Architecture:

- **Image Encoder:** EfficientNet.
- **Text Encoder:** BERT-based transformer.
- **Training:**
    - Contrastive learning aligns images and noisy captions (web-scraped).
    - Handles extremely large datasets (hundreds of millions of pairs).

Key Features:

- Scales well with noisy data.
- Excellent performance on retrieval and classification benchmarks.

Use Cases:

- Image-text retrieval.
- Image classification with textual queries.

Bootstrapping Language-Image Pre-training (BLIP)

BLIP aims to unify vision-language tasks using bootstrapped pre-training, which uses both vision-to-language and language-to-vision tasks.

Architecture:

- **Vision Encoder:** Vision Transformer.
- **Text Encoder:** BERT-style transformer.
- **Training:**
  - Combines image-text matching, caption generation, and question answering tasks.
  - Uses both contrastive and generative losses.

Key Features:

- Versatile architecture: supports retrieval, captioning, and Visual Q&A.
- Bootstrapping helps improve data quality by filtering noisy captions.

Use Cases:

- Visual question answering.
- Image captioning.
- Image-text retrieval.

Facebook AI (FLAVA)

FLAVA is a multimodal, multi-task model that can handle unimodal (just text or just images) and multimodal inputs.

Architecture:

- **Image Encoder:** ResNet or ViT.
- **Text Encoder:** Transformer.
- **Fusion Module:** Combines image and text embeddings.
- **Training:**
  - **Multi-task objectives**: uni-modal and multimodal masked language modeling, contrastive learning, and image-text matching.

Key Features:

- Handles unimodal and multimodal tasks simultaneously.
- Flexible backbone for various downstream tasks.

Use Cases:

- Visual question answering.
- Image captioning.
- Single-modality tasks (image classification, text classification, and so on).

VideoBERT

VideoBERT extends BERT-style pretraining to the video domain by jointly modeling video and associated language. The key idea is to discretize video into "*visual tokens*" (via vector-quantized CNN features) and treat them like words alongside speech transcripts from the video. VideoBERT's architecture is basically a standard BERT (bidirectional Transformer) that takes a sequence of tokens mixing visual tokens and word tokens. During training, some tokens (video or text) are masked out, and the model learns to predict the masked content. An auxiliary alignment task uses the [CLS] token to predict whether the text and video segments are aligned in time. In effect, VideoBERT jointly encodes the temporal dynamics of video and co-occurring speech text.

VideoBERT yields rich high-level video representations and "*learns to anticipate*" video content from text and vice versa. It was shown to improve downstream tasks such as video action classification, video captioning, and open-vocabulary video understanding. For instance, when pretrained on cooking videos with recipe transcripts, VideoBERT could perform zero-shot action recognition and generate captions. It achieved state-of-the-art performance on video captioning and significantly improved open-set video classification.

- **Modalities:** Video + text (speech captions).
- **Key features:** Single-stream Transformer (BERT) over mixed tokens; video frames quantized into discrete tokens (via vector quantization); trained with masked token prediction and cross-modal alignment loss.
- **Core use cases:** Unsupervised video representation learning; video captioning and understanding; action recognition; predicting future video frames; any video-language task benefiting from large-scale pretraining.

Evaluation Strategies

Multimodal Transformer Models are evaluated differently depending on the task and modalities involved. We summarize the key metrics, benchmark datasets, and qualitative techniques for each major task category. Where possible, we highlight strengths and weaknesses of each metric and best practices for interpreting results.

Image–Text Retrieval

Retrieval is typically evaluated with Recall@K (R@1, R@5, R@10, and so on) and median rank. Recall@K is the fraction of queries for which the correct match is among the top K retrieved items. (For example, in image-to-text retrieval, R@1 measures the percentage of images whose true caption is the top candidate.) Higher recall is better; low values (especially at K=1) indicate difficulty. In some cases, Mean Reciprocal Rank (MRR) or mean rank is also reported. Now, we will take a deep dive into different multi-modal tasks and discuss the relevant metrics for them.

Image Captioning

Generative captioning is evaluated primarily with NLG metrics: BLEU, METEOR, ROUGE-L, CIDEr, and SPICE.

- **BLEU** (n-gram precision, usually up to 4-grams) measures n-gram overlap with references. It ranges from 0–1 (often shown as 0–100). BLEU is fast and interpretable but ignores recall (missing words) and semantic equivalence; grammatical correctness is not directly measured. Small changes in wording (synonyms, paraphrase) can yield low BLEU despite good captions.
- **METEOR** combines unigram precision and recall into an F-score, with higher weight on recall. It includes stemming and synonyms, addressing some BLEU limitations. METEOR correlates better with human judgment at the sentence-level than BLEU.
- **ROUGE-L** (Longest Common Subsequence recall) emphasizes recall of word sequences. It captures fluency to an extent but also suffers from overlap bias.
- **CIDEr** weights n-grams by their rarity in the corpus (TF-IDF) and measures consensus with multiple references. It was designed to correlate with human consensus and often outperforms BLEU/METEOR in that regard. For example, MS COCO's leaderboard uses the "CIDEr-D" variant.
- **SPICE** parses captions into scene-graph fragments (objects, attributes, relations) and compares on that semantic level (no simple citation listed here). SPICE captures meaning better but can be brittle and is slower.
- **RefCLIPScore/CLIPScore:** A **reference-free** metric using CLIP embeddings. CLIPScore computes the cosine similarity between an image and a caption in the CLIP embedding space. Hessel et al. showed that CLIPScore correlates highly with human judgments, outperforming CIDEr and SPICE on caption quality. CLIPScore focuses on *image-text compatibility*, complementing overlap-based metrics. (RefCLIPScore adds reference contexts to CLIPScore for even higher correlation.)

- **BERTScore** uses contextual embeddings (BERT) to compare candidate and reference texts, capturing semantic similarity beyond surface n-grams.

Visual Question Answering (VQA)

VQA is usually evaluated with accuracy (fraction of correctly answered questions). In the VQA v1/v2 datasets, each question has 10 human answers; the official accuracy formula gives partial credit if some annotators agree. For multiple-choice formats, plain accuracy (or top-1 accuracy) is used. For open-ended ones, an exact match to the "*consensus*" answer is typical.

Visual Grounding (Referring Expression Comprehension)

Grounding tasks require predicting a bounding box (or region) given a referring expression. The standard metric is Accuracy@0.5 IoU: the prediction is counted as correct if its Intersection-over-Union (IoU) with the ground-truth region exceeds 0.5. Many papers report this accuracy at IoU≥0.5 (often denoted Acc@0.5). Some also report stricter thresholds (Acc@0.75, Acc@0.9) or the mean accuracy over thresholds. When multiple objects match an expression, evaluation usually considers the ground-truth referent only.

Speech Recognition (ASR)

The de facto metric is Word Error Rate (WER). WER is defined as (Substitutions + Deletions + Insertions)/(Number of words in reference), computed via alignment (Levenshtein distance at word level). It ranges from 0 (perfect) upward (over 100%). WER directly measures the fraction of words mistaken. Character Error Rate (CER) is analogous at the character level, useful when word segmentation is unclear (for example, languages without spaces or noisy output). Lower is better.

Speech Translation (ST)

Speech translation produces text in a different language. The output is evaluated like a written translation, using BLEU (usually BLEU-4). BLEU measures n-gram overlap between the translated speech and a human reference translation. Sometimes METEOR or TER is used as well. In multilingual benchmarks, SacreBLEU is used to standardize BLEU computation (tokenization, normalization) across studies.

Video Captioning

Video captioning evaluation largely reuses image captioning metrics: BLEU, METEOR, ROUGE-L, CIDEr, SPICE. For example, MSR-VTT and MSVD benchmarks report

BLEU-4, METEOR, ROUGE-L, and CIDEr. These measure n-gram overlap between the generated caption and reference captions. Because videos add a temporal dimension, some works also compute Video-specific CIDEr variants or use multiple captions per video (some datasets have 20 references).

Video Retrieval (Video–Text Retrieval)

Similar to image-text retrieval, video-text retrieval is evaluated with **Recall@K**. For a query video (or text), one retrieves matching sentences (or videos), and measures R@1, R@5, R@10, and so on, plus median rank. For example, retrieval on MSR-VTT or MSVD uses these metrics.

Video Question Answering

Generally accuracy (or F1) on answers. Datasets may be multiple-choice (choose A/B) or open-ended (short answers). For multiple-choice VQA, accuracy is straightforward. For open-ended answers, accuracy (exact match) or soft accuracy (such as in VQA) is used. Some video QA datasets use special metrics: for example, WUPS (Wu-Palmer similarity) to allow synonyms, or precision/recall for counting questions. But most simply use accuracy.

Text-to-Image Generation

Unlike discrete text outputs, generated images are assessed with both distributional metrics and compatibility metrics. Common quantitative metrics include:

- **Inception Score (IS):** measures diversity and objectness using a pre-trained Inception classifier. Higher is better, but IS can be gamed by generating varied but less realistic images.
- **Kernel Inception Distance (KID):** an unbiased variant of FID (works with small samples).
- **Precision and Recall (PRD):** measures how well the generated distribution covers the real data (precision = how realistic samples are, recall = how much of the real data is covered).
- **CLIP-based metrics:** Similar to CLIPScore for captioning, one can use CLIP to measure image-text alignment. For a prompt and generated image, the **CLIPScore** (cosine similarity) estimates whether the image matches the text. CLIP Directional Similarity measures whether the direction of change in CLIP space aligns with the prompt's semantics. These metrics have shown high correlation with human preference for text-to-image quality in some studies.

Audio-to-Text Generation (Audio Captioning)

Metrics: Audio captioning (describing an audio clip in words) is evaluated like image captioning, using text metrics: BLEU, METEOR, ROUGE-L, CIDEr, SPICE, and so on. These measure overlap between generated and reference captions. A new metric, FENSE, was proposed, and very recently, MACE (Multimodal Audio-Caption Evaluation) incorporated audio features alongside text. However, most published results still use the NLG metrics from captioning.

Best Practices and Pitfalls

- **Use Multiple Metrics:** No single metric captures all aspects of performance. For text generation tasks (captioning, translation, and so on), combine precision (BLEU) and recall (METEOR, ROUGE, CIDEr)-based scores, and consider embedding/compatibility scores (CLIPScore, BERTScore) for semantics. For retrieval, report at least R@1, R@5, and median rank. If possible, include confidence intervals or standard deviations to convey variance (especially important for metrics such as FID that are sample-dependent).
- **Understand Metric Biases:** Every metric has blind spots. BLEU and similar n-gram metrics can reward safe, repetitive output and penalize valid paraphrases. CIDEr improves on consensus but can be dominated by common n-grams in the reference set. Accuracy-based metrics (VQA, QA) assume exact matching and can be fooled by dataset biases. FID/IS depend on the pre-trained network (ImageNet) and can mis-evaluate new domains. CLIP-based scores inherit CLIP's training biases. Therefore, interpret results in context: a small gain in one metric might be meaningless if unaccompanied by other evidence (see image captioning survey).
- **Benchmark Consistency:** Use standard datasets and splits, and run official evaluation scripts when available. For example, use the COCO evaluation server for captioning/CIDEr to ensure consistency. Report whether you used the standard evaluation (for example, VQA official accuracy). For retrieval, ensure that the gallery set matches published protocols (some papers differ in test size). Always clarify any differences (for example, extra training data, ensembling).
- **Human Evaluation:** Whenever feasible, include human judgments. For open-ended generation (captions, images, audio), automatic metrics are only proxies. Structured human eval (for example, Likert scales for relevance/fluency, pairwise preference tests) is the gold standard. Even limited human evaluation on a subset of examples can validate whether metric gains are meaningful. Tools such as DrawBench/PartiPrompts exemplify how to conduct crowdsourced image evaluation.

- **Qualitative Examples:** Always complement metric tables with example outputs. For instance, when claiming an improvement in captioning, show cases where the new model succeeds and the baseline fails (and vice versa). This avoids "*gaming*" metrics (for example, producing generic captions with high BLEU) and gives readers intuition.

Task-Specific Tips:

- For ASR, carefully normalize text (lowercase, remove punctuation, or speak them out) before computing WER. Consider reporting both WER and CER in languages with many short tokens.
- For translation/ST, use SacreBLEU for replicable BLEU scores.
- For retrieval, note random or trivial baselines (for example, recall of 0 with random ranking). Report per-query category if data permits (some retrieval tasks have multiple correct answers).
- For QA tasks, check for annotation artifacts (for example, repeated answers) that might inflate accuracy.

Thus, by combining complementary metrics and including qualitative analysis, one can obtain a fuller picture of model performance. Remember that automatic metrics are guides, not arbiters. Discrepancies between metrics and human judgment are common, so use them with caution and transparency.

Business Case Studies in the Healthcare Segment

Here are some case studies for leveraging multimodal systems for medical diagnosis.

Radiology + EHR Fusion

- **Pulmonary embolism detection (Huang et al., Sci Rep 2020):** A deep learning model fused CT imaging and electronic health record (EHR) data (for example, demographics, lab results) using early and late data fusion strategies. This multimodal integration improved accuracy and AUC compared to models based on imaging alone.
- **Clinical transformer model (Zhou et al., arXiv 2023):** Processes unstructured text (chief complaints), structured labs, and radiographs in a unified Transformer. It achieved 12% better disease identification and 29% better COVID-19 outcome prediction than unimodal models.

Neurodegenerative Disease Diagnosis

- **Multimodal Alzheimer's model (Nature Comms 2022):** Combines MRI and FDG-PET imaging to distinguish normal, mild cognitive impairment (MCI), and Alzheimer's disease with ~85% accuracy, outperforming single-modality baselines.
- **MADDi framework (Golovanevsky et al., 2022):** Integrates imaging, genetic data, and clinical records via cross-modal attention to achieve 96.9% accuracy and demonstrated that omitting clinical data reduced performance by ~7.9%.

Video + Sensor Input in Vestibular Diagnosis

BPPV diagnosis (BMC Med Inform Decis Mak 2024): Uses patient eye-movement video plus head-position sensor data in a cross-attention multimodal model. Tested on 518 patients, the system achieved 81.7% diagnostic accuracy, outperforming unimodal approaches.

Cardiology: ECG + Echocardiography Fusion

LVH-fusion model (PMC 2022): Fuses ECG time-series with ultrasound-based echocardiography to diagnose left ventricular hypertrophy. Combining electrical and imaging signals resulted in better diagnostic precision than using either modality in isolation.

Oncology: Prostate Cancer Treatment Planning

Artera platform (Time/Business Insider 2024): Integrates biopsy imaging and historical patient records to guide personalized prostate cancer treatments. Adopted as a standard of care by the National Comprehensive Cancer Network, the platform aims to optimize therapy decisions (reducing overtreatment risk).

Clinical Workflows + Admin Support

AI-augmented radiology reports: Companies such as Bayer and Rad AI are integrating LLMs with radiological images and patient records to automate report drafting and patient communication, freeing radiologists to focus on interpretation.

Key Takeaways

- Combining imaging with structured (EHR/labs) and unstructured (text, sensor) data boosts diagnostic accuracy—typically by 10–30% over single-modality models.

- Cross-modal attention and unified Transformers enable nuanced interactions between data types (for example, video + clinical readings).
- Proven applications include neurology, cardiology, otolaryngology, oncology, and radiology, supporting both diagnosis and clinical workflow improvement.

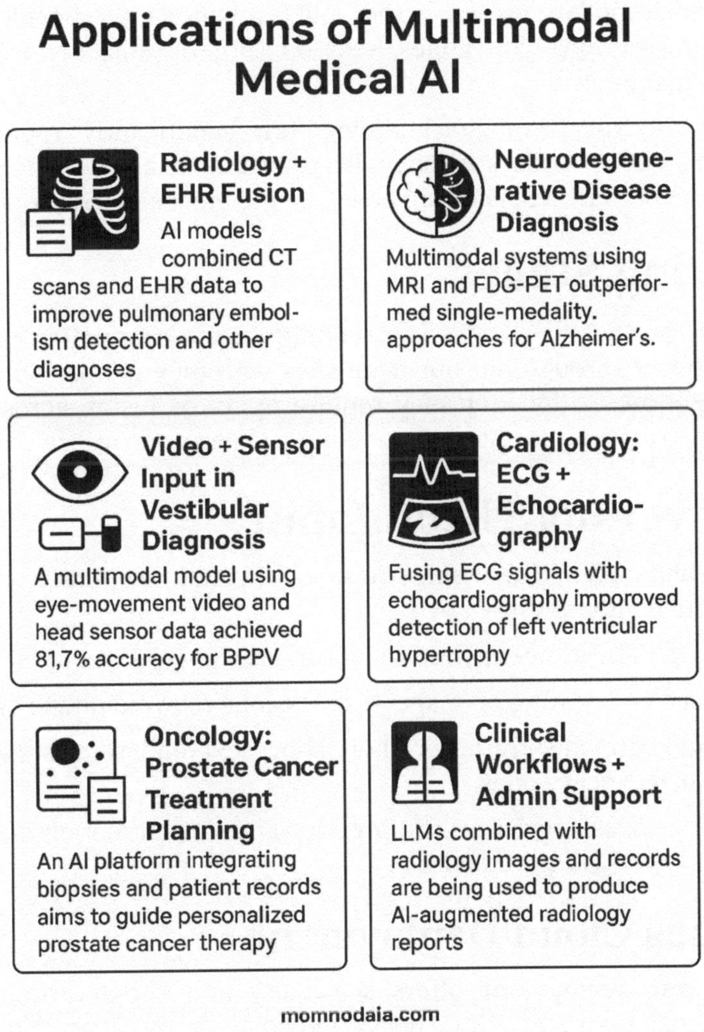

Figure 11.10: *Summary of multi-modal applications in healthcare*

Deployment Trade-Offs

Deploying multimodal Transformers—those handling combinations such as text+image, audio+video, or all three—presents unique trade-offs across hardware, latency, resource management, and accuracy. Here is an enhanced summary of key deployment considerations:

Decoupled Model Splitting (Image versus Text Nodes)

- Large multimodal systems often split into modality-specific nodes: image encoders on GPU-rich nodes, text on CPU-optimized nodes, and shared decoding modules.
- Modality aware routing/scheduling can significantly reduce latency by avoiding queue stalls, for example, prioritize image-text requests, balance image-heavy batches, and skip head-of-line blocks in text nodes.

Co-locating Stages

Co-locating image encoding and text decoding on the same GPU can reduce data transfers and boost throughput, but it must be carefully managed to prevent GPU resource contention. Co-location may require operator fusion across encoder and decoder stages to achieve seamless scheduling and resource utilization.

Latency versus Throughput

- Image and video processing burdens throughput–image encoders often dominate compute time.
- Balancing TTFT (time-to-first-token) and throughput requires:
    - Prioritized routing of image-text sessions to avoid queue backlog.
    - Mixed batching strategies where short text-only requests are not delayed by image-heavy ones.
- On edge devices, aggressive compression and smaller models may be necessary to meet latency requirements.

Edge versus Cloud Deployment

- **Cloud-first deployment** offers scalability and simpler orchestration, but multimodal models are GPU/heavy and costly to run at scale continuously.
- **On-device/edge deployment** can lower latency and enhance privacy but is constrained by memory bandwidth, compute power, and power budgets (for example, Snapdragon 8, Hexagon NPUs).
- Achieving on-device performance may require:
    - Sparse, quantized models.

  - Neural Architecture Search (for example, ElasticViT) to find efficient yet capable variants.
- Amplified by low-power hardware (EdgeBERT, vision NPUs), but designs still struggle with large image or video transformer layers.

Cost and Scalability

- Cloud inference costs can escalate rapidly due to GPU usage, especially for image/video tasks.
- Techniques to reduce cost include:
  - Model compression
  - Elastic autoscaling (spin resources up/down based on demand)
  - Modality-aware scheduling to efficiently utilize resources
- Edge-side deployments, though limited by hardware, avoid cloud bandwidth and compute charges but require upfront integration and device-specific tuning.

Best Practices

- Apply modality-aware batching and routing to avoid idle compute or queue jams.
- Compress all encoders consistently, ensuring modality alignment is preserved.
- Perform scheduled co-location on GPUs to minimize overhead between encoding stages.
- For cloud, use elastic scaling to match irregular traffic and reduce idle costs.
- For edge, employ efficient architecture search (for example, ElasticViT) and hardware-specific optimizations for on-device viability.
- Use dimensionality reduction techniques to reduce the feature set.

Mock Interview

Let us walk through the system design for a couple of multimodal systems in healthcare. This time, the interviewer explains the use-case and asks the candidate to discuss specific key aspects.

Interview Question

Interviewer: *Design a system that assists radiologists in diagnosing chest pathologies such as pneumonia, tuberculosis (TB), and lung cancer—by ingesting chest X-rays (images) and structured EHR data (labs, demographics, vitals, clinical notes).*

Key Requirements:

- *Describe the data ingestion and preprocessing pipelines for both modalities.*
- *Sketch the model architecture, specifying fusion methods (for example, early, late, cross-attention).*
- *Define training strategy, metrics, and dataset splits.*
- *Explain deployment architecture, considering real-time inference in a hospital* PACS *(medical imaging store) environment.*
- *Address regulatory, privacy, and maintenance expectations.*

Candidate:

Data Pipelines

- **Images**: Fetch chest X-rays from PACS; DICOM is standard medical imaging format. Hence apply DICOM-to-JPEG conversion, apply lung segmentation using U-Net, resize, and normalize.
- **EHR Data**: Ingest vitals, labs, and demographics; standardize units; impute missing values; embed categorical fields; optionally encode unstructured notes via a clinical text encoder.
- **ETL Setup**: **HL7** (*Health Level Seven*) is one of the oldest and most widely used healthcare data standards. **FHIR** (*Fast Healthcare Interoperability Resources*) is the *modern* version of HL7. Use HL7/FHIR connectors feeding into preprocessing pipelines (for example, Spark or AWS Clean Rooms).

Model Architecture

- **Vision Encoder**: *ResNet* or *Vision Transformer* outputs vector v.
- **EHR Encoder**: MLP or embedding + MLP produces e.
- **Fusion Layer**: For example, a cross-modal Transformer where queries come from the EHR encoder attending to image patches or vice versa. Alternatively, fuse via concatenation followed by a joint Transformer with subsequent projection and classification head.
- Uses binary/multi-label classification over pathologies and optional severity regression.

Training Strategy

- Split the dataset into patient-wise train/dev/test sets.
- Use multi-label AUC-ROC per pathology, plus overall accuracy, sensitivity, and specificity.
- Monitor per-pathology metrics to ensure rare conditions are not overlooked.
- Use 5-fold cross-validation if the dataset size is limited to ensure robustness.

Deployment Design

- **Edge inference**: push vision encoder + fusion model close to image source (on-prem GPU) to minimize latency streaming.
- **Microservice API**: REST/gRPC interface providing image+EHR input, outputs top probabilistic diagnoses.
- **Monitoring/Logging**: continuous tracking for latency, throughput, and error patterns.
- **CI/CD**: model retraining triggered on drift detection or batch performance drop.

Regulatory and Privacy

HIPAA (Health Insurance Portability and Accountability Act) is the main U.S. law that protects patient health information (PHI). If the AI system handles medical data (x-rays, lab results, notes, patient identifiers), we must follow HIPAA rules. When hospitals want to collaborate on AI training, they cannot simply send patient data to each other – HIPAA and local laws forbid that. So we use privacy-preserving machine learning techniques.

- Every file containing PHI must be encrypted *before or during storage.*
- Use *differential privacy* or *federated retraining* for inter-institutional models without sharing raw data. Differential Privacy ensures no single patient's data can be reverse-engineered from the model. Federated Training happens inside each hospital, only sending model updates—not patient data.
- Document model will not replace clinicians; used only as decision support.
- Maintain explainability via attention heatmaps and text summarizations to aid clinical validation.

Interviewer: *Build a real-time clinic tool that can tell if a patient has dizziness caused by BPPV. It should use a video of the inside of the ear and head-movement sensors, work while the doctor does the Dix–Hallpike test, and give a clear yes/no answer.*

Tasks:

1. *Describe video + sensor streaming and synchronization.*
2. *Design the model, preprocessing, and fusion.*
3. *Define deployment requirements (for example, latency <200 ms).*
4. *Plan data collection, validation, and regulatory compliance.*

Medical Terms- Explanation

- **Benign Paroxysmal Positional Vertigo (BPPV)**: A common inner-ear problem that makes people feel dizzy or like the room is spinning, especially when they move their head.
- **Otoscopic video**: A video taken with a small camera (otoscope) that looks into the ear.
- **Positional sensor data (IMUs)**: Tiny motion sensors placed on the patient's head that track how the head moves and its position.
- **Dix Hallpike manouver**: A specific head-movement test doctors use to trigger dizziness and check if someone has BPPV.

Candidate:

Data Ingestion

- **Video Stream**: USB otoscope camera at 30 FPS; synchronized via timestamped IMU frames.
- **Sensor Data**: 3-axis accelerometer and gyro sampled at ≥200 Hz.
- Use time-aligned buffering to ensure both modalities share the same real-world timestamp.

Preprocessing and Model

- **Video**: Apply cropping, illumination normalization; extract optical flow or motion key points pre-model.
- **Sensor Stream**: smooth noise, extract features (for example, jerk, tilt angles).
- **Model Architecture**: mid-fusion multimodal Transformer:
  - Video patches + sensor feature tokens fed into a shared Transformer.
  - Use cross-modal attention to align sensor patterns with visual cues (for example, nystagmus movements).
- Binary classification head outputs P(BPPV) + severity confidence.

Training and Evaluation

- Collect a balanced dataset from patients, with clinician-labeled ground truth (as in real-world BPPV studies).
- Use accuracy, sensitivity (recall of true BPPV), specificity, and F1.
- Use 5×5-fold cross-validation (5 repeated 5 cross validations) to account for heterogeneity (age, movement style).

Deployment Architecture

- **On-device GPU**: NVIDIA Jetson Nano or equivalent to achieve ≤200 ms per-frame inference.
- Preload model to GPU; run pipeline: capture → preprocess → inference → output.
- Output is displayed live to the clinician; positive BPPV flags are saved to the health record.
- Use watchdog monitoring to restart on dropped frames or decode failures.

Regulatory and Maintenance

- ISO-13485 quality assurance for medical devices; FDA classification.
- Implement versioned deployment with rollback capability.
- Regular calibration: Schedule data input tests weekly using synthetic replay.
- Record all inputs/outputs with logs for post-market performance review.
- Provide UI explainability: show which frames triggered a positive detection.
- Plan human-in-the-loop override before final diagnostic labeling.

Conclusion

In this chapter, we explored the design and deployment of multimodal diagnostic systems in healthcare—a domain that increasingly demands the fusion of images, text, audio, and structured data to improve diagnostic accuracy and workflow efficiency. We crafted a series of mock interview questions that emphasize real-world challenges such as data ingestion, cross-modal alignment, model architecture, evaluation strategies, and deployment considerations in clinical environments.

Through detailed end-to-end system design exercises, we examined the complexities of combining modalities such as chest X-rays with EHR data and otoscopic videos with sensor readings. We highlighted not only the technical decisions—such as transformer-based fusion architectures—but also the critical aspects of latency, interpretability, privacy, and regulatory compliance, all of which are paramount in healthcare settings.

Designing these systems requires a holistic understanding of both machine learning modeling and production system engineering, underscoring the importance of bridging the gap between data science research and real-world clinical implementation. Candidates preparing for ML system design interviews in this domain should be well-versed in cross-modal attention mechanisms, projection networks, evaluation metrics tailored to healthcare, and deployment trade-offs, as well as the ethical and regulatory frameworks that govern healthcare technologies.

Thus, by mastering these design frameworks, engineers can build diagnostic systems that are not only technically robust but also safe, interpretable, and aligned with the needs of clinicians and patients, alike.

References

The following is a curated list of references that cover foundational concepts, architectures, and tutorials relevant to multimodal transformers and healthcare diagnostics:

- **Radford et al., 2021** *Learning Transferable Visual Models From Natural Language Supervision* https://arxiv.org/abs/2103.00020 (Introduces CLIP and multimodal vision-language models.)
- **Huang et al., 2023** *What Makes Multi-modal Transformers Effective?* https://arxiv.org/abs/2302.00923 (Analyzes different fusion strategies for multimodal transformers.)
- **Zhang et al., 2020** *Cross-modal Attention for Vision-and-Language Tasks* https://arxiv.org/abs/2004.14806 (Detailed explanation of cross-modal attention mechanisms.)
- **Huang et al., 2023** A *Survey on Multi-Modal Pre-training for Vision-Language Understanding* https://arxiv.org/abs/2303.15347 (Comprehensive overview of multimodal architectures and pre-training tasks.)
- **FDA Guidance** *Clinical Decision Support Software* https://www.fda.gov/regulatory-information/search-fda-guidance-documents/clinical-decision-support-software (Essential for understanding regulatory aspects of diagnostic systems.)
- **MIMIC-IV Clinical Database** *Medical Information Mart for Intensive Care* IV (MIMIC-IV) https://physionet.org/content/mimiciv/ (A widely used dataset for EHR-based diagnostic research.)
- **PyTorch Blog** *Deploying Transformers on Edge Devices* https://pytorch.org/blog/optimizing-transformer-models-for-mobile-and-edge/ (Practical considerations for deploying transformer models in resource-constrained environments.)
- **HIMSS Privacy Guidelines** *Healthcare Data Privacy and Security* https://www.himss.org/resources/privacy-security (Guidance on maintaining privacy and compliance.)

Index

A

Adapter Layers 77
ALIGN 330
Amazon 166
Audio Captioning 336
Audio Processing 318
Autoencoders 177
Automatic Metrics 264
Automatic Metrics, types
  BLEU 264
  ROUGE 264

B

BART 256
BART, configuring 257
BART, modalities
  Correct Attention Mechanism 261
  Encoder Architectures 258
  Right Decoder 259
  Right Positional Encoding 260
  Right Tokenizer 259
BERT 256
BLIP 331

C

Chain-of-Thought (CoT) 26
CLIP 327
Clustering 142
Clustering, algorithms
  Density-Based 145
  Gaussian Mixture Model (GMM) 146
  Hierarchical 144
  K-Means 143
  Latent Dirichlet Allocation (LDA) 148
CNNs, architecture 211
CNNs, characteristics
  Hierarchy Features 211
  Local Connectivity 211
  Weight Sharing 211
CNNs, evolutions 212
CNNs, layers
  Activation 211
  Convolutional 211
  Fully Connected 211
  Input 211
  Output 211
  Pooling 211
CNNs, sources
  EfficientNet 212
  MobileNet 212
  SqueezeNet 212
Coherence 151
Coherence, steps 151
Cold Start Problem 185
Cold Start Problem, terms
  Cross-Domain Knowledge Transfer 186
  Engagement Data 186
  No Interaction Data 186
  Personalization 185
Collaborative Filtering 170
Collaborative Filtering, terms
  Item-Based 171
  User-Based 170
Content-Based Filtering 169
Contrastive Learning 322
Convolutional Neural Networks (CNNs) 211
Cosine Similarity 138

CRM, applications
  Customer Support Analysis 153
  Feedback/Review Analysis 153
  Marketing Personalization 154
CRM, case studies
  Algorithm Selection 157
  Business Requirement 155
  Data Curation 155
  Deployment 160
  Evaluation/Iteration 160
  Feature Engineering 156
  Model Evaluation 160
Cross-Modal Attention 325
Customer Relationship Management (CRM) 152

D

Data Annotation 242
Data Annotation, challenges
  Ambiguity 243
  Dialogue Data 242
  Domain/Distribution Mismatch 243
  Parallel Corpora 242
  Speech Data/Transcription 242
Data Annotation, frameworks
  Doccano 245
  ELAN 247
  Label Studio 246
  LightTag 247
  Prodigy 246
Data Annotation, solutions 243
Data Annotation, techniques
  Crowdsourcing 245
  Data Augmentation 244
  Synthetic Data Generation 245
Databases 44
Databases, types
  Document 46
  Graph 48
  Redis 50
  Relational 45
  Vector 47
Data Labeling 99
Data Labeling, techniques
  Crowdsourcing 99
  Historical Data 99
  Manual 99
  Sem-Supervised Learning 99
  Synthetic Data 99
Data Optimization 218
Data Optimization, configuring 218
Data Optimization, techniques
  Lightweight Model Design 225
  Mixed Precision 220
  Pruning 221
  Quantization 219
  Sparsity/Low-Rank Approximations 227
Data Parallelism 302
Data Parallelism, configuring 302, 303
Data Preprocessing 318
Data Processing 214
Data Processing, architecture 215
Data Processing, components 216, 217
Decision Trees 105
Deep Learning-Based 177
Deep Learning-Based, approaches
  Autoencoders 177
  Graph Neural Networks (GNNs) 179
  Neural Collaborative Filtering (NCF) 177
  Recommendation Systems 178
  Transformer-Based Models 178
Deep Learning (DL) 7
Density-based Clustering 145
Density-based Clustering, steps 145
Design Interviews 14

Design Interviews, concepts
Curveballs Interviewers 16
Discussion Phase 15
Problem Statement 15
Whiteboarding 16
Design Interviews, terms
AI Fields 15
AI Initiatives 14
Distance Algorithms 134
Distance Algorithms, categories
Cosine Similarity 138
Euclidean 137
Hamming 136
Mahalanobis 138
Manhattan 137
Distance Algorithms, configuring 135
Distance Algorithms, illustrating 140, 141
Distributed Training 302
Distributed Training, frameworks 307
Distributed Training, objectives
Data Parallelism 302
Model Parallelism 304
Pipeline Parallelism 305
Tensor Parallelism 306
ZeRo/Sharded Optimizers 306
Distributed Training, strategies 307
DL, approach
DL-Based Spam 8
ML-Based Spam 8
DL, challenges
Computational Demands 7
Cost Concerns 8
Data Requirements 7
Document Databases 46
Document Databases, disadvantages 46
Document Databases, principles 47
Domain-Specific Data 282
Domain-Specific Data, sources
APIs/Open Data Sources 282
Proprietary Data 282
Public Corpora/Open Datasets 282
Web Scraping 282
Domain-Specific LLM 281
Domain-Specific LLM, case study
Data Collection/Preparation 310
Legal-BERT 312
Model Design 311
Researchers Evaluated 311
Training 311
Domain-Specific LLM, deploying 309
Domain-Specific LLM, frameworks 309
Domain-Specific LLM, metrics
Accuracy/F1 Score 308
BLEU/ROUGE 308
Perplexity 308
Domain-Specific LLM, responsibilities
Bias/Ethical Pitfalls 289
Copyright/Licensing 289
Legal Contraints 290
Privacy/PII Removal 289
Proprietary Considerations 290
Domain-Specific LLM, terms
Domain-Specific Data 282
Normalization 284
Supervised Learning 288
Tokenization 285

E

Early Fusion 320
EDA, aspects
Explainability 101
GDPR/CCPA 100
EDA, components
Data Cleaning 98
Data Collecting 97
Data Labeling 99
Outlier Detection 98
Prediction/Fraud Detection 97

EDA, considerations 100
EDA, preventing 117-120
Efficiency Metrics 116
Efficiency Metrics, resources 116, 117
Euclidean Distance 137
Evaluation Metrics 80
Evaluation Metrics, categories
  Efficiency 116
  Offline 114
  Online 115
Evaluation Metrics, challenges 81
Evaluation Metrics, strategies
  LLM-Specifc 83
  Task-Specific 82
  Text Quality 82
Exploratory Data Analysis (EDA) 97

F

FastText 142
Few-Shot Prompting 26
Fine-Tuning 72
Fine-Tuning, case studies
  Customer Support 85
  Finance 84
  Healthcare 83
  Legal Domain 85
Fine-Tuning, configuring 73-75
Fine-Tuning, domains
  E-Commerce 72
  Education/EdTech 72, 73
Fine-Tuning, frameworks
  Hugging Face Transformers 87
  Scaling Training 88
Fine-Tuning, steps 86
Fine-Tuning, techniques
  Adapter Layers 77
  Full Fine-Tuning 79
  Instruction 76
  Low-Rank Adaptation (LoRA) 77
  Parameter-Efficient 76
  Prompt/Prefix 79
  Quantized LoRA (QLoRA) 78
Fine-Tuning, terms
  FastAPI 89
  ML Project 89
  Transformer-Based Models 88
FLAVA 331
FM, architecture 173
FM, techniques
  Alternating Least Squares (ALS) 173
  Non-Negative 173
  Singular Value Decomposition (SVD) 173
FM, terms
  Item 174
  User 173
Full Fine-Tuning 79

G

Gaussian Mixture Model (GMM) 146
Generative Captioning 333
Generative Captioning, metrics 333
GMM, steps 147
GNNs, architecture
  Graph Representation 179
  Message Passing 179
GNNs, predictions
  Edge-Level 180
  Graph-Level 181
  Node-Level 179
GNNs, techniques
  Graph Attention Networks (GAT) 179
  Graph Convolutional Network (GCN) 179
Gradient Boosting 106
Graph Databases 48
Graph Databases, configuring 48, 49
Graph Neural Networks (GNNs) 179
Graph-of-Thought (GoT) 29
Guardrails 33

Guardrails, levels
In-Process 34
Irrelevant Queries 33
Output 34

H

Hamming Distance 136
Hamming Distance, cons 136
Hamming Distance, pros 136
Hierarchical Clustering 144
Hierarchical Clustering, steps 144
Histogram Oriented Gradients (HOG) 142
Hugging Face Transformers 87
Hugging Face Transformers, steps 87
Hybrid Deployment 36
Hybrid Deployment, benefits 37
Hybrid Deployment, drawbacks 37
Hybrid Deployment, principles 37

I

Image Annotation 207
Image Annotation, challenges 208
Image Annotation, strategies
Active Learning 209
Crowdsourcing 209
Data Augmentation 209
Pre-Annotating 209
Transfer Learning 209
Image Annotation, tools
AI-Assisted/Automated Annotation 208
Cloud-Based 208
Open-Source 208
Image Classification 204
Image Classification, case study
Industrial Defect Detection 230
Pest Classification 228
Precision Farming 229
Remote Medical Diagnosis 229
Wildlife Conservation 230
Image Classification, configuring 205
Image Classification, process
Data Collection 206
Model Selection 206
Model Training 207
Performance Evaluation 207
Image Classification, recommendations
Data Collection 232
Deployment 234
Metrics Evaluation 234
Model Selection 233
Requirements Gathering 231
Image Classification, terms
Feature Extraction 210
Tradition Machine Learning 210
Image Classification, types
Binary 206
Hierarchical 206
Multi-Class 206
Multi-Label 206
Instruction Fine-Tuning 76

K

K-Means 143
K-Means, steps 143

L

LangChain 58
LangChain, steps 59
LangChain, terms 59
LangGraph 61
Large Language Models (LLMs) 10
Late Fusion 321
Latent Dirichlet Allocation (LDA) 148
Lazy Prompting 25
LDA, steps 148, 149
Least-to-Most (LtM) 27
Lightweight Model Design 225
Linear Regression 104
LlamaIndex 58
LLMs 21
LLMs, architecture 35
LLMs, breakdown 11
LLM-Specific Metrics 83

LLMs, stages
Generative Models 10
Multi-Modal 10
Pre-Trained Models 10
Small Lanuage Models (SLMs) 11
LLMs, steps
Data Collection 11
Deployment 12
Fine-Tuning 12
Model Evaluation 11
Optimization 12
LLMs, strengths 21, 22
LLMs, types
Hybrid 36
Private 35
Public 36
LLMs, workflow
Command-Line Engines/ Quantization 24
Ecosystem Integrators 24
Hosted APIs/Hardware Backends 24
Hugging Face Hub/ Transformers 23
Offline/Local Workflows 24
Logistic Regression 105
Long Short-Term Memories (LSTMs) 249
Low-Rank Adaptation (LoRA) 77
LSTMs, configuring 251, 252
LSTMs, ensuring 252, 253
LSTMs, functionality 250
LSTMs, gates
Forget 249
Input 250
Output 250
LSTMs, integrating 254, 255
LSTMs, state
Cell 249
Hidden 249

M

Machine Learning (ML) 5
Mahalanobis Distance 138
Manhattan Distance 137
Matrix Factorization (FM) 172
Meta-Prompting 29
Microservices-Based Architecture 62
Microservices-Based Architecture, terms
Docker Container 63
Kubernetes Orchestration 63
Mixed Precision 220
ML/DL, stages
Data Collection 9
Deployment 9
Experimentation 9
Model Building 9
Model Evaluation 9
ML/DL System Design, differences 8
ML, sources
Continuous Adaptation 7
Data-Driven Learning 6
Personalization 7
Scalability 7
Model Parallelism 304
Model Parallelism, configuring 304
Multimodal Architectures 327
Multimodal Architectures, sections
ALIGN 330
BLIP 331
CLIP 327
FLAVA 331
VideoBERT 332
Whisper 328
Multimodal Data 316
Multimodal Data, case study 337
Multimodal Data, configuring 317
Multimodal Data, considerations
Co-Locating Stages 340
Decoupled Model Splitting 340
Multimodal Data, modalities
Contrastive Learning 322
Cross-Modal Attention 325
Early Fusion 320
Late Fusion 321
Projection Networks 324
Multimodal Data, pitfalls 336

Multimodal Data, preventing 341-343
Multimodal Data, strategies
- Audit Captioning 336
- Generative Captioning 333
- Retrieval 333
- Speech Recognition (ASR) 334
- Speech Translation (ST) 334
- Text-to-Image Generation 335
- Video Captioning 334
- Video Question Answering 335
- Video Retrieval 335
- Visual Grounding 334
- Visual Question Answering (VQA) 334

Multimodal Data, takeaways 338
Multimodal Data, tips 337
Multimodal Data, types
- Audio Processing 318
- Data Preprocessing 318
- Video Data 319

Multi-Task Prompting 28

N

Netflix 165
Neural Collaborative Filtering (NCF) 177
Neural Networks 111
Neural Networks, layers
- Hidden 111
- Input 111
- Output 111

Normalization 284
Normalization, terms
- Deduplication 284
- Domain Data 284
- Noise Removal/Filtering 284
- Preserve Structural Makers 285

O

Offline Metrics 114
Offline Metrics, types
- Classification 114
- Regression 115

Online Metrics 115
Online Metrics, applications 116

P

Parameter-Efficient Fine-Tuning 76
Pipeline Parallelism 305
Pipeline Parallelism, configuring 305
Private LLM 35
Private LLM, benefits 35
Private LLM, challenges 35
Projection Networks 324
Prompt Engineering 20
Prompt Engineering, case study
- Agriculture 40
- CRM 39
- Finance-Automate Earnings 38
- Law 40
- Medical 38

Prompt Engineering, tasks
- Guardrails 33
- Prompt Optimization 32
- Prompt Parameters 32
- Prompt Template 31

Prompt Engineering, techniques
- Chain-of-Thought (CoT) 26
- Few-Shot 26
- Graph-of-Thought (GoT) 29
- Lazy 25
- Least-to-Most (LtM) 27
- Meta 29
- Multi-Task 28
- Role 28
- Self-Consistency 27
- Tree-of-Thought (ToT) 29
- Zero-Shot 25

Prompt Engineering, tools
- Hardware/Orchestration 21
- Hugging Face Hub 21
- Local Tooling 21

Prompt/Prefix Tuning 79
Pruning 221
Public LLM 36
Public LLM, benefits 36
Public LLM, limitations 36
Purity 152

Q

Quantization 219
Quantized LoRA (QLoRA) 78

R

RAG 51
RAG, architecture
  Agentic/Multi-Agent 54
  Multimodal 54
  Multi-Stage/Iterative 54
  Retrieve-and-Rank 53
  Speculative/Corrective 54
RAG, case study
  Customer Support 65
  Healthcare 65
  Legal Domain 64
RAG, components
  GENERATOR 53
  INDEX 53
  QUERY 52
  RESPONSE 53
  RETRIEVER 53
RAG, configuring 51, 52
RAG, integrating 66, 67
RAG, section
  LangChain 58
  LangGraph 61
  LlamaIndex 58
RAG, terms
  Caching/Routing 57
  Chunking Strategy 56
  Distributed Generation, embedding 56
  Evaluation/Monitoring 57
  Hybrid Retriever 57
  Index Maintenance 57
  Scalable Storage 56
Random Forest 107
RDBMSs, configuring 45
Recommendation Systems 165, 178
Recommendation Systems, algorithms
  Collaborative Filtering 170
  Content-Based Filtering 169
  Deep Learning-Based 177
  Matrix Factorization (FM) 172
  Rule-Based Systems 169
  Two-Tower Neural Network (TTNN) 175
Recommendation Systems, architecture 167
Recommendation Systems, features
  Data Drift, handling 193
  Multi-Armed Bandit (MAB) 192
  Running A/B Tests 192
  User Feedback Loop 192
Recommendation Systems, outcomes
  Accuracy-Based Metrics 183
  Business KPIs 185
  Engagement Metrics 185
  F1-Score 184
  NDCG 184
  Precision 184
  Recall 183
Recommendation Systems, platforms
  Amazon 166
  Netflix 165
  Spotify 167
Recommendation Systems, points
  Diversity/Serendipity 187
  Explainability 190
  Fairness/Bias Mitigation 189
  Privacy/Security 191

Recommendation Systems, scenarios
- Algorithm 195
- Business Requirements 193
- Computational Costs 197
- Data Collection/Labelling 194
- Evaluation 200
- Hybrid Approach 199
- Knowledge Graph Construction 195
- Ranking 196
- Real-Time Inference 198

Recommendation Systems, sector
- Education 167
- Finance 167
- Healthcare 167

Recommendation Systems, use cases 167
Recurrent Neural Networks (RNNs) 248
Redis 50
Redis, configuring 50, 51
Relational Databases (RDBMSs) 45
Retrieval 333
RNNs, configuring 248
Role Prompting 28
Rule-Based System 5
Rule-Based System, challenges 6
Rule-Based System, configuring 5
Rule-Based Systems 169

S

Self Consistency 27
Semantic Similarity 55
Semantic Similarity, variations
- Feedback/Active Learning 56
- High-Quality Embeddings 55
- Multi-Vector 55
- Query Transformation/ Expansion 55
- Semantic Chunking 55

seq2seq Model, application
- Machine Translation 239
- Media/Research Summarization 240
- OpenAI 240
- Question Answering (QA) 240
- Speech Transcription 240

seq2seq Model, case study
- CNN/DailyMail 267
- Data Preprocessing 267
- Fine-Tuning 269
- Serving Deployment 271
- Summarization Model 270

seq2seq Model, revolution
- BART 256
- BERT 256
- Long Short-Term Memories (LSTMs) 249
- Recurrent Neural Networks (RNNs) 248
- Transformer Parallelism 255

seq2seq Model, strategies
- Automatic Metrics 264
- Human Evaluation 266
- Learned Metrics 265

seq2seq Model, tips 275
Sequence-to-Sequence (seq2seq) Model 239
Serving Deployment, aspects
- FastAPI/Model Serving 271
- Scaling Optimization 273
- Summarization Service 273

SHapley Additive exPlanations (SHAP) 102
Silhouette Coefficient 150
Silhouette Coefficient, steps 150
Spam Detection 12
Spam Detection, terms
- Contextual Enhancing 12
- Generative Models 12
- Multi-Modal Advantages 12
- Real-Time Adaptability 12

Speech Recognition (ASR) 334
Speech Translation (ST) 334
Spotify 167
String Data 141

Supervised Algorithm, comparing 112
Supervised Algorithm, terms
- F1 Score/Accuracy 113
- Imbalanced Data, handling 113
- Inference Time 112
- Interpretability 113
- Less Data, handling 113
- Multi-Dimensionality 113
- Training Time 112

Supervised Learning 96
Supervised Learning, insights
- Claims Modeling 96
- Credit Scoring 96
- Fraud Detection 96
- Insurance Underwriting 96

Supervised Machine Learning 103
Supervised Machine Learning, algorithms
- Decision Trees 105
- Gradient Boosting 106
- Linear Regression 104
- Logistic Regression 105
- Neural Networks 111
- Random Forest 107
- Support Vector Machines (SVMs) 109

Supervised Machine Learning, aspects
- Classification 103
- Regression 103

Supervised Machine Learning, flow
- Gather Data 103
- Predict 103
- Test 103
- Train Model 103

Support Vector Machines (SVMs) 109
SVMs, components
- Contour Lines 110
- Data Points 109
- Decision Boundary 110
- Interpretation 110
- Margin 110
- Support Vectors 110

System Design 2
System Design, architecture 5
System Design, configuring 2, 3
System Design, ensuring 3, 4
System Design, integrating 16, 17

T

Task-Specific Metrics 82
Tensor Parallelism 306
Tensor Parallelism, configuring 306
Text Quality Metrics 82
Text-to-Image Generation 335
Tokenization 285
Tokenization, ensuring 286
Transformer Architecture 291
Transformer Architecture, configuring 292
Transformer Architecture, terms
- Attention Model 294
- Design Recommendations 301
- Encoder Class 296
- Hiddent Dimensions 299
- Language Translation 297

Transformer-Based Models 178
Tree-of-Thought (ToT) 29
TTNN, configuring 175
TTNN, workflow 176, 177
Two-Tower Neural Network (TTNN) 175

U

Unsupervised Learning 133
Unsupervised Learning, case study
- Anomaly Detection 154
- Customer Segmentation 154
- Topic Modeling 153

Unsupervised Learning, metrics
- Coherence 151
- Purity 152
- Silhouette Coefficient 150

Unsupervised Learning, scenarios 133, 134

Unsupervised Learning, terms
  Clustering 142
  Distance Algorithms 134
  Image Data 142
  String Data 141

V

Vector Databases 47
Vector Databases, configuring 47, 48
VideoBERT 332
Video Captioning 335
Video Data 319
Video Data, configuring 319
Video Question Answering 335
Video Retrieval 335
Vision Transformers (ViTs) 213
Visual Grounding 334
Visual Question Answering (VQA) 334
ViTs, configuring 213, 214
ViTs, variants
  DeiT 214
  MobileViT 214
  TinyViT 214

W

Whisper 328

Z

ZeRO 306
ZeRO, configuring 306
Zero-Shot Prompting 25